THE ANTISOCIAL PERSONALITIES

THE ANTISOCIAL PERSONALITIES

David T. Lykken
University of Minnesota

LEA LAWRENCE ERLBAUM ASSOCIATES, PUBLISHERS
1995 Hillsdale, New Jersey   Hove, UK

Lawrence Erlbaum Associates, Inc., Publishers
365 Broadway
Hillsdale, New Jersey 07642

Library of Congress Cataloging-in-Publication Data

Lykken, David Thoreson.
    The antisocial personalities / David T. Lykken.
        p.   cm.
    Includes bibliographical references and index.
    ISBN 0-8058-1941-X (alk paper). -- ISBN 0-8058-
1974-6 (paper : alk. paper)
    1. Antisocial personality disorders.   I. Title.
    RC555.L95   1995
    616.85'82--dc20   95-12891
                                                    CIP

Books published by Lawrence Erlbaum Associates are printed
on acid-free paper, and their bindings are chosen for strength
and durability.

Printed in the United States of America
10 9 8 7 6 5 4 3 2 1

Contents

Introduction

Although antisocial personality disorder (APD) is treated in the *Diagnostic and Statistical Manual of Mental Disorders* (*DSM–IV*; American Psychiatric Association, 1994) as if it were a single entity, most knowledgeable people, whether they hold the union card of a psychiatrist, psychologist, or criminologist, agree that APD is a heterogeneous category. People[1] can meet the criteria for this diagnosis in a variety of ways and for different reasons. Some persistently or seriously antisocial people do not meet APD criteria at all. One of the major but officially unrecognized subcategories of APD consists of the *psychopathies*, people whose antisocial tendencies result in large part from biological differences, quantitative differences in temperament, and in some cases, perhaps, qualitative differences in brain function, differences that make it unusually difficult to socialize these individuals when they are growing up. Since the 1950s, an extensive and impressively consistent experimental literature has accumulated concerning one of the psychopathies, the *primary psychopath*, and one main purpose of this book is to survey this literature.

The antisocial personalities who are responsible for most crime, including violent crime, in the United States are not psychopaths but rather *sociopaths*, persons of broadly normal temperament who have failed to acquire the attributes of socialization, not because of innate peculiarities in themselves, but because of a failure of the usual socializing agents, primarily their parents. A second main purpose of this book is to document this claim, to show how recent cultural changes have contributed to the increase in the incidence of incompetent parenting and to the resulting marked and continuing increase in the incidence of crime and violence.

Part I of this book outlines a theory of socialization based on evolutionary and genetic concepts, a theory that demands a different and more discriminating diagnostic scheme than that provided by *DSM–IV*. In chapter 1, I discuss what the

---

[1]Because most criminals and most psychopaths are males, I usually avoid the awkwardness of "he or she" and "him or her" throughout this volume.

process of socialization entails and contrast my assumptions about crime and criminality with those of traditional criminology. Only other bull terrier owners will understand at once the logic of devoting chapter 2 of a book on crime to a discussion of that breed. Chapter 3 attempts to counteract the tendency for discussions of criminality to create a picture of "the criminal" that does not do justice to the rich variety of individuals who fall within this rubric. In place of many varied and detailed case histories, for which there is not enough space, I provide instead an illustrative, armchair taxonomy of criminal "types" to give at least some sense of the heterogeneity of the people whom we are trying here to understand.

With this taxonomy, we first separate those few individuals whose crimes are a by-product of genuine psychosis and another group of psychologically normal offenders whose crimes can be attributed to situational factors, including restricted options, easily rationalized temptation, or excessive provocation. This leaves the main body of persistently antisocial offenders, the family of *antisocial personalities*. The largest genus within this family consists of the sociopaths but we shall also identify several species of psychopaths as well.

The three chapters of Part II provide the evolutionary and genetic basis for my analysis of the causes of crime and violence. Our human species was designed by natural selection to live relatively amicably in extended family groups. Just as we evolved an innate readiness for learning language, so we evolved a proclivity for learning and obeying basic social rules, for nurturing our children and helping our neighbors, and for pulling our own weight in the group effort for survival. But, like the ability to acquire language, our innate readiness to become socialized in these ways must be elicited, developed, and practiced during childhood, otherwise we should remain permanently mute and also, perhaps, permanently unsocialized.

Traditional societies in which children are socialized communally, in the manner to which our species is evolutionarily adapted, have little intramural crime and any persistent offender is likely someone whose innate temperament made him or her unusually difficult to socialize. These are the people I call *psychopaths*. Our modern society no longer entrusts this basic task of socializing children to the extended family, but rather to that child's two biological parents collaborating as a team. Increasingly, however, this vital responsibility is currently entrusted to single parents, usually single mothers, often single mothers who are immature and/or unsocialized themselves. The feral products of indifferent, incompetent or over-burdened parents are the people I refer to as *sociopaths*.

As suggested earlier, the new discipline of evolutionary psychology seems to me to provide a fresh and illuminating perspective on many of the traditional areas of psychological thinking. Chapter 4 introduces evolutionary psychology and then proceeds to consider socialization and crime from an evolutionary point of view.

Unlike cystic fibrosis or Huntington's disease, criminality as such is not inherited, yet traits that make a child more or less difficult to socialize undoubtedly have strong genetic roots. I have been doing behavior–genetic research since 1970 and have been associated since 1979 with the landmark study, by my colleague T. J. Bouchard Jr., of twins separated in infancy and reared apart. Along with other twin and adoption studies, at my university and elsewhere, these researches have revolutionized psychology's view of human differences and of the way in which the genetic steersman in each of us tends to choose which formative environments we select and to decide the different ways in which we are affected by the same environments. This new formulation of an old problem, which I call the "nature *via* nurture" perspective, is discussed in chapter 5, preceded by a more general introduction to behavioral genetics.

Genetic differences may prove to be somewhat less important in determining our levels of socialization than in determining our aptitudes, our temperaments, or even our position, left to right, on the political spectrum. But genetic factors are important in relation to crime as in almost all of human affairs and this issue is considered in chapter 6.

Part III introduces the psychopathic personality and discusses the relevant experimental literature in some detail. Chapter 7 provides a brief historical introduction and chapter 8 discusses the problem of identifying "the psychopath" for purposes of studying him. In chapter 9, I introduce my own "low fear quotient" theory of the etiology of primary psychopathy and review the evidence pertaining to this theory. The more recent theory promulgated by Don Fowles and Jeffrey Gray, discussed in chapter 10, can be regarded as a modern version of the Lykken low-fear theory with various improvements. One such addition is the concept of secondary psychopathy that flows from the Fowles–Gray model. Chapters 11, 12, and 13 discuss the work of R. D. Hare, the leading researcher in this area, the "septal-rat" theory of J. P. Newman and related theories of frontal lobe dysfunction, the "low serotonin syndrome" of dysphoric impulsivity, and another speculative proposal of my own, the "hysterical psychopath."

Part IV is concerned with the sociopathic personalities who, while perhaps less interesting psychologically than the psychopath, are vastly more numerous and, therefore, constitute the larger social problem. In chapter 14, I discuss the sociopath or common criminal in some detail, because he is the reason for the recent and alarming increase in the crime rate in the United States and in other Western countries. In chapter 15 I come to grips with the fact that African Americans, who constitute only one eighth of the U.S. population, are responsible for about one half of the crime (and for virtually all the crime within the Black community itself). Because I have an African-American daughter-in-law and four grandchildren whom society, in its curious way, will classify as "Black," this problem is of personal concern to me. I try to demonstrate that Black sociopaths are being created in the same way as White sociopaths, that the same preventive strategies will be required in both cases, and that genetic racial differences probably do not play a major role.

Finally, in chapter 16, after a brief summing up, some suggestions regarding the treatment and prevention of antisocial personality are discussed. I argue that rearing a child at risk for psychopathy is like rearing an average youngster only harder and more demanding and a few practical guidelines are suggested. In the final section, concerned with the prevention of sociopathy, I consider what might be done to try to stem this criminal tide within both the White and Black communities. The social policies I propose there are much more radical than anything currently being discussed and, for that reason, they will be controversial (to say the least). That these policies are needed and that they should work if properly implemented seem to me to be plausible in the light of the psychological and demographic facts to be reviewed in this book but I do not pretend that these proposals follow in any rigorous way from the facts in hand. I would argue, however, that the less radical remedies that have been proposed by others are plainly implausible on current evidence and that the kinds of remedies I suggest should at least to be seriously discussed if we are ever to find the solutions to the problems that confront us.

ACKNOWLEDGMENTS

One advantage of working in an academic department of the first class is that the colleagues one prevails upon to read drafts of a work can be counted on to ferret out errors and suggest valuable improvements. Professors T. J. Bouchard, Jr., I. I. Gottesman, W. Grove, W. G. Iacono, M. McGue, A. Tellegen, and Regents Professor P. E. Meehl, as well as my former student, Dr. S. Lilienfeld, read and commented upon all or portions of this manuscript. Faced with the common problem of wanting to acknowledge their generous help without burdening them with responsibility for the product, I can say that, although each would have written a different and perhaps better book himself, *this* book was vastly improved through their assistance. Numerous graduate students have puzzled over earlier drafts and their comments and suggestions have been helpful. My wife, Harriet, and my sons, Jesse, Joseph, and Matthew, provided the perspectives, respectively, of an intelligent lay person and former social worker, an expert in juvenile corrections, a physicist, and a lawyer. For all of their help I will add the reader's thanks to my own.

—*David T. Lykken*

PART I

CRIME AND VIOLENCE: WHO ARE THE PERPETRATORS AND WHY DO THEY DO IT?

1

The Psychopathology of Crime

During most of the 20th century, psychiatric diagnosis was an impressionistic art form and studies showed that even experienced practitioners often could not agree in classifying the same patients except in a very general way. Diagnoses sometimes were based on highly subjective inferences about the patient's unconscious impulses and motivations or on the clinician's unsystematic and even quirky observations accumulated over years of practice. The American Psychiatric Association (APA) published its first *Diagnostic and Statistical Manual (DSM)* in 1952 but it was not until the third edition, known as *DSM–III*, appeared in 1980 that some measure of diagnostic consistency was finally achieved. This was accomplished in *DSM–III*, in the subsequent revision, *DSM–III–R*, and in the current *DSM–IV*, published in 1994, by formulating diagnostic criteria that were relatively objective and noninferential. For the most part, the criteria were arrived at by consensus of committees of clinicians rather than by statistical analysis of empirical data.

Antisocial Personality Disorder

In this diagnostic scheme, antisocial personality disorder (APD) takes the place of such earlier labels as psychopathy, sociopathy, and dyssocial personality. To be diagnosed with APD, an individual must show (a) "a pervasive pattern of disregard for and violation of the rights of others occurring since age 15 years," and (b) the person must be at least 18 years of age. Moreover, there must be (c) "evidence of conduct disorder with onset before age 15." In addition, (d) "the occurrence of antisocial behavior is not exclusively during the course of Schizophrenia or a Manic Episode" (APA, 1994, pp. 649–650). In *DSM–III–R*, Criterion C could be satisfied by any 3 of 12 quite specific facts about the individual's behavior before age 15 (e.g., "was often truant") and Criterion A required evidence of at least 4 of 10 relatively specific adult behaviors (e.g., "lacks ability to function as a responsible parent, as indicated by one or more of the following: (a) malnutrition of child, ... (f) repeated squandering, on personal items, of money required for household

3

necessities"). No special psychiatric knowledge or insight was required to make a diagnosis on the basis of these guidelines, a fact that no doubt accounts for the good reliability or interrater agreement achieved by *DSM–III–R*.

In *DSM–IV*, the four general APD criteria recur but the specific criteria are fewer in number and somewhat less specific in content. Because at least some degree of judgment is required in using the new criteria, reliability may diminish slightly but it seems likely that the epidemiological and other findings relating to APD that were gathered using *DSM–III–R* criteria will hold as well for the new ones. The *DSM–IV* criteria for APD are as follows:

301.7 Antisocial Personality Disorder

A. There is a pervasive pattern of disregard for and violation of the rights of others occurring since age 15 years, as indicated by three (or more) of the following:
    (1) failure to conform to social norms with respect to lawful behaviors indicated by repeatedly performing acts that are grounds for arrest.
    (2) deceitfulness, as indicated by repeated lying, use of aliases, or conning others for personal profit or pleasure.
    (3) impulsivity or failure to plan ahead.
    (4) irritability and aggressiveness, as indicated by repeated physical fights or assaults.
    (5) reckless disregardful for safety of self or others.
    (6) consistent irresponsibility, as indicated by repeated failure to sustain consistent work behavior or honor financial obligations.
    (7) lack of remorse, as indicated by being indifferent to or rationalizing having hurt, mistreated, or stolen from another.
B. The individual is at least age 18 years.
C. There is evidence of Conduct Disorder with onset before age 15 years.
D. Occurrence of antisocial behavior is not exclusively during the course of Schizophrenia or a Manic Episode. (APA, 1994, pp. 649–650)

The cookbooklike, relatively objective character of this list of criteria is obvious; what is not so apparent is the fact that there is no theoretical nor empirical basis for supposing that this scheme carves Nature at her joints. Because there may be a variety of psychological causes for a given action, classifying people by their actions rather than their psychological dispositions or traits, although perhaps natural for the purposes of the criminal law, is less useful for the purposes of psychiatry or science. Note that the cut-off age of 18 years for the APD diagnosis makes more sense in legal, rather than in psychiatric terms; in most of the United States, 18 is the age of legal responsibility although, of course, it is absurd to suppose that delinquent youth undergo some psychological transformation on their 18th birthday. In view of the alarming recent increase in the number of homicides and other major crimes by youngsters under age 18, many of them now being tried as adults and incarcerated for long periods, it is noteworthy that none of them could be classified as APD.

As one might expect from reviewing these diagnostic criteria, a large proportion of those heterogeneous individuals we call common criminals could be classified as APD as well as many feckless citizens who do not commit serious crimes. Consider, for example, persons meeting Criteria A1, A2, A4, and A7; these might be the garden-variety sociopaths who populate most jails and prisons. Persons who meet Criteria A3, A5, and A6, but not the others, might also be diagnosed APD although they are not criminals but, rather, drifters or addicts or drunks. APD is plainly a heterogeneous category in respect to etiology and also in respect to the psychological characteristics that give rise to the varied patterns of socially deviant behavior that serve to meet the criteria.

The incidence of APD is twice as high among inner-city residents as among persons living in small towns or rural areas, and more than five times higher in males than in females (among Blacks, however, the gender rates are less divergent; Robins, 1978a). APD is higher among first-degree relatives of APD probands and higher still if the proband is female. The prevalence of APD was estimated at 3% in males during the early 1980s but had risen to 4.5% by 1990 for reasons that are explained later (Robins, 1978a, 1978b; Robins, Tipp, & Przybeck, 1991). Robins found that about 70% of the adolescents in her samples who met criteria for conduct disorder as children were not classifiable as APD as adults, although many of them showed other psychiatric problems. However, at least up to the time when the *DSM–III* criteria were formulated, she knew of no documented instance of an adult sociopath who had not also displayed antisocial behavior during childhood (Robins, 1978a).

For its first 150 years or so, psychiatry attempted to account, not for ordinary criminals, but for that subset of amoral, often criminal individuals, the people who are classified here as *psychopaths*, who came from apparently normal middle-class backgrounds and who therefore were harder to understand than the unsocialized offspring of parents who were themselves unsocialized. With *DSM–III* and the concept of APD, however, American psychiatry took a sharp turn toward conventional criminology. In their quest for diagnostic reliability through the use of specific and noninferential criteria, they devised a category into which most common criminals will comfortably fit. It seems evident that the people who fall within this category must be psychologically heterogeneous, their antisocial dispositions widely varied as to etiology. Identifying someone as "having" APD is about as nonspecific and scientifically unhelpful as diagnosing a sick patient as having a fever, or an infectious or a neurological disorder.

In spite of the heterogeneity of the group classified by the *DSM–IV* criteria, APD does demarcate a category of individuals that is socially important because many of these people are the reasons why we lock our doors, stay off the streets at night, move out of the cities and send our children to private schools. A majority of inmates in our prisons meet these criteria for the diagnosis of APD[1] so it is not unreasonable to conclude that these criteria identify more than half of the men whom we normally refer to as common criminals. The largest and most important subcategory of APD includes those people who, in this volume, are called *socio-*

---

[1]See Harpur, Hare, and Hakstian (1989, p. 9). The overlap of APD with criminality is much lower for women, perhaps because ASP criteria are male-oriented: In the large Epidemiologic Catchment Area (ECA) study reported by Robins and Regier (1991), 55% of male but only 17% of female ASPs were criminal.

paths. This is the group that is growing—metastasizing—so rapidly that it already threatens to overwhelm our criminal justice system. Wolfgang and associates studied two cohorts of boys born in Philadelphia, the first in 1945 and the second in 1958 (Tracy, Wolfgang, & Figlio, 1990). Of the 1945 cohort, 6% became chronic criminals responsible for 61% of the Uniform Crime Report (UCR) Index Crimes (from 69% to 82% of the violent crimes). Of the 1958 cohort, 8% were chronic recidivists, accounting for 68% of the UCR Index Crimes. Based on the 50% increase in the incidence of APD since 1984, we can estimate that perhaps 12% of the males born in Philadelphia in 1970 may be recidivist criminals by now. According to the broader ECA study, the incidence of childhood conduct disorder (CD) among males born from 1961 to 1972 was nearly three times higher than the incidence among men born from 1926 to 1945 and the incidence of adult APD, which by definition must be preceded by CD, has increased in parallel.

In the 1958 birth cohort, the dangerous recidivist group comprised 3% of the White males and 11% of the Black. Because Blacks and Hispanics are greatly overrepresented among these unsocialized predators, the extraordinary improvements in minority opportunities and interracial harmony that have been achieved since the 1940s in the United States are being threatened. That young man you see approaching along the deserted city street at night—the odds are much higher that he makes his living mugging people if he is Black than if he is White (Levin, 1992). Such facts must inevitably lead to a recrudescence of the very racism that we have tried so hard as a society to overcome.

The Psychopath

In her important study of mental illness in non-Western, primitive societies, Murphy (1976) found that the Yupic-speaking Eskimos in northwest Alaska have a name, *kunlangeta*, for the

> man who, for example, repeatedly lies and cheats and steals things and does not go hunting and, when the other men are out of the village, takes sexual advantage of many women—someone who does not pay attention to reprimands and who is always being brought to the elders for punishment. One Eskimo among the 499 on their island was called *kunlangeta*. When asked what would have happened to such a person traditionally, an Eskimo said that probably "somebody would have pushed him off the ice when nobody else was looking." (p. 1026)

Because traditional methods of socialization are so effective in tribal societies, where the extended family rather than just a particular parent-pair participate in the process, the *kunlangeta* probably possesses inherent peculiarities of temperament that make him unusually intractable to socialization. Such a man I classify as a *psychopath*, an individual in whom the normal processes of socialization have failed to produce the mechanisms of conscience and habits of law-abidingness that normally constrain antisocial impulses.

In 1957 I published an experimental study of this type of antisocial character. Since then, a substantial research literature on the psychopath has accumulated and, in this book, I summarize what we know now about these warped character defects seem to have a biological basis. Yet, as on current state of crime and violence in the United States, it is cl... played by the primary psychopath is only one small part of this broader picture.

The Sociopath

In Western, and especially in Western urban society, the socialization of children is entrusted largely just to the parents, often to a single parent, and if the parents are overburdened or incompetent or unsocialized themselves then, as I document below and in Part IV, even a child of average temperament may grow up with the antisocial tendencies of a psychopath. In this book I use the term *sociopath* to refer to persons whose unsocialized character is due primarily to parental failures rather than to inherent peculiarities of temperament. The psychopath and the sociopath can be regarded as opposite endpoints on a common dimension with difficult temperament maximized at the psychopathic end and inadequate parenting maximized at the sociopathic end.

I believe that it is both scientifically interesting and socially important to continue to improve our understanding of the psychopath and most of this book is dedicated toward that end. However, the pure case psychopath is relatively rare; there was only one among the 499 residents of Murphy's Eskimo community. Those whom I call sociopaths, on the other hand, who are just as dangerous and as costly to society as psychopaths, occur in Western society in ever-increasing numbers, especially in our cities. We know of no cure for either condition. The best we can do with a truly unsocialized 20-year-old is to sequester him until late middle age when his antisocial impulses begin to wane in strength (or, perhaps, to "push him off the ice"!). We can probably find ways of preventing potential psychopaths from developing first into delinquents, then into criminals, once we better understand the nature of the inherent differences that make them so difficult to socialize. But I believe that we could certainly and substantially reduce the incidence of sociopaths in our society, whom we are currently producing with factorylike efficiency and at enormous cost. To do this will require that we find ways to reduce the numbers of children in each generation who are raised by—or domiciled with—incompetent parents. I discuss these social policy issues and propose what I think would be a workable solution—perhaps the *only* workable solution—briefly in chapter 16.

In the remainder of this first chapter, I explain how I intend to define the basic concepts of *socialization* and *criminality*, then introduce the simple *diathesis-developmental* model of criminality which is the main thesis of this treatise.

SOCIALIZATION

Socialization is defined as the aggregate of an individual's acquired habits of conformity to the rules and expectations of the society in which he lives. Socialization includes three principal components:

1. Conscientiousness: This is a general disposition to avoid antisocial behavior. This avoidance normally results from fear of punishment, including the self-inflicted punishments of guilt and shame, together with the tendency to reject, on rational utilitarian grounds, the criminal alternative. This does not mean that socialized people are continually confronting and overcoming temptation. For most adults, crime avoidance becomes automatic; we are not often tempted to strike out, to just take what we want, or to drive off without paying, because doing the right thing, obeying the rules, has become habitual. One reason crime rates peak during late adolescence is that these habits have not yet been consolidated in many teenage youngsters.

2. Prosociality: The second component of socialization is a general disposition toward prosocial behavior; it includes all of the individual's nurturant, affectional and altruistic impulses and it is accomplished through the cultivation of his or her ability to empathize with others, to participate in and to enjoy affectionate relationships, and to admire prosocial role models and wish to emulate them.

3. Acceptance of Adult Responsibility: The third component of socialization consists in the motivation and associated skills required to "pull one's own weight" in the communal effort; it involves the acquisition of the work ethic, the aspiration to achieve through personal effort, and the acceptance of conventional family and social responsibilities.

If the first obligation of parenthood is to provide basic nurturance, to feed, shelter, and protect the offspring, then one can say that the second most important function of parents is the socialization of their children. I argue that socialization (hence, also, conscientiousness) is a product of two factors, *parenting* and *innate characteristics*. By *parenting* I mean to refer to all the learning experiences tending away from antisocial behavior and tending toward prosocial activities; the most important of these experiences are usually at the hands of a parent or parents. Parenting is perhaps one of the most difficult tasks that humans undertake in this modern world[2] and some parents are much better at it—more successful in socializing their children—than other parents are.

> Families of antisocial children are characterized by harsh and inconsistent discipline, little positive parental involvement with the child, and poor monitoring and supervision of the child's activities. (Patterson, DeBaryshe, & Ramsey, 1989, p. 329)

As Patterson and his colleagues have documented, the child who is poorly socialized at home tends to be rejected by the normal peer group and to fail

---

[2]My colleague, Auke Tellegen, asked me, "How can parenting be so difficult if wolf and monkey mothers do it so successfully?" He points out that, under the tribal circumstances to which our ancestors became adapted, most human parents probably also did their jobs well enough by doing what came naturally. It is in the more complex conditions of modern life, to which we are not well adapted by evolution, and in which they must function without the support of the extended family, that many parents find the task too hard for them.

academically in school. The nearly inevitable progression in such circumstances is into membership in deviant peer groups or gangs where antisocial behavior is both learned and reinforced, whereas normal or prosocial behavior is discouraged or punished. Moreover, there are certain innate characteristics that make some children harder than others to socialize. As a rule, children who are more venturesome, impulsive, or aggressive, less intelligent or less talented, are harder to socialize successfully.

Conscientiousness Versus Criminality

Socialization is a multifaceted concept and only one of the facets consists in the avoidance of criminal behavior. Some well-socialized persons, under extreme circumstances, will commit crimes; it is a paradox of prison life that murderers, if that one impassioned act is the only blemish on their records, often make the best trusties. Some habitual criminals are conscientious workmen, loving husbands or fathers, or trustworthy members of some dyssocial subculture. Many noncriminals, on the other hand, are shiftless or mean and hard-hearted, lack prosocial motivation, and are bad citizens. Some psychopaths, especially those with talent and who are born to privilege, manage to achieve gratifying professional success through more or less normal channels. That is, talented persons who are well rewarded for their success in school and in their later professional pursuits can develop good work habits and strong, goal-directed aspirations without the benefit of effective parenting and also without the goad of conscience or the fear of failure. Those who do acquire this component of socialization can often successfully simulate the other components and conceal their lack of a restraining conscience. Because some criminals are in other respects well socialized, whereas many poorly or partly socialized people are not overtly criminal, it is necessary to distinguish criminality from socialization.

CRIME AND CRIMINALITY

The classical theory of criminology, as promulgated by Bentham, argued that human behavior is directed toward the pursuit of pleasure and the avoidance of pain. Because some of the things we might do to pursue pleasure or avoid pain are defined by law as criminal, from this perspective crime is in a sense natural. The so-called "control" theories of criminology therefore focused on providing sanctions that would make the consequences of crime sufficiently painful so that crime would tend to be avoided. Thus, the classical theory tended to ignore individual differences in criminality.

Sociological theories, like that of Sutherland and Cressey (1978) which dominated criminological thinking during much of this century, took the diametrically opposite tack, holding with Rousseau that crime is a violation of man's natural impulses and must be learned. These *cultural deviance* theories contended that, "except for the idiot and the insane, who cannot know what they are about, the universal experience of mankind is conformity with the norms of the groups into which they have been socialized and to which they owe allegiance. People never violate the norms of their *own* groups, only the norms of other groups" (Kornhauser, 1978, p. 29). Like most theories in this area, this one contains at least a kernel of truth. A boy allowed to run wild on the mean streets may become socialized according to the norms of his delinquent peers and, while remaining loyal and supportive to the members of his gang, may become a predator with respect to the larger society. But, as a general theory of crime, social deviance theory fails and it fails in part because, like the classical theory, it ignores individual differences.

Gottesman and Goldsmith (1994) represented the probability of crime or anti-social behavior as a multiplicative function of genetic and environmental factors. Although one cannot argue with the descriptive truth of this formulation, I prefer not to conflate, as this scheme does, the early developmental environment, which is, or should be, dominated by parental interactions, with the current environment of neighborhood and peers. An alternative formulation, which I favor, is to think of antisocial behavior as a multiplicative function of antisocial proclivities or *criminality* interacting with the temptations or protections of the immediate environment. Then, criminality in turn can itself be thought of as a product of genetic factors interacting with early experience, especially experience with parental figures.

By claiming that criminality is a function of innate antisocial proclivities combined with inadequate parenting, I seem to be asserting a leaden platitude. But it is a very important first principle that will point us in the right direction. Many social scientists, sociologists, and anthropologists assume something quite different. Anthropologists since Franz Boas have been "taught to hallow" the idea that "all human behavior is the result of social conditioning" (Turner, quoted in Freeman, 1992, p. 26). We have seen that the cultural deviance theorists believed that there are no individual differences in the degree of socialization. Some psychologists, like Walter Mischel, have assumed that behavior is primarily situational and that person-factors—individual differences in traits like socialization or criminality—are unimportant. The classical studies of Hartshorne and May (1928) left generations of psychologists with the belief that "honesty," which sounds very much like "socialization," is also situational, that honesty is not in fact a trait unity. And many people, including some psychologists, still subscribe to Rousseau's idea that the child is a kind of noble savage, naturally good until corrupted by social influences. Rousseau was able to maintain this inverted image of reality because he abandoned his own children to the care of their mother but it is difficult to understand how anyone who has actually reared a little boy could sustain such a notion. We shall return to this issue later in the discussion of crime from the perspective of evolutionary psychology.

All of these assumptions are violated in some degree by my contention that most important criminal behavior can be understood in terms of an acquired trait called *conscientiousness* interacting with the criminal impulse, which varies with both the individual and the situation. That is, I assume that yielding to criminal temptation means that, at least momentarily, the impulse is stronger than the forces of restraint.

As seen in Part II, children differ innately in characteristics that influence both sides of this equation. Fear of the consequences is an important restraining force and some children are innately more fearful than others. I argue later that relatively fearless children tend to develop an effective conscience less readily than most children do and therefore may be less constrained, not only by fear, but also by guilt. Unusually impulsive children may act before they think about the consequences and thus fail to experience their internal restraints until it is too late.

Other innate differences among children influence the impulse side of the equation. A hot-tempered child is more sorely tempted to strike out than is one of a more placid disposition. For some children, risk itself is a powerful attraction because it can produce in them an excited "high" that is intensely gratifying—and many forms of criminal behavior provide this risk-produced high just as reliably as any bungee jump. Unsocialized people tend to do a poor job of socializing their own children. For this reason, people with hard-to-socialize temperaments tend to produce children with a double liability, children with difficult temperaments whose parents are unable or unwilling to socialize them.

Figure 1.1 illustrates the differences between psychopathy and sociopathy and how these two troublesome syndromes are related to genetic factors and to parenting. The bell-shaped curve at the left of the figure indicates that most people

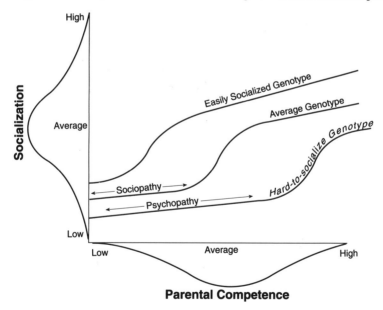

FIG. 1.1. Degree of socialization as a function of parental competence, plotted for three genotypes. The child with an easy-to-socialize temperament and aptitude is likely to make it even with relatively incompetent parents. Really hard-to-socialize children are likely to grow up as psychopaths unless their parents are very skillful or unless strong socializing incentives are provided from other sources in their rearing environments. The majority of persons who have average genotypes, may remain unsocialized, hence sociopaths, if their parents are incompetent or indifferent.

are in the broad middle range of socialization with a few saintly people very high on this dimension whereas a few more, the criminals, are very low. The horizontal axis represents parental competence and the curve at the bottom assumes that most parents are average, some are incompetent, and a few are super parents.

The top curve in the body of the figure represents what might happen to a child, call him Pat, whose innate temperament makes him truly easy to socialize; he is bright, nonaggressive, moderately timid, with a naturally loving disposition. Like all little boys he starts out life essentially unsocialized and, if his parents are totally incompetent, his neighborhood a war zone, and his peers all little thugs, Pat might remain marginally socialized. But boys like Pat tend to avoid conflict and chaos, they are attracted by order and civility, and they tend to seek out socialized mentors and role models. With even poor parenting, the Pats of this world tend to stay out of trouble.

The middle curve in Fig. 1.1 represents Bill, a boy with an average genetic make-up, moderately aggressive, moderately adventurous. Because he is average, we can safely anticipate that average parents, living in an average neighborhood, will be able to raise Bill to be an average, law-abiding citizen. Incompetent parents, however, living in a disruptive neighborhood, will not succeed with Bill who will remain a sociopath.

Mike, the bottom curve in the figure, is really difficult to socialize; he may be fearless, or hostile and aggressive. The great majority of parents would find Mike too much to cope with, a perennial source of worry and disappointment. Mike's curve goes up on the far right of the figure because really talented parents or, more likely, a truly fortuitous combination of parents, neighborhood, peer group, and subsequent mentors, can sometimes socialize even these hard cases.

The important fact that I was not clever enough to symbolize in Fig. 1.1 is this; the Bills in each generation, because they are average, are vastly more numerous that either the Pats or the Mikes. Most youngsters have average genetic tempera-ments like Bill and therefore, even though only a minority of parents are truly incompetent, the total number of Bills (and Marys) who reached adolescence and adulthood still unsocialized—the number who become criminal sociopaths—is much larger than the number of psychopaths like Mike. Moreover, because un-socialized people tend to become incompetent parents themselves, the number of sociopaths is growing faster than the general population, faster indeed than we can build reform schools and prisons.

In modern times, dog owners who want their pets to learn to come, sit, heel, and stay, enroll in dog obedience classes where they are told at the outset that: "This class is to teach *you* how to teach your dog." Many modern parents undertake the socialization of their children without prior instruction of any kind and without effective help. Our species was not designed to learn the rules with such ineffectual instruction. There is a lot to learn about the process of socialization from partnering a puppy in an obedience class and a lot to learn also about individual differences in aptitude for socialization from comparing the different breeds of dog that one will find there—as is seen in the next chapter.

2

An Animal Model: The Bull Terrier

Having owned two bull terriers over the years, I have found my acquaintance with this breed more useful to an understanding of criminality than the perusal of most texts on the subject. The bull terrier was created as a fighting dog in the early 19th century by cross-breeding the English bulldog, for its strength and resolution, with the white English terrier, for its agility and grit. The bull terrier's quickness and tenacity, his powerful jaws, his relative fearlessness, and high pain threshold made him a formidable gladiator. But this breed's unusual appearance and lively personality proved attractive to many dog fanciers and for the past 100 years or so the bull terrier has been bred primarily as a companion animal.

Not everyone, however, is equipped with the patience and determination to cope successfully with a bull terrier pup. In dog obedience classes, where the herding and the hunting breeds keep their eyes on their masters, waiting for instructions and kind words, the bull terrier has a different agenda. He wants to romp and raise hell and he is relatively indifferent to punishment. With his great jaws he can reduce wooden chairs to kindling, destroy shoes and leather briefcases in a light-hearted moment, and create chaos in a hurry. The unsuspecting owner who just wants a dog around the house and chooses a bull terrier because he fancies the breeds' distinctive muzzle is in for a shock when he discovers that he has adopted a juvenile delinquent.

On the other hand, the bull terrier (Bully or BT to his friends) is outgoing, fun-loving and sociable, free of neurotic inhibitions. Polly Peachum, our first BT, matured to take a place in our affections like one of our own children and Slick Willy, the current incumbent, is making his way toward the same goal. Willie's pedigree shows that he is by *Cry Havoc* out of *One Tough Cookie*, which tells you something right there (about BTs and their owners) Because Willie is less than 1 year old, I am forcibly reminded each day of the parental attributes required to help him reach that goal of happy socialization. These include, on the one hand, my determination to be the boss, to refuse to tolerate unacceptable behaviors, and a willingness to take the time to enforce each lawful command. Little by little, as

Polly did before him, Willy is slowly coming to realize that I am bigger and stronger than he is—that I am the Alpha dog in his pack—and that he will have to do what I say in the end. I have had to smack him a few times to get that point across; it is hard to hurt a bull terrier and Willy has never yelped nor appeared to be frightened, but when he is leaping and biting with youthful glee I do what is required to make him stop, now, and to display canine submission to superior authority.

Let me be clear that we really do like Willy; we enjoy his company when he is behaving himself and we enjoy playing with him and making him happy. We take him for walks and for rides and we let him watch television with us on the couch and he sleeps on my bed. The carrot is at least as important as the stick. Willy's obedience training is based largely on positive reinforcement; he sits and stays and comes because he's praised for doing it and wants to do it, and because he is gradually learning that, in the end, he will have to do it anyway. It is hard work to socialize a BT and it demands a certain amount of good sense and self-restraint. When Willy occasionally dashes out of the yard, willfully ignoring my "Willy! Come!," and I have to chase after him, often in my stocking feet, there is a strong temptation to belt him once I get my hands on him and it is difficult to say "Good boy, Willy" and bestow instead a friendly pat when finally he does come to me. But it would plainly be dumb to punish him when, his brief display of independence over, he does come to my command, just because I'm mad about his freedom dash which he has now put behind him. When Willy chews the top off a plastic bottle and floods the basement with a gallon of bleach, one has to be able to rinse off his feet, shut him up in his cage, and get out the mop with no more than a few muttered imprecations.

Parenting Styles

In her widely cited research, Baumrind (1971, 1980) has identified four styles of parenting that I believe would produce predictably different results if adopted by the surrogate parents of a young bull terrier. The *authoritarian* parent emphasizes dominance and the stick while neglecting the carrot. Although BTs are relatively hard to intimidate, I have no doubt that I could bully Willy sufficiently to make him restrain himself when I am nearby. But, instead of being an outgoing and friendly animal, I feel sure that Willy would in time become surly and potentially dangerous in my absence or, once I am enfeebled by age and no longer tougher than he is, even dangerous to me. A truly antisocial parent (not one of Baumrind's types) might actively encourage the BT's aggressiveness, setting him upon stray cats and dogs or even people to stimulate his blood lust. Willy has the makings of a lovable companion or a fearsome attack dog; either suite of qualities could be cultivated by appropriate training.

The *permissive* parent tries to be loving and affectionate but fails to set limits. I remember Susie, a middle-aged BT female whose middle-aged permissive owner brought her to a gathering of owners and dogs brought together for a kind of BT beauty contest. Susie was uncontrollable, barking and lunging on the end of her chain (Susie bit through ropes or leashes in a hurry) while her poor owner strove to hang on and maintain her balance. In the end, she had to lock up Susie in the car and wistfully depart because there was no way that Susie could be taken into the ring with the other dogs. Canids and, I believe, all social animals including homo sapiens tend to form dominance hierarchies. Every dog trainer knows that it is essential to establish and maintain an ascendant position; either the human or the dog will be dominant and it is in both their interests for the human to assume that role. Susie's owner failed that test and they both suffered for it.

The *neglecting/rejecting* parent should be prevented by law from acquiring a bull terrier who, left to roam without supervision or effective restraint, having no affectionate relationship to elicit and enlarge his prosocial impulses, will almost inevitably become an outlaw. He will discover his ability to dominate other animals and he will become a bully and a thief. It will not be long before he ends up in the pound or shot dead on the street.

But, reared by an *authoritative* parent, one able to set firm limits while providing affectionate reinforcement for acceptable alternative behavior, that same animal could become a favorite of the neighborhood as Polly was and Willy (I hope!) will also be in his turn. It is important to understand that there is no incompatibility between dominance and love. Both Polly and Willy acknowledged me as the Alpha or dominant animal but both Polly once and Willy now welcome my return with exuberant enthusiasm. My own father was the Alpha male in our family and his five sons unquestioningly acknowledged his authority and loved him unreservedly. One important function of the dominance instinct is to avoid conflict; my father never laid his hand on me in anger and spoke harshly to me on very rare occasions. It did not occur to any of his sons to challenge his authority and it was therefore seldom necessary for him to assert it.

The suggested consequences of inept or indifferent parenting would not apply with equal force to all dog breeds. Herding and hunting dogs, because of the docile temperament and behavioral predilections that have been bred into them, are easier to control and to train, they need less restraint, are simply easier to socialize than BTs are and have less potential for outlawry. Bull terrier breeders are expected to identify the occasional pup that proves to be overly endowed with the ancestral belligerence and either euthanize it or at least make sure that it is neutered. Willy is considerably more aggressive than Polly was; males of most species, including our own, are more inclined toward violence than females. Male dogs (and cats), except for a few special animals to be used for show or breeding purposes, are routinely neutered, one purpose of which is to reduce their subsequent aggressiveness. Without proper training, however, any dog will be at least a nuisance and just where he ends up on the continuum of canine criminality will depend largely on his innate tendencies interacting with the accidents of circumstance and especially with the characteristics of the other dogs and people in his immediate environment.

What Has Training Dogs to Do With Raising Children?

Developmental psychologists do not suppose that the role of parents in the socialization of children is just a matter of using judiciously the carrot and the stick (Maccoby, 1992). They speak of the attachment between mother and child that is established during the first 2 years of life, a bond that may affect other relationships the child forms later on. They explain that, as the child's competencies grow, the good parent will provide opportunities for self-regulation and encourage his or her participation in decision making. Unlike puppies, after all, children develop complex concepts of themselves and then tend to behave in conformity with those self-concepts. A good parent helps to insure that this self-concept is a socialized one.

On the genetic side of the equation, the dog–human parallel is more obvious. The differences in temperament and behavior tendencies observed between the nearly 800 breeds of the domestic dog reflect the variability latent within the genetic material of their common ancestor, *canis lupus* (Mech, 1970). Across individuals of our human species there is at least as much genetic diversity as that seen among the canids.

But, dog and wolf pups need to be socialized as do human children. Because children are more complex than puppies and because they have language and self-concepts, children are socialized not only by the puppy rules of conditioning and reinforcement but by more cognitive principles as well. Parenting is plainly harder than dog training, yet do not suppose that it is irrelevant or demeaning to compare the two. If your neighbor's dog is out of control and their little boy seems feisty and adventurous, you have a legitimate cause for concern about what that child will be like in adolescence.

A Gedanken Experiment

Suppose that every parent of a young child were to be given also a puppy to care for. Three or 4 years later we will do a census to see how those animals have turned out. If the pups were to be allocated randomly, then we should expect to find many tolerably socialized canine companions, some even graduates of obedience classes who proudly show off their acquired skills. But there will also be some frightened dogs with broken spirits, others who are not even house broken, and some dogs who are vicious or destructive. The happy, well-adjusted dogs, and also the neurotic ones, are likely to be collies and shelties and spaniels, breeds with easy, tractable temperaments. Bull terriers will be more numerous among the outlaws.

Now let us change the experiment and match the temperament of the pup to the temperament of the owners, in the same way that Nature matches the temperament of the child to that of the parent. Now most of those lucky shelties and spaniels will be raised by responsible, law-abiding masters and most of the bull terrier and rottweiler pups will be placed with masters least competent to raise them properly. No Humane Society would countenance such an experiment, of course. This is one inhumane experiment that we can do—are doing—only with human puppies.

3

A Classification of Criminal Types

In this chapter I present a kind of rogues' gallery of criminal types for the purpose of giving an illustrative overview of the complex etiology of criminal behavior. There seems to be an almost irresistible tendency for criminological theorists to oversimplify the causes of crime, to underestimate the variety of psychological peculiarities that can contribute to the underlying disposition for criminal behavior. Crime has been said to result from unemployment and exposure to bad company, from "mesomorphic" physique and "somatotonic" personality, from "anomie" or from an unconscious need for punishment, from excessive or displaced rage and aggression, and so on and on. In their valuable *General Theory of Crime*, Gottfredson and Hirschi (1990) posited that the defining characteristic of the criminal temperament is low self-control. Although each of these notions may contribute to our understanding of some criminals, none of them apply to all criminals. As an antidote for this urge to oversimplify, it would useful if we could introduce here the case histories of, say, 1,000 consecutive admissions to the state and federal prison systems. But each case would require a novella to do justice to the variety of interacting factors that determine the course of real lives and so this approach is impractical. Instead I shall picture in broad strokes a zoo of caricatures, each inmate representing one of the host of psychological characteristics that may contribute to criminality. As anticipated in the earlier discussion, the disposition toward criminal behavior usually results from a complete or partial failure of socialization, either due to parental non-, mis-, or malfeasance, to innate temperamental peculiarities that make the child difficult to socialize, or to a combination of these. Moreover, even a tolerably well-socialized individual may commit crimes under unusually strong provocation.

In zoology, carnivorous mammals are grouped together under the *Order Carnivora* into subgroups called families such as the *canidae, felidae, ursidae,* and so on. The felidae, in turn, include many genera such as the lions, tigers, civets, lynx, and the like. I shall borrow this Linnaean scheme for the classification of my rogues' gallery. These groupings are not seriously proposed as real "types" or taxa in the

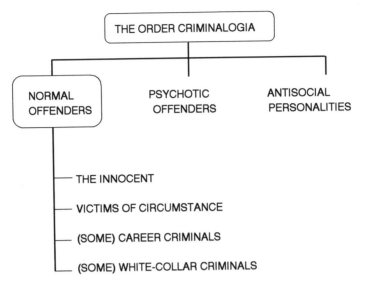

FIG. 3.1. The order of criminal offenders includes three main families: offenders who are psychologically normal; a few who are genuinely psychotic; and (the largest family) offenders who have never been adequately socialized, either because they were difficult to socialize due to inherent peculiarities of temperament or disposition, or because the usual socializing agents, primarily the parents, were incompetent or unsocialized themselves. The family of normal offenders includes several "genera" as listed in the figure and described in the text.

sense of disease entities; the zoological analogy is for heuristic purposes only. Nor is this taxonomy intended to be exhaustive. The main message is that "the criminal" consists of more than just one breed of cat.

The *Order Criminalogia* will be taken to include all criminal offenders, major and minor, one-timers and recidivists, the imprisoned and the not-yet caught. These may be subdivided into the *Families of the Order Criminalogia*, which include the three main categories shown in Fig. 3.1.

PSYCHOLOGICALLY NORMAL OFFENDERS

Some prison inmates were tolerably well socialized as children and have temperaments within the broadly normal range, although they are likely to be at the low end of that range on the traits of harmavoidance and constraint and toward the high end on risk-taking. Some (albeit few) are actually innocent, wrongly convicted, and not criminals at all. Among the guilty majority, some find themselves behind bars because they happened to encounter a situation that was especially provocative or a temptation that was irresistibly alluring or because they found themselves in circumstances where the licit options were unappealing in comparison to opportunities whose illegality could be easily rationalized.

The Innocent Inmate

Although most prison inmates claim to be innocent, at least of the particular offense for which they were convicted, we should not forget that a few, let us hope a very few, are innocent in fact. Through my work as a critic of the polygraph test—the mythical "lie detector"—I have been involved in a number of cases of men who were convicted, largely on the basis of having failed polygraph tests, sentenced to prison and then, years later, proved to have been innocent. Their alleged crimes included rape, sexual abuse of children and, in several cases, homicide. Floyd Fay, for example, was arrested in 1975 and charged with robbing a convenience store in Toledo, Ohio, and shooting the proprietor, who made a tenuous death-bed identification of the masked robber. Fay had no previous criminal record and, absent other evidence linking him to this crime, the prosecutor offered to drop the charges if Fay would take and pass a polygraph test; Fay was required to stipulate, however, that the results could be used against him in court should he fail the test. Floyd subsequently failed two successive tests by different examiners and this was sufficient to lead the jury to convict him of aggravated murder.

Sentenced to life in prison, Fay read up on the polygraph test, found my name in that literature and wrote to me asking for assistance. Meanwhile, however, a bright young attorney volunteered his help and, like a real-life Perry Mason, uncovered evidence leading to the identification and confession of the real killers (Cimerman, 1981). A free man again after serving 2 years in an Ohio prison, Floyd told me that he was glad his alleged crime had been murder "because then at least you get some respect."

Victims of Circumstance

Some crimes, especially "crimes of passion," are committed by essentially normal people reacting atypically to a uniquely provocative situation. The defining property of these individuals is that, if they were to be allowed to return to a normal environment, their likelihood of committing subsequent crimes would be no higher than for any random citizen of their age and gender.

Although I am known for my sweet disposition, there was one occasion when, as a young man, I put my hands around the throat of another man and tried my best to strangle him. Fortunately, I was forestalled in my ambition by the fact that he was a better street fighter than I was. It was the one time in my life when I truly "lost my temper" and I can remember having no concern whatever about anything except the need to attack this person and that, for the few minutes that the fit lasted, I had no sense of volitional control. Had I managed to hurt my opponent, I would have felt later that we both had been victims of the same unavoidable accident.

The Career Criminal

This genus consists of people who may not be pathological psychiatrically or psychologically, in their appetites or even in their moral values, but who have chosen a criminal career because it seems to be the best course open to someone with their abilities and opportunities. This category includes tens of thousands of young men, many of them minorities, who are confronted with the choice of an entry-level job in the private sector, at perhaps $200 a week, versus an entry-level job in the drug trade at several times that amount, tax free. By spending billions in the futile "war on drugs" we have created a multibillion dollar industry that conspires to divert the boldest, most ambitious, and entrepreneurial of these young people onto a path leading to prison or death in some alley. Absent the lure of the illegal drug trade, the less socialized of these young men would turn to other forms of crime but some at least might be salvaged.

To understand the psychology of the people in this genus, another thought experiment might help. Let us identify a random sample of 100 young men, college graduates in their 30s who are now firmly established in middle management or some profession and with excellent prospects. Suppose that we could transport them each back in time to age 18 and put them in a situation in which further education was not an option. Now we let them choose between a job at McDonald's or in a car wash versus one selling drugs at which they earn, say, $1,000 per week. The latter position carries risks, from the police and especially from other drug dealers, but it also entails opportunities for advancement to positions of higher status and much greater remuneration.

Will all of these 100 bright and ambitious young men reject the drug-selling option because it is illegal? Many of them will make that choice, for religious or moral reasons or because drug dealing entails more stress than they can handle. But I think that some of the more competitive, aggressive, and daring—the more entrepreneurial—of the 100 would make the other choice and, if they survive, become what I call *career criminals*. Ten years later they will have become inured to the harsh necessities of that profession. Like the banker who must foreclose on some poor debtor's mortgage, they may have foreclosed on the life of a police snitch or an aggressive competitor. They may be kind to women and children, loyal to their friends, contributors to the United Fund, differing from the men they would have become but for our time machine only in the fact that they would be unlikely to invite their son or daughter to spend a day with them at the office.

The White-Collar Criminal

People with broadly normal temperaments and backgrounds are sometimes lured into crime by environmental circumstances that constitute a kind of Devil's offer that they cannot (or do not choose to) refuse. They may be politicians offered gifts, trips, or interest-free loans by lobbyists who affect to be just friendly or admiring, in circumstances where the expectation of a quid pro quo is so implicit as to be almost undetectable. They may be police officers who "know" the suspect is guilty so that their perjured testimony accomplishes what they believe to be a just result. They may be businessmen or lawyers, company executives, or stock speculators who see a chance for profit with little risk, and where there is no sentient victim who must bear the loss, men who find it difficult to distinguish this case from any other, licit, entrepreneurial opportunity. They are not often caught and, when they are, they may suffer the same shame and guilt that you or I might feel in the circumstances. One is more likely to succumb to these Devil's offers if one has a temperament similar to that of the psychopath with whom we will get acquainted later.

THE PSYCHOTIC OFFENDER

Due to their delusional misinterpretation of reality, the behavior of these individuals is inappropriate to the actual circumstances and may be criminal. Most psychotic persons are not violent and, indeed, are more likely to be victims than assailants. However, the probability of assaultive behavior among psychotics is significantly higher than for an unselected population (Monahan, 1993), especially for those living on their own, often among the ranks of the homeless, who are unlikely to regularly take their antipsychotic medications.

THE ANTISOCIAL PERSONALITIES

This is by far the largest and most complex family. Its members are characterized by a persisting disposition toward antisocial behavior. Because this disposition can usually be dated from adolescence, this family includes those individuals who qualify for the psychiatric diagnosis of APD—as described in *DSM–IV* (APA, 1994)—as well as some others who do not meet APD criteria.

I identify three genera within this family as well as several species and subspecies within each genus. But we must not get carried away with this taxonomic exercise. I believe that one might find in the prison population people who fit comfortably within each of these "species" but it is important to remember that this is really intended to be a taxonomy of etiological factors that are conducive toward crime. Most actual criminals will represent mixed etiologies.

I refer to the largest and most important subgroup as the genus of sociopathic personalities. Some sociopaths had reasonably normal temperaments but especially incompetent or indifferent parents; others are aggressive or fearless, stimulus seekers or Machiavellian manipulators, people who, as children, posed too great a problem for their well-intending but overmatched parents to cope with. Because "sociopath" and "psychopath" are no longer included in the official psychiatric nomenclature, and because these terms have never been clearly or usefully defined in the past, I take the liberty of using them here to emphasize an important distinction between antisocials with abnormal temperaments (psychopaths) and antisocials who were badly socialized (sociopaths).

Although most sociopaths are broadly unsocialized, there is considerable variation within this genus and we shall identify several species, people for whom the distinguishing feature is an alienation from some or all of their fellow humans, others who specialize in dominance and sadism, still others who are socialized but to the mores and values of a dyssocial outgroup.

The genus of psychopaths includes people for whom we can say that, if they are unsocialized, the fault lies not so much with their parents as with themselves. These include the primary psychopaths who, from their childhood, possessed temperaments that were truly difficult to manage. I have already referred to such people in discussing some members of the sociopath genus above and some individuals belong to both of these clubs.

Some psychopaths, however, are at least superficially socialized, some have learned the rules and do generally obey them. Especially if they are talented or privileged, they may do well in school, hold a job, succeed in a profession. But there remains lurking in the background an antisocial disposition that manifests itself from time to time. In some cases, as illustrated by the species of distempered psychopaths, a reasonably socialized matrix of habits and restraints is overmastered periodically by a kind of brainstorm. Finally, the species of secondary and hysterical psychopathy are more speculative categories. The former includes those Dionysian individuals for whom the attraction of Eve's apple is just too potent to resist. They are more soberly described in due course.

An earlier generation of psychiatrists might have classified many criminals as members of the genus of character neurosis, people who are deviant neither in socialization nor in temperament. These were people whose antisocial behavior was thought to constitute the acting out of unconscious, neurotic conflicts. Psychotherapy that was intended to provide the patient with insight into these conflicts too often failed to produce any useful change in the behavior, however, and this classification has gone rather out of fashion. Yet, as we shall see, there are some individuals who can usefully be classified under this heading.

The Sociopathic Personality

This is the largest genus of all, consisting of young men—and increasing numbers of young women—who were simply never adequately socialized during childhood and adolescence. Many members of this genus also possess impulse peculiarities or habit patterns that are traceable to deviant learning histories interacting, perhaps, with deviant genetic predilections. Some illustrative species and subspecies are listed in Fig. 3.2 and described below.

The Common Sociopath

Sometimes called *subcultural delinquents*, this is the main species of the largest genus of antisocial personalities and, because of the rising incidence of incompetent parenting, they are increasing in number. They have a weak and unelaborated conscience, are not shamed by much of what would shame you and me. They have a weak future perspective because they have grown up under circumstances in which the future was unpredictable and only the pleasures and pains directly at hand could be relied on. They take pride in rule breaking rather than in rule observance and are like feral children grown up, gratifying impulses of the moment, disinterested in long-term goals. They are the natural result of weak parental bonding, weak parental control, and bad parental example. Most commonly they also display the effects of being turned loose in the streets to run with other sociopathic children where they assimilate the atavistic social structure of the street or of the adolescent gang. These individuals are feral creatures, undomesticated predators, stowaways on our communal voyage who have never signed the Social Contract.

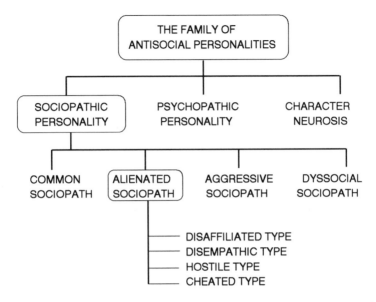

FIG. 3.2. The family of antisocial personalities includes three main "genera": the sociopathic personalities, the psychopathic personalities, and the character neuroses. The most common species of sociopathic personality is the ordinary sociopath. Other variants include the alienated sociopath (of which four subspecies are listed in the figure), the aggressive sociopath, and the dyssocial sociopath. All four species and subspecies are described in the text.

Crystal Taylor

Susan Sheehan's (1993a, 1993b) true-life account of this teenage resident of the South Bronx provides a graphic picture of how the young of our species can be expected to develop in the absence of parental socialization. Crystal was the eldest of Florence Drummond's six children, all illegitimate, by four different men. Florence too was illegitimate and had been brutalized by her borderline psychotic mother and then shunted around from one foster-care placement to another from the time she was 6 years old.

Florence met Crystal's father, Wesley Taylor, just before he entered the service and when Crystal was born during his absence, Florence applied for welfare. Wesley returned from the Vietnam War addicted to heroin. During the ensuing 20 years, Wesley's only job was for a few months as a parking lot attendant, yet he fathered several children by at least three different women and was alternately supported by them or by his mother until his death from AIDS in 1991. Florence also became a heroin addict, served short jail terms for welfare fraud and shoplifting, and helped support her habit by selling drugs in a small way. She frequently kept Crystal home from school to care for the younger children while she herself went out, often not returning until late at night. Crystal herself started using drugs before she entered her teens and one morning smoked a bag of PCP before going to school where she attacked her eighth-grade teacher and had to be held down by several adults until taken by ambulance to the hospital.

At this time, Crystal, her mother, and her four younger half-siblings were living in a filthy one-bedroom apartment with Florence's cousin, Hazel, Hazel's daughter, and current boyfriend. When Crystal was 13, Daquan Jefferson, a small-time drug dealer 9 years older than she, met the attractive girl on the street, invited her to the movies, and then took her to a hotel room where she pocketed $40 that dropped from his pockets when he undressed. Not long afterward, Daquan took Crystal to come share his bed in his parents' apartment in a Bronx housing project. There, within the next few months, Crystal became pregnant with Daquan Jr. who was delivered 2 months prematurely when his mother was 14.

Crystal agreed to place little Daquan in foster care while she herself was placed in a group home run by a Catholic agency and housing five other "adjustment-disordered" girls between 16 and 18 (at a cost, in 1985, of $25,500 a year each). Although the girls were required to attend school, Crystal usually missed her first class and

> some days, instead of going to school she and two friends from the group home traveled to Manhattan by bus and subway and went to the movies on Forty-second Street; the journey was only slightly longer than the one to school ... and from Crystal's point of view there was more to look forward to when she reached her destination. (Sheehan, 1993, p. 64)

Soon after her 16th birthday, Crystal visited a boyfriend who supplied her with marijuana and she was arrested when the police busted the friend's place of business. A few months later, she and two girlfriends were apprehended by department store security personnel for shoplifting clothes. When Crystal was 5 or 6, her mother often took her to Bloomingdale's where she would steal clothes to sell for drugs and Crystal herself was an experienced shoplifter at 16. It was not that she lacked money; the group home provided a clothing allowance and men friends gave her cash "presents." Crystal's view was, "Why buy when I can just take? I can get me a new outfit and still have money in my pocket" (p. 66).

Although Daquan Sr. continued giving Crystal spending money, she soon decided that he was too old and too short to hold her interest. She was attractive and maintained an active social and sex life with a variety of young men including Diamond, a drug dealer with whom she again became pregnant at age 16. At the time of her first pregnancy, Daquan Sr. and his mother both counseled her against an abortion: "You don't be needing no abortion; them things are dangerous" (p. 68), but this time she terminated the pregnancy. During that spring, Crystal was late to school 36 times and absent altogether 30 days from January to May. She visited little Daquan at his foster home from time to time but realized she had no desire to spend much time with him: "I've got no parently patience" (p. 72).

Although petite and generally good natured, Crystal did not shrink from violence when aroused. She cracked her mother's roommate, Hazel, over the head with a two by four once when Crystal was just 13 and, with Daquan Sr.: "We did a lot of punching and grabbing over the years. ... When I was 15, I hit him over the head with a glass ashtray shaped like a gingerbread man. When I was on the phone with my male friends, he'd try to listen: I'd smash him over the head with the phone." Once when she dawdled in the hall with friends after her math class had begun, the teacher at first would not let Crystal in so she smashed the glass pane in the door and told that teacher off: "The bitch was scared" (p. 69). Crystal felt that school was unreasonably strict: "I got written up for every little thing—like cutting some guy with a pocket knife after gym class—and the dean was unreasonable" (p. 70).

By the time her story ends at age 21, Crystal had spent 4 years in the group home, 2 years sharing an "independent living" apartment with another group home alumnus, and 3 years in an apartment of her own. Her modest earnings in a job addressing envelopes scarcely cover her rent, phone bill, and the monthly cost of her beeper (Crystal doesn't want to miss any interesting invitations that come when she's away from home). But she has had a succession of male friends, most of them drug dealers, all willing to keep her supplied with reefers and money for nice clothes, jewelry, and other necessities. Crystal claimed to have been really in love with Diamond, and when Diamond was killed in a drug-related altercation, she took the week off from work to attend his funeral. But she had spent the previous 2 days and nights with another dealer, Troy, and it was Troy who took her to buy a new outfit and escorted her to Diamond's wake. Crystal valued these muscular and adventurous young men who admired her; she enjoyed being with them in bed and out but her sense of loss when one died or went to jail does not seem to have been deep.

Crystal's life so far has been a reasonably happy one, partly because she is blessed with a happy temperament and is unburdened by a nagging conscience or by apprehensions about the future. But her future can only be described as bleak. Since puberty, Crystal has been vivacious and attractive to men whose attentions have helped to maintain her self-esteem ("I'se lovable," she admits) and have provided her with money, little luxuries, admiring companionship, drugs, sex, and other forms of entertainment, and the envy of other girls, which Crystal values. But the bloom that has attracted all these suitors is beginning to fade. With her poor work habits and lack of skills, Crystal cannot support herself honestly without help. Unlike many of her friends, she has avoided burdening herself with children to care for but that may change when her beeper stops beeping and the boys stop coming by with presents. And as she says herself, Crystal lacks "parently patience" and any children who in the future may be reared by her are unlikely to be more socialized than she is. Her involvement with drugs, both using and selling, seems likely to increase in future years. Like her mother before her, her involvement in crime is likely to be small-time and nonviolent, more because of lack of opportunity and because she is a woman than because of active avoidance on her part of such alternatives. If she does contribute in future to the statistics of important crime, it is likely to be either as a victim (she has already been shot once, in the hand, by a jealous boyfriend) or by producing one or more male children during the next two decades and choosing to rear them herself with AFDC support.

Crystal could not be called an evil person, a "bad seed." She is of average intelligence, healthy (so far), and with a happy disposition; had she been the daughter of real parents in a real family there is every reason to suppose that she would now be educated, socialized, and ready to become a functional, independent member of society. Instead, she will always be a social burden and a costly one. Daquan Jr. spent many weeks in a hospital intensive care unit after his premature birth and hundreds of weeks since then in expensive foster care. We can hope that Daquan will turn out to be better socialized than either of his parents but the odds are assuredly not as good as they would have been if he had been a full-term baby raised by two mature biological parents in a stable and healthy environment.

The Alienated Sociopath

Here I refer to an individual with an undeveloped ability to love or to affiliate with others. A failure of empathy or affectional attachment is plainly a risk factor for antisocial behavior because one of the important protective factors that lead us to avoid predatory crime is our inclination to identify with and care about the victim. There are several variants.

The Disaffiliated Type

The absence of a nurturant parent during a critical period may prevent the development of the normal capacity for love and attachment that, as social animals, we all presumably possess. We know that children whose innate proclivity for language is not developed during the early years may never learn to speak and it seems likely that our native affiliative tendencies also require stimulation and reinforcement early in childhood. There are children who seldom or never have nurturant, loving, or happy interactions with other human beings or whose approaches to their parent are unpredictably punished so that they become extinguished. Such a child will not develop the prosocial components of socialization and their inability to relate emotionally to other people makes his or her adult adjustment problematic. This incapacity for fellow-feeling may be as intractable as any innate defect of temperament, yet I classify such people as sociopaths rather than as psychopaths because their condition can be prevented in the same way that other forms of sociopathy could be prevented, by reducing the frequency of non-nurturant, incompetent parents.

The Disempathic Type

This individual is capable of emotional investment in his family, his mate or, perhaps, his dog, but has a constricted "circle of empathy" and reacts to most people only as objects. Although it is clear that, unlike most other mammals, our species is capable of empathy, capable of sharing to some extent the pain and the joy of other human beings and even other species, it is also clear that this capacity must be cultivated by experience. There are, moreover, wide individual differences in the breadth or inclusiveness of people's circles of empathy. My wife shares the pain of all creatures from children, wolves, and elephants to ladybugs and spiders but human hunters, trappers, and most lawyers and politicians fall outside her circle of empathy. A child reared by parents who dislike animals as well as most of their neighbors is likely to have a constricted circle of empathy. When we are exposed too long and too often to stress and the suffering of others, most of us defensively constrict our empathic tendencies. One suspects that even Mother Teresa, like Albert Schweitzer before her, has developed emotional calluses to partly shield her from the human suffering she has devoted her life to assuaging.

It is an interesting question whether television plays a useful role in this aspect of socialization. One hallmark of the disempathic person is his or her inability to get much involved in TV drama; to enjoy either soap operas or "Masterpiece Theater" requires an ability to care about at least some of the characters. I am convinced that I am far better able to empathize with people of color after years of vicarious acquaintance through television. By the same token, one expects that those African Americans who habitually watch TV programs involving mainly White actors must feel a greater kinship with Whites than those who have not been thus exposed. When they came home from school for lunch, unless they had some more important school happening to report on, my children watched a TV soap opera ("As the World Turns," called in our family "As the Stomach Turns") with their mother at the kitchen table. At the age of 6 or 7, they each were deeply involved in the endless tribulations of those characters and we felt it was a socializing experience for them.

We do not know whether there are significant innate differences in the talent for empathy although the best guess is that there are, because all human attributes seem to be apportioned in varying amounts to different people. But a relative failure of empathic development may result from dyssocial rearing and thus be equivalent to the dyssocial personality discussed later in this chapter.

The Hostile Type

Some alienated individuals, feeling rejected by the community or unable to succeed according to its rules, repudiate the society of others and adopt a hostile, aggressive, or destructive attitude toward the group and all its members. It is a little recognized truth that feeling angry is more agreeable than feeling frightened or sad or depressed. Most people, if they try, can identify occasions or circumstances in which they self-indulgently permit themselves to cultivate and express irritation; driving alone in traffic is a situation in which many of us enjoy muttering criticisms about the skills, character, or parentage of other drivers. I can get reliably irritated reading the letters to the editor or certain columnists in the newspaper and there is no doubt that I feel stronger, more vigorous and self-confident when I am irritated than I do when I am feeling worried or apprehensive or discouraged.

Adolf Hitler is said to have ranted about the unfairness of the Versailles Treaty and other rage-inducing topics in order to wrench himself out of an occasional funk. I can remember at least a couple of times, when my children were small, when I guiltily realized that I was being sharp and irritable with them, not as a responsible parent but because it made me feel better than I had felt before they gave me the excuse to get angry. Many people can be seen to hoard grievances and develop a kind of chronic irritability as they get older because, when one is irritated, the juices start flowing and one feels stronger, more puissant. A good fictional example of a sociopathic offender whose adjustment to life is based on this principle is in Tony Hillerman's (1989) novel, *Talking God.*

The Cheated

Freud speaks somewhere about the individual who feels disadvantaged by appearance or physical disability, by social or class origin, minority status, or in some other way and who rationalizes his failure to follow the social rules on the grounds that, having been thus cheated at the outset, those rules do not apply to him. It is an interesting and important fact that most of the diverse criminal types suggested here do tend to justify their conduct in one way or another, at least to themselves. One 15-year-old, now residing in a local juvenile facility, took a bus to a suburban neighborhood, hoping to locate a party he had heard about. Unsuccessful, he found that the next bus home would entail an hour's wait. Having brought his pistol along, he lurked near some cars parked by a store and, when a woman came out with her infant and opened her car door, the boy demanded her keys at gunpoint and drove off. Explaining his offense to the corrections officers, he expressed exasperation: "How else was I s'posed to get home, man?"

The Aggressive Sociopath

Some people learn to enjoy hurting, frightening, tyrannizing others; they derive from it a feeling of power and importance. Katz (1988) described rapists, muggers, and other violent criminals who report that they derive strong gratification from their sheer dominance and control over their victims. To be bold, tough, brash, and unflinching is admired and reinforced in the society of the streets and may become an entrenched personal style in those who have the temperament to carry it off. A muscular, aggressive male is more likely to take this course and become one of the Alpha baboons of his peer group.

The following excerpt from a letter illustrates extreme aggressiveness in a young child:

> I am deeply concerned about an 8-year-old boy in our neighborhood. I have a son the same age, and I am worried this boy (I'll call him Brad) will harm my child or some other youngster. Brad is cruel and destructive. He destroys property, steals toys from his playmates and tells his mother he found them in the garbage. I have seen him urinate on the front lawn and in the street. When I mentioned this to his mother, she said "I have been having trouble with him about that. Brad urinates anywhere he feels like it. He has ruined some good furniture in our living room." The boy uses obscene language and when he is angry he kicks, punches and hits his playmates and exhibits frightening, savage behavior. I have never seen a child act out so viciously. He is also cruel to animals. His own pets are scared to death when you try to pet them. (Letter from a worried mother, 5–8–90)

Richard Allen Davis, the sociopath who kidnapped and killed Polly Klass in Petaluma, California, in 1993 exemplifies such a child grown up. Although Davis' father was an alcoholic who "packed a gun all the time, and sometimes at night he'd go outside and shoot at hallucinations" (Toobin, 1994, p. 40), the boy's mother was even worse, so the father was given custody when the parents divorced. During Davis' teenage years, "Everyone feared him. … He did an awful lot of cruel things to animals. He would douse cats with gasoline and set them on fire. He made a point of letting people know that he carried a knife, and he used to find stray dogs and cut them up" (p. 40). During one of his many prison terms, Davis proved to be an excellent sheet-metal worker: "the best press-break operator we've ever had here ... Rick had a lot of potential. With his skills, he could have made $45 an hour" (p. 46). But Davis was interested in taking rather than earning and he never held a job on the outside. After one criminal spree, he told the judge that "'If I felt bad about it I wouldn't have done it.' ... 'You don't—it doesn't bother you at all?' asked the judge. 'No,' Davis replied. 'If it did I wouldn't have done it'" (p. 43).

The satisfactions of interpersonal dominance may motivate not only criminals but other bullies who happen to be parents, teachers, employers, bureaucrats, police officers, and so on. I once belonged to a political organization in which one member, a business executive, intimidated all the rest of us. His aggressive, domineering manner was so habitual and practiced—and so effective—that one felt the only way he could be resisted would be to hit him with a brick. There are disadvantages to this personal style; this man's wife confessed to my wife that she had given up trying to invite people over. But it is an effective style in some fields of endeavor on both sides of the law.

Sadism that is specifically sexual may involve some sort of brain dysfunction as suggested earlier. However, in view of the powerful reinforcement provided by orgasm, it is easy to suppose that boys whose first sexual experiences (or whose early masturbation fantasies) involve coercion might grow up to be men who rape.

The Dyssocial Sociopath

Here we have persons who are normal, both temperamentally and psychologically, but whose allegiance and identification is with a (possibly predatory) subculture having norms and mores that are foreign to and often antithetical to the norms and mores of the establishment culture. These are Fagin's children, the offspring of the Mafia, traditional European gypsies, or the ghetto guerrilla who has been brought up to regard established society as an occupying foreign power. Members of any political underground movement or revolutionary terrorist group are thus "dyssocial sociopaths" from the point of view of the established authority.

In most inner-city street gangs there are boys capable of loyalty, of feeling guilt and shame, boys who care about their colleagues and who are capable of altruism within their own limited circle, boys who do honor a set of social rules but they are the wrong rules. It seems likely that such boys could more easily learn a new set of rules than that their truly "unruly," unsocialized confederates could learn to be rule-governed at all; therefore, it seems appropriate to classify these former individuals separately, as *dyssocial sociopaths*.

It is likely that most dyssocial sociopaths one finds incarcerated are young men belonging to the group whose antisocial tendencies tend to be "adolescence-limited" (Moffitt, 1993). During normal childhoods, they were tolerably socialized and acquired basic educational skills but, during the long "time warp" of adolescence, they mimicked the pseudo-adult attitudes and behaviors of their more truly

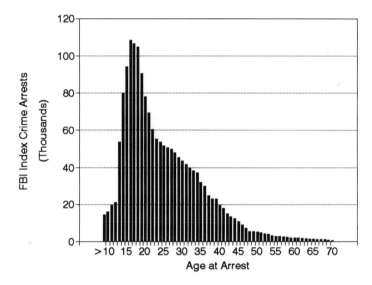

FIG. 3.3. Total police arrests in 1991 for "index" or serious crimes, plotted by age of the arrestee. Note that the number of offenders aged 12 years old was greater than the total number of offenders aged 40 to 49. Moffitt (1993) believes that many of the more than 750,000 teenagers arrested each year are victims of our unnaturally protracted adolescence; in place of the adult role models employed by our ancestors at this age, modern adolescents tend to imitate the psuedo-adult models provided by their more unsocialized peers (source: FBI, 1992).

antisocial peers. As Moffitt pointed out, *most* teenage males in our society engage in some sort of criminal behavior during this period, accounting for the sharp bulge in the crime rate from the ages of 15 to 25 as is illustrated in Fig. 3.3. If the youngster is unfortunate enough to be caught in these forays—caught by the police, by a drug habit, by an unwanted pregnancy, or by some other ball and chain—they may require to be classified as sociopathic and, in view of the etiology, as dyssocial sociopaths.

An Afterword on Sociopathy

Socialization involves: (a) monitoring the child's behavior, (b) recognizing deviant behavior when it occurs, (c) punishing that deviant behavior, (d) encouraging and selectively rewarding prosocial alternatives, and (e) explaining what is right and what is wrong, that is, socialization by precept. When these manifold responsibilities are grossly neglected by the parents (or parent)—and they are difficult responsibilities, not easy to fulfill—and when no other community resource takes over the socializing role, then sociopathy is a natural consequence.

Not all children in this situation become criminal, of course. Some are shaped up by outside influences (e.g., by a stint in the Marine Corps) and others have temperaments that make socialization almost automatic. But children who have any of the attributes that make socialization difficult—children who are risk-takers, fearless, aggressive and tough, who are not very bright, who are preternaturally charming and successfully manipulative, who are highly sexed or have violent tempers, and so on—need consistent socialization and are most likely to progress from feckless, disorderly homes to the streets to the prisons. For the purposes of this taxonomy, I am using *sociopath* to refer to persons whose lack of socialization is primarily attributable to neglectful or incompetent parenting, reserving *psychopath* for those whose antisocial behavior is due primarily to innate characteristics that either overmaster their socialization from time to time or which make them difficult to socialize even within a traditional two-parent family structure. It should be clear, however, that there is a continuum from sociopath to psychopath with intermediate cases that could reasonably be assigned to either or both categories.

During the protracted period of adolescence, which is an artifact of modern times to which our species has not been properly adapted by our evolutionary history (see chap. 4) some youngsters with tolerably competent parents and reasonably normal biological equipment fall prey to bad luck and bad companions and find themselves trapped in dyssocial sociopathy.

The Psychopathic Personality

The label *psychopath*—psychologically damaged—seems strangely nonspecific but it has probably persisted because it insists that the source of the psychopath's deviant behavior lies in his psyche rather than in his situation. The media tend to use "psychopath" to designate a criminal whose offenses are especially abhorrent and unnatural but that is not its original psychiatric meaning nor my usage here. The group that I call *distempered psychopaths* are likely to be at least intermittently dangerous but the primary and secondary psychopaths are better thought of as vehicles without effective brakes, dangerous only when chance or some auxiliary peculiarity gets them headed in the wrong direction. Some subtypes of psychopathy are listed in Fig. 3.4.

Distempered Psychopaths

These may be well-socialized individuals afflicted with an episodic organic disorder in the presence of which they are emotionally distraught or mentally unbalanced to a degree that, in some cases, might even justify their being considered to have diminished responsibility for any antisocial behavior emitted during the episode.

Epileptic Equivalents

Certain brain lesions (tumors, hematomas, and the like) can produce abnormal behaviors, sometimes antisocial behavior, as can some forms of epileptic brain storm of which the rare *epileptic furor* is an extreme and dangerous example (e.g., Virkkunen, 1987). It has been claimed that the hormonal imbalance associated with the premenstrual period can, in some women, induce such intense and aversive emotional reactions as to lead to uncharacteristic and irrational behavior over which

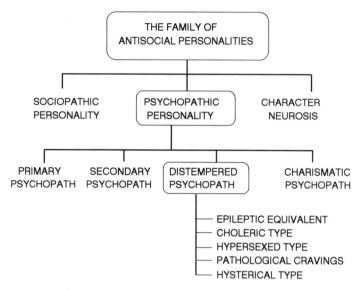

FIG. 3.4. The genus of psychopathic personalities includes at least four species, as shown here. The various subspecies of the distempered species may have a socialized conscience and value system that is overmastered, however, from time to time by their abnormally strong emotional, appetitive, or dissociative tendencies.

the sufferer has little control. There are cases on record in which serious violence, including homicide, has been attributed to premenstrual syndrome. These are two examples of organic brain or hormonal disorders that might sometimes lead to sporadic episodes of violence.

Another possibility might be the short-circuiting of the brain mechanisms for sex and aggression. This idea is wholly speculative and included primarily to suggest that more variants of this species are likely to be identified in future. There is no doubt that violent aggression is an essential or, at least, a preferred accompaniment to sexual expression in some men. It is likely that this association can be learned, perhaps in the same way that sexual fetishes become conditioned. Consider friendless, lonely Thomas Schultz who, in 1993, murdered the woman he had met through a lonely hearts ad and then spent 2 hours mutilating her body. Even in grade school, he said, "I'd get attracted to a girl and for some reason even without knowing them I'd want to hurt them." His sexual appetites grew increasingly violent, finally demanding murder and mutilation for satisfaction (Casseno, 1993).

It is also possible that forcible rape was a normal and adaptive component of male sexuality in ancestral times, that this anachronistic tendency remains latent in most men, and that certain patterns of experience can make it manifest and dominant (just as certain training could elicit aggression and blood lust in my bull terrier.) However, the biographies of some serial killers begin with the sexualized enjoyment of the torture of animals in childhood and are strongly suggestive of some sort of cross-wiring of the motivational systems at the level of brain architecture.

Choleric Temperament

Schmidt chased Villalobos into the street from a party at Schmidt's home and struck him five times with the blade of a shovel. Villalobos died of head injuries two days later. Schmidt had 12 previous convictions for crimes that include assault with a knife in 1986 and with a baseball bat in 1989. ("Unlucky 13th," 1991)

Although it is a commonplace that some people are more choleric than others, it is embarrassing for a psychologist to have to acknowledge how little we really know about individual differences in this area. Are the people who get angry most easily also the ones whose rage is most intense? Do the shortest fuses produce the biggest explosions? Like Othello, I claim to be not easily roused "but, once wrought, perplexed in the extreme." In the 40 years since my own attempt at homicide, described earlier in the discussion of normal offenders, there has been no repetition. But if I was capable of that one incident, there must be other people who fly into a similar frenzy more easily and more often. (The use of steroids for muscle-building purposes is said to increase the likelihood of murderous aggression.) Such a choleric person might have to be regarded as having a "persisting disposition toward antisocial behavior." Thus it seems necessary to identify a subspecies of distempered psychopath consisting of persons at the high end of the normal distribution of rage readiness or rage intensity.

Hypersexuality

A similar problem arises when we consider biologically determined differences in sexuality. Every man of my advanced age understands what is meant by biologically determined intraindividual differences in sexuality but I have always been fascinated by how little we know scientifically about interindividual differences in the "strength of the sex drive." As in the case of the anger disposition, we do not really know whether there exists one dimension or several. Does the frequency of sexual arousal predict the maximum intensity of sexual hunger? Is the typical strength of sexual excitement during coitus predictive of the number of orgasms required for satiation? What we do know is that some males are capable of astonishing feats of sexual energy and that others (or perhaps the same ones?) seem to be obsessed by sexual urges during a large part of their waking lives. Most men would acknowledge that, at least in the privacy of the conjugal bedroom, there have been times when they were sufficiently aroused as to neglect the possible consequences of their actions, to neglect contraception for example. Judging from the accounts in his biography, the serial rapist–murderer known as the Boston Strangler (Frank, 1966) seems to have been in such a state much of the time every day. Just as for the choleric individual just discussed, such a person would seem to be at high risk for certain types of antisocial behavior, a subspecies of distempered psychopath consisting of men at the very high end of the distribution of sex drive intensity.

Pathological Cravings

Powerful cravings for illicit indulgences constitute risk factors for sociopathic behavior. Drug addiction is an obvious example. Pedophilia is another as is the curious phenomenon known as kleptomania which, like pedophilia, may be a displacement of the sexual impulse. Still another, much more important, example is the craving for risk itself. Stress elicits the secretion of certain endogenous opioids whose analgesic effects help us tolerate pain and fatigue. These compounds are the source of the enjoyable "high" experienced by many long-distance runners at the end of their ordeal. They also seem to be one explanation for many forms of deliberate risk-taking (Gove & Wilmuth, 1990). For some individuals, the excitement of sports parachuting or bungee-jumping seems to elicit the copious secretion of these endorphins or enkephalins which, in the absence of the resulting pain that they were "meant" to allay, produce instead an experience of delight. In a recent study of active burglars:

> the informants almost unanimously reported a "rush" upon entering the site. Some referred to the feeling as a "rush of adrenaline." All found the feeling very pleasurable. … "I know that once I'm inside, everything I can find is mine. I can have anything there. It's like Christmas." (Cromwell, Olson, & Avary, 1991, p. 63)

As Apter (1992) and Katz (1988) pointed out, many forms of, especially, violent crime produce this gratifying state in susceptible individuals, for whom crime may be said to be its own reward.

The Primary Psychopath

It has been recognized for more than a century that there are some persistently antisocial personalities who do not fit in any of the categories so far considered. They are not necessarily afflicted by abnormal appetites or urges or by uncontrollable emotional storms. Neither are they people who are normal psychologically and who have simply elected some form of crime as the profession best suited to their opportunities and talents. They may resemble the unsocialized products of incompetent parenting and bad environments but, because they are so resistant to socialization, they derive also from middle-class, traditional families with long-suffering parents who have attempted to provide good environmental opportunities.

Monster

Kody Scott, also known as Sanyka Shakur, was a member of the Eight-Tray Gangster Crips in South Central Los Angeles, where he was known as "Monster," is currently serving a 7-year sentence in solitary confinement in a northern California prison. His autobiography (Shakur, 1993) required little editing because Monster is intelligent and remarkably articulate, especially considering his negligible education. Kody was initiated into the Eight-Trays when he was 12 and shot his first victim that same night. The name "Monster" resulted from an incident when, while in his early teens, a victim Kody was mugging attempted to fight back so Kody stomped him to a bloody pulp.

Kody's mother, Birdie, at 21 was a single mother of two, living in Houston, when she met a 33-year-old visitor from Los Angeles and later moved there to marry him. The marriage was unstable and violent but Birdie produced four more children before it broke up. At least one of these four, Kody, was fathered by Dick Bass, a professional football player with the L.A. Rams, with whom his mother had a brief affair. Kody never knew his biological father and his mother's husband was gone for good when Kody was just 6.

Kody's mother was a hard worker, mostly at bar-tending jobs, and the family's circumstances were lower middle class, the mother, six children, and miscellaneous animals living in a two-bedroom house. There were gangs in the vicinity and an older brother was briefly involved while in seventh grade; he was caught stealing a leather jacket and spent a night in a juvenile detention center; that one experience stayed with him and he never joined a gang. Kody was different:

> Kody was always the daredevil. "He was like a demolition derby," his sister Kendis says, "reckless, wild, and intriguing." "He had no fear," says his older brother Kerwin. Kody built wooden ramps on the street and raced his bike at top speeds, jumping crates like a junior Evil Knieval. "No one else would do it," Kerwin says, "but he would." (Horowitz, 1993, p. 32)

A bright, muscular, adventurous boy with no fear and no father, a boy who might have become a professional athlete if his real father had been there to guide and inspire him, or a boxer or policeman or soldier, perhaps even an astronaut, but he became "Monster" instead, a classic example of primary psychopathy in its second-most dangerous form. The *most* dangerous form is exemplified by Ted Bundy, the handsome, ingratiating, serial killer whose psychopathy was compounded with a perverse sexualized blood lust. Although Kody Scott was reared without a father in a gang-infested neighborhood, his siblings were apparently adequately socialized; this is why I would classify him as a psychopath rather than a sociopath although he exemplifies the frequent overlap between the two groups.

Other Variants

In some primary psychopaths, the first component of socialization discussed earlier, the disposition to inhibit antisocial behavior, has been accomplished reasonably well but without the development of a strong and effective conscience. Clever children of certain temperaments or under certain parenting regimes can learn the rules of social living intellectually and may find that observance of those rules is consistently rewarded and leads to gratifying social achievement. So far, this is the developmental pattern we would hope for with most children. But most children now and then slip-up and are punished and their fearful apprehension of the disapproval of the Big People leads, by the mechanisms already discussed, to the introjection of the Big People's values and the development of conscience. With potential primary psychopaths, however, such punishment is not effective so that the only forces pointing down the path of virtue are motives of expediency; honesty is accepted to be the best policy most of the time but the truth is that the Golden

Rule does not always apply in real life. There are times when crime does pay, when the utility of cheating or lying or stealing is clearly greater than the disutility unless the disutility equation includes significant components of fear or shame or guilt. Hence, there are some hard working, even altruistic and likable people who simply break the rules now and then when it suits their convenience.

In some of the more interesting cases, the indifference to conventional morality may be successfully masked behind an appearance of social compliance, or combined with prodigious talent so as to seem more eccentric than criminal, or it may be manifested on such a large scale or directed toward such important ends as to be classified as leadership rather than as criminality. Thus, this species of primary psychopathy may include certain unincarcerated leaders of commerce and industry, some police officers or other members of the criminal justice system, certain artists, politicians, or statesmen.

Judge Wachtler

In 1992, a wealthy divorcee named Joy Silverman began receiving letters containing blackmail demands and threatening to kidnap her 14-year-old daughter (Franks, 1992). The anonymous writer knew intimate details of Mrs. Silverman's Park Avenue apartment and of her current relationship with a New Jersey attorney, David Samson. Other letters, allegedly from a woman in New Jersey, reported that she had hired one David Purdy, a private investigator from Texas, to spy on Samson. This woman reported that Purdy had obtained photographs and tapes of Silverman and Samson and planned to use them to blackmail Mrs. Silverman. A man dressed in Texas garb left messages at both Samson's and Silverman's apartment buildings. Mrs. Silverman began receiving threatening phone calls from a man whose voice seemed disguised. She appealed to the FBI for help in dealing with this escalating and frightening harassment.

The FBI obtained a court order enabling the telephone company to "trap and trace" any calls that were made to the Silverman apartment. When the first call came through, it was traced to the car phone belonging to Sol Wachtler, the 62-year-old chief judge of the State of New York. Wachtler had been Silverman's longtime lover before she broke off the relationship a year earlier because she had come to feel that he "had increasingly tried to control her, both emotionally and financially, as trustee of the $3 million she had inherited from her stepfather." Silverman was stunned: Wachtler "had fallen into a rage when she began seeing Samson, but she could not really believe that he would do this to her."

After her marriage had failed, Silverman had turned to Wachtler although she was much younger than he and his wife was her cousin. Wachtler was the most powerful judge in the state, "said to be a very ambitious guy, who got to the top by assiduously and methodically cultivating those who could help him." I do not know that Wachtler was a primary psychopath; one would need more information about his early life to make a differential diagnosis. But, on the evidence available, this classification seems a good guess.

Because of Wachtler's status, an army of FBI agents collaborated in an attempt to catch him in the act. Because of his meticulous planning and ingenuity, the task was difficult but ultimately successful. Agents found in his possession the typewriter on which the letters were written, the electronic device he had used to disguise his voice on the phone, the cowboy hat and string tie he had worn while posing as "David Purdy." When finally arrested, Judge Wachtler "looked calmly at the assembled law-enforcement officials and shook hands all around."

The Secondary Psychopath

In his studies of the personality patterns of violent criminals, the English psychologist, Ronald Blackburn (1975) identified a group whom he called "secondary psychopaths" who were aggressive, impulsive, and undersocialized, like his primary psychopaths, but who were also introverted, withdrawn, and guilt-prone, in marked contrast to the primaries. The theories of primary psychopathy proposed by Fowles and by Gray (discussed in chap. 9) flow from a neurophysiological model which suggests that impulsive, psychopathic behavior might result not only from a weak "behavioral inhibition system" (BIS) but also from an overactive "behavioral activation system" (BAS), the former leading to primary psychopathy and the latter to a syndrome that might be expected to resemble Blackburn's secondary psychopaths. The BAS-driven psychopath is a risk-taker and yet he is likely to be stress-reactive, worried, irritable, dissatisfied with his life and with himself. Because he tends to live on the edge, where the action is, where the risks are, he is confronted by more stress than is the average person yet, unlike the primary psychopath, he may be as vulnerable to stress as is the average person.

The Charismatic Psychopath

In Meredith Wilson's *The Music Man*, Harold Hill, the protagonist, induces River City parents to buy band instruments and uniforms on the pretense that he is a gifted musician and will mold their offspring into a marching band. His intention, however, is to simply take the money and run. He is a charming and attractive liar, a confidence man. People my age can get a sense of how this species of psychopathy originates by reflecting on the personality of little Shirley Temple. The 1930s films of this gifted and enchanting youngster illustrate the ability of certain rare, precocious children to beguile and manipulate adults. Ms. Temple had a strong-willed mother who did not permit herself to be manipulated; she saw to it that Shirley confined her role-playing to the screen.

With different parents, such a child might easily become a kind of con artist, employing her charms to get her way just as a physically precocious boy might bully other children to get his way. "Marjo" was an attractive, curly-haired child who became a revivalist preacher before the age of 10; that this was manipulation rather than true religious commitment is suggested by the fact that he later became a Hollywood actor specializing in psychopathic roles. The Reverend Al Sharpton, similarly, became a gospel preacher before his voice had changed and has made his way ever since by exploiting his fast-talking manipulative skills. Neither of these individuals may be psychopaths, but they make it easy to see how similarly gifted children might move in that direction.

David Koresh, the leader of a religious cult whose members met a fiery death in Waco, Texas, in 1993 seems to have possessed this dangerous charismatic gift of being able to persuade others to believe whatever he said and to follow wherever he led. As I write this, a Minneapolis jury has just convicted 48-year-old Michael Blodgett of bilking 250 mostly well-to-do investors of more than $25 million by selling them rare coins for grossly inflated prices, using the old Ponzi scheme. His victims, many of them hard-headed business and professional people, trusted him implicitly and some say they can't help liking him still.

I once spent an evening with one of these top-flight confidence tricksters, a Frenchman who had swindled my father of the foreign rights to the fine-grinding machinery my father had patented. On our first trip abroad, my wife and I had dinner with M. Lecher who turned out to be soft-spoken, sober, and totally convincing. As he described a project he then had in hand, I had the queer feeling that I would invest in his scheme if he asked me (and if I had any money which, fortunately, I did not) even though I had known going in that he was a swindler. In *The Music Man*, after his fraud has been revealed and in a rare moment of candor, "Professor" Harold Hill tells a disillusioned little boy: "I always think there's a band, kid." I suspect that people with this fatal gift of charm and suasion often do come to believe in their own fictions, thus adding to their irresistibility.

The Hysterical Psychopath

In my own clinical work, I think I have encountered another species of this genus of psychopathic personality, individuals who sometimes exhibit the psychopath's headlong indifference to the consequences of his or her actions but who, in between, display quite normal feelings of apprehension or regret. Since Freud, we have generally accepted that the mind is capable of *repressing* awareness of unpleasant ideas or impulses. Once again, it appears that this capacity varies from person to person and those individuals at the high end of this continuum used to be called "hysterics." In a normally socialized young person, an impulse to do some forbidden thing tends to be aborted because the thought of the consequences of that action elicits fear or guilt. If that unpleasant thought can be repressed, however, the temptation is more likely to be yielded to. My clinical impression is that this repression involves some sort of effortful inhibitory mechanism that is subject to exhaustion and that during these periods of exhaustion the hysterical psychopath presents as a normally vulnerable person, often racked by regret for earlier behavior.

Character Neurosis

Since Franz Alexander's (1930) discussion of the "neurotic character," psychodynamic theorists have attempted to account for sociopathic behavior in terms of a basically neurotic etiology with important unconscious determinants. Karl Menninger's (1938) *Man Against Himself* and Lindner's (1944) *Rebel Without a Cause* are examples of this approach. The implicit assumption of this psychoana-

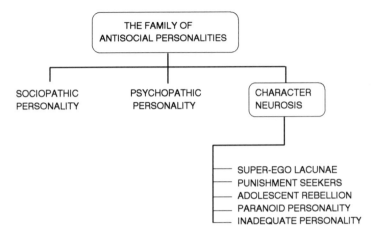

FIG. 3.5. The species of character neurosis is a wastebasket collection of persons who break the rules, usually in a rather minor way, for various reasons of personal or social maladjustment. This is the one group of antisocial personalities that is likely to benefit from some form of counseling or psychotherapy.

lytic view is that the patient has been normally socialized and that his antisocial behavior must therefore be accounted for in terms of some aberrant, unconscious emotional complex, dating from childhood, which somehow overmasters what would otherwise be normal behavioral tendencies. Because we know that some children are never adequately socialized, so that their "normal behavioral tendencies" are feral and often antisocial, we should not expect these psychodynamic explanations to apply generally or to account for an important proportion of antisocial offenders. Moreover, not many psychological theorists any longer take seriously "the dynamic centralism of such motivants as the unresolved Oedipus situation or castration anxiety" (Lindner, 1944, p. 285). However, there are certain patterns of experience that might plausibly lead to intermittent or focal antisocial behavior in an otherwise socialized individual who, because he cannot give a coherent account of his motivations, seems to be expressing neurotic, unconscious impulses. Illustrative examples are listed in Fig. 3.5 and discussed below.

Super-Ego Lacunae

The child analyst, Adelaid Johnson (1949), described a form of conduct disorder resulting from the fact that the parent gets vicarious satisfaction from certain forms of the child's misbehavior and therefore unconsciously reinforces such behavior so that it persists. One of her examples was a boy brought in for treatment because of his habit of running away—often far away—from home. The boy's father had been an over-the-road truck driver who had given up that profession when he married. As the boy recounted his latest escapade, involving a long hitch-hiking trip to a distant city, the father's grim demeanor changed to one of fascinated interest and it seemed clear to Dr. Johnson that the behavior had been shaped by these unconscious signals of approval even though both the boy and his father thought that the father disapproved. I know at least one man whose son became a neighborhood bully because his father, who overtly deplored the boy's conduct, covertly admired his feistiness. More than one mother has unwittingly led her daughter into sexual promiscuity through her own vicarious enjoyment of the daughter's escapades.

Punishment Seekers

Suppose a laboratory rat lives in a box with a grid floor, an overhead light and a movable lever. Three times a day the signal light is turned on and then, after some lengthy and unpredictable time has elapsed, a strong electric shock is administered through the grid floor, and the light is turned off. If the rat presses the lever while the light is on, these events occur at once; the shock is delivered and the light is extinguished. The rat will learn these contingencies in time so that, when first placed in the box, he will avoid the lever but, when the light comes on and the tension produced by the impending shock increases, a point will be reached where he brings matters to a head, presses the lever and turns out the light. The rat has learned to emit behavior that produces punishment.

   This may be analogous to a not uncommon pattern of parent–child interaction that involves a crescendo of acting-out behavior, "testing the limits," until at last the overly permissive parent is stressed beyond endurance and retaliates by punishing the child, perhaps severely, and this is followed in turn by an emotional reconciliation with tearful protestations of love and regret on both sides. What the child may learn from such encounters is that the tension of increasing alienation and guilt can be relieved by punishment because it is punishment that leads to forgiveness and reconciliation. To an observer who sees only part of the sequence, it may appear that this child is displaying flagrantly improper, even intolerable conduct as if inviting parental retribution.

Adolescent Rebellion

The complex and difficult relationship of parents with their children can encourage misconduct in other ways as well. Acting out by the child can also serve to punish the kind of parent who is more concerned about "what the neighbors will think" than about the needs of the child. Defiant rejection of the parents' norms and rules is an effective way for the overly controlled youngster to establish a sense of personal identity. Flagrant acting out is also one method by which a youngster can "break through" to his or her parents who may be overly preoccupied with their own affairs, a way to get their attention and establish contact.

Paranoid Personality Disorder

Paranoid personality disorder is rather mysterious as to etiology. Some people, without actual psychosis, are able to see themselves (and/or their group or party) as on the side of good and all those who oppose them as evil so that, as in war, any tactic is justified. Thus, for example, it is all right for us to interfere in the internal affairs of other countries because we are good; all right for me to lie because my side is the right side and the other, evil, side probably lies too, and so on. I know a professor who has lied in print and committed perjury on the witness stand, yet who plainly believes that he wears the white hat, that those who disagree with him are scoundrels, and that his dishonest conduct is in the service of a greater good.

Inadequate Personality

A familiar scenario is the adolescent girl who feels unloved at home and has poor self-esteem but finds that she can obtain acceptance and a simulation of love and human closeness by making herself sexually available and then drifts gradually into a tawdry underworld of vice. Her lonely male counterpart may steal money in order to buy friends and later become a subordinate gang member to win peer approval. When I was doing my dissertation research at a Minnesota reformatory, one inmate, in his late 20s, had just been recommitted for the fourth or fifth time; it was the spring of the year and the beginning of the baseball season and this man's only success in life had been as a pitcher for the prison's softball team. His most recent offense was to smash a jewelry store window and run off with a handful of watches, only to be apprehended minutes later. He made it back to prison just in time for spring training.

I suspect that mechanisms of this type seldom serve as the proximal causes of serious criminal behavior but, rather, serve to instigate sexual acting out, experimentation with alcohol and drugs and, most ominously, affiliation with other troubled youth, gangs, and other sociopathic elements that, in their turn, can lead ultimately to serious criminal involvement. Patty Hearst did not rob banks because she felt alienated from her parents; rather, she drifted into drugs and bad company until vulnerable enough to be taken over by a group of radical Black Nationalists with a truly criminal agenda.

Conclusions

The reader is reminded that this taxonomy was not constructed by sophisticated statistical or "taxometric" methods from a basis of empirical data but, rather, it was concocted by me from the armchair, mainly for the purpose of emphasizing the probable complexity of psychological motives, temperamental peculiarities and personality configurations that can contribute to criminal behavior. The official diagnostic categories of American psychiatry also were arrived at largely from the armchair, although it was a chair big enough for a committee of clinicians rather than just one. There are other, more systematic classification or diagnostic schemes that have been used in classifying criminal offenders, some of which I discuss in chapter 8, but it must be admitted that this problem is far from solved.

The major categories in this taxonomic scheme are illustrated in Fig. 3.6. They are (a) the psychopathic personalities, distinguished by biological differences that make them difficult to socialize, differences probably in temperament (hence, they are plotted at the "distempered" end of the horizontal axis in the figure); (b) the

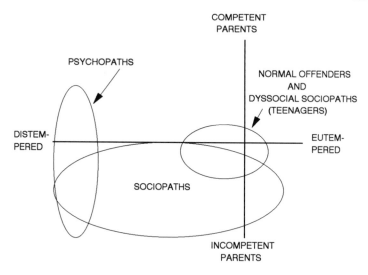

FIG. 3.6. The principal categories in our armchair taxonomy, plotted on a horizontal axis representing ease of socialization (i.e., at the "distempered" end, inherent temperamental characteristics that make consistent socialization difficult). The vertical axis represents parental competence. The large group of sociopaths had relatively inadequate parenting and many of them were also difficult to socialize, hence there is considerable overlap between the sociopaths and the psychopaths. The "genus" of normal offenders and the "subspecies" of dyssocial sociopaths (which includes many not-yet-socialized adolescents) are plotted to suggest that difficult temperaments and less-than-ideal parenting probably increases susceptibility to antisocial behavior in these groups as well.

sociopathic personalities, whose parents were not up to the task of equipping them for life as full members of society; (c) the normal offenders for whom their sort of crime is a rational career choice, and (d) the dyssocial sociopaths caught in the teenage time warp who, in the absence of "old heads," real adult mentors and role models, mimic instead the false maturity of their antisocial peers.

Human nature being as complex as it is, I believe that even an ideal taxonomy will yield "fuzzy" and overlapping types. A hostile or sadistic sociopath can also be a distempered psychopath. Many primary psychopaths, like Kody Scott, are broadly unsocialized and are therefore classifiable as sociopaths. A primary psychopath can also be a secondary psychopath. Nor has every relevant peculiarity of endowment or of learning history been touched upon here. In thinking about crime or, indeed, any other aspect of human nature or behavior, there seems to be a strong tendency to oversimplify, to seek a single underlying principle or explanation. This chapter is intended primarily to counteract that tendency.

PART II

THE GENETIC AND EVOLUTIONARY BACKGROUND

4

Crime From an Evolutionary Perspective

By the second birthday children from many cultures show uncertainty with regard to broken or flawed objects, empathy with the distress of another, and anxiety over possible task failure. Because it is unlikely that parents across the world begin to socialize these acts at the same time, the temporal concordance implies a biologically based preparedness to judge acts as right or wrong, where "preparedness" is used in the same sense intended by linguists who claim that two-year-old children are prepared to speak their language.

—Jerome Kagan (1987)

The genes sing a prehistoric song, which must sometimes be resisted, but which cannot be ignored.

—Bouchard et al. (1990)

Evolutionary psychology is an important new paradigm, a fresh and provocative way of looking at the problems of modern social science. Even many creationists accept that primitive hominids did exist, that they were different from ourselves in many ways, and that our ancient ancestors grew to be more and more like us over the eons by a process of natural selection; those genetic qualities that were more adaptive in those prehistoric times were more likely to be passed along to succeeding generations.

WHAT IS EVOLUTIONARY PSYCHOLOGY?

Evolutionary psychology is based on the idea that, when our species was evolving during the Pleistocene, we developed by natural selection not only morphological adaptations like bipedality and the opposable thumb but also psychological ones. Our brains got much bigger, which testifies to the fact that our species depended for survival more on brain power than on brawn or speed or protective coloration.

45

These big brains that we developed were not merely general-purpose computing machines, however. We also developed "mental organs" (Chomsky, 1986; Tooby & Cosmides, 1992), analogous to the read-only memories (ROMs) that are supplied with many modern computers, packets of programming that provide these computers with certain basic skills that facilitate later programming. These evolved ROMs in our human brains are not fully orchestrated instincts like those that govern insect behavior but, rather, they are innate dispositions toward certain kinds of learning. It is now generally acknowledged that our brains (but not those of other primates) have an innate ROM or "deep structure" that facilitates our learning language. Some of our ROMs are more complete, more instinctlike. Humans, for example, like the other primates, can more easily be taught to fear snakelike or spiderlike objects than to fear guns or electric sockets, because snakes and spiders were a source of danger in the Pleistocene but guns and sockets were not. As Darwin himself recognized and as Ekman and others have documented (Ekman, 1985; Ekman & Friesen, 1974), the ways in which we express the several basic emotions are qualitatively the same across cultures and appear to be hard-wired.

We humans also display evolved deep structure that is associated with our being social animals (which itself, of course, is evidence of an evolved behavioral disposition—to be social animals.) Another innate fear disposition that seems universal in our species is stage fright, finding one's self the focus of attention of a multitude of eyes. Few actors or speakers would feel the same apprehension if they could perform standing at the back of the hall with the audience gazing, say, at slides projected on a screen. Among other primates (and in some human cultures), a sustained direct gaze is a threat signal and the occasions when our ancient ancestors found all eyes focused on them were likely to have been dangerous situations calling for escape or avoidance behavior. One reason we admire "high-talking chiefs" and are inclined to accept their leadership is that they have the unusual ability to function with apparent confidence before an audience of eyes. The large portion of evolutionary psychology that is concerned with such innate predispositions for responding to other persons, and with other social behaviors, is called *sociobiology* (E. Wilson, 1975, 1978).

Why We Need Evolutionary Explanations

When the Minnesota Twins baseball team won the World Series in 1987, and again in 1991, 3 million otherwise rational Minnesotans acted as if something wonderful and important had happened. People who had never attended a Twins game, who could not previously have named a single player on the team, were glued to their televisions. Walking my dog one chilly evening during the 1987 series, I could hear the sound of people cheering inside their closed-up houses in my quiet neighborhood. We groaned when the other team got a hit, cheered when one of our boys made a good play, and generally acted as if we believed that those 25 highly paid athletes, born in other states or even other countries, none of whom we had ever met, were all members of our family and that the National League players were enemy invaders. In all of the press talk about the fans' reaction to those games, no one ever asked the most obvious and puzzling question: "Why did we care?" Those boys were not "our" boys at all; the team belonged to a rich banker, not to us. Why did we agonize, cheer, exult with pride? What actual difference could the result of those games possibly make in our individual lives? The fact that most of us reacted the same way makes the question sound silly at first: of course we cared. But when we take a second look there is really no denying that—unless we had bet the farm on the team's success—our reaction to that event was irrational. And yet it was also somehow deeply inevitable and natural. The only way I can make sense of such phenomena is to remember that the ROMs that we now carry around with us evolved when our ancestors lived in small bands of hunter–gatherers and the fate of the band depended on the success of the band's young men in combat with the young men of other bands.

The entire U.S. Congress standing and cheering lustily the entrance of President Bush at the conclusion of the 1991 Gulf War requires a similar explanation. On the other side of the world, "our boys" had killed a lot of Iraqis so as to permit a feudal monarch to return from European resorts to reclaim his burning oil wells and rebuild his palaces. Why did most of us feel that we had done something wonderful? The answer lies in a process that was effected thousands of years ago.

These innate dispositions that are characteristics of our species evolved because they were adaptive to the Pleistocene environment, a context vastly different from that confronted by most modern humans as a consequence of the complex cultural and technological developments that have happened too recently, in the evolutionary time scale, for much additional evolutionary change to have occurred. Especially for this reason, I believe that evolutionary psychology provides a new and provocative vantage point from which to consider many problems of psychological theory as well as valuable insights regarding their solution. This chapter is an introductory essay on evolutionary psychology, an excursus that returns to the main themes of this book in the section titled "The Evolution of Sociality." Readers already knowledgeable about evolutionary psychology may wish to proceed to that section directly.

The Relation of Evolutionary Change to Genetic Diversity

A basic principle of evolutionary theory is that the organism is the gene's way of reproducing itself (Dawkins, 1976). Just as humans do today, the ancestral hominids differed from one another genetically, due both to the occurrence of random mutations and also to the new genetic configurations that are created at every conception when a random half of the mother's genes combine with a random half contributed by the father. We know today that virtually every psychological trait that can be reliably measured owes an appreciable part of its variation in the population to genetic variation (see chap. 5). Therefore, we can safely assume that our earliest ancestors, because of their genetic variability, also varied one from another in their behavioral tendencies. Those genetically influenced behavior tendencies that increased the likelihood of viable children and grandchildren (or nieces and nephews) were for that reason likely to be more frequent among succeeding generations.

Genetic variations that confer important adaptive advantages will become fixed characteristics of the species, given sufficient environmental stability and enough time for all the less adaptive variants to disappear from the gene pool. Why is there then so much genetic variation left in so many of the psychological traits of modern humans? First, there has not been enough time. Our species has been in place for only 50,000 years or so, which is not long as time is reckoned by evolutionists. Second, the environment has been far from constant. The psychologically relevant environment embraces all of human culture and technology (and is much broader than the aspects of environment that influence physiological development) and it has been changing at an ever-increasing pace. Many human talents and propensities that are important now were irrelevant in far ancestral times so that evolutionary pressures could not act upon them. If a child with Shakespeare's or Newton's genetic blueprint (*genome*) had been born in some band of Paleolithic hunter–gatherers, it is not at all clear that he or she would have been considered to be special or, if special, wonderful.

Moreover, many psychological traits may turn out to be genetically complex, involving configurations of genes that are *pleiotropic*, that is, genes that have other functions apart from their contribution to the trait in question. Such traits are hard to get to "breed true," whether natural selection is doing the job or a human breeder of domestic animals. The record-setting thoroughbred Secretariat provides one example; his unique racing ability was never recaptured in any of his 400 offspring, all of whose dams were themselves highly selected (Lykken, Bouchard, McGue, & Tellegen, 1992). Many human traits have presumably become less variable over the millennia, such as the traits of socialization that are considered here. Other psychological traits may have an even greater range of genetic variation now than in ancient times (e.g., there may be more very smart humans now than there once were, due to assortative mating for intelligence).

Evolutionary psychology is perforce a speculative enterprise. Voltaire's Dr. Pangloss blithely asserted that we were given noses to provide a perch for eyeglasses and it has been suggested (Lewontin & Gould, 1978) that much of evolutionary psychology is Panglossian in character. Although it is difficult to think of experimental ways of testing one's conjectures in this area it is, however, not impossible. Hypotheses about ancestral times that are advanced in order to account for behavior tendencies observed in modern peoples sometimes can generate predictions of other tendencies or relationships not hitherto noticed and such predictions can be tested. Daly and Wilson (1988), for example, formulated an integrated set of hypotheses concerning the evolution of impulses and inhibitions governing homicidal aggression and then tested predictions derived from these hypotheses using modern crime statistics. To illustrate, an older child, having survived infancy, is more likely to live to pass on his or her genes; therefore, Daly and Wilson predicted that an older child should be valued by its parents relatively more than an infant and, thus, be less likely to be killed or abandoned by them. At least some of these predictions were unexpected (I would have supposed, for example, that parents would favor a helpless infant over an older child) so that their confirmation increases one's confidence in the theory as a whole.

Moreover, there is a considerable and important difference in the plausibility of Dr. Pangloss' conjecture about the nose and evolutionary speculations about our susceptibility to stage fright or to snake or spider phobias. A useful scientific theory is one that provides the best available coherent and plausible account of a set of related observations. Thus, for example, from a "sexual strategies theory," based on evolutionary considerations, Buss and Schmitt (1993) were able to generate 22 specific predictions about mating behavior and preferences that they proceeded to confirm by experiment.[1] In considering almost any psychological question, I think it is useful to keep in mind that the machinery whose workings we study as psychologists evolved during the Pleistocene because it was adaptive to environmental—including social—conditions that prevailed then. The adaptability of these ancient inclinations to the very different conditions in which we find ourselves today is contingent and precarious. Therefore, I think it appropriate to ruminate briefly on the probable origins of crime in our evolutionary past and on the mechanisms that we evolved for socializing the young and for controlling crime.

SOCIAL ANIMALS

The social insects, the honeybees, ants, and termites, are characterized by *eusociality*; individualism and selfishness is almost nonexistent, individuals work out their lives for the group, the specialist ant soldiers literally sacrifice their lives for the group. Except possibly for Mother Teresa, few humans ever manage to consistently display the Christian ethic nearly so well as the ants and the termites do. Evolutionists believe that this is achieved by the bees and the ants by making all but the queen (plus a few no-account males) sterile so that the only way a worker or a soldier ant can achieve genetic immortality is by helping the colony and, in particular, her sisters. These sisters share three-fourths of her genes and one or more of her sisters will ultimately become a queen and pass those genes along. Among some of these insects, the queen secretes a pheromone that keeps the workers sterile and certain workers have the job of passing this around, like a nurse handing out medicine, sterilizing themselves in the process.

The naked mole rat of East Africa is the only mammal that seems to have independently evolved a eusocial adaptation similar to that of the *hymenoptera* (Sherman, Jarvis, & Braude, 1992). We humans can claim only to have approximated the ultrasociality of the bees and the mole rats. Remember that the driving

---

[1]One prediction is that, in their search for mates, men should be more interested in a woman's fecundity and health, as indicated by her youth and good looks, whereas women should be more interested in a man's potential as a provider. Ira Gershwin's lyric expresses the principle: "Your pa is rich and your ma is good lookin', so hush, little baby, don't you cry." It is perhaps not surprising that these deep structures laid down by evolution should be more readily accessible to poets than to scientists (D. Buss & Schmitt, 1993).

force of evolution is successful reproduction, producing babies who carry half of your genes and helping those babies survive so that they can do the same thing in their turn. The only way the sterile honeybees can achieve this ultimate objective is by nurturing their relatives who share three-fourths of their genes. Mole rats within the same colony share about 80% of their genes because the queen mates mainly with her own siblings and offspring. Most individuals of both sexes never breed and yet their industrious pursuance of their various specialized tasks is rewarded, in an evolutionary sense, by the survival of their queen's pups who are genetically more similar to each worker than most mammals are to their own biological parents.

Humans, like most animals, can pass their genes along directly, and we have therefore evolved tendencies that facilitate successful mating and childrearing. We seek status and attractiveness, and we males aspire to be physically tough and dominant, so that we can compete successfully for mates. But these are *individualist* tendencies aimed at successful competition with our conspecifics and some of them could be regarded as antisocial or at least asocial.

Nurturing the Young

It is important, however, to distinguish between the distal and the proximate causes of evolved behavior tendencies. Because young animals are vulnerable and relatively helpless, we, like other mammals, evolved a tendency for parents to behave in a nurturant and protective way toward their offspring; the greater probability that nurtured and protected offspring would survive to breed themselves was the distal cause of this evolved tendency. But the actual mechanism that evolved to yield this useful tendency is relatively nonspecific; like many other mammals, we seem to have an innate disposition to be protective of the helpless and vulnerable generally. A mother dog can sometimes be induced to accept a nursing kitten and, once used to the idea, becomes maternally protective of the foundling. Although it is true that human infants are more often killed by, for example, stepfathers or the mother's new boyfriend than by their biological parent (e.g., Daly & Wilson, 1988), it is a fact that most human adults feel an innate tenderness toward an infant, even an infant not related to themselves and, having once accepted responsibility for its care, will come to love it as their own. My guess is that nurturing helps to generate love, as well as the other way around. Doing things for an infant, a younger sibling, a pet animal, seems to enhance its value to us as well as our feelings of empathy.

This nonspecific feeling of tenderness toward the helpless and vulnerable, this innate pleasure that we take in their nurturance and care, constitutes the proximate cause of parenting behavior. It did not presumably evolve because it was nonspecific but, rather, it evolved as a nonspecific tendency because that was sufficient to accomplish the evolutionarily important result of inducing parental nurturance. But because it is nonspecific, this tendency may have unanticipated consequences. It may explain, for example, the curious fact that many humans can feel the full range of parental emotions and nurturing impulses toward pet animals, a tendency that seems unlikely to have evolved on its own.

The important principle that this example illustrates is this: Adaptations, including behavioral dispositions, that were selected because they increased inclusive fitness in ancestral times, may have effects wholly extraneous to those effects that were responsible for their original selection in the "environment of evolutionary adaptiveness" (Bowlby, 1969), effects that, under the greatly altered conditions of modern life, may even detract from reproductive fitness.

Xenophobia

Human xenophobia, for example, our innate distrust and animosity toward persons different from ourselves, probably had its beginnings in the need to defend a hunting and living area from invaders. Neighboring tribes sometimes raided one another's camps, trying to kill the men and the children and carry off the young women. Primitive peoples still living in New Guinea, Africa, and South America, dress and paint or mark themselves in group-specific ways so that the members of one group are easily recognized by their cohorts and easily distinguished from strangers. By thus adopting a distinctive group appearance, group solidarity and security is enhanced. This same tendency is obvious among modern humans in the uniforms of armies, the uncomfortable formal attire of fashionable adults, the often weird appearance adopted by teenagers, and the color-coding of street gangs. Ancestral young men who were successful, both as raiders and as defenders of the home territory, were more likely to have grandchildren. Individuals who feared strangers and avoided them or, if they could, killed them—individuals, that is, who were xenophobic—were more likely to have grandchildren. And those who failed to produce grandchildren are not included among our ancestors.

This xenophobic tendency has been responsible for all manner of maladaptive strife and warfare during human history, including the ethnic and interracial conflict of the modern era. The mechanism of xenophobia depends on the impression of difference or strangeness and this can be moderated by coexperience. Whites and Blacks who play together as children are less likely to experience mutual xenophobia as adults.

A related example is the tendency of children reared together to avoid mating with one another when they grow up. This characteristic of our species evolved because it avoided consanguineous matings that tend to produce offspring with recessive genetic defects but, because of its nonspecificity, because it works not just with siblings but with any children reared together, this mechanism has had the locally maladaptive effect of preventing the intermarriage of nonrelated children reared together in Israeli kibbutzim.

Gangs

Still another example, one more relevant to our topic of crime, concerns the tendency of human adolescents, under certain circumstances, to form close-knit groups or gangs that are often organized in a hierarchy of authority and characterized by strong mutual loyalties, by "team spirit," and a tendency toward rivalry with other groups or gangs. This proclivity is almost certainly related to our evolved tendency, which we share with the canids and with other primates, to organize in mutually supportive family groups led by an elder parent, usually a father or grandfather. We evolved this inclination because it contributed to our "inclusive fitness" by improving the odds that the genes that we share with other family members will be propagated, not only through our own offspring but also through our nephews and nieces. But, again, the mechanism by which this was accomplished was nonspecific. Our inherent inclination to be a part of a family can be satisfied within a familylike grouping of unrelated individuals and we are likely to be drawn to such substitute families if our biological family is fractionated, rejecting, or nonexistent. Hinde (1986) made a similar point.

In 1992, Frederick Goodwin was forced out as chief of the Alcohol, Drug Abuse, and Mental Health Administration for suggesting that young males, like adolescent male Rhesus monkeys, may have an innate tendency to roam about in gangs characterized by a high level of interpersonal violence. He could as easily have referred to the example of primitive peoples still living much as our Pleistocene ancestors lived. In these societies young males compete, often violently, for status and to demonstrate their courage and puissance. Members of neighboring tribes are most often the victims of this status-driven aggression.

This last point is important: Although the young men of many traditional cultures may display violence, they are seldom criminal in the sense of violating the rules of their own communities. Those who do break the rules are rare and treated as pariahs, as Murphy's Eskimos treated the man they called a *kunlangeta* (see chap. 1). Crime is rare among peoples who still live as our ancestors lived in the late Pleistocene because that extended family system of communal socialization is the one to which our species became adapted for the suppression of crime.

Thus, having a tribal culture, a "hive"—with its accumulated knowledge of the world, its mutual support and defense, its opportunities for division of labor and its attendant efficiencies, and so on—also contributed to genetic fitness, both to our ability to pass on our genes directly and also to our inclusive fitness, passing on our genes indirectly through our near kin. But to live peacefully within a structured social group required that we find ways of curbing our self-seeking individualism. In place of the sterilizing treatment, which is the way the social insects restrain the anti- and asocial tendencies associated with direct reproduction, we evolved a disposition toward a certain basic set of social impulses (e.g., the capacities for love, empathy, and nurturance, the apparently innate hunger for approval) and restraints (e.g., the capacities for shame and guilt, our apparently innate tendency to march with the group and take orders). The same basic pattern of moral codes, much like the Ten Commandments, can be found in most cultures, albeit sustained by a remarkable diversity of traditions and supernatural beliefs.

This suggests that dispositions to acquire the same basic pattern of behavioral constraints became part of our common genetic heritage because these constraints proved adaptive to human social living during ancestral times. Evolutionary psychology would not say, however, that we have evolved a package of "morality genes" nor that socialization is somehow automatic. It would say merely that, perhaps unlike the solitary mammals such as the porcupine and the wolverine, we have acquired some innate capacities, which vary in strength from person to person, that provide the necessary substrate for socialization.

Religion

Anthropology tells us that religion is an ubiquitous feature of human culture and archaeology reveals that this has been true since human culture first evolved. A naturalistic explanation of the universality of religion might invoke our species' unique awareness of personal mortality and our penchant for seeking causal explanations of phenomena. Most religions provide some sort of explanation of why we are here and of the vicissitudes of existence, as well as a reassuring hope of continuing existence after death. But, for the religious tendency to have evolved, it must have somehow enhanced the relative survivability of the offspring of those ancients who possessed this tendency most strongly.

Underlying the exotic variety of deities and ceremonials, there is a common theme among the world's religions consisting in support for the established social order. Because belonging to a cohesive, mutually supportive group or tribe plainly was adaptive, a genetic inclination tending to enhance group solidarity and the individual's adherence to rules would be adaptive also. This suggests that our ancient ancestors must have differed genetically, one from another, in religious proclivity: could that be possible? My colleagues at the University of Minnesota, using data from a very large sample of adult twins, including twins reared apart, have shown that, in modern Western culture, variation in religiosity has strong genetic roots (Waller, Kojetin, Bouchard, Lykken, & Tellegen, 1990). From a secular point of view, therefore, religion may have evolved because it provided supernatural authority and justification for the particular form of social contract, often including the political system, governing the interactions of a given people.

By analogy, another cultural universal, marriage, evolved to support the practice of pair-bonding that was essential for the survival of the uniquely altricial (helpless, slow to reach maturity) human infant. Because pair-bonding came first, it seems likely that the evolved instincts and emotions that tend to result in pair-bonding served as the inspiration for the invention of marriage. Because they were instinctive and compelling, these impulses must have seemed preordained and right, as indeed they were from an evolutionary point of view. Therefore, their expression became enshrined in custom and ceremony and their violation came to be considered wrong.

Pursuing the analogy, the universal religious impulse may have its roots in our evolved tendencies as social animals, tendencies to learn and to adhere to the rules and customs of the group. These innate proclivities, which include deference to a leader, the experience of guilt for violation of the rules, feelings of well-being associated with altruistic behavior, as well as fear of and hostility toward nonadherents, may constitute that which is common to the world's religions (including, of course, the secular religions such as Marxism). In brief, we seem to have evolved the capacity to acquire a conscience in order to facilitate our adaptation as complex social animals and the possession of a conscience, with its internalized rules, rewards, and punishments—its "still, small voice"—is a mysterious experience. Religion both rationalizes this experience and supports the social contract.

Whether these evolutionary speculations have merit or not, it is a fact that religion and socialization are closely intertwined. A child who fully and genuinely accepts the religious teachings of his society is unlikely to be an antisocial child. Religious faith may be one of the more dependable counterindicants of delinquency and criminal behavior (Gorsuch, 1988). The converse of this rule does not hold, however, because there are many nonreligious people who are highly socialized. Perhaps because we are a complex and versatile species, Nature has provided alternative routes to at least the most important of her ends.

Traditionalism

Other social mammals—from elephants to chimpanzees—have ROMs that tell them to cooperate in fending off aggressors, protecting each other and especially their young. If they were to take up baseball, gorillas and baboons would probably cheer "their guys" in the Simian World Series just as fervently as we do. As we have seen, however, our ancestors took social cooperation considerably further in the direction of the bees and ants. The younger members of the human tribe stood to benefit greatly from the accumulated wisdom of the elders, passed along from *their* elders, often in the form of traditions and taboos and myths. This tendency to accept the received wisdom and opinions and outlook of the ruling establishment was an adaptation that probably paid off in most circumstances and thus could evolve by natural selection. This tendency is now expressed in traits like Traditionalism, Conservatism, and Authoritarianism, traits that are strongly correlated with each other and also strongly genetically determined.

Multiculturalism

This buzz word of political correctness, "multiculturalism," is an oxymoron (Wagenbichler, 1993). The current explosive splitting asunder in Eastern Europe of unnatural agglomerates of peoples and cultures, although bound together for generations by totalitarian forces, is not merely an expression of human xenophobia. The whole point of being social animals, of living cooperatively together within our hive or tribe, is for mutual assistance and support and the security of group solidarity. Solidarity requires the mutual predictability provided by a common set of social rules, by common values, a common language—by a common culture. The ambition of the planners of the European Community is to compete on equal terms with Japan but Japan, with its ancient and homogeneous culture, has evolution on its side. The signers of the Maastricht Treaty, in contrast, are attempting to swim against the evolutionary current, to turn a Tower of Babel into a strong and integrated socioeconomic organism. My prediction is that it won't work.

Part of the romance of American tradition is the idea that we benefited greatly from the cultural diversity of the immigrants who came to join in our experiment. Perhaps we did benefit from their diversity but only because, during the first 200 years, the new arrivals understood their obligation to become a part of the new culture that we were building here, to learn the language, the laws, the social rules, and folkways. Evolutionary considerations argue, and human history both ancient and modern confirms the argument, that human social groups—nation-states—cohere and thrive only when there is a common culture. The United States has demonstrated that we can tolerate considerable diversity, different skin colors, different gods, but we know there is a limit. We know that if the 48 contiguous states had been separately settled by immigrants from 48 different countries, retaining their Old World languages and customs, there would be no United States today. Our evolved capacities for adapting to cooperative living within a social group are what set the tolerable limits of within-group diversity and it is as dangerous to press those limits as it would be to adopt chimpanzee habits of sexuality.

PAIR-BONDING PRIMATES

Chimps and bonobos (the "pygmy chimps" of Zaire), our closest primate cousins, are sexually promiscuous and use gifts of sex as well as food or grooming to restore peaceful relations within the group. As far as we can tell, chimpanzee youngsters cannot identify their own fathers (or vice versa). Exclusive love relationships between primate fathers and mothers and between fathers and their offspring, the emotions that facilitate pair-bonding for the protection of the young and what we call altruism, seem to have evolved strongly only in the hominid line.

Archaeologists have found bones of large animals around the ancient home-base camp sites of our hunter–gatherer ancestors. Mellen (1981) inferred from this something quite interesting. The hominid males were specialized for hunting, stronger and more venturesome than the females, and hunted cooperatively. To kill a large animal like a 2-ton dinotherium must have required an extended foray lasting days, to find the quarry, injure it, and follow the blood-spoor until the creature could be finally dispatched. Why then did our ancestral fathers go to all the work of carving off great haunches of the meat and then carry them back miles and miles to the home-base? Why not just camp locally and consume those proteins themselves? Mellen argued that they carried the meat home *because they wanted to*, because they had begun to develop the rudiments of parental and spousal affection. Hominid infants were much more dependent than even chimp infants. They could not cling to Momma's fur and be nourished easily with the forest vegetation. Fathers who pair-bonded, helping to feed and protect their mate and her child, were more likely to produce viable young—hence the tendency to pair-bond evolved by natural selection.

Many present-day birds and mammals bring back food to their young but these are rather specific instincts, evolved over millions of years. The great apes, from whom we sprang, had no such instincts because they lived in the pantry of the forest where food was everywhere available. When the protohominids moved out onto the savannas and became more carnivorous, that instinct to bring the meat home was not already part of their built-in repertoire.

Mate Selection

Recent research on human mate selection has revealed an interesting and surprising fact about pair bonding in our species. In cultures where young people are permitted to make their own marital choices, there is a strong impression among the participants that real selectivity is being exercised and most people find a mate whom they feel, at the time, is ideally suited to themselves. The criteria employed in mate selection presumably derive from some combination of genetic and learned characteristics of the choosers. Identical twins share both identical genomes and very similar histories of experience; therefore, one would expect that the spouses "chosen" by pairs of identical twins should resemble one another, at least in respect to the particular characteristics that were criterial to the twins who "chose" them.

My colleague, Auke Tellegen, and I found, however, that the spouses of monozygotic (MZ) twins were no more similar than the spouses of dizygotic (DZ) twins and, indeed, hardly more similar than random pairs of persons of the same age and sex. Moreover, although MZ twins tend to understand and approve of their cotwins' choices of clothes, vacations, jobs, and friends, when an MZ twin falls in love with the person they will eventually marry, their cotwin is as likely to dislike as to like the mate their twin has chosen. That is, very similar people, who make similar choices in most other areas of living, do not tend to agree on their choices of mates (Lykken & Tellegen, 1993).

We also asked the singleton spouses of these middle-aged MZ twins to rate how they felt about their spouse's twin at the time of their own marriage. These spouses report that, at the time when they were most "in love" with their chosen twin, they felt no special attraction even to a virtual clone of the mate they had selected. These findings seem to indicate that human mate selection, unlike other human choice behavior, is not predictable either from the characteristics of the chooser or the characteristics of the chosen. Tellegen pointed out that human romantic infatuation thus resembles the phenomenon of imprinting in geese and other precocial birds and he speculates that we evolved this susceptibility to infatuation because it tended to facilitate pair bonding and to sustain the bond long enough for the more enduring bonds of companionate affection to mature.[2]

A Note on the Utility of the Evolutionary Paradigm

Science proceeds most efficiently when it is theory-driven, when research is designed to test specific conjectures rather than as mere exploration. The most successful researcher is one who can generate plausible hypotheses that are capable of surviving such experimental test and evolutionary psychology can sometimes

---

[2]Many previous studies had shown that spouses tend to be similar to one another in IQ, stature, personality, interests, socioeconomic status (SES), and attitudes; spousal correlations were positive for every one of the 88 variables measured by Lykken and Tellegen (1993). But these correlations are too small, even in the aggregate, to account for specific mate choice. What the spousal similarities most likely show is that we are attracted to potential mates who are similar to ourselves so that, when Cupid's arrow strikes, the couple who are seized by infatuation tend to be somewhat more like one another than would be a random man and woman.

provide a basis for evaluating the plausibility of competing hypotheses. For example, many anthropologists believe that romantic love was invented by Europeans during the Middle Ages and has been passed down succeeding generations as a cultural artifact (summarized in Jankowiak & Fischer, 1992). The considerations concerning human pair-bonding and mate selection that were just discussed, however, make it seem likely that the tendency for romantic infatuation evolved in our species much earlier because it served an adaptive function. Subsequent cultural developments have reinforced that function with courtship traditions and marriage laws both religious and secular. Therefore, the cultural artifact hypothesis can be seen to be less plausible than the conjecture that the romantic tendency is a universal, innate human disposition. That proposition, in turn, can be tested by seeking evidence of romantic infatuation among contemporary cultures that have remained relatively free of European influence. Anthropologists Jankowiak and Fischer (1992) conducted just such a search of the ethnographic literature, using relatively stringent criteria, and found clear evidence of romantic infatuation in more than 85% of some 166 different cultures.

Jealousy

An innate disposition that we share with many other species is *jealousy*, defined as an emotional state "that is aroused by a perceived threat to a valued relationship or position and motivates behavior aimed at countering the threat" (Daly, Wilson, & Weghorst, 1982, p. 12). In species like our own, where the male normally participates in supporting and rearing the young, an emotional resistance on the part of the female to her mate's interest in some other female is adaptive to the extent that it may tend to prevent the loss of that parental assistance. In all species where fertilization and gestation occurs inside the female's body, males have the special problem of ensuring paternity and thus avoiding the investment of care and resources in infants who do not carry their own genes. Male sexual jealousy therefore is thought to have evolved as a (fallible) solution to this special problem. Reasoning from these assumptions, Buss conjectured that men should experience relatively greater distress in response to the thought of their loved one's sexual infidelity than in contemplating the idea of their mate's forming an emotional attachment to another man. Women, on the other hand, having no similar doubts about whether the fruit of their loins actually carries their genes, should display relatively greater jealousy to affectional, rather than sexual, infidelity. D. Buss, Larsen, Westen, and Semmelroth (1992) confirmed these predictions using both ratings of the relative aversiveness of the two possibilities and also measures of the physiological arousal induced by having their subjects contemplate the two scenarios in turn.

If male sexual jealousy is intended to prevent investment in a child who does not carry one's own genes, then a man should be only half as disturbed by his wife's infidelity with his brother or his father as he is by her dalliance with a stranger, because his father's or his brother's child is genetically half as similar to himself as his own child would be. Moreover, if the jealousy mechanism is specific to its presumed evolutionary purpose, a man should feel no jealousy at all upon discovering his mate in *flagrante delicto* with his identical twin! But brothers are in fact jealous of one another, even twin brothers, so sexual jealousy is another illustration of the principle that evolution accomplishes its ends by means of proximate mechanisms that serve Nature's purpose but which can have unexpected side effects.

THE EVOLUTION OF SOCIALITY

Thus, our ancestors evolved the intelligence required for adapting to complex social living, an instinct for imitation, some as yet poorly understood predisposition toward respect for authority, for the prevailing mythology, and for the established ways of doing things. They also evolved the emotional equipment and the innate social needs and response tendencies that were necessary for their young to learn to obey the rules and generally to conform to the requirements of social living. Like every other human characteristic, these evolved species-specific instincts and predilections are bound to exist in varying degrees in different people. All of them must also be susceptible to modulation through learning. How modifiable our evolved tendencies are, and at what cost, is an important question that deserves discussion next.

Rising Above Our Ancestral Adaptations

During the "hippie" era of the 1960s, I was approached in my role as a psychotherapist by a young couple who had been unhappily cohabiting for more than 2 years. They were agreed that it was the young man, Craig, who was the main source of the problem; when he wasn't acting cold and aloof toward Sally he was downright mean and angry. He hated his behavior as much as she did and it seemed plain to me that the two were genuinely in love. Because neither understood the problem, they had reluctantly turned to professional help. I saw them four times, first together, then a separate hour with each, and a final joint session. In our brief time together, all three of us learned something important.

In the liberated spirit of their time, these young people firmly believed in an equal and open relationship. They had met in a Bohemian subculture devoted to freedom and experimentation—ideological, artistic, sexual, and pharmacological. She was somewhat more experienced with this life than he was but they both were true believers. Although they now lived together as a couple, they both continued to have casual affairs. On our fourth encounter, I rather diffidently offered my simple-minded diagnosis:

> You kids live in a world that's foreign to me but I know that if I were Craig I couldn't help feeling jealous about Sally's making-out with other men and I think it would make me feel hurt and mad and generally miserable. I know you two think that people shouldn't feel this way but I think people do feel this way, especially men, because that's the way we are made, we can't really help it.

I had feared they might be derisory but Craig's eyes teared and his voice choked while Sally reacted with maternal solicitude: "I don't have to do those things, Baby; I didn't think you cared!" It was one of my few triumphs as a therapist.

What I learned from this episode was that our species is not wholly plastic, that we have certain proclivities as humans that tend to obtrude themselves unexpectedly and in spite of our intellectualized values and intentions. This is not to say that all our atavistic inclinations must be yielded to. Although we are carnivorous animals, many people, including my wife and sons, are vegetarians and it is interesting that their physiology accommodates in time so that the smell or taste of meat becomes aversive to them. My species-specific hunting instinct, which once sent me out into the woods with gun or bow and arrow has long been quiescent due to a change of attitude (which I owe to my wife) about the ethics of killing things for sport. Our xenophobia can be reduced by frequent and agreeable exposure to people who are different from ourselves. I have an African-American daughter-in-law and four "Black" grandchildren and can attest that, although I was never a card-carrying racist, my own "circle of empathy" and affection extends much further than it once did.

I do not doubt that some couples can adjust to living in what is called an "open marriage" but I think it is risky. I know that some children have been successfully and happily raised by single parents but I know that is risky; the statistics I consider in chapter 14 make that very clear. It has been proven beyond doubt that some women can succeed and flourish in what were once thought to be occupations suitable only for men and thus it is plain that all doors should be open regardless of gender. But it is absurd to imagine that the two sexes have evolved to be psychologically identical, that the manifest differences in the interests and behavior of most little boys and most little girls are due only to the gender-shaping imposed on them by their parents, or that the relative preponderance of male to female engineers is due solely to persisting gender biases in a sexist society.

A question more relevant to our present topic is the cultural relativist notion that the traditional stable, two-parent family was an invention of the Victorians that is no longer relevant to our time. Conservatives have the right instinct on this issue whereas the liberals' fondness for what is novel and innovative—and their related belief in the unlimited malleability of human nature—leads them astray here. On the issue of the importance of the family, there is no doubt at all that, with respect to the importance of parenting and the role of the father, "Dan Quayle was right" (Whitehead, 1993). I shall return to this issue later.

Some evolutionary theorists argue, however, that in times of persisting stress and uncertainty those of our ancestors who were able to abandon the constraints of socialization, including pair-bonding, may have had greater success in transmitting their genes to succeeding generations. According to this theory (Belsky, Steinberg, & Draper, 1991; see also Harpending & Sobus, 1987), our species therefore evolved a mechanism that, in effect, presets the course of development of the individual child toward greater or lesser socialization as a function of the stress and instability experienced during childhood. Whatever the merits of this theory, the array of facts that it embraces seems well established. Stressed and overburdened parents provide inconsistent and negative parenting; the children of such parents form insecure attachments and display unsocialized, opportunistic behavior, and they also tend to become sexually mature and sexually active at an earlier age. As adults, the offspring of such parents tend themselves to form unstable marital relationships and provide inconsistent nurturing to their own children, thus replicating the process in the next generation. In ancestral times, this "every man (or woman) for himself" pattern might have had an adaptive advantage during, for example, periods of environmental stress or change. Subsequently, however, under more settled conditions, the advantage would revert again to organized social living, to stable pair-bonding and parental nurturing.

THE EVOLUTION OF CRIME

Social Rules

Because of their big brains, our ancestors were able to divide responsibilities in useful ways, to exchange favors, to barter and make deals, and thus to become increasingly interdependent. As hominid society became more complex in these ways, it became necessary to make rules and to enforce them. The old primate dominancy hierarchy—the one rule of "Don't make Big Brother mad at you"—was no longer sufficient to meet the needs of hominid group living. *It was when rules were invented that crime began,* because crime is the breaking of the social rules. Some of our prosocial instincts or ROMs were in place already; when those first commandments came down from the mountain we were probably already capable of affection and love and altruism and nurturance.

Some criminologists and other theorists tend to assume that criminality is *created* by learning. Some kinds of experience (e.g., being reared in the ghetto or by abusive parents) may indeed increase the strength of antisocial dispositions. There is no doubt that specific techniques of crime—how to pick a lock, hot-wire a car, where to sell stolen merchandise or buy drugs for resale, and so on—have to be learned and, once learned, the possession of these skills somewhat increases the probability that they will be exercised. But there can be no doubt that many basic antisocial impulses are part of every normal child's repertoire. Children tend to take what they fancy and strike out when thwarted. Every normal boy has the instincts of a vandal because breaking things and despoilation generally satisfies his normal effectance motivation, his need to stir things up, make things happen. Most young children tend to be heedlessly cruel to insects and small animals and, indeed, to other children smaller than themselves. If one has no sense of empathy for other creatures and no notion that such behavior is considered to be wrong, it is quite natural to do things that produce an interesting and lively reaction or that give one a sense of control over these salient objects in one's environment. Empathy and guilt have to be learned. My own children had stopped stepping on ants and pulling the cat's tail by the time they were 2 and, by age 3, would show empathic distress if the dog yelped from being accidentally pinched; developmental psychologists now believe that the human child possesses a readiness to learn how to empathize and to feel guilt but, for most children, this readiness must be cultivated by consistent training, precept, and example.

A basic mechanism of social learning involves the tendency of children (and adults) to imitate the behavior of others, an instinct we share in some degree with most higher animals. The young tend to eat what the parents eat, to fear what the parents fear, to behave as the parents do. The process of learning operant or voluntary responses requires that the response must first be elicited before it can be selectively reinforced. The tendency to imitate ("Can you say 'daddy?'—dah dee?") greatly expedites this process. The young of many species will avoid food rejected by an adult or that makes another sick and a child will fear and avoid a hot stove without having to be burned herself if she sees another touch it and display a pain reaction.

The Process of Socialization

Second only to basic nurturance, the primary responsibility of parents is the socialization of their children. This difficult and demanding task involves monitoring the child's behavior, recognizing and consistently punishing antisocial behavior when it occurs, and modeling, encouraging, and then positively reinforcing prosocial behavior. We assume that punishment of rule breaking does two things: (a) by a process of Pavlovian conditioning, punishment causes us to *fear* stimuli associated with that punishment, including the impulse to emit the behavior that was punished, which in turn leads us to avoid those stimuli in future; and (b) by a less well-understood process, punishment administered by a disapproving authority figure causes us to experience *guilt* the next time we engage in the behavior that was punished.

Guilt and shame are two emotional capacities that are central to the process of socialization. It is curious that modern psychology has no generally accepted theory of shame and guilt, not even an official set of definitions (see Zahn-Waxler & Kochanska, 1988, for a survey). My own usage is based more-or-less on Freudian concepts as interpreted by Dollard and Miller (1950).

Guilt

Humans are capable of internalizing the values of authority figures so that we can feel guilty even when no one knows what sin we have committed. A housebroken dog who soils the carpet because no one was around to let him out seems to suffer agonies of guilt when the master discovers the infraction. Is this distress merely apprehension of imminent punishment or does the dog feel guilt right after the forbidden act and before his master discovers the evidence? Do chimpanzees experience real guilt or is this ROM uniquely human? I don't know the answer but developmental psychologists believe that the human capacity for guilt, like our capacity for language learning, is built upon a biological "deep structure" (Kagan, 1987) and is at least more complex than that of other animals. We socialized humans experience guilt when we break the social rules and this requires our being able to learn the rules and to value them.

The process of internalizing the values of our social group is a learning process. We learn through prior punishment what the master (or parent) disapproves of so that we can predict his or her displeasure. Typically during the third year of life, "children begin to experience specific negative emotions associated with their behavioral transgressions and continue, almost universally, to feel distress, arousal, discomfort, uneasiness, or deviation anxiety after having committed, or when about to commit an act of wrongdoing" (Kochanska, 1993, p. 329). However, if our bad behavior is not detected, or if it is not consistently punished, then we are less likely to develop an effective repertoire of potential guilt reactions—unlikely, that is, to develop an effective conscience. The process is complex, however, and there is evidence that internalization works best when parental disapproval is moderate; then the result is more likely to be: "This was wrong," or "I feel bad because I did something wrong," rather than: "This makes Mom really mad and I better not do it again when she's around!"[3] Even with normal parenting, a child who is uninhibited and relatively fearless, and therefore less than normally distressed by punishment, will be slow to develop this key component of socialization.[4]

Shame

I define *shame* as a threat to self-esteem. As a natural part of our evolution as complex social animals, we developed the capacity to admire other people, people with qualities that were valuable to the tribe, people we would like to associate with, whom we would follow into battle, whose advice we value, and so on. We also developed self-awareness, the ability to picture ourselves as having certain individual qualities, and we naturally tend to judge ourselves according to the same criteria we use in judging others. We feel good when we or other people see in us qualities that we admire and we feel bad—we feel shame—when we or other people see in us qualities that we disdain in others.

But notice that a positive self-concept can provide a strong socializing influence without invoking guilt or fear. If you see yourself as a good person, an honest person, a courageous person, and if you value that good opinion of yourself, then you will tend to avoid actions that conflict with that self-image. Research has shown that psychopaths may fail to learn to avoid responses that produce a painful electric shock—apparently because they do not fear the shock as much as most people would—but they will learn the same avoidance promptly when the punishment is the loss of something that they value and want to keep, in this case money (Lykken,

---

[3]Hoffman (1988) and Dienstbier (1984), from different angles, converge on the conclusion that moderate parental disapproval or punishment are more likely to lead the child to internalize the prohibition, whereas overpowering disapproval or punishment leads instead to a more episodic learning: "Don't do that again when she's around!"

[4]Kochanska (1991) showed that skillful parental discipline at age 2 predicted effective consicence development by ages 8 to 10, but not in temperamentally less fearful children.

1957; Schmauk, 1970). One of the techniques of good parenting is to actively facilitate the child's development of a positive self-image: "I liked the way you told the truth about that, Billy; you are a brave and honest boy!" or "Thank you for clearing the table, Sarah; you are such a kind and helpful child I don't know what I'd do without you!" Once a child has accepted the idea that she is the kind of person who doesn't do this, or he is the kind of person who always does that, and that these kinds of persons are admirable, then that self-image becomes a beneficent internal steersman that directs behavior toward prosocial and away from antisocial conduct. Kochanska (1993) made a similar point.

Lying

As it is natural to do what makes you feel good, to take what you want, to dominate those weaker than yourself, so too is it natural to tell people what you want them to believe rather than telling them the truth. Some theorists believe that one reason we developed language—one important way in which language was adaptive—was because language facilitates deception; we learned to talk in order to be able to tell lies. It is interesting that, at least in English, there is a plethora of synonyms for *credulous* (e.g., gullible, naive, green, simple, a dupe, gull, mark, pigeon, sucker, etc.) but no word at all for the precise antonym.[5] Moreover, most of us are not very effective as human lie detectors, the talent that this antonym of credulous would name (Ekman, 1985), which may be why our language provides many names for bad lie detectors and no name for good ones. As the Eskimo language provides many names for different depths and qualities of snow, so too are there many names (at least in English) for people who are especially frequent or skillful liars and it seems likely that in this, as in most areas of human endeavor, skill and frequency are correlated. Some children have a much greater native talent for dissembling than others do and the reinforcement for successful lying is immediate while honesty is often punished. Thus, it seems certain that lying is as natural as drawing breath and that veracity is a habit that must be, with some difficulty, learned.

Adolescence

In an important theoretical paper, Moffitt (1993) pointed out that, in ancestral times, the precarious period of adolescence began later and ended sooner. Just since the early 1900s, youngsters in developed countries are attaining puberty nearly 3 years earlier, due to improved health care and nutrition. During the same period, educational requirements for entry into the adult world of work have greatly increased, trapping today's adolescents in a "*maturity gap*, chronological hostages of a time warp between biological age and social age" (Moffitt, 1993, p. 687). In ancestral times, the transition from childhood into man's (woman's) estate was accomplished relatively quickly after that late puberty, probably marked by a

---

[5]*Skeptical*, for example, means "inclined to doubt" rather than "able to distinguish truth from falsehood."

rite-of-passage of the sort observed by most traditional societies of today. These newly accredited adults then took their places as apprentices in the adult community, learning adult ways and skills by imitating and being guided by their elders.

Today's adolescents, in contrast, are required to remain for as long as 10 years in a "time warp" in which they are adult in physique and inclination but not in occupation or status. During this period, most importantly, their social community consists largely, not of adults disposed to teach them the ways of the larger community, but of their adolescent peers, from whom they are likely to learn less useful and constructive lessons. As Moffitt pointed out, the risky and antisocial behavior of some adolescents tends to be mimicked by others because it gives the *appearance* of adult status and, perhaps, because youngsters of that age are programmed to imitate the behavior of their associates because that was how our ancestors of that age learned adult ways. Because this protracted and insular adolescence was not a feature of ancestral life, our species has not evolved healthy and adaptive ways of accommodating to this interlude.

Summary

As a species, therefore, we are xenophobic, jealous of our mates, competitive for status, and inclined toward violence. When it serves our purposes, we have the impulse to lie, cheat, and steal. We have an instinctive tendency to affiliate in groups, to identify group leaders and to follow them, even when they lead us into mindless conflict with other groups. Even in ancestral times, when our tools and weapons were relatively primitive, we exceeded all other species in our capacity for wanton destruction. We have evolved the capacities to curb and channel these impulses but these capacities evolved in a context in which children were reared in an extended family with already socialized adults who, by their example and by selective reinforcement, passed along the social rules and restraints to succeeding generations. The fact is, therefore, that most children require socialization experiences, love and nurturance, consistent punishment of misbehavior, role models to imitate and positive reinforcement of prosocial behaviors, encouragement of empathic identifications with other living things, a knowledge of and a respect for the rules of civilized society, and so on—if they are to be good citizens when they grow up.

Plausible speculations about our evolutionary origins suggest that we are a species designed to live in small, interdependent social groups having a sufficiently complex structure so as to require the establishment, and enforcement, of both affirmative and inhibitive social rules. Unlike the eusocial insects and even the naked mole rats, our species depends more on our large, extraordinarily adaptable brains than on a repertoire of hard-wired instinctive behaviors so our social rules have to be learned. We are, however, equipped with innate talents and dispositions for the learning of the rules. These include our talent for imitation of role models, our capacity for affectionate relationships, for empathy, for nurturance, for self-awareness and, therefore, for a sense of pride, and our capacity for internalizing the values of parental role models and experiencing guilt when we violate those values. Our ancestors must have exhibited individual differences in all of these dispositions in order for these proclivities to have been selected for by evolution. And we still differ, one from another, in the strength of both our prosocial and of our antisocial tendencies. Therefore, it is to be expected that now, as in the beginning, some young members of our species are harder to socialize than others. It is also to be expected that, after their too early puberty, today's adolescents should feel themselves unfairly deprived of adult privilege and status and that they should feel alienated from the members of that club which they are not yet allowed to join.

The rearing environment in which we were designed by evolution to learn the rules, to become socialized, probably involved both a female and a male parent as primary agents but certainly also involved an extended family group. In that extended family, children learned the rules by imitation and by what must usually have been a reasonably consistent pattern of discipline; with all those aunts and uncles around, it would have been difficult to get away with much. Older children also had an opportunity, also by observation and imitation, to learn the skills of parenting. Those societies today that most resemble the ancestral pattern of our species—we like to call them *primitive*—are in fact the most successful in socializing their children and in preventing crime.

For more than 70 years, the Israeli kibbutzim have been experimenting systematically with a system of collective early child care (Aviezer, Van IJzendoorn, Sagi, & Schuengel, 1994). The most successful arrangement has been one in which the children sleep in their parents' home but spend their days in the "children's house" under the supervision of full-time caregivers. Perhaps because it is more like the ancient system to which we are evolutionarily adapted, this system works. These children seem to flourish and grow up to be contributing members of the community. In particular, they grow up with a bare minimum of delinquency and crime; the children of the kibbutz become socialized naturally and, as in Murphy's Eskimo community, with rare exceptions.

5

Genes and the Mind

Equality in spite of evident nonidentity is a somewhat sophisticated concept and requires a moral stature of which many individuals seem to be incapable. They rather deny human variability and equate equality with identity. Or they claim that the human species is exceptional in the organic world in that only morphological characters are controlled by genes and all other traits of the mind or character are due to "conditioning" or other nongenetic factors. Such authors conveniently ignore the results of twin studies and of the genetic analysis of nonmorphological traits in animals. An ideology based on such obviously wrong premises can only lead to disaster. Its championship of human equality is based on a claim of human identity. As soon as it is proved that the latter does not exist, the support for equality is likewise lost.

—Ernst Mayr (1963, p. 649)

In the previous chapter, I argued that, in contemplating most psychological problems, it is helpful to begin with some understanding of the innate psychological tendencies and constraints that we all share because they were adaptive to the simpler hunter–gatherer lifestyle in which our common ancestors evolved. I believe even more strongly that most psychological problems cannot be adequately understood without a clear appreciation of how much we differ still from one another psychologically or without realizing that these individual differences are determined largely by genetic differences among us. Like the previous one, this chapter is an excursion from my main theme, an essay on behavioral genetics in which the so-called nature-versus-nurture controversy is reviewed and evaluated in relation to recent twin and adoption research, much of it from my own university. Readers who are already comfortable with the neo-hereditarian position advocated here may wish to turn directly to the section titled "Nature *Via* Nurture," where I return to the main themes of this book.

NATURE VERSUS NURTURE

Both Charles Darwin and Gregor Mendel knew, of course, that the offspring tend to resemble the parents; that had been understood since the beginnings of human agriculture. Mendel's insight had to do with the mechanism of transmission. The great controversy over Darwin's *Origin of species and ... the descent of man* was not about whether people's physiognomy and character tended to reflect their ancestry; like the invention of the wheel, the origins of that idea date back to prehistory. Animal breeders well knew that temperament, as well as running speed in horses or milk production in cows, reflected the animal's parentage and every dog fancier was aware that terriers were aggressive and sheep dogs inclined to herd things and that these behavioral traits tended to breed true.

Throughout most of our history, people have assumed that the same thing is true of humans, that smart parents tend to have smart children, the offspring of athletes tend to enjoy sports, that mean parents often have mean kids. One of the first to seriously question this assumption was the 19th-century British philosopher, John Stuart Mill.

John Stuart Mill

Mill was the oldest child of James Mill, a brilliant Scots historian and philosopher and James educated his oldest son himself. Little John Stuart was reading by the age of 3, he was reading Greek at 5, and by the age of 8 he had read all of Herodotus and all of Plato's Dialogues in the original. By the ripe old age of 12, John Stuart had mastered algebra and Euclid's geometry, he had read all the standard Greek and Latin classics in those languages, and he was beginning the serious study of Adam Smith, Ricardo, and other political economists.

Not surprisingly, in his later life Mill was inclined to attribute his own intellectual achievements to that extraordinary and intensive early training and he became one of the first *radical environmentalists*. What Mill did not take into account, however, was that he had benefited—not only from his father's determined and ambitious educational efforts—but also from having received a half-helping of his brilliant father's genes.

It was not until the 20th century, however, that significant numbers of intellectuals took up the notion that, unlike the case of any other species, the human nervous system is unaffected by the same heritable variation that is obvious in the body's morphology. It follows from this postulate of radical environmentalism that every normal human child, however distinctive in size, shape, and appearance, must arrive equipped with a brain that is essentially identical in structure and capacity with every other new brain, just as all new Macintosh computers are essentially identical when they arrive from the factory. What differences in intellect, character, or personality are to be found later in the adult must, in this view, be attributable solely to differences in subsequent experience or programming.

Extending the computer analogy, it is conceivable that a time may come when even the personal computer is so powerful and so fast that hardware development will cease and the only differences between your computer and mine will be in the software that we happen to be running. The implicit assumption of radical environmentalism seems to be that this stage in the evolution of the human brain has already been achieved so that the only differences between one adult's brain and another's consist in the programming, in the residue of the different experiences that the two individuals have been exposed to since birth. Thus, for example, Jacques Ruffié (1986) asserted that: "The beginning of mankind's psychosocial development represented the end of biological evolution. This is the meaning of the occasional comment: 'Man has no nature, he only has a history'"(p. 297).

Expressed in this way, these wildly counterintuitive assumptions of radical environmentalism make it hard to understand how such a notion could have been so widely accepted by educated people, by political thinkers, and even by most social scientists. But of course these implicit assumptions have seldom been explicitly articulated. What has happened instead is that different thinkers, wishing to account for different aspects of human diversity, hit upon plausible but different principles of environmental influence, and then made the human mistake of overgeneralizing and concluding that their account was the complete one.

Marxism.   Karl Marx wanted to refute the prevailing assumption that the existing class structure of society was somehow preordained by God or human nature. Like many non-Marxist economists of today, he saw human individuals as fungible pawns at the mercy of economic forces and his utopian vision required that these same pawns, arrayed on a different board with different rules, would all behave differently and in their mutual interest. Lamarckian notions about the possible inheritance of acquired characteristics, echoed in the pretensions of Trofim Lysenko (1898–1976), provided what appeared to be a mechanism for achieving a new world order and became a part of neo-Marxist dogma.

Liberalism.   Liberals, too, were concerned about the evils of oppression, both political and economic, and believed that the achievements of the privileged classes were largely a consequence of that privilege rather than of some innate superiority. They reacted especially against Herbert Spencer's *Social Darwinism* and his claim that the structure of Victorian society reflected the "survival of the fittest," the workings of a natural law which we cannot change and with which we should not tamper. Upper class white males took for granted the genetic superiority of their race and gender and considered their dominant social position to be a birth right. The liberals believed that, with better living conditions and equivalent education, many children from the lower classes could excel in life's race over many scions of the aristocracy.

Anthropology and Margaret Mead.   American cultural anthropology, led by Franz Boas (1858–1942), "declared war on the idea that differences in culture derived from differences in innate capacity" (Degler, 1991, p. 62). This view may at first have been in reaction to prevailing assumptions about racial differences but, by 1915, Alfred Kroeber, one of Boas' leading students, was asserting a broader dogma: "Heredity cannot be allowed to have acted any part in history" (Degler, 1991, p. 84). This position was most clearly articulated by another Boas disciple, Margaret Mead, whom he sent as a graduate student to the South Pacific with the aim of demonstrating that adolescence was less stormy and stressful in Samoa than in the United States because of cultural differences and, in particular, because of the greater sexual freedom allegedly enjoyed by young Samoans. Mead's (1928) book, *Coming of Age in Samoa*, the most widely read anthropological treatise ever published, propelled her into the front rank of social thinkers and her views were strongly stated and widely influential. "We are forced to conclude," she wrote later, "that human nature is almost unbelievably malleable, responding accurately and contrastingly to contrasting cultural conditions" (cited in Degler, 1991, p. 134). In her book *Male and Female*, Mead explicitly asserted the radical assumption of the computer analogy given earlier: "Learned behaviors have replaced the biologically given ones" (Mead, 1949, p. 216).

Part of the impetus for Mead's work throughout her distinguished career was her conviction that prevailing assumptions about psychological sex differences were mistaken and that cultural stereotypes, rather than innate genetic factors, play an important (she would say a decisive) role. We now know that Mead's Samoan research was superficial and that her conclusions were based largely upon innocent deceptions practiced upon her by her young female Samoan informants (Freeman, 1992). On the other hand, there is no doubt that there are marked differences in sexual attitudes and practices across human cultures and, indeed, one of the facts that I lament in this book is the recent change in our own culture that has increased the frequency of children having children. Mead was assuredly correct in insisting upon both the malleability of human culture and the important role that the culture plays in affecting human behavior. Her mistake, it seems to me, was in conflating human culture, which is relatively easy to change, with human nature, which is not.

Behaviorism. The middle half of the 20th century was the heyday of behaviorism or stimulus–response (S–R) psychology and many behaviorists tended to be radical environmentalists. One obvious reason for this tendency was the reluctance of behaviorists to theorize about mental mechanisms; if there are no theoretical constructs referring to the organism, if one deals only with S–R relationships rather than with S–O–R relationships (where O stands for the organism or person), then it is difficult to account for individual differences, much less for genetically determined differences. The founder of the movement, J. B. Watson (1924), is famous for his claim:

> Give me a dozen healthy infants, well formed, and my own specified world to bring them up in and I'll guarantee to take any one at random and train him to become any type of specialist I might select—doctor, lawyer, artist, merchant-chief, and, yes, even beggar-man and thief, regardless of his talents, penchants, tendencies, abilities, vocations, and the race of his ancestors. (p. 128)

Nearly 60 years after Watson, the geneticist, Richard Lewontin (1992), made an even more extravagant claim:

> Our genetic endowments confer a plasticity of psychic and physical development, so that in the course of our lives, from conception to death, each of us, irrespective of race, class, or sex, can develop virtually any identity that lies within the human ambit. (from author's precis of the book on the jacket)

By claiming nearly limitless plasticity for both psychic and physical development, Lewontin suggested that ambitious parents can aspire to make their child, not only into a doctor, lawyer, or merchant-chief at will, but also into a tennis champion or an NBA forward, if that is what the child aspires to. Watson had only hubris and wishful thinking to back up his assertions. Lewontin's challenge was greater because he had 60 years' accumulation of data to contend with, most of it adverse to his startling hypothesis. That he chose to state it anyway is a triumph of ideology over reason and evidence. If it were true, Lewontin's claim would impose a heavy burden of guilt on the parents of children who fail to achieve whatever "identity" they hoped for; because it is not true, it seems to me that Lewontin's claim is a kind of scandal.

Skinnerism.   Although most psychologists were also liberals and sensitive to the intellectual *Zeitgeist*, I believe that the chief source of their radical environmentalism was a kind of professional *chutzpah*. As a psychology graduate student in the early 1950s, I can remember writing a patronizing response (happily never published) to an article in *Harpers* by an elder statesman of psychiatry in which he said that, if he were a young man starting over, he would focus his education on genetics and biochemistry. My fatuous rejoinder asserted that he would do better to apply himself to the study of modern learning theory that we now "knew" could account for all varieties of human behavior, normal and pathological. The great B.F. Skinner, at the end of his long and distinguished career, remained frustrated by the failure of society to fully appreciate and implement the power of the methods of behavior modification that he had developed and demonstrated.[1] I remain sympathetic to Skinner's views and, if I controlled the core curriculum required of every educated person, I would include in it a semester course in Skinnerian behavior analysis, confident that it should produce better parents, better social policymakers, and better citizens generally. Based on these principles, one could change a back ward of a 1950s mental hospital from a snake pit into a relatively clean, orderly, humanized environment. With these methods one could run a more effective school and a more rehabilitative prison. But behavior modification has its limits; it will not cure schizophrenia nor will it achieve Watson's goal of making any random child capable of getting through law school.

---

[1] Some of the most eminent behaviorists (e.g., both Skinner and Clark Hull) explicitly assumed that the parameters of the laws of learning could be expected to vary across individuals for genetic reasons.

Nazi Racism. The views and deeds of Adolf Hitler may have had more influence on the nature–nurture question than Marx or Mead or any other thinker. Nazi notions about racial differences and Aryan superiority, the cruel experiments on twins conducted by Dr. Mengele and, above all, the barbaric "final solution" for the millions alleged to be genetically inferior, made it difficult for an entire generation of civilized people to be dispassionate about the role of heritable differences in human affairs. One minor but significant casualty of the Hitler period was the loss to our language of the innocent and useful word, *eugenics.*

The Decline and Fall of Radical Environmentalism

The long night of radical environmentalism seems, however, to be coming to an end. Throughout the period, occasional studies appeared showing that adoptees resembled psychologically their biological parents more than the adoptive parents who reared them. Twin and family studies accumulated, showing that the degree of resemblance of pairs of related individuals tends to parallel their degree of genetic relatedness. In recent years there has been a crescendo of twin and adoption studies with mutually corroborative results and the pendulum of informed public opinion seems to be swinging in the direction toward which these findings point. After briefly outlining the basis of the twin method for assessing genetic and environmental influences on metrical human traits, I very briefly review some of the findings with emphasis on those most relevant to criminality. After then considering some of the common misunderstandings and criticisms of behavior genetic research, I explore the obvious question posed by the harvest of accumulated findings, namely: By what means can individual differences in genes, whose function it is to code for structural proteins and enzymes, produce individual differences in complex psychological traits such as IQ, extroversion, conservatism, or criminality?

Estimating Heritability From Twin Data

Monozygotic (MZ; one-egg or identical) twins are produced about three times in every 1,000 births and result from the splitting of the embryo, for as yet unknown reasons, into two identical and viable halves sometime during the first week or two after conception. In about one third of such cases, the embryo splits early, before it has attached itself to the wall of the uterus. In these instances, the two halves attach independently and develop separate placentas just as do the embryos of dizygotic (DZ) twins, which result from the fertilization by different sperms of two different ova. When the embryo splits after attachment, only one set of placental membranes is produced and the MZ twins must develop together with the same chorionic sac. In a few percent of cases, both twins are confined within the same inner sac or amnion and still later separation, toward the end of the second week after conception, is likely to be incomplete, producing conjoined or "Siamese" twins.

Because some two thirds of MZ twins must develop under the crowded conditions within a single chorion, they are subject to greater prenatal stress and a higher incidence of developmental anomalies even than DZ twins. One example is the transfusion syndrome, resulting from an arterio-venous shunt that causes one twin in effect to bleed continuously into the other so that one twin experiences a shortage of hemoglobin during development. The environmental effects of development within the same womb and at the same time can also work to affect both twins in the same direction. Maternal alcohol abuse, for example, might have similar deleterious effects on both twins. Based on an appraisal of these various possibilities, however, Price (1950) concluded that the prenatal environment more often works to decrease, rather than to increase, the postnatal similarity of MZ twins.

Twins Reared Apart

An especially powerful natural experiment[2] is provided by those rare occasions when MZ twins are for some reason separated in infancy and reared apart (MZA twins.) All differences observed in later life within pairs of MZA twins have to be attributed to differences in environmental influences beginning in the womb. The similarity of twins with respect to any metrical variable, Z, is measured by the *intraclass correlation* that varies typically from zero, indicating that the twins are no more alike in Z than random pairs of persons, to 1, which would indicate that Twin A had the identical score as Twin B in each pair. (Negative values of the twin correlation would indicate that Twin A's score is likely to be high if Twin B's score is low; in practice, negative twin correlations are small and usually indicate random sampling fluctuations around a true value that is zero or low positive.)

A variable like stature that is strongly affected by genetic constitution will have a high correlation—.90 or so—among MZ twins reared together (MZT twins.) The correlation is less than unity for at least three reasons: (a) There is always at least some error of measurement that acts to decrease the correlation; (b) a proportion of MZ twins differ in size from birth due to such prenatal environmental effects as transfusion syndrome; and (c) stature actually varies slightly over the course of a day so that either twin might be a bit taller or shorter than usual at the time of measurement. The correlation of stature among MZA twins will approximate the MZT values unless one member of some MZA pairs experienced significant deprivation during early childhood.

Heritability

The total variance in any trait, the variation among people of a given group or population, can be expressed as the sum of the variance that is due to environmental factors (external influences beginning in the womb but especially experiences during childhood and later) plus the variance that is due to genetic differences

---

[2]More accurately, MZA twins are a natural *quasi-experiment* because the twins to be separated are not chosen randomly from among all twin pairs nor are the adoptive parents randomly selected.

among the members of the given population. The *heritability* of the trait, then, is the proportion of the total variance due to genetic variation. It is important to see that heritability must increase when environmental variance decreases; when environmental differences are reduced, the total trait variance gets smaller, so the same genetic effect becomes a larger fraction of the total.

The MZ correlation, R_{MZ}, on trait Z equals the heritability of Z (because MZ twins share the same genes) plus any additional component of similarity that has resulted from the twins' having shared the same experiences, as in being reared in the same home. Because the twin correlation for stature of MZA twins is about equal to that found for MZT pairs, it appears that the only environmental factors that normally contribute to variation in stature are the pre- and postnatal experiences shared both by MZT twins and by MZA twins prior to their separation.

If we can assume that the MZA cotwins were placed randomly for adoption in uncorrelated homes (I evaluate this assumption later in this chapter), then the correlation, R_{MZA}, of the cotwins on some trait, Z, directly provides an estimate of the heritability of trait Z. As explained earlier, perinatal influences can affect twin—including MZA—similarity but these influences more often decrease rather than increase the correlation; therefore, R_{MZA} usually provides a conservative or underestimate of the true heritability of the trait.

The most extensive study of twins separated in infancy and reared apart began at the University of Minnesota in 1979 under the leadership of T.G. Bouchard, Jr. (see Bouchard, Lykken, McGue, Segal, & Tellegen, 1990). More than 120 sets of reared-apart twins or triplets, including individuals from all over the United States, Great Britain, and Australia, one each from China, Germany, and New Zealand, plus a set of Swedish triplets, have visited the labs in Minneapolis for a full week of intensive assessment. Some of the many variables measured have also been assessed in twins reared together, either by the Minnesota investigators or by others, and Bouchard et al. reported that the MZA and MZT correlations appear to be substantially the same, on anthropometric and psychophysiological variables, on personality traits, on occupational and recreational interests, and even on religiosity and measures of other social attitudes.

The Heritability of IQ

There have been five major studies of the similarity of MZA twins in respect to IQ or the general factor measured by tests of mental ability, [3] in addition to the controversial study by Cyril Burt (see later). The first three of these studies each employed two independent assessments with different tests, and Bouchard et al. reported three separate estimates of IQ. Pedersen, Plomin, Nesselroade, and McClearn (1992) estimated IQ from the first principal component factor extracted from a battery of mental ability tests. The MZA IQ correlations ranged from .64 to .78 (median .74) and the grand average correlation over all five studies, totaling

---

[3]See Newman, Freeman, and Holzinger (1937); Shields (1962); Juel-Nielsen (1965); Bouchard et al. (1990); and Pedersen et al. (1992).

163 pairs of MZA twins, weighted for sample size, is equal to .75. This value is less than the mean correlation found in the 34 published studies of MZT twins reviewed by Bouchard and McGue (1981) but those studies involved primarily children or adolescents and we know that siblings become somewhat less similar in IQ as they grow older and leave home, presumably as the effects of common rearing dissipate and unshared experiences accumulate (McCartney, Harris, & Bernieri, 1990). In their unprecedented population-based study of Swedish twins, Pedersen et al. (1992) administered the same tests of mental ability to 46 pairs of MZA and 67 pairs of MZT twins, all in late middle age and matched for age, sex, and county of birth: The MZA correlation was .78, while the MZT value, .80, was not significantly different.

Sir Cyril Burt, Britain's first professional psychologist, claimed to have measured the IQs of 53 pairs of reared-apart MZ twins, finding a value for R_{MZA} of .77. Suspicions raised by Leon Kamin and others led Burt's designated biographer, Hearnshaw (1979), to investigate the authenticity of this study. Hearnshaw's conclusions, which were widely accepted, were that Burt had forged the twin data, that he had invented his supposed collaborators, and that he became a deeply twisted and dishonest man. Joynson (1989), however, argued that Hearnshaw's scholarship was careless, tendentious, and prosecutorial and Fletcher's (1991) independent analysis makes it clear that some of Burt's critics were bloody-minded and unreliable. It is interesting to compare the scientific contributions of those who collaborated in the posthumous destruction of Burt's reputation with any one of his classic studies such as *The Young Delinquent* or *The Backward Child*; the comparison puts one in mind of jackals gnawing on the carcass of a dead lion. It is especially interesting to note that the five undisputed studies of twins reared apart yield findings essentially identical to those that Burt reported, R_{MZA} for IQ of .75 versus Burt's .77. The "Burt Affair" has been recently reviewed by Jensen (1991).

The Near Equivalence of R_{MZT} and R_{MZA}

The fact that, for most variables of interest, adult MZA twins appear to be about as similar as MZ twins reared together has at least two important implications. The first is that, for most variables, the influence of shared environment, of being reared together in the same home, appears to be negligible. Unrelated children reared in the same home correlate in IQ about .30 when studied prior to adulthood but this similarity decreases to zero when they grow up and leave home. Even DZ twins, who correlate .58 in IQ when tested in adolescence (Bouchard & McGue, 1981), are substantially less similar later in life. Pedersen and her colleagues (1992) tested 100 pairs of DZA twins and 89 pairs of DZT twins in their Swedish sample at an average age of 65 years, finding IQ correlations of .32 and .22, respectively. Many other studies of personality, interests, and attitudinal variables in adult twins have confirmed the—at first surprising—conclusion that being reared together does not tend to make siblings more like one another psychologically as adults (Plomin & Daniels, 1989). (This conclusion is less surprising when one remembers that most sensible parents do not try to squeeze their offspring into some predetermined common mold. Except perhaps for the basic traits of socialization, the best parents try to help each child to develop his or her own unique potentialities.)

A second important implication of the approximate equivalence of MZA and MZT correlations is that it justifies, in most situations, the use of the MZT correlation as a direct estimate of heritability. As we have seen, R_{MZT} equals the sum of the variance in the trait due to genetic factors plus the variance due to shared rearing environment. On the assumption that this second component is important, it has been customary to estimate heritability as twice the difference between the MZ and the DZ correlations. The effect of this formula is to use the DZT correlation to remove the presumed contribution of common rearing from the MZT value.[4] Estimating heritability in this way not only requires testing of an equal number of DZT pairs but, due to the much greater unreliability of difference measures, this method also requires many times as many of both types of twin to yield the same precision of estimate obtained directly from a given sample of MZA twins. Twins reared apart are of course rare and expensive to assess but, because it now appears that R_{MZA} and R_{MZT} are approximately equal for most variables, accurate as well as efficient estimates of heritability can usually be obtained directly from correlations of (adult) MZ twins reared together (Lykken, Bouchard, McGue, & Tellegen, 1993). (As I argue later, this rule does not apply to subcultures where many home environments have an unusually strong effect upon the trait in question.)

Estimating heritability from R_{MZT} has the added advantage of including the effects of both additive and nonadditive genetic variance. It has been generally assumed for years that most metrical traits, such as stature, are influenced only by additive polygenic effects, that is, by the sum of the effects of all the "tall" genes one has in one's genetic blueprint. When that assumption is correct, and when there is no assortative mating[5] for the trait in question as well as no common environment effect, then the MZT correlation will equal twice the DZT value, because MZ twins share 100% of their genes while DZs share only 50% on average.[6] We now know that common environment effects are about zero for most traits in adults but the other assumptions cannot always be defended. For some psychological traits, we

---

[4]The Falconer (1989) formula for estimating heritability is

$$h^2 = 2(R_{MZT} - R_{DZT})$$
$$= 2[V_g + V_{se}) - (\tfrac{1}{2}V_g + V_{se})]$$
$$= 2(\tfrac{1}{2}V_g)$$
$$= V_g,$$

where h^2 is the estimated heritability (i.e., the proportion of variance associated with genetic variation), R_{MZT} and R_{DZT} are the correlations of MZT and DZT twins, V_{se} is the proportion of variance attributable to shared experience, and V_g is the genetic variance (i.e., the quantity sought).

[5]Assortative mating means that like marries like; bright women tend to mate with bright men so that spouses correlate about .40 in IQ. Where there is assortative mating, as there is for IQ, then DZ twins and other siblings will resemble each other somewhat more than half as much as MZ cotwins do.

[6]DZ twins, like you and I, share 100% of their monomorphic genes, the ones that make us humans rather than apes. Other genes, called "polymorphic," vary from person to person and produce genetic variation. DZ twins and other siblings share about 50% of these polymorphic genes but some pairs, by chance, share many fewer than 50%, whereas other pairs share many more than 50% and may be hard to distinguish from MZ twins.

now know that R_{DZT} tends to be less than half the MZT value and, for some variables, R_{MZT} is substantial while R_{DZT} is essentially zero. This can occur when the relevant genes combine configurally or nonadditively and the result can be an "emergenic" trait (Lykken, 1982b; Lykken et al., 1992) with the curious property of being strongly genetic while yet tending not to run in families. In such cases, use of the Falconer (1989) formula (heritability = $2(R_{MZ}—R_{DZ})$) will overestimate the actual heritability; therefore, R_{MZT} alone provides both a more efficient and a more accurate estimate.

Nongenetic Interpretations of MZ Similarity

Can the remarkable similarity of MZ, and especially MZA, cotwins be explained without reference to their genetic identity? Are there pitfalls in the study of twins reared apart or in the twin method generally that compromise genetic inferences based on the findings? Publication of part of the Bouchard study in *Science* in 1990 elicited representative criticisms and alternative interpretations that are worth addressing in detail. Because these critiques are most commonly directed toward claims about the heritability of IQ, I focus on this trait in the following discussion.

Selective Placement

It has been suggested that the similarity of MZA twins in IQ could be explained environmentally if there was a tendency for the twins to be placed for adoption in similar homes. There is in fact a small correlation (0.3), within pairs, for both the educational attainment and the SES of the adoptive parents of these twins reared apart. But these same correlations equal 1 for DZ twins and other siblings who have been reared together; selective placement therefore cannot explain why MZA twins are so much more alike than non-MZ siblings reared in the same home. Moreover, like Scarr and Weinberg (1978), Bouchard and his colleagues found that the education and SES of the adoptive parents did not correlate at all with the IQs of the twins whom they reared.

It might be supposed that there may have been some other common feature of the adoptive homes, a feature that we did not identify or measure, that caused the IQ similarity that we observed. This unspecified variable, let us call it X, with respect to which the adoptive homes are thought to have been strongly correlated, must be virtually unrelated to parental education or SES because these variables were only weakly correlated between paired homes. X must be known to and easily assessed by social workers and others who make adoption placements because the supposed strong similarity in X of the adoptive homes is thought to have been deliberately achieved by these persons. Finally, X must be a variable that can, by environmental influence, control the IQ of normal children over a range of at least 60 points. Critics have alluded to this mysterious but potent variable for years but they have never identified it. I believe they never will.

Many of the Minnesota MZA pairs were in fact reared under what appeared to be significantly different circumstances. The marked difference in background of an MZA pair from Britain was immediately apparent; one twin had a distinct

Cockney accent while the other spoke like the Queen. One had been adopted by working class parents and attended a secondary modern school which she left at 16; the adoptive father of the cotwin was a university professor and she was educated in a posh private school—yet the twins' IQs were almost identical. The largest IQ difference in the Minnesota MZA sample, a difference of 29 points, was found in a pair of older men, one of whom was informally adopted by illiterate parents and quit school himself at 13 to work in the family trade. The cotwin was reared by better educated parents and had received technical training in the military. These pairs may illustrate the principle that it is easier to lower the IQ than to raise it. On the other hand, these twins were taken prematurely by caesarean section after their mother had been gravely injured and it is possible that perinatal trauma contributed to their difference in adult IQ.

The attempt to account for MZA similarity in terms of the modest similarity of the adoptive homes is further confuted by existing data on biological first cousins. Surely the homes in which adopted-away twins are placed are not in fact more similar, in their intellectually stimulating propensities, than are the homes in which ordinary first cousins are separately reared? First cousins share about .125 of their genes by common descent and the IQs of first cousins correlate about .145, very close to what one might expect on purely genetic grounds.

Other commentators have suggested that the similarity in IQ (and other variables) of the MZA twins might be accounted for by the fact that, although raised in different homes, both members of most pairs were reared within the same general culture where they "learn a particular language, interact with adults, learn the same taboos, use the same eating implements, in short, are subject to the same environmental and experiential factors as are all individuals who share the same culture."[7] The fact that this argument would require, for example, that most North Americans should be as much like one another as identical cotwins seems to me to detract from its plausibility.

Pre- and Postreunion Contact

Could the similarity of the MZA twins be due to their mutual contact prior to separation or after their adult reunion? One critic of Bouchard's study pointed out that all the MZA pairs had developed in close literal contact in the same womb. Others argued that, because the MZA twins were separated at an average age of 5 months, the Minnesota study proves not that genetic factors are important but, rather, that human psychological characteristics are substantially determined by environmental factors during the first few months of life. Thus, MZA twins are so similar as adults in ability, personality, and interests because they were shaped in similar molds during the perinatal period. One of the many problems with this notion is that it predicts DZ twins to be as similar as MZ pairs, whether reared together or apart. A vast literature shows that DZ twins are much less similar than MZs are.

---

[7]This hypothesis, from two professors of statistics (!), was offered in a letter sent to *Science* and dated December 17, 1990.

Some of the MZA twins spent considerable time together after their adult reunion but before we assessed them. This should not have made any difference if it is true that within-pair similarity is fixed by shared perinatal experiences but, because we reject the latter hypothesis, we did look for a relationship between within-pair similarity in IQ and the amount of contact both prior to separation and after adult reunion—but we found none. For all the variables we have investigated, the correlation between similarity and degree of contact is negligible. The Swedish researchers also found that the resemblance of their MZA twins was independent of age at separation, degree of contact, and of number of years separated (Pedersen et al., 1992).

Effect of Physical Appearance

Perhaps the remarkable physical similarity of MZ twins causes them to be treated in the same way by parents and others and this, in turn, causes the twins to become so alike psychologically? This raises the important question of gene–environment correlation, to which I return later. The specific idea that look-alikes act alike because they are treated alike, however, is an old and rather simple-minded notion. As an "explanation" for MZ similarity in IQ, it assumes, among other unlikely propositions, that different parenting styles, adopted in response to the child's appearance, are capable of generating the full range of adult IQs. To explain the similar high IQs exhibited by some of the MZA pairs, for example, this hypothesis requires us to suppose that two sets of adoptive parents, unacquainted with each other—couples who could have produced dull or average children had they started with infants having different physiognomies—did in fact react to these particular infants in a way that, if we could only copy it, would reliably yield IQs on the order of 130 in other children also. It is not surprising that this implausible conjecture has found no empirical support (e.g., Burks & Tolman, 1932; Matheny, Wilson, & Dolan, 1976).

Representativeness of Twin Data

Can we safely generalize from twins to singletons or from adopted-away twins, reared as singletons, to people in general? As we have seen, twins are more vulnerable than singletons to pre- and perinatal trauma. The effect of this increased vulnerability is to make twins, and especially MZ twins who are especially vulnerable, more dissimilar within-pairs than they would otherwise have been, absent these early developmental difficulties. Price's (1950) exhaustive analysis of this problem led him to conclude that, "In all probability the net effect of most twin studies has been the underestimation of the significance of heredity in the medical and behavioral sciences" (p. 293). In respect to IQ specifically, Munsinger (1977) reanalyzed various published data sets in which both IQ and birthweight data were available. Among MZ, but not DZ twins, lower birthweight was associated with lower adult IQ and large within-pair differences in birthweight, more common among MZ than DZ twins, were associated with large differences in adult IQ, but only for the MZ twins. Munsinger attributed these findings to the transfusion syndrome, a problem affecting about 22% of MZ pairs. Thus, most published IQ correlations for MZ twins, not having controlled for this environmental effect that is unique to MZ twins, may underestimate the true similarity to be expected between individuals with identical genomes.

Persons reared by their biological parents experience what has been called *passive gene–environment correlation* (Plomin, DeFries, & Loehlin, 1977). For example, a child of athletic parents is likely to receive both "athletic genes" and also athletic stimulation and training and athletic role models and this going together of the genetic and environmental effects is "passive" in the sense that neither the parents nor the offspring make an effort to bring it about. Passive gene–environment correlation probably accounts for part of the small increment in IQ correlation for MZ twins reared together as compared with those reared apart.

An Important Limitation of Most Heritability Studies

Remember that the total variation in a trait such as IQ across the group of people under study is equal to its heritability, the effect of genetic variation within the group, plus the trait's *environmentality*, the variation due to differences across people in the environmental factors that affect that trait. The amount of genetic variation in a population is relatively constant unless real selective breeding is going on. But the amount of environmental variation can change radically from time to time or from one group to another. Most studies of the heritability of IQ have included subjects who were reasonably representative of the broad middle class, people of mainly European extraction. Therefore, the findings of these studies can reasonably be generalized to perhaps 90% of society.

The true underclass of American society, however, has been largely omitted from these study samples because such people are less accessible to researchers and less likely to volunteer to take psychological tests and the like. Suppose we were to repair this omission by locating and testing 100 pairs of adult MZ twins, and 100 pairs of DZs, who were born to and reared by mothers, many of them poorly educated, living on welfare in the inner cities of this country. It is likely that the genetic variation that is related to IQ will be less among this segment than in the population generally due to truncation at the high end. But we shall certainly find that the relevant environmental variance is greater in this group. More of these twins will have received poor prenatal care, more of these mothers will have been badly nourished or substance abusers, more of the births badly managed with greater risks of cerebral anoxia and other perinatal trauma. More of these youngsters will have been abused or neglected. Fewer of them will have been read to and talked to, trained and encouraged to learn. More of them will have been frequently truant and early school drop-outs. All of these differences are at least potential environmental contributors to IQ variation. Although the study has not been attempted, I think that even the most committed hereditarian psychologist would expect it to show a substantially greater component of environmental variation— and, hence, a lower heritability—than has been found in the many studies of the "mainstream" population.

Moreover, incidentally, I think one would expect another difference, namely, that there would likely be a significant lasting effect of common home environment. That is, the DZ twins would prove to be more than half as similar in IQ as the MZ twins. Mothers who neglect or abuse one twin are likely to treat the other one the same way. Prenatal and perinatal deficiencies are likely to affect both babies. Dedicated mothers who, in spite of all the obstacles, nurture, protect, and encourage one youngster will tend to treat the other similarly.

Although this study has not been done, the expectation that it would show stronger effects of environment—and therefore lower heritability—is supported by two small adoption studies conducted in France. In one of these, 34 children were located who had been abandoned by working-class parents and adopted into upper class homes (Schiff, Duyme, Dumaret, & Tomkeiewicz, 1982). On average, these youngsters scored 12 points higher on an IQ test than did 20 of their siblings reared in the lower class environments of the biological parents. In the second study, four small groups of adoptees were found, two each consisting of children born to lower or upper class parents; one group of each pair had been adopted and reared by lower class, and the other by upper class, parents (Capron & Duyme, 1989). The appropriate comparisons indicated that upper class rearing of the lower class children increased IQ about 12 points whereas lower class rearing of upper class children lowered IQ an equivalent amount.

It is important to note that these adoption studies do not permit us to assess the possible effects on IQ of the different prenatal and perinatal environments of children with biological parents at opposite ends of the socioeconomic scale. However, another finding in this study was that the adoptees with upper class biological parents had IQs 15 points higher than those with lower class origins. McGue (1989) pointed out that this difference may be due in part to pre- and perinatal environmental differences prior to adoption but is likely due also in part to true genetic differences between parents who rise to or remain in the upper stratum and those who sink to or remain in the lower one.

All things considered, therefore, it seems reasonable to conclude that heritability estimates based on twin studies, including twins reared apart, slightly underestimate the true values that characterize the broad segment of the largely Caucasian population from which these twins were drawn. However, it is likely that the heritability of IQ (and, as we shall see, of socialization) is lower among the true underclass of society due to the greater frequency of deleterious environmental factors that impinge on children born and reared in those circumstances.

NATURE VIA NURTURE

We cannot yet begin to trace the many steps that intervene between the protein-making activities in which the genes are directly engaged and their ultimate influence upon individual differences in complex psychological traits. We assume that behavioral differences are associated with nervous system differences. Some of the later undoubtedly are "hard-wired," biological differences. We can imagine, for example, that some brains work faster or more consistently than others (e.g.,

Reed, 1984) or that the inhibitory mechanisms that subserve phenomena like habituation are biologically stronger or more reliable in some brains than in others. But surely many of the brain differences that account for differences in personality, interests, and attitudes are differences in the "software," are the result of learning and experience? Yet, if nurture or experience is the proximal cause of individual differences in these traits, how can one explain the strong association between these differences and genetic variation (i.e., nature)?

A major insight of behavior genetics is that one important way in which the genome exerts its influence upon the brain is indirect; the genes help to determine the effective environment of the developing child through the correlation or the interaction of genes with environment (Plomin et al., 1977; Scarr & McCartney, 1983). Passive gene–environment correlation has already been discussed. Partly for genetic reasons, some infants are fussy and irritable whereas others are happy and responsive; these differences elicit different responses from their adult caretakers. This process, which of course continues throughout life as our (primarily social) environment reacts differentially to our innate temperament, talents, and physical appearance, is called *reactive* or *evoked* gene–environment correlation. Partly for genetic reasons, different children attend to different aspects of their environment, and seek out or create environments attuned in some way to their genetic make-up. These are examples of *active* gene–environment correlation. The first day in school or a first roller-coaster ride will be a pleasurable excitement for some children, stimulating growth and self-confidence, but a terrifying and destructive experience for other children; as Allport (1937) put it, the same fire that melts the butter hardens the egg—this is gene–environment *interaction.*[8]

Some Illustrative Examples

A distinguished ornithologist of my acquaintance was relieved to learn, at age 11, that he was adopted; this discovery explained for him why he was so different from his parents and their relatives. His adoptive parents did not read or own books but the boy always had a library card and used it regularly. The parents had no talent for nor interest in sports but the youngster, in summer, always carried his baseball mitt with him in case of the chance for a game and won recognition for his prowess at basketball and tennis. This man's biography is a chronicle of active gene–environment correlation and his quest for experiences compatible with his innate proclivities contrasts with his failure to respond to influences that were readily available but to which he did not resonate. One interest that the other members of his adoptive family shared was in religion but our acquaintance never joined with them in this.

This man's adoptive parents, like most parents, were "permissive" in the sense that they did not determinedly or effectively shape his behavior nor influence him

---

[8]Purists will note that reacting differently to the same experience is a main effect and not an interaction. One could introduce two levels of the independent variable by adding, say, a ride on the merry-go-round, and thus satisfy the purist to the mystification of the ordinary reader.

by their provocative or charismatic example. They might have prevented him from engaging in sports but they merely did not encourage these activities. Had they been readers themselves with quick minds and lively intellectual interests, they might have given different or additional directions to his reading and thought. Had their religious practices been either emotionally or intellectually stimulating, he might well have been more interested in them. Had this man, in adulthood, found his MZA twin reared by a different set of similarly "permissive" adoptive parents in some other U.S. town, I believe they would have discovered that they shared, not only similar aptitudes and interests, but similar developmental histories. Had the cotwin been adopted by Joe Kennedy, however, or the father of John Stuart Mill, or by Dickens' Fagin, or a Mafia Godfather then, having traveled such a different epigenetic landscape (Waddington, 1957), the cotwins' differences might be as interesting as their residual similarities.

One of Bouchard's MZA twins has been a professional pianist although her cotwin cannot play a note. One of the adoptive mothers was a piano teacher who gave lessons in her home; the other parents were not musical. But it was the latter parents who produced the pianist! The piano-teacher mother offered lessons but did not insist, whereas the other adoptive mother, not musical herself, was determined that her daughter would have piano lessons and determined also that she would make the most of them; she shaped her daughter's early environment with a firm, consistent hand.

Many other youngsters (myself among them), with similarly determined mothers, have sweated through years of piano lessons with no useful result. It can hardly be doubted that these discordant twins shared a native talent for playing the piano that most children do not have, a talent sufficient for the first twin to have once appeared as soloist with the Minnesota Orchestra, yet not strong enough, by itself, to lead the other twin even to join one of her own mother's classes. If their talent had been of Mozartian dimensions, however, who can doubt that the second twin also would have learned to play? The discordance in pianistic skill of this MZ pair, like the concordance of other pairs on other attributes, seems to me to be strongly suggestive. What it suggests (e.g., about the relative effectiveness of different parenting styles) needs, of course, to be tested by systematic research. Much of the value of the study of twins reared apart resides in such heuristic implications.

It is useful to think of the themes or tendencies latent in the genome as each having a certain press or "push," sufficient to allow them to become manifest in certain developmental environments—certain epigenetic landscapes—but not in others. The remarkable similarity of MZA twins on so many psychological traits suggests that the rearing environments provided by most adoptive parents are "functionally equivalent" (e.g., Scarr & Weinberg, 1978), meaning that both identical genotypes are able to seek out very similar effective environments, similar "epigenetic pathways." But the previous example shows that the right kind of intervention with certain children can elicit surprising potentialities which, unsolicited, might have remained latent and unrecognized.

Is IQ All There Is to Intelligence?

It is a fact that virtually all potential measures of intelligence that have ever been investigated turn out to be positively intercorrelated. The British psychologist, Charles Spearman, argued long ago that this "positive manifold" can be understood if we assume that all such measures are influenced by a common underlying factor he called "general intelligence" or g. It is important to understand that g—which is estimated by the IQ score—is not all there is to intellectual ability. Psychologists are coming around to the view that the brain is not just a general purpose computer but, rather, that there exist in the brain various special purpose mechanisms, such as a language processor, whose efficiency can vary independently of that of the main computer. Autistic persons, for example, seem to be innately deficient in the specialized ability to process social cues while, at the same time, some autistic people—savants—have extraordinary powers of vivid visual imagery (some have the related capacity of perfect pitch) and may be gifted artists. Others possess extraordinary mnemonic, musical, or mathematical talents (see Sacks, 1995). Such observations suggest that there are numerous dimensions of intellectual capacity and that one can be well-endowed with certain of these talents while less well endowed with others. But the general-purpose computer function of our brains seems to orchestrate the functioning of these more specialized "mental organs" and Spearman's g may represent the power, speed or accuracy of this central computer; g may not be all there is to intelligence but it is very important.

It seems reasonable to suppose that g is associated with the hardware, with as yet unidentified neuronal or whole-brain parameters that are genetically determined. The cerebral hardware can be affected by such environmental factors as pre- and perinatal trauma, inadequate nutrition, environmental poisons, and the like. The *IQ*—the best measure we yet have of g—clearly is determined by the software as discussed earlier. Deleterious environmental effects on cerebral software can be profound: I have already alluded to the (environmental) effects on some MZ twins by the restriction of blood oxygen due to the transfusion syndrome. Moreover, of course, any of the persons celebrated in the lists of human genius would have produced low IQ scores had they been reared in a cage without intellectual stimulation (cf. Skeels, 1966). Positive environmental effects can therefore be profound to the extent that they involve the *prevention* of deleterious effects.

For example, in the developed countries of the world, there has been a substantial increase in average IQ test score in recent decades, an improvement especially in abstract reasoning ability or "fluid" intelligence rather than in verbal or numerical ability (Flynn, 1987). For example, in the Netherlands where the military administers a 40-item version of the Ravens Matrices test to all healthy 18-year-old men annually, the estimated mean IQ has increased about 6 points per decade since 1952. Flynn argued that the Dutch cannot actually have become that much smarter or someone would have noticed. If the entire IQ distribution—the Dutch "Bell Curve"—had shifted upwards as much as the average score has, then the number of Dutch men with IQs in the genius range (150 and above) should have increased more than 50-fold from 1952 to 1982; "The result should be a cultural renaissance too great to be overlooked" (Flynn, 1987, p. 187). A more likely possibility is that the increase in the mean score consists primarily in a reduction in the frequency of low scores as a consequence of improved nutrition, better prenatal care, and the like. No method has as yet been identified that can produce significant and lasting increases in the IQ of well-nourished, healthy children of below-average intelligence (e.g., Spitz, 1986).

The Interplay of Genetics and Environment

Conduct disorder and criminality are software disorders that are commonly associated with parametric deviations in the hardware—deviations expressed as impulsiveness, aggressiveness, adventurousness, muscular physique, a low "fear IQ" (Lykken, 1957), and so on—deviations that are not necessarily defects in themselves. Twin studies have confirmed that criminality and antisocial personality have a genetic component (e.g., Wilson & Herrnstein, 1985, pp. 90–96) and we know from Robins' (1978a) classic studies that nearly all antisocial adults demonstrate antisocial behavior as children, although fewer than half of juvenile delinquents become criminal adults.

In a recent review, Lytton (1990) marshals a strong case for the proposition that much of the destructive or ineffectual parental behavior that leads to conduct disorder in children consists of aggressive and rejecting—or passive and permissive—*reactions* by the parent to the strong-willed temperament of the child in infancy and to his aggressive, defiant behavior later on. Because punishment is frequently effective, we often forget how much we depend on punishment in the socialization of children. When a child's temperament is such that the usual punishment-based methods fail, parents may either intensify the punishment or give up altogether; that is, they may react to the child in ways that appear to cause the child's subsequent delinquency. And the parent's behavior is causal while at the same time is caused itself by the child's intransigent temperament. The potential psychopath is not "born bad" but he is born *difficult* and he is likely to become "bad" unless his parents are skillful, or have skillful help, so that they can avoid the usual "coercive cycles" (Patterson, 1982) of this kind of gene–environment correlation. The biography of Captain Sir Richard Burton (Rice, 1990), the Victorian explorer and adventurer, illustrates the way in which a psychopathic temperament, combined with great talent, privileged birth, and the opportunities of empire—a rather specialized epigenetic landscape—could lead to a knighthood rather than to gaol.

It is not difficult to see how certain innate talents and energies can create the environments that transmute the talents into skills and the energies into interests. It is harder to guess what sorts of innate traits would lead a child to seek out experiences conducing toward religiosity (Waller et al., 1990) or conservatism (Martin et al., 1986). But we know that for all of these traits much or most of the stable variance is genetic variance and where else might we conceivably look for an explanation of this remarkable fact except to the mechanisms of gene–environment correlation and interaction? The challenge of understanding these phenomena, and of devising effective interventions argues against wasting further time on the nature–nurture controversy.

The traditional argument over nature versus nurture is plainly fatuous, like asking whether the area of a rectangle is more dependent on its length or on its width. You cannot construct a building with only a blueprint or with only bricks and mortar; you need both. Without environmental inputs, your genome would have created nothing more than a damp spot on the carpet. Nature works *through* nurture, even in the fabrication of bone and neurons. In creating the mental software that is the essence of human individuality, the nature via nurture coupling is looser, leaving greater room both for both accidental and selective intervention.

Does Parenting Matter?

The studies at Minnesota, like those of other investigators, indicate that being raised together in the same home by the same parents in the same general environment usually does not make children more alike. There is nothing surprising about this when we realize that two genetically different children in the same environment may experience very different *effective* environments. One source of this difference, the importance of which has only recently begun to be appreciated (Dunn, 1992; Dunn, Brown, Slomkowski, Tesla, & Youngblade, 1991; Dunn & Plomin, 1990), is the fact that each sibling constitutes a salient part of the effective environment of the other. Nor should we be dismayed by this because good parents do not try to treat each different child the same way. Sensible parents are not radical environmentalists who expect every child to have the same problems and possibilities, nor do they assume that their child, because he or she is theirs, must be a little replication of themselves. Wise parents remember that each child is unique, unprecedented, and they try to discern its individual needs, liabilities, and potentials (see also R. Wilson, 1983).

Scores on the Aggression scale of the Multidimensional Personality Questionnaire (MPQ)[9] show no significant shared environmental influence—DZ twins are not more than half as similar as MZ twins, for example—yet it seems very likely that many children grow up less (or more) aggressive than their genomes might have inclined them to be, as a result of their parents' reactions to the child's aggressive (or unaggressive) proclivities. Some parents may effectively and unselectively discourage (or encourage) aggressiveness in all their children; my wife and I did not allow our boys or our animals to fight and our sons are not aggressive men (we do still have to keep an eye on the bull terrier and one psychopathic cat). Studies have proven that excessively aggressive children can learn to moderate their behavior if the problem is addressed early and in the right ways (Lore & Schultz, 1993; Pepler & Rubin, 1991). But, because shared environment contributes negligibly to the

---

[9]The MPQ measures 11 basic traits of personality plus 3 high-order traits or superfactors (viz., positive and negative emotionality and constraint; see Tellegen & Waller, 1994). The MPQ has been widely used in the Minnesota twin studies (e.g., see Tellegen et al., 1988).

population variance in this trait, we know that parents who use these methods effectively are rare. The data suggest instead that many parents fail to control the aggressiveness of those children in whom the innate tendency is extreme.

Fearfulness or "harmavoidance," although half its variance is attributable to genetic variation, can assuredly be influenced by environmental manipulation and therefore by skillful parenting. Wise parents use careful desensitization and confidence-building manipulations to help their innately shy or fearful children, culminating perhaps in experiences like the Outward Bound program or a Dale Carnegie course. But few parents strive, as Joseph and Rose Kennedy seem to have done, to make all of their children less fearful, more dominant, more aggressive, or more conservative—and few parents are as effective as the Kennedys were.

I have argued that the proximal cause of individual differences in cognitive, personality, and character development is the effective environment toward which the child is attracted and to which he or she reacts in idiosyncratic ways, and that each youngster possesses a unique genetic steersman that directs this process. The parent's job is to get to know this steersman and to facilitate its actions in some ways, subverting or overriding it in others. Whether a child is intellectually gifted or afflicted with Down syndrome, skillful parenting can make a profound difference in that child's ultimate attainment, productivity, and quality of life. A willful, aggressive, relatively fearless child, like a bull terrier pup, can become an outlaw if he is left to run wild or trained by methods suitable to poodles or pomeranians. Handled with consistent, patient, loving firmness, however, the bull terrier can grow up to be the neighborhood favorite. Similarly handled, emphasizing pride rather than punishment, constructive rather than antisocial risk taking, the potential delinquent can grow up to be a hero rather than a hood, a leader rather than a psychopath.

Like the great Japanese wood carvers, the wise parent seeks out the strengths and patterns implicit in each unique specimen. *Of course* parenting makes a difference, but it makes the most useful, helpful difference when it works with nature, fertilizing here, pruning there, bending (gardeners call it "training") but not breaking. Like the great Japanese wood carvers, parents this wise and skillful seem to be rare (and, unhappily, parents too incompetent to even socialize their children are altogether too numerous).

I believe that it is no longer intellectually respectable or scientifically acceptable to offer interpretations of important human psychological phenomena that leave genetic influences out of account. Just one example, chosen because it is recent and important, is a prospective study of the relationship of physical abuse in childhood to subsequent violent behavior by that child grown up (Dodge, Bates, & Pettit, 1991). As DiLalla and Gottesman (1991) pointed out in relation to another study of the same problem (Widom, 1989), the probability that the offspring of violent, abusive parents will be prone to violence themselves even without having been reared and abused by those parents is not even considered. Do we really think that there is less stigma associated with being violent because one was abused as a child than because of one's heritage? Is it easier to remediate violence proneness if it is due to a history of abuse rather than genetic factors? Or is it better to address this (or any other) problem armed with facts rather than with fantasy?

Some Myths About Genetic Differences

Facing facts is not always easy but it is, I think, always better than not facing them. Moreover, many of the feared consequences of facing the genetic facts are phantasmagorical and disappear once we take a good look under the bed. To acknowledge the importance of genetic variation in human individuality does not imply any of the unhappy consequences discussed here.

Biological Determinism

(We are all puppets dancing on strings manipulated by our once and only genes.) If genes affect the mind in part by probabilistically determining one's environment, then surely we can affect the mind (our own mind, our child's mind) by environmental intervention, some aspects or traits being more malleable than others. The fact that most of the MZA twins developed so similarly is evidence of the functional equivalence of the rearing environments provided by this collection of adoptive homes.

If an MZA study had been conducted in 19th-century Europe, when there were peasants and princes and the mean absolute difference between random pairs of rearing environments was greater than it is today, many of the MZA correlations would presumably have been smaller than those found during the 20th century. Where there is a strong class structure in society, the social class in which one has been reared may be obvious in the adult; if twins were separated as infants and placed, one with a middle-class Minnesota family and the other with an 18-year-old unmarried mother living on AFDC in the South Bronx, the twins will surely differ 30 years later.

Clearly, the adoptive parents of the Minnesota MZA twins do not represent the extremes of environmental deprivation that still exist in Western society. They do represent, however, a broad socioeconomic range that includes most English-speaking peoples of European descent and the findings indicate that what appear to be important differences between these families were in fact not very important psychologically to the twins reared in their midst. In the absence of a strong external influence working to systematically determine the course of experience, the child's own genetic individuality is the one consistent steersman over the epigenetic landscape; with identical drivers and such a relatively homogeneous landscape, it is little wonder that MZA twins tend to arrive at similar destinations.

Therapeutic Nihilism

(If a tendency is genetic, like the diathesis for schizophrenia or bipolar affective disorder, then there is no hope for a cure).[10] It seems extraordinary that psychologists especially should suppose that the effects of experience are easier to modify or ameliorate than those of genetic origin. I agree with Dawkins (1982): "What did the genes do to deserve their sinister, juggernaut-like reputation? Why do we not

---

[10]The fallacy of therapeutic nihilism was thoroughly autopsied (but, alas, not laid to rest, humankind's fondness for the fallacious being what it is) by Meehl (1977).

make a similar bogey out of, say, nursery education or confirmation classes? Why are genes thought to be so much more fixed and inescapable in their effects than television, nuns, or books?" (p. 13)—or, one might add, than prenatal or infant experience or being reared by a "schizophrenogenic" mother?

We know that half of the MZ cotwins of schizophrenic or psychopathic individuals do not develop the disorders (Gottesman, 1991). The hopeful and the only responsible approach is to continue the search for the mechanisms, especially the manipulable mechanisms, that make the difference, rather than to invent environmental pseudo-explanations for the high MZ concordance—to explain why the glass is half empty rather than attempting to explain away the fact that it is certainly half full.

Social Programs Will Not Be Funded

(Why bother with preschool, drug education, assertiveness training, or the Outward Bound experience if "it's all in the genes?"). We are accustomed to viewing the nature–nurture question as a competition; if one becomes more impressed with the importance of genetic factors, one should become correspondingly less impressed with the role of the environment. If that part of the observable variance that is due to environmental variation is smaller, then it is undeniably true that, for a particular population, the proportion attributable to genetic variance must be correspondingly larger. But, whereas the total genetic variance is relatively stable, the environmental variance for any trait can be increased or decreased by environmental manipulations. Thus, the heritability of ponderosity (fatness) is undoubtedly greater in Zurich, where the prosperous Swiss get all they want to eat, than it is in Haiti or Somalia, where only the rich or powerful are well-fed while many people are thin because of deprivation rather than because of genetic factors affecting either their physiology or their consummatory behavior.

Consider next the heritability of criminality, which will be highest among Jane Murphy's Eskimos, lower among White, middle class Americans, lowest among members of our underclass living in an urban ghetto. In the Eskimo community, environmental variation in both socialization and in criminal provocation or temptation is minimized because of the homogeneity of the society and of the experiences of its members and because responsibility for the socialization of children is shared by the group and its results are therefore homogeneous also. In the ghetto, the socialization of children varies from remarkable to negligible while criminal provocation and temptation is much higher and therefore more variable also. Variation in the genetic factors that are relevant to criminality is presumably about the same within each of the three populations. Therefore, because the relevant environmental variance (Cattell's *threptic* variance) is lowest among the traditional Eskimos and highest in the ghetto, so the heritability of criminality will be highest among the Eskimo and lowest in the ghetto. The heritability of a trait often tells us as much about the culture as it does about human nature. It tells us about the relative effectiveness of the relevant environmental variations that prevail in the culture.

Genetic factors presently determine about 75% of the reliable variance in IQ among the White population of the Western democracies. This tells us that Western society is doing a moderately good job of providing equality of opportunity for the intellectual development of its (White, middle-class) citizens. This heritability statistic tells us nothing, however, about how well we are doing in providing compensatory treatment for, say, retarded or dyslexic children; such effects would be measured by a decrease in total phenotypic variance. If methods could be found to improve the socialization of underclass children, the incidence of criminality in this group would decrease while the heritability of criminality among inner-city residents would increase. But whether such effective environmental manipulations can be found depends on the trait and the nature of the organism and, as Baumrind (1993) has pointed out, cannot be predicted from genetic studies.

One must accept, of course, that there are limits to intervention, that no imaginable training or experience could have made Everyman into a Mozart, a Ramanujan, or a Shakespeare, that it is harder to raise IQ than to lower it, and that it is neither necessary, possible, nor indeed desirable to change all shy persons into extroverts. The point to emphasize is that social intervention will be most effective when it is designed and allocated in a way that takes into account individual differences in genetic proclivities.

Social Darwinism

(Science endorses the inevitability of the status quo; the evils of social stratification are unavoidable; people have to learn to accept their "place" in the natural scheme of things.) On the contrary, the neohereditarian position does not open the door to fascism, racism, and related evils. Consider social class differences, for example. It is not true that "good" genes migrate upwards to become the birthright of a ruling elite while "bad" genes sink into the gutter. *Individuals* rise and fall partly as a consequence of their genetic endowment; that is social mobility. Because of that mobility, there are social class differences in IQ, stature, physical vigor, and the like but the offspring quickly regress toward the mean. We are all familiar with the Adams family of Boston which contributed presidents and statesmen over a 100-year span, but that family was notable as a family precisely because it was so exceptional. Successful families do not remain on top for long and what hysteresis there is results largely from the advantages that money buys; that is, the status achieved by the founders of the family is sustained by later generations mainly because of environmental rather than genetic factors—and not even the money lasts for long. Cornelius Vanderbilt, who had planned to build a family dynasty, was the richest man in the world when he died in 1877. "When 120 of the Commodore's descendants gathered at Vanderbilt University in 1973 for the first family reunion, there was not a millionaire among them" (Vanderbilt, 1989, p. ix).

At the other end of the social scale, however, at the level of the underclass, the hysteresis is considerable. Illegitimate children reared in poverty tend to breed more illegitimate children who remain in poverty. Grandparents who fail to socialize their children tend to have grandchildren who are unsocialized, and so on and on. This is the society's problem, both because the larger society pays for and suffers from this problem, and also because the larger society, partly because of misguided good intentions, has helped to create and to sustain the problem.

If those underclass grandparents were handicapped by "bad" genes—if their mental and physical talents were below average and if their innate temperaments made them difficult to socialize—their children and especially their grandchildren will tend to be less handicapped than they were in these ways, their genomes will tend to "regress toward the mean" of the population at large. But unless better methods of social intervention are employed to prevent the intergenerational transmission of dyssocial habits and values, too many of those grandchildren will remain trapped within the underclass. Even now, without much outside assistance, some of those grandchildren rise up into the mainstream of society and even to its headwaters. Emergenesis (Lykken et al., 1992), in particular, urges us to recognize and cultivate talent wherever it sprouts.

The Hegemony of Barbarism

(If our psychology is rooted in our genes then, because our human genome evolved during the Pleistocene and has not much changed since neolithic times, the next millennium—if our species survives it—will be as irrational and violent as the last one.) I suspect that this assumption may be responsible for some of the antagonism directed toward the fields of evolutionary psychology and behavior genetics. I wish I could be as confident about refuting this concern as I am about the other four. "The genes sing a prehistoric song that must often be resisted but cannot be ignored" (Bouchard et al., 1990, p. 228). Much of what constitutes "civilization" is only skin deep and its fabric is rent easily and often. Even as I write, Christian Serbs are attacking Christian Croats and Muslim Bosnians with genocidal intent in the former Yugoslavia. Every sub-Saharan nation of Africa is periodically torn by tribal conflicts while Hindus and Moslems are at each other's throats throughout India as are Arabs and Jews in the Mideast.

But it is also true that the genes' "prehistoric song" *can* be successfully resisted. Our forefathers were cruel, xenophobic, reflexively obedient to the authority of their alpha males, and treated women as property. Many men now manage to resist these instincts, most of the time, at least during the interludes of peace. I believe that, in order to control these atavistic impulses, it is necessary (albeit not sufficient) to be aware of them and to understand their origins.

Conclusions

Thus, the neohereditarian platform does not belittle the importance of social intervention, of good parenting, of psychotherapy, good public education, and the like. It is not in conflict with liberal values nor does it necessarily conflict even with the Marxist views espoused by some of the more prominent radical environmentalists. On the contrary, many who believe that much of human individuality is prefigured in the genes could happily adopt the Marxist slogan: "To each according to his needs; from each according to his ability." As a prescription for parents, if not for governments, it is a neo-hereditarian maxim, suitable for framing.

Like the late Cold War between East and West, the war between the radical environmentalists and the hereditarians is an anachronism; we should agree that it is over, that both sides have won, and that the influence of genetic variability on the human psyche, although pervasive and important, is *itself* dependent on the effective environment during development. The time has come to tear down the Wall and turn our energies to the difficult but fascinating study of the mechanisms by means of which the brain writes its own software.

6

The Heritability of Criminality

What heredity determines are not fixed characters but developmental processes.

—T. Dobzhansky (1956)

In 1983, 265 pairs of high school-aged twins were recruited by mail to respond to 25 questions about their own delinquent or antisocial behavior ("How often have you: –stolen something worth more than $50? –started a fight? –deliberately broken a window? –lied about your age?" etc.; Rowe, 1983). Within-pair correlations for the extent of self-admitted antisocial behavior were about .64 for MZ twins and .49 for DZs. Genetic model testing rejected all nongenetic models, giving the usual finding of a significant genetic influence. But what is unusual about this study, was that Rowe could not reject the possibility that normal-range adolescent antisocial behavior, unlike most psychological traits, is influenced by shared environmental effects. Those DZ correlations are larger than half the MZ values and this suggests either that there is considerable assortative mating for the genetic factors that tend to elicit antisocial behavior, or that the common home environment tends to socialize both twins of each pair in the same way.

The estimated heritability of adolescent antisocial behavior, as self-reported in Rowe's study, was .30. A meta-analysis of the literature on the genetics of delinquency, published in the same year, came to the same conclusion; the grand average heritability was .30 and, as in Rowe's research, Gottesman, Carey, and Hanson (1983) also concluded that delinquency, unlike most psychological traits, shows substantial influence of shared home environment.

In this chapter I show that adult criminality, also, is influenced to an important degree by genetic factors. This is because the more basic psychological characteristics that make children difficult to socialize and that conduce toward crime, characteristics like relative fearlessness, aggressiveness, stimulus-seeking, muscular body build, and below-average IQ, are themselves strongly influenced by genetic variation. But, unlike most psychological traits, criminality is also strongly influenced by characteristics of the rearing environment, as Rowe's data suggest.

92

The most important feature of the rearing environment is the competence of the rearing parents in their basic task of socialization. I show later that the absence of the father is one of the most important risk factors for inadequate socialization, partly because parenting is such a demanding job that many single parents are unable to cope adequately on their own, and partly because fathers seem to play a specially important role in matters of discipline. Before I consider the genetic data in detail, I mention here just one further study, rather similar to Rowe's in that it concerns self-confessed antisocial behavior in noncriminals, which alerts us to just how sensitive this process of socialization is to the presence of the father in the home.

In the early 1960s, Siegman (1966) recruited a group of male, first-year medical students whose fathers had been away from home for a year or more in the armed services during World War II when these boys were from 1 to 4 years old. For his comparison group, Siegman located other students in the same class whose fathers had not been out of the home for an extended time during that early childhood period. Only students whose parents were currently living together were included. All subjects filled out an anonymous questionnaire asking about a variety of antisocial behaviors ranging from truancy to vandalism, premarital or extramarital sex, and theft. Although both groups consisted of high achievers from stable, two-parent families, and although the fathers' absence was dictated by wartime conditions rather than paternal or marital instability, the group whose fathers had been absent during the son's early childhood reported significantly more antisocial behavior than the group whose fathers had been present during that period.

The Genetics of Crime

Crime, like boxing, is primarily a man's game; the male:female ratio ranges from 4:1 to 20:1 over many diverse cultures (and this wide range suggests the importance of cultural influences on socialization). And crime is primarily a young man's game; as shown in Fig. 6.1, we could avoid two thirds of all crime simply by putting all able-bodied young men in cryogenic sleep from the age of 12 through 28. Also like boxing, crime attracts mainly mesomorphs, young men with a muscular, athletic body type and the action-oriented, competitive personalities that often go with that type.

Thus, although "criminal" is a heterogeneous category, the bulk of criminal offenders are mesomorphic young men. Some are intellectually handicapped. Many are adventurous, relatively fearless sensation-seekers; many are aggressive and able to dominate their peers. All of these precursor traits, as we shall see, are strongly influenced by genetic factors. Therefore, it is not too surprising that even when we use such a crude and heterogeneous classification as "criminal" in our studies, we might still find a significant genetic effect.

Twin Studies

A dozen different studies have located criminal or antisocial twins and then examined their cotwins. A review of nine older studies, involving 231 MZ and 535 DZ pairs, all males, found that the MZ twins averaged 55% concordance for being

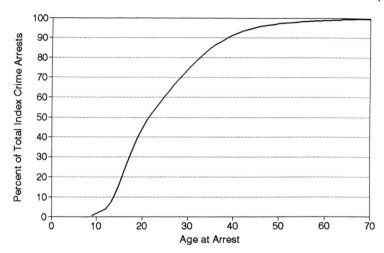

FIG. 6.1. Ages of persons arrested in the United States for "index" or serious crimes during 1991, plotted cumulatively. Some two thirds of all those arrested were between 12 and 28 years of age at the time of arrest (source: FBI, 1992).

criminal or antisocial (i.e., if John's MZ twin is antisocial, then there is a 55% chance that John will be classified as antisocial himself). The average concordance for DZ twins was 13% (Eysenck & Eysenck, 1978; see also Gottesman et al., 1983). These older studies are suspect, however, because the ascertainment may have been biased. Unless one systematically determines whether every inmate who passes through the prison is a twin and, if so, the status of his cotwin, one is likely to notice concordant MZ pairs and fail to discover other pairs who are discordant. An alternative to determining the twin status of every prisoner is to determine the criminal status of every twin, that is, to begin with a comprehensive sample of the twins in a population and then determine which twin individuals are criminal.

Christiansen (1968, 1977) identified all twin pairs born in Denmark between 1880 and 1910 and followed them through official police and court records. He defined as "criminal" those convicted of acts corresponding roughly to our felonies. The follow-up was reported at various stages of completion and the final follow-up was reported by Cloninger and Gottesman (1987). These data are shown in Table 6.1.

The twin correlations given in Table 6.1 estimate the within-pair similarity in the underlying risk for criminality and they suggest that criminality has a heritability of more than 50%. As in Rowe's study, however, the DZ correlations are also high, indicating a significant effect of common family rearing.

Carey (1992) applied a sophisticated behavior–genetic analysis to these data, one that allows for the possibility that twins reared together reciprocally influence one another, MZs more than DZs, in respect to their pro- or antisocial behaviors. When this is the case, and when the continuous trait in question is partly genetic (as risk for criminality is here), the MZ variance will exceed the DZ variance. This means that the incidence of criminality will be greater in the MZs than in the DZs

TABLE 6.1
Twin Concordance for Criminal Conviction

	Pair Members Who Were Criminal			Proband-Wise Concord.	Twin Corr.
Type of Twin	Both	One	Neither		
MZ males	25	48	292	51%	.74
DZ males	26	120	554	30%	.47
MZ females	3	12	332	33%	.74
DZ females	2	26	662	23%	.46
DZ opposite gender	14	200	3,918	7%	.23

Note. In 90% of the opposite-gender pairs who were discordant for criminality, it was the male, rather than the female twin who appeared on the criminal register. Based on Cloninger and Gottesman (1987, Table 6.6, p. 99).

(as will also the incidence of extreme prosocial adjustment). Using elegant model-fitting methods, Carey found that there is reciprocal interaction (the model that assumes none is statistically rejected) and that, if this is stronger for MZs than for DZs (which these data could not powerfully test) then the heritability estimates decrease from .50 or higher down to about .40.

In the Washington University Twin Study of Psychopathology, 81 twin individuals diagnosed as APD were recruited from consecutive admissions for psychiatric treatment and the cotwins of these probands[1] were also examined. The proband-wise[2] concordance rates were .65 for MZ twins and .40 for DZs, yielding a heritability estimate of .30 for APD (DiLalla & Gottesman, 1993). As seen in chapter 1, nearly half of the males with APD can be classified as criminal and a majority of male criminals meet the criteria for APD, which suggests that both the Washington University and the Danish twin studies were concerned with essentially the same disposition, namely criminality. (Remember, however, that being classified as *criminal* requires criminal behavior—plus being apprehended by the police—and criminal behavior results from the combination of criminality plus environmental circumstances conducive to crime. Not all criminals are high on criminality and not all persons high on criminality are criminals—yet.)

Adoption Studies

In 1972, Schulsinger reported on the first Danish adoption study of psychopathy, finding a higher incidence of the disorder in the biological families of adopted-away psychopathic probands than in a control group of nonpsychopathic adoptees. But the numbers are small (e.g., 5 affected fathers of 54 probands vs. 1 father of 57 controls). Crowe (1975) started with 41 female reformatory inmates in Iowa who had given up their child for adoption. A control sample of adoptees, matched for age, sex, race, and age at adoption, was selected from the adoption registry. Eight of the adopted-away

---

[1]The *proband* is the affected family member first identified, whose twin or other relatives are then sought out to see if they are also affected.

[2]The probandwise concordance rate is the probability that, if I am affected, my twin is also affected.

offspring of criminal mothers had arrest records compared to just two of the controls; these 8 had totaled 14 arrests, whereas the 2 had only one each.

Hutchings and Mednick (1974) screened file data on 1,145 male adoptees in Denmark who were then adults; 185 or 16% of these men were listed on the criminal register. Of these, the investigators were able to identify the fathers of 143. They proceeded to locate 143 control adoptees matched for age and SES of the adoptive father. Starting with these adult adoptees then, Hutchings and Mednick obtained the criminal records of their biological and adoptive fathers, getting results that seemed to indicate that criminality in the biological father nearly doubled the risk in the adopted-away son while criminality in the adoptive father had no effect unless the biological father also was criminal, in which case the risk in the son was doubled again.

This was a striking finding that seemed to make very good sense. Although the causes of crime may be many and varied, the criminal fathers as a group possessed higher than average criminality, a heterogeneous psychological trait that is in part heritable. The biological offspring of these criminal fathers, sharing half the fathers' genes, should therefore also be at greater risk for crime. But the most interesting aspect of this study is that criminality in the adoptive fathers has a multiplicative effect, substantially increasing criminality in biologically susceptible adoptive sons but having little effect on the others. This is, in fact, the outcome predicted by the model advocated here. Criminality, according to this model, varies directly with the aggregate strength of innate lawless tendencies and inversely with the quality of parenting. Criminal tendencies involve or are facilitated by aggressiveness, impulsiveness, sensation-seeking, by fearlessness, and so on, and these traits are in part genetically determined. Therefore, for genetic reasons, the offspring of criminal parents are likely to be harder to socialize than average children are and the success of this parental function is especially in doubt when the rearing father is himself criminal.

Unfortunately, the results of the Hutchings and Mednick study, which are so congenial theoretically, were based on too small a sample to be statistically reliable. The authors therefore expanded their survey to include all of Denmark, rather than just the Copenhagen area surveyed in 1974 (Mednick, Gabrielli, & Hutchings, 1984, 1987). This increased the total sample of adoptees sixfold and the results, although less striking in percentage terms, were now statistically significant (see Table 6.2).

TABLE 6.2
Criminality in Male Adoptees Representing all of Denmark, as a Function
of Criminality in Their Biological and Their Adoptive Parents

	Criminal Status of Parent			
	Neither	*Adoptive*	*Biological*	*Both*
Proportion of adoptees who were criminal	13.5%	14.7%	20%	24.5%
Total adoptees	2492	204	1226	143

Note. Data from Mednick, Gabrielli, and Hutchings (1984).

Gottfredson and Hirschi (1990), however, pointed out that, if the cases studied in 1974 are subtracted from the 1984 totals, the remainder—the new data that could be regarded as a replication of the 1974 study—do not show the same effect; that is, the replication fails! On the other hand, it would not be unreasonable to assume that, in Denmark as in the United States, the incidence of criminality is higher in the urban areas and that the additional, mostly rural fathers added in 1984 therefore had less criminality to pass along to their sons than the city dwellers in the 1974 sample. Thus, it does not seem unreasonable to take the 1984 totals as representative of Denmark as a whole and to accept Mednick et al.'s interpretation, namely, that criminality is modestly heritable and that poor socialization by the adoptive parents has more deleterious effects on boys whose genetic temperaments make them difficult to socialize. A study of several hundred adoptees in Iowa and Missouri (Cadoret, Cain, & Crowe, 1983) found a similar result, that the combination of adverse factors in both the biological and adoptive families produced a higher incidence of antisocial behaviors in the adoptees than could be easily explained by the sum of the two factors acting independently.

By means of a *path diagram*,[3] we can estimate the correlation between actual criminality in fathers and sons from the heritability of criminality. Based on the St.Louis twin data, the father:son correlation would be .15, whereas the Danish twin date yields an estimate of .20. If we estimate this same correlation from the adoption data in Table 6.2, we get a value of about .17, close enough to expectation to suggest that the heritability of criminality is in the neighborhood of .30 to .40.[4]

This conclusion is supported in a latter comprehensive analysis, by Baker, Mack, Moffitt, and Mednick (1989) of the data for Mednick's 13,000 Danish adoptees,

---

[3]Since the directions of the causal arrows are not in doubt in this case, the correlation between the criminality in fathers and sons can be predicted from a *path diagram* as follows:

$$r_g = .50$$

Father's $- -$ Son's
Genes   Genes
   | |
$r_{gp} = .63$ | | $r_{gp} = .63$
   \|/ $r_{fs} = (.63)(.5)(.63) = .20$ \|/
Father's $- -$ Son's
Criminality   Criminality

In the diagram, r_{gp} represents the correlation between genotype and phenotype; its square is equal to the heritability of the phenotypic trait, the proportion of variance in the observable trait that is associated with genetic variance. We know that $r_g = .50$ (because fathers and sons share half their genes). If we suppose that the heritability of criminality is about .40 as suggested by Carey's reanalysis of the Danish twin data, then $r_{gp} = (.40)^{1/2} = .63$ as in the path diagram, and the correlation, r_{fs}' between actual criminality in fathers and sons will be equal to the product of the other three correlations around the path: (.63)(.50)(.63) or .20. Based on the St. Louis twin data, the father:son correlation would be (.55)(.50)(.55) = .15.

[4]Cloninger, Sigvardsson, Bohman, and von Korring (1982) reported an adoption study from Sweden that produced results similar to those from Denmark. However, the number of criminal adoptees was small, only 39 in total, and the incidence of criminality in both the biological parents and in the sons in the Swedish study is only about one fourth that reported by Mednick et al. for Denmark, suggesting oddly different criteria in the two studies.

which included the females as well as the males, and their biological and adoptive parents. In this large sample, more than five times as many men as women had received a criminal conviction, indicating either that the propensity for criminality is weaker in women than in men or that the threshold is higher in women, that is, that social and other factors tend to inhibit the expression of criminality in women unless their innate proclivity is considerably higher than that which is sufficient to tip the average male over the edge into criminal behavior. Baker et al. were able to show that it is this second hypothesis that is correct. Adopted-away children of criminal mothers were shown to be at significantly greater risk for criminality themselves than adoptees whose biological father had been convicted of crime. Moreover, 48% of the convicted female adoptees had at least one criminal biological parent, compared with 37% of the criminal male adoptees, indicating that female criminals carry a stronger biological diathesis than male criminals.

About 28% of the biological parents in this large sample had at least one criminal conviction, compared to just 6% of the adoptive parents, confirming that persons who are unwilling or unable to raise their own children tend to be less well socialized than average. For the male adoptees, having at least one criminal biological parent increased risk of criminality in the offspring by 64% while the increased risk resulting from being reared by adoptive parents at least one of whom is criminal was 41%.

Criminality

These Scandinavian twin and adoption studies suggest that the underlying risk for crime has a heritability of 30% to 40% (among the Danes and Swedes at least; remember that the heritability of a trait depends as much upon the culture as on human nature). In these studies, what was actually assessed was the dichotomous attribute "criminal/noncriminal" and the underlying risk factor of criminality was inferred. The Socialization (So) scale of the California Psychological Inventory (CPI) was constructed to distinguish between delinquent and nondelinquent youth and thus may be said to measure at least some aspects of criminality directly. Among middle-class adults, the heritability of scores on the So scale is from .43 to .53.[5]

The Psychopathic Deviate (Pd) scale of the Minnesota Multiphasic Personality Inventory (MMPI) was constructed to distinguish antisocial from law abiding adults and is thus another estimator of underlying criminality. The heritability of the Pd scale in the general population is in the range from .50 to .60 (Gottesman & Goldsmith, 1993; Willerman, Loehlin, & Horn, 1992).

The (negative) correlation between So and Pd is substantial (−.53; Gough, 1987) but not high enough to claim that the scales measure the same thing. It should be emphasized that neither the Pd scale nor the So scale, in spite of its name, attempts to measure all three components of socialization that we discussed in chapter 1 (the

---

[5]Horn, Plomin, and Rosenman (1976) administered the CPI to 99 pairs each of MZ and DZ adult male twins. They found twin correlations on So of .43 and .23 for MZs and DZs, respectively. On the Minnesota sample of adult MZA twins, R_{MZA} was .53 for socialization (Bouchard & McGue, 1990).

disposition to avoid antisocial behavior, the disposition toward prosocial behavior, and the acceptance of the work ethic with the related desire to pull one's own weight). I defined *criminality* as the inverse of the first of these components and it seems plausible to suppose that a factor common to both the So and Pd scales is closely related to criminality. The data reviewed above suggests, that this common factor has a heritability on the order of .50, somewhat higher than the estimate, .30 to .40, derived earlier from the studies of actual criminal behavior. However, as explained in the next section, there is reason to think that these psychological measures would prove to have a lower heritability, with more of their variance accounted for by environmental factors, if measured within the criminal subculture.

On the Heritability of Measures of Socialization/Criminality

An important consideration in evaluating estimates of the heritability of criminality is the cultural relativity of such estimates, alluded to earlier. Do we want to estimate the heritability of criminality among Danes, or Merit Scholars, or among Americans in general—or among criminals? Only two of the more than 250 reared-apart twins in the Minnesota study had criminal records and they were a pair of DZA twins. In a society that includes a high proportion of incompetent parents and bad rearing environments, there will be proportionately more criminals and the majority of those criminals will come from those bad environments, environments that are substantially less propadeutic to socialization than the families in which most twins, including adopted-away twins (or most Danes) are raised. If a very few of Loehlin and Nichols' 1,700 Merit Scholar twins have turned to crime (as far as I know, none of them have), it is likely that assessment would reveal that they had truly unusual temperaments, that they were what we shall later refer to as primary psychopaths. Among the broadly middle-class population of families whose children win academic prizes, as among Jane Murphy's Eskimos, environmental influences toward socialization are relatively homogeneous; when the environmental variation is minimal, the heritability of criminality must be relatively high.[6]

The question that we really want answered is this: To what extent is criminality determined by genetic factors and, therefore, how much of the variance in criminal tendency remains that we might hope to influence by improving the parenting practices of those parents whose offspring now become delinquent and later criminal? To answer this question, we must estimate the heritability (or its complement, "environmentality") of criminality among the offspring of these target parents, that is, among the population who are now at high risk to become (or who have become) criminal. If we were persuaded that the So scale (inverted) measured criminality, then the way to estimate heritability of this trait-cluster in the criminal population would be to select a sample of twins born into families comparable in

---

[6]The same point was made by Herrnstein (1973) in relation to IQ; in a society that has succeeded in providing everyone, from early childhood, with good nutrition and equal intellectual stimulation, very little environmental variation will remain to influence IQ so that most of the residual variation in that phenotype would have to be attributed to genetic differences.

parental incompetence and other crime-relevant risk factors to the families of criminals generally. Some of these would be well-socialized, two-parent families but the sample would include a much higher proportion of dysfunctional or single-parent or unsocialized families than exists in the population at large. Therefore, the environmental variance (what Cattell[7] called the "threptic" variance) of criminality would be increased and the heritability consequently decreased to a value lower than we estimate based on twins in general.

The studies of criminal twins or adoptees mentioned earlier would seem to have this correction built into their design since, by starting with a criminal proband, they sampled from the subpopulation of families that produce criminals. These studies, however, sampled probands reared in the criminogenic families of Scandinavia during the first part of the 20th century and these families did not include nearly as high a proportion of truly incompetent parents—teenage parents, single parents, sociopathic parents—as exists among the criminogenic families of the contemporary United States. On this reasoning, therefore, the best guess is that the heritability of criminality in the United States today is less than .3 to .4, as found in these studies, and certainly less than the .5 to .6 suggested by the studies of the So and the Pd scales using twins from the general population.

Traits That Contribute to Socialization/Criminality

In a recent survey of the literature on the causes of crime and violence, sponsored by the National Research Council, we find a statement of the theme of this section: "Temperament may explain why only a proportion of children from high-risk homes and neighborhoods develop antisocial or violent behavior" (Reiss & Roth, 1993, p. 366). In their reanalysis of the Gluecks' classic longitudinal study of 500 delinquent boys and a matched control sample, Sampson and Laub (1993; S. Glueck & E. Glueck, 1950) showed that the delinquents more often were "difficult" from infancy, more often displayed temper tantrums, and the like, even when various differences in parental behavior (poor supervision, harsh discipline, rejection, parental misconduct) are controlled for.

If we ask what traits of temperament make children "difficult" and hard to socialize, four come quickly to mind: fearlessness, aggressiveness, impulsiveness, and adventurousness or sensation-seeking. There are not many shy, fearful inmates in our prisons or reform schools but there are many who are aggressive and impulsive "hip-shooters," many who are experienced fighters or bullies, and many who like to stir up excitement and who are attracted by adventure and risk.

---

[7]"In using the term *threptic* we employ a word which only a minority of researchers have yet used, but which assists clarity of thought. Threptic means *that part of the variance of a trait which is the result of variance in the environment.* To call this environmental variance, which has often been done, is to confuse the variance *in the environment itself* (e.g., in the social status of subjects, their years of training, and the number of accidents they have suffered) with the variance *in the person,* that is, in the individual's *traits, due* to the environment. ... I chose the term *threptic* ... as used by Aristotle in *De Anima* (and later by Galen), meaning 'nourishing and promoting growth'" (Cattell, 1982, p. 59).

Fearlessness

Innate differences in fearfulness or harmavoidance are important because most socializing agents rely heavily on punishment as a technique and punishment works, when it works, by eliciting fear when the impulse to do something that was previously punished occurs the next time. Relatively fearless children are not easily intimidated by punishment which means that, on the average, such children are likely to be less well socialized. In the Cambridge Study in Delinquent Development, it was found that the best predictor of criminal convictions at age 14 to 16 was being rated as "daring" at age 8 to 10 (as the best predictor of criminal conviction at age 21 to 24 was conviction at age 14 to 16; Farrington, 1986). The Los Angeles gang leader mentioned in chapter 3, author of the autobiography *Monster*, was described by his siblings as having been "absolutely fearless" as a youngster.

Moreover, even among reasonably socialized adults, a relatively fearless person may be more likely to yield to certain criminal temptations than would someone with a livelier fear of the possible consequences. In chapter 9, the role of fear and punishment in socialization is discussed in detail and I argue that children truly at the low end of the normal distribution of innate fearfulness may develop the syndrome of primary psychopathy even when reared in a typical, well-socialized, two-parent family.

Individual differences in fearfulness can be identified early in life and are quite stable over time. Even young children, aged 20 to 30 months, can be reliably classified as shy (about 30%) or as uninhibited and relatively fearless (also about 30%) and most of them will be classified the same way 5 years later (Kagan, 1994). We know that shy or fearful children can be helped to be less fearful by methods of systematic desensitization. For example, when my own sons were little, I made a practice of swinging them by their arms, up and back between my legs, trying each time to take them to the edge of fear but never across it. With experience, they became used to the rush of sensation and could gleefully tolerate the most vigorous swinging of which their perspiring father was capable. It is also probable that relatively fearless children could be made more harmavoidant by the reverse procedure of overstimulation, although one cannot imagine a good parent wanting to do such a thing. Relative fearlessness can be an asset, after all, and a good parent can find ways of socializing such a child that do not depend so heavily on punishment.

In the absence of skilled parental intervention, however, what tends to happen instead is that the initial differences in fearfulness become exaggerated through the process known as *active gene–environment correlation*. Fearful children tend to seek out safe, unstimulating environments, thus avoiding the kinds of experience that would toughen them up. More daring children, in contrast, take progressively greater risks—they climb up on the chair, then the table, the fence, the tree, the roof—and become progressively more risk-tolerant in consequence.

Numerous self-report instruments are available for measuring, in adults, individual differences in "anxiety" but these turn out to be primarily measures of

TABLE 6.3
Intraclass Correlations for Crime-Relevant Scales of the Multidimensional
Personality Questionnaire for MZ Twins Reared Apart and the 10-Year
Cross-Twin Correlations for Young Adult MZ Twins Reared Together

MPQ Scales	MZA	MZT[a]	Stability[b]	MZT/Stab
Number of twin pairs	54	79	254	
Aggression	.30	.43	.54	.80
Control[c]	.49	.45	.55	.82
Harmavoidance	.43	.43	.64	.67
Constraint	.56	.46	.59	.78

[a]These twins were tested at age 20 and again at age 30; correlations shown are correlations between Twin A's (B's) score at age 20 and Twin B's (A's) score at age 30. Values shown in Columns 2 and 3 taken from Table 4 of McGue, Bacon, and Lykken (1993, p. 104).

[b]These are the within-person correlations over the 10-year interval for the 254 individuals retested.

[c]Persons with low scores on the MPQ's Control scale are impulsive, inclined to leap before they look.

neuroticism or *negative emotionality*. Back in the 1950s, I constructed a scale called the Activities Preference Questionnaire (APQ) that was intended to assess fearfulness specifically, based on the respondent's choice of nonfrightening but onerous activities in preference to experiences that are risky or frightening (Lykken, 1957; Lykken & Katzenmeyer, 1964). The differences between the APQ and measures of anxiety or neuroticism are detailed later in chapter 9. Items from the APQ were employed in the Harmavoidance scale of Tellegen's MPQ which has been used extensively in the Minnesota studies of twins reared together and apart. Twin correlations for the relevant scales and superfactors of the MPQ are shown in Table 6.3.

The first column of Table 6.3 gives the correlations for Bouchard's MZ twins reared apart (MZA twins). The second column shows the cross-twin/cross-time correlations for a sample of MZ twins reared together (MZT twins) and tested twice, at age 20 and again at age 30; that is, the correlation of Twin A's (B's) score at Time 1 with Twin B's (A's) score at Time 2.

The third column in the table shows the long-term stability of these traits over the third decade of life as these twins settled into maturity independent of their rearing families and, largely, of each other. Dividing the cross-time twin correlation in Column 2 by the stability coefficient in Column 3 gives an estimate of the heritability of the stable component of each trait; we see in Column 4 that more than two-thirds of the *stable* variance in these traits is genetically determined. But Column 3 shows that about 40% of the total variance in these traits is not stable over the 10-year period but is determined instead by the vicissitudes of individual experience.

An example of a relatively fearless child at risk for developing an antisocial lifestyle is provided in the following excerpt from a letter I received after an article of mine on fearlessness appeared in a popular magazine (Lykken, 1982a).

Your article on fearlessness was very informative. I was able to identify with many of the traits. However, being thirty-six and a single parent of three children, I have managed to backpack on the "edge" without breaking my neck. I have a 14-year-old daughter who seems to be almost fearless to anything in her environment. She jumps out second-story windows. When she was in first grade, I came home from work one afternoon and found her hanging by her fingers from our upstairs window. I "calmly" asked her what she was doing. She replied that she was "getting refreshed." Later, she stated that she did things like that when she needed a lift—that she was bored and it made her feel better. Nancy is bright, witty, attractive, charismatic, and meets people easily. She tends to choose friends who are offbeat, antisocial, and into dope, alcohol, etc. During her month's visit here with me, she stole money from my purse, my bank card, etc., etc. (Letter from a single mom, 8–25–82)

The main point of this section is that individual differences in fearfulness are evident in early childhood, are quite stable across the developmental years, and are substantially related to genetic variation among people. Because low-fear children are more likely to become criminal, the criminal population includes more relatively fearless—and fewer fearful—individuals than the population at large.

Aggressiveness

Individual differences in aggressiveness, in the tendency to launch verbal or physical attacks, also are remarkably stable from childhood to adulthood and this stability is found across cultures (Eron & Huesman, 1984, 1990; Huesman, Eron, Lefkowitz, & Walder, 1984; Olweus, 1979). Children who are aggressive at the age of 8 to 10 tend to become violent teenagers and violent adults (Farrington, 1991; Hamparian, Davis, Jacobson, & McGraw, 1985; Huesmann, Eron, Lefkowitz, & Walder, 1984; Reis & Roth, 1993). If we can assume that scores on a self-report device such as the Aggression scale of the MPQ measure at least the more civilized degrees of this same attribute, then we see in Table 6.3 that, in normal adults, the heritability of aggression is about .30 based on the data of the middle-aged MZA twins but somewhat higher based on the younger twins reared together. On the other hand, about 80% of the *stable* component of aggressiveness is genetically determined. In their 22-year longitudinal study, in which averaged peer ratings were used to measure aggressiveness, Huesmann et al. (1984) found that the parent's aggressiveness at age 8 correlated .65 with offspring's aggressiveness at the same age, indicating that aggressiveness is strongly familial, perhaps because aggressive parents not only pass along "aggressive genes" but also set an aggressive example.

A number of twin studies, studies that used poorer measures of the aggressive trait than the MPQ Aggression scale, however, have indicated rather weak heritability for aggression Twin studies on aggression have been reviewed by Plomin, Nitz, and Rowe (1989). Moreover, the one observational study, in which 216 twin children whose average age was about 8 were, in effect, incited to knock around a large, inflated "Bobo doll," the twin correlations for ratings of how enthusiastically they responded to this incitement were substantial but about equal for MZs and DZs, suggesting zero heritability but substantial effects of shared environment (Plomin, Foch, & Rowe, 1981). I think the other evidence, cited herein, of the heritability of aggression is too strong to be blown away by a bunch of 8-year-old twins banging on Bobo dolls, but I also agree with Plomin and his colleagues that "aggressiveness may prove to be a particularly interesting trait" (Plomin, Nitz & Rowe, 1989, p. 128). And it would be hard to deny their conclusion that aggression, unlike most psychological traits, is significantly affected by shared experiences growing up in the same family. Like Traditionalism and Religiosity, traits equally relevant to ultimate socialization, aggression seems to be affected by genetic factors and also by shared home environment and it may well be that sibs and DZ twins are more than half as similar as MZ twins because the extent of their mutual influence is proportional to their initial genetic differences. I think it likely that a genetically aggressive (or traditionalist) sibling exerts a greater influence on a genetically nonaggressive (or nontraditionalist) sibling than on a sibling who shares the same tendencies.

The link between childhood aggressiveness and adult antisocial personality is further shown in a study of 37 adopted-away youngsters who were diagnosed with aggressive conduct disorder (Jary & Stewart, 1985). Of the biological parents of these children, 30% of the fathers and also 30% of the mothers qualified as APD, compared to none of the adoptive parents. In a control sample of 42 nonadopted children with aggressive conduct disorder, 33% of the fathers (but none of the mothers) were antisocial.

An aggressive child is more likely to respond coercively to parental interference, with tantrums or attacks, which may deter many parents from consistently enforcing the rules and may thus result in less adequate socialization. As Huesmann et al. (1984) conclude: "What is not arguable is that aggressive behavior, however engendered, once established, remains remarkably stable across time, situation, and even generations within a family" (p. 1133). Moreover, as is true also for relative fearlessness, hyperaggressiveness even in a tolerably socialized adult can sometimes lead to antisocial outbursts.

Impulsiveness and Sensation-Seeking

Impulsiveness and sensation-seeking have not been studied as such in young children although it seems likely that some youngsters who are called *hyperactive* would be classified as high on these traits. Satterfield (1987) followed up a group of youngsters diagnosed as hyperactive while aged 6 to 12 plus a group of normal control children, all of them residents of Los Angeles County. By age 18, 47% of the hyperactives had been arrested for one or more serious criminal offenses, compared to about 7% of the controls; 25% had been institutionalized versus just 1% of the controls. Satterfield estimates that more than 60% of all boys committed to the California Youth Authority were hyperkinetic as children.

It is especially noteworthy that the hyperactive boys who did not show associated EEG and other neurologic abnormalities were the ones who had the worst prognosis for antisocial behavior in adolescence. This suggests that many youngsters diagnosed by physicians as hyperactive do not have a developmental neurological disorder at all; rather, they are by temperament impulsive and sensation-seekers, probably relatively fearless and perhaps also aggressive, whose parents have been unwilling or unable to monitor and control them. This interpretation squares with findings from recent studies showing that antisocial personality and conduct disorder, previously reported to be elevated in the parents and sibs of hyperactive children, are in fact elevated only among relatives of children who show both hyperactivity and conduct or oppositional disorder themselves (Biederman et al., 1992; Gottesman & Goldsmith, 1994).

Zuckerman's (1989) Sensation Seeking Scale (SSS) is a principal marker of what that author regards as the underlying diathesis for crime. Studies with the SSS in adult twins indicate that more than half of its variance is genetically determined.[8] As might be expected, sensation-seekers tend to be impulsive and relatively fearless. In fact, whatever the SSS measures seems to be psychometrically equivalent to what is measured by one of the three MPQ superfactors called "constraint," people high on constraint tend to be fearful, not impulsive, and endorsers of traditional values and, as might be expected, they are unlikely to be criminal. People who get low scores on constraint tend to be sensation seekers. We found that the SSS correlated −.60 with constraint on a sample of 251 mature adults (the Minnesota twins reared apart and their spouses) and the subscales of the SSS correlate as strongly with constraint as they do with each other.

As can be seen in Table 6.3, nearly 80% of the stable variance in both control (impulsiveness) and in the constraint superfactor is genetically determined although, as discussed earlier, the heritabilities of all these trait variables that conduce toward criminality are likely to be lower within the population of families whose offspring are at the highest risk for delinquency and crime.

Another letter prompted by my article on fearlessness in *Psychology Today* (Lykken, 1982a) came from an inmate of a Florida prison. He qualifies as a sensation-seeker but he and I would agree that his basic attribute is relative fearlessness:

I am an inmate at Lake Butler Reception and Medical Center, serving a ten year sentence for drug trafficking. Prior to my arrest and conviction, I taught in the public school system, sold real estate, and owned a construction company. In retrospect, I believe that one of the main reasons that I left teaching was the lack of risk. As you know, there is a great deal of risk associated in real estate, running a business, and there certainly is a great deal of risk in drug trafficking and smuggling. I knew a long time ago that the thrill of facing the fear of failure and succeeding were far more important to me that the financial rewards. One group of people that I am familiar with that you might find interesting is surfers. I have surfed for the past 15 years in many parts of the world, meeting surfers from all parts of the globe, and many countries. The one common thread that I find in the group is the total disregard for fear, in fact, it is as if all of us seek it for the adrenalin "rush" you can get, how close to losing your life, and still escape. Witness surfers that ride ten foot waves that break in three feet of water over an urchin-infested coral reef. There certainly is no financial reward, it all must come from the thrill. Needless to say, not all surfers are as fearless as others, but the common thread is there. For years, when smuggling "kingpins" have

---

[8]Heritability of the SSS based on twins reared together is about .60 (Fulker, Eysenck, & Zuckerman, 1980) and the SSS correlates .54 on the Minnesota MZA twins.

wanted fearless men to do the actual smuggling, they often have chosen their men from the ranks of the surfing population. It is no accident that many "kingpins" are surfers or ex-surfers themselves. (Letter from a surfer, 9–9–82)

Intelligence

It is now well established that offenders, whether juvenile delinquents or adult prison inmates, have lower IQs than nonoffenders, a mean IQ of about 92 compared to the general population value of 100 or to the estimated mean for nonoffenders of about 102. Offenders, moreover, are especially likely to have a lower verbal than performance IQ (J. Wilson & Herrnstein, 1985). The relationship of criminality to intelligence is curvilinear, peaking in the borderline range from IQ 70 to 80 and decreasing in both directions. As we have seen, the heritability of IQ in Western societies is on the order of .75. Once again, however, the heritability even of IQ is likely to be somewhat lower among high-risk families because children of less competent parents often receive less intellectual stimulation. Where there is greater variance in relevant environmental factors, there will be less of the total variance attributable to genetic differences.

Body Type

Hollywood bit-players specializing in hoodlum or gangster roles have one thing in common: They all look tough and menacing. That is to say, they all have muscular bodies or, as a physical anthropologist might say, they are mesomorphs rather than endomorphs (soft and roly-poly) or ectomorphs (thin, fragile looking.) This stereo-type of the criminal as tending to be mesomorphic makes good sense; if you plan to make your living mugging people or robbing banks, then you had better be strong, fit, and fast on your feet. The psychiatrist, William Sheldon (1949), believed that each of the three extremes of body type (somatotype) have associated with them a characteristic pattern of personality traits. Sheldon published a study of 200 persistingly delinquent young men whom he found to be predominantly meso-morphs, well-muscled with broad shoulders and narrow hips. On follow-up, 30 years later, although most of these men had problems of one kind or another, only 14 of the 200, 10 of them mesomorphs, had become criminal adults (Hartl, Monnelly, & Elderkin, 1982). S. Glueck and E. Glueck (1956) somatotyped 500 juvenile delinquents plus 500 nondelinquent boys matched with the delinquents for family background and other characteristics. Once again, the delinquent boys were mainly mesomorphs, more mesomorphic and less ectomorphic that the nondelin-quent boys. Cortés and Gatti (1972) reported even more striking differences when their delinquent sample was restricted to young men convicted of serious crimes. Several studies agree in showing that Black males, who are disproportionately represented in criminal populations, are on the average more mesomorphic than Whites (J. Wilson & Herrnstein, 1985).

Although few psychologists take seriously Sheldon's claims of close ties be-tween body type and personality, the fact that criminals (including female crimi-nals; Epps & Parnell, 1952) are predominantly built along mesomorphic lines has been well established. We can say, therefore, with some confidence, that mesomorphy is a risk factor for a career in sports, or in ballet—or in crime. I know of no studies of the heritability of body type as such but we know that the components of body type—height, weight, ponderal index or fatness, and so on—are strongly heritable, and it seems safe to conclude, based on common observation, that mesomorphy runs in families.

Interests

Our Minnesota group administered inventories of occupational and recreational interests, and of self-rated talents, to some 900 pairs of middle-aged adult twins, to 54 pairs of adult MZ twins reared apart (MZA), and slightly modified inventories to 231 pairs of 17-year-old male twins (Lykken et al., 1993; the retest and the adolescent data have not previously been reported). Of the adult twins, 198 pairs retook the inventories from 2 to 3 years later so that we could estimate twin similarity on the stable components of these interests. Several of these interest/talent factors, including three that seem especially relevant to potential criminality, are listed in Table 6.4.

Interest in gambling (card games, casinos, race tracks, etc.) is strongly heritable (the MZA correlation is .54) but there is substantial effect of common home environment, both for adolescents still living at home and for adults. The Thrill-Seeking factor in the adult inventories involved such activities as mountain climbing, parachute jumping, hang gliding, and the like. For the 17-year-olds, this factor included items like: "Doing something on your own that could get you arrested," "Hanging out at a mall or a drive-in with friends," and "Climbing around high places where most people get scared." The 17-year-old DZ twins were just as similar as the MZs on this factor.

TABLE 6.4
Twin Correlations on Eight Interest/Talent Factors for Middle-Aged Adults
and Adolescent Males

	Middle-Aged Twins					17-Year-Old Male Twins	
	Single-Test		Mean of Two[a]				
	MZ	DZ	MZ	DZ	MZA	MZ	DZ
No. of pairs	513	390	105	93	54	150	81
Cultural interests	.75	.34	.81	.37	.60	na	na
Width of interests	.47	.18	.51	.24	.48	.41	.27
Self-esteem	.50	.20	.55	.13	.38	.44	.27
Dating, flirting	.45	.21	.55	.30	.50	.57	.22
Blood sports	.58	.34	.60	.48	.60	.78	.48
Gambling	.57	.42	.66	.45	.54	.59	.40
Thrill seeking[b]	.50	.27	.62	.27	.44	.40	.44
Religiosity	.60	.38	.65	.49	.66	.67	.49

[a]"Mean of two" are correlations based on the means of two scores obtained 2.6 years apart.
[b]The Thrill-Seeking factor for the 17-year-olds included explicitly illegal activities.

It is a surprising but well-established fact that individual differences in religious interests, attitudes, and values are strongly determined by genetic variation (Martin et al., 1986; Waller et al., 1990). It also seems reasonable to assume that religious interest and commitment acts as a strong protective factor against antisocial conduct. Interest in religious and church-related activities can be seen in Table 6.4 to be strongly correlated in MZ twins, including MZ twins reared apart, but the correlation in DZ twins reared together also is high which presumably indicates that siblings growing up together influence each other's religiosity, especially if their genetic inclinations are rather different initially.

For most of the interest factors that we studied, the DZ correlations were half or less than half of the MZ values, indicating a lack of effect of being reared in the same home. Like religiosity and like thrill seeking in adolescents, however, the gambling factor is an exception to this rule; $R_{MZT} = .55$ while $R_{DZT} = .41$. Because R_{MZA} (.48) is nearly as high as the R_{MZT} value, this predilection seems to be in part genetic in origin, but the high R_{DZT} suggests that family attitudes respecting gambling may have a lasting effect on children reared in that family. This is interesting because interests in gambling, risk-taking, and in religion are all relevant to criminality and the theory of criminality promulgated here requires that this trait should be an exception to the rule of no shared family influence that seems to characterize most psychological traits.

Conclusions

The bottom line is that virtually every psychological characteristic that can be reliably measured in adult subjects—reliable both in the sense of internal consistency and retest stability—appears to have an appreciable fraction of its variance associated with genetic variation between people. The average heritability of psychological traits seems to be about 50%, based on single measurements, and perhaps 70% when based on estimates of the stable component of the traits (e.g., on the means of repeated measurements). A highly consistent and stable trait like IQ has a heritability on the order of 75% for single measurements, rising to perhaps 85% when corrected for instability. IQ may be relevant to criminality because we know that the mean IQ of prison inmates and adjudicated delinquents is somewhat lower than the population average, although it is probable that some of the brighter offenders are not included in these averages because they have avoided getting caught. For traits of personality, temperament, and interests that seem specifically relevant to criminality, we can estimate that perhaps 50% to 70% of the stable variance is genetically determined within the general population and somewhat less than this—perhaps 30% to 40%—among the population now at high risk for delinquency and crime.

Whether a child who is innately fearless or aggressive or a risk-taker becomes delinquent and then criminal, however, depends largely on the skill and dedication of his or her parents. Aggressive children (like aggressive bull terriers) can be taught to moderate and control their aggressiveness.[9] Relatively fearless children can be

---

[9]See Lore and Schultz (1993) and Pepler and Rubin (1991) for methods of moderating aggressiveness in children overendowed with this propensity.

led to take advantage of their daring in socially approved-of ways. Risk-takers can become crime fighters, for example, rather than criminals.

It is because these basic traits are substantially heritable that we find that the complex trait of criminality itself is heritable. Suppose all human parents were equally feckless and neglectful of their parental duties; then most mesomorphic, aggressive, relatively fearless boys would remain unsocialized and the heritability of criminality would approach 100%. Suppose all human parents were equally dutiful and skilled; then only the most extremely mesomorphic, aggressive, fearless boys would remain unsocialized—and the heritability of criminality would again approach 100%. It is because there is a wide range of variation in the quality of parenting that the heritability of criminality is less than the heritability of the more basic psychological traits. And it is the case that, if we could somehow prevent the most unskilled and indifferent of young adults from becoming parents, then we would, paradoxically, increase the heritability of criminality, while drastically reducing the number of criminals in the next generation.

PART III

THE PSYCHOPATHIC
PERSONALITIES

7

The Psychopath: An Introduction
to the Genus

Not deeply vicious, he carries disaster lightly in each hand.

—Hervey Cleckley (1955)

Since the beginnings of psychiatry in the early 19th century, it has been recognized that there are persons whose persisting antisocial behavior cannot be understood in terms of mental or emotional disorder, neurotic motivations, or incompetent parenting. Psychiatric befuddlement is evident in the diagnostic labels used to classify these people. The father of French psychiatry, Phillipe Pinel (1745–1826), noted that they seemed to behave crazily without actually being crazy and, in 1801, he coined the phrase *manie sans delire.* Not long afterward, Benjamin Rush (1845–1913), the first American psychiatrist, described patients with "innate preternatural moral depravity" (Rush, 1812). J. C. Pritchard (1786–1848), an English physician and ethnologist, employed a similar label, "moral insanity," in 1835.

The German systematists, like Koch (1843–1910), first used the term *psycho-pathic* for a heterogeneous collection of what we would now call personality disorders and Kraepelin (1856–1926), in the seventh or 1915 edition of his influential textbook, first used *psychopathic personality* specifically to describe the amoral or immoral criminal type. An American psychiatrist, Partridge (1930), pointed out that these people had in common a disposition to violate social norms of behavior and introduced the term *sociopath.* However, I use this term differently in this book to refer to antisocial personalities whose behavior is a consequence of social or familial dysfunction. I use *psychopath* to refer to these people who have puzzled psychiatry for so long, whose antisocial behavior appears to result from a defect or aberration within themselves rather than in their rearing.

THE PRIMARY PSYCHOPATH

More than 100 years after Pinel and Pritchard, an American expert on criminal psychiatry concluded: "When all of the cases which I group under symptomatic psychopathy are removed and accounted for, there would still remain a small group which may be designated as primary or idiopathic psychopathy" (Karpman, 1941, p. 113). As outlined in chapter 3, there seem to be several "species" of psychopath; that is to say there are several innate peculiarities of temperament or endowment that conduce toward a complete or partial failure of socialization or toward intermittent lapses of socialization and to antisocial behavior. Many of these endogenous vagaries—choleric temperament or hypersexuality, for example—can be easily identified but the etiology of what Karpman called primary psychopathy is more mysterious and has been the subject of extensive research and debate.

Cleckley's Contribution

In his classic monograph, *The Mask of Sanity*, Hervey Cleckley (1941, 1982) illustrated the problem of understanding the primary psychopath by means of a collection of vividly described case histories from his own practice. Here were people of good families, intelligent and rational, sound of mind and body, who lied without compunction, cheated, stole, casually violated any and all norms of social conduct whenever it suited their whim.   Moreover, they seemed surprisingly unaffected by the bad consequences of their actions, whether visited upon themselves or on their families or friends.

Cleckley also cited several examples from literature of the kind of individual he had in mind, including Shakespeare's Iago and Falstaff, Ibsen's *Peer Gynt*, and Molnar's character, *Liliom*, the prototype of Billy Bigelow in Rogers and Hammerstein's musical, *Carousel*. Unaccountably, however, he neglected the Shakespearean character who best epitomizes the primary psychopath, *Richard III* who, in the first speech of Scene 1, declares himself bored, looking for action:

> Now is the winter of our discontent. ... Why, I, in this weak piping time of peace, have no delight to pass away the time ...

In the next scene, the Lady Anne enters with the corpse of her husband, Henry VI, born by bearers. It was Richard who killed Henry and Anne fears and despises him, yet he commands the bearers to set the coffin down while he proceeds to make love to the grieving widow! Richard talks her around in just three pages—surely one of the greatest tours de force ever assayed by a dramatist or by an actor—and then he gloats:

> Was ever woman in this humour woo'd? Was ever woman in this humour won? I'll have her; but I will not keep her long. What, I, that kill'd her husband and his father, to take her in her heart's extremest hate, with curses in her mouth, tears in her eyes, the bleeding witness of my hatred by; having God, her conscience, and these bars against me, and I no friends to back my suit withal but the plain deveil and dissembling looks. And yet to win her, all the world to nothing!

Some female psychopaths in literature include Mildred, in Somerset Maugham's *Of Human Bondage*, Sally Bowles in *Cabaret*, Ibsen's *Hedda Gabler* (Hedda is a nice example of the "secondary" psychopath), and Bizet's *Carmen*. We can see primary psychopathy in the character played by the actor, Jack Nicholson, in numerous movies including: *Five Easy Pieces, Chinatown, The Last Detail*, and especially in *One Flew Over the Cuckoo's Nest*. Harry Lyme as portrayed by Orson Welles in the film *The Third Man* conveys the eerie combination of charm and menace found in some of these individuals. The character played by child actress Patty McCormack in the film *The Bad Seed* and the eponymous hero in Thomas Mann's *The Confessions of Felix Krull, Confidence Man* are contrasting portraits of the psychopath as mendacious manipulator. The brother in Graham Greene's novel, *The Shipwrecked*, is a good example of the feckless, self- and other-deluding, poseur type of psychopath as is the protagonist's father in John Le Carre's *The Perfect Spy*, a character said to be based on the author's own father. The psychopath in youth can be found as the hero of E.L. Doctorow's book, *Billy Bathgate*, which also provides a more dangerous version in the character of the gangster, Dutch Schultz.

As used by the media, *psychopath* conveys an impression of danger and implacable evil. This is mistaken, however, as suggested by Cleckley's comment in this chapter's epigraph. Like the unsocialized sociopath, the psychopath is characterized by a lack of the restraining effect of conscience and of empathic concern for other people. Unlike the ordinary sociopath, the primary psychopath has failed to develop conscience and empathic feelings, not because of a lack of socializing experience but, rather, because of some inherent psychological peculiarity which makes him especially difficult to socialize. An additional consequence of this innate peculiarity is that the psychopath behaves in a way that suggests that he is relatively indifferent to the probability of punishment for his actions. This essential peculiarity of the psychopath is not in itself evil or vicious but, combined with perverse appetites, or with an unusually hostile and aggressive temperament, the lack of these normal constraints can result in an explosive and dangerous package. Examples of such combinations include the serial killer, Ted Bundy (see Anne Rule's *The Stranger Beside Me* or Winn and Merrill's *Ted Bundy: The Killer Next Door*), Gary Gilmore (see Norman Mailer's excellent *The Executioner's Song*), Diane Downs (in Ann Rule's biography, *Small Sacrifices*), and the sex murdering RAF officer, Neville Heath (see Playfair & Sington's *The Offenders*).

Perhaps the best collection of examples of criminal psychopaths and vignettes of psychopathic behavior can be found in Hare's excellent *Without Conscience* (1993). Professor Hare is the leading researcher in this area and we shall have much more to say about his work later in this section.

In marked contrast to these dangerous characters, and illustrative of why psychologists find such fascination in the psychopath, is the case of Oscar Schindler, the savior of hundreds of Krakow Jews whose names were on *Schindler's List*. Opportunist, bon vivant, ladies's man, manipulator, unsuccessful in legitimate business by his own admission but wildly successful in the moral chaos of wartime, Schindler's rescue of those Jews can be best understood as a 35-year-old con man's response to a kind of ultimate challenge, Schindler against the Third Reich. Any swine could kill people under the conditions of that time and place; the real challenge—in the words that his biographer may have put in his mouth, the "real power"—lay in rescuing people, especially in rescuing Jews. Some parts of Stephen Spielberg's film do not fit with my diagnosis of Schindler as a primary psychopath, especially "the scene near the end in which Schindler (portrayed by Oscar nominee Liam Neeson) breaks down and cries while addressing his Jewish workers." British film maker, Jon Blair, whose earlier documentary film, "Schindler," was truer to history than Spielberg's feature film, noted this same discrepancy. "'It was slightly out of character, and, of course, it never actually happened,' Blair said" (Richmond, 1994).

Some other biographies of colorful primary psychopaths include N. von Hoffman's *Citizen Cohn*, Neil Sheehan's *A Bright Shining Lie: John Paul Vann and America in Vietnam*, and Daniel Akst's *Wonderboy: Barry Minkow, the Kid who Swindled Wall Street*. Some historical figures who, I believe, had the "talent" for psychopathy but who did not develop the full syndrome and achieved great worldly success include: Lyndon Johnson (see Robert A. Caro's biography, *The Years of Lyndon Johnson*, 1982, 1988), Winston Churchill (see Carter, 1965; Manchester, 1988), the African explorer, Sir Richard Burton (see biographies by Farwell, 1963, or Rice, 1990), and Chuck Yeager (see Tom Wolfe's *The Right Stuff* and *Yeager*, an "assisted autobiography").

The fact that many of these illustrative characters were not adjudicated criminals reminds us that we are talking here about a class of actors rather than a pattern of actions. Psychopaths are at high risk for engaging in criminal behavior but not all of them succumb to that risk. Even the identical twins of criminal psychopaths, with whom they share all their genes and many of their formative experiences, do not necessarily become criminal themselves. To mention Churchill, Johnson, Burton and Yeager in this context may seem especially surprising but all four set out as daring, adventurous, unconventional youngsters who began playing by their own rules early in life. Talent, opportunity and plain luck enabled them to achieve success and self-esteem through (mainly) licit rather than illicit means. Johnson and Burton were borderline psychopaths, if we can believe their biographers, while Churchill and Yeager seem merely to have shared what I call the "talent" for psychopathy, that is, an inherent temperament that makes a child very difficult to socialize and therefore consitutes a risk for psychopathy. What I believe to be the nature of this talent will be explicated later in this chapter.

Cleckley's Criteria

In order to summarize what he thought to be the essential features of what others have called the primary psychopath, Cleckley formulated the 16 diagnostic criteria listed in Table 7.1. Beginning with my own study published in 1957, the Cleckley criteria have been widely used in research on primary psychopathy. They have been incorporated into a psychometrically sophisticated diagnostic instrument, the Hare Psychopathy Checklist (PCL; Hare, 1991). Compared to the APD criteria of

TABLE 7.1
Cleckley's 16 Diagnostic Criteria for Primary Psychopathy

Superficial charm and good intelligence
Absence of delusions and other signs of irrational thinking
Absence of "nervousness" or other neurotic manifestations
Unreliability
Untruthfulness and insincerity
Lack of remorse or shame
Inadequately motivated antisocial behavior
Poor judgment and failure to learn by experience
Pathological egocentricity and incapacity for love
General poverty in major affective reactions
Specific loss of insight
Unresponsiveness in interpersonal relations
Fantastic and uninviting behavior
Suicide rarely carried out
Sex life impersonal
Failure to follow any life plan

Note. From Cleckley (1982, p. 204).

DSM–III–R, some of these criteria are inferential (e.g., "lack of remorse" or, in the PCL, "lack of empathy") but Hare and his colleagues have shown that they can have good diagnostic reliability and evidence has accumulated to show that they identify a more homogeneous subgroup of people than do the APD criteria.

Theories of Primary Psychopathy

Cleckley's View

Cleckley concluded that the primary psychopath lacks the normal affective accompaniments of experience, that the raw feel of his emotional experience is attenuated much as is the color experience of people who are color-blind. Where Pritchard and Rush believed there was an innate lack of moral sensibility, Cleckley took the more modern view that moral feelings and compunctions are not God-given but must be learned and that this learning process is guided and enforced by the power of emotional feelings. When these normal feelings are attenuated, the development of morality—the very mechanism of socialization—is compromised. Thus, we can see that Cleckley regarded the primary psychopath as someone for whom the normal socializing experiences are ineffective because of an innate defect which he compared with *semantic aphasia*, a condition sometimes seen in brain-injured patients who can speak in coherent sentences but do not seem to grasp the meaning of their own words (Cleckley, 1955). As we acknowledged at the outset, some children are harder to socialize than others and a child whose capacity for emotional experience is innately very weak would presumably be especially difficult.

There is no real evidence, however, that the primary psychopath is incapable of genuine emotion. He seems clearly able to feel anger, satisfaction, delight, self-esteem—indeed, if he did not have such feelings, it seems improbable that he would do many of the things, proper and improper, that he does do. As Gilbert and Sullivan pointed out:

> When the felon's not engaged in his employment, or maturing his felonious little plans, his capacity for innocent enjoyment, is just as great as any honest man's!

Other investigators have tried to identify more focal defects to explain the Cleckley type of psychopath. Five of these conjectured species of this genus are described here and are treated in more detail in later chapters.

Lykken's "Low Fear-Quotient" Theory

One of the first alternative proposals was my own suggestion (Lykken, 1957) that the primary psychopath has an attenuated experience, not of all emotional states, but specifically of anxiety or fear. We are all endowed with the innate tendency to fear certain stimuli—loss of support, snakelike or spiderlike objects, strangers, fire—and to associate or *condition* fear to stimuli and situations that have been previously experienced together with innately fearful stimuli, including pain and punishment. Like all biological variables, fearfulness or what I have called the innate "fear quotient" (FQ), varies from person to person. Some individuals have a very high FQ and are victimized from childhood on by fearful inhibitions. It is noteworthy that such individuals are especially unlikely to become juvenile delinquents or adult sociopaths.

My theory of primary psychopathy is that people at the low end of this same distribution of innate fearfulness are at risk to develop primary psychopathy. I discuss this notion in more detail later, but the basic idea is that, because much of the normal socialization process depends on punishment of antisocial behavior, and because punishment works, when it works, by the fearful inhibition of those impulses the next time that temptation knocks, then someone who is relatively fearless will be relatively harder to socialize in this way. "Harder to socialize" does not mean "impossible to socialize" and it is interesting to note that being less fearful than the average person is not necessarily a disadvantage. A child with a low FQ, whose parents nonetheless succeed in instilling the essentials of good citizenship, would grow up to be the kind of person one would like to have on hand when stress and danger threaten. I believe, in short, that the hero and the psychopath may be twigs on the same genetic branch.

Duane

One psychopath of my acquaintance, whom I will call "Duane," easily met criteria for the diagnosis of APD having spent most of his adolescence and young manhood in reform school or prison. He also met at least 14 of the 16 Cleckley criteria although he became a well-qualified pilot and a successful businessman so he did "follow a life plan" as well as most people do and he could be reliable when it suited his purposes. Duane was the youngest of three boys and was still a toddler when his footloose father tired of the strains of family life, got on his motorcycle, and disappeared, leaving his unfortunate and rather feckless wife to cope as best she could on welfare. She did well with the two older boys who grew up to be law-abiding, self-supporting family men. The mother could not cope with Duane, however, and their relationship was never close. In the streets and in reform school, Duane learned to more than hold his own in the subculture of other delinquents and was respected in prison as someone who could not be intimidated.

While Duane was on parole, in his 20s, relatives helped him to acquire training in one of the building trades. Duane was a quick learner and his fearless self-confidence helped give him status in that male society. He learned for the first time the satisfactions of being more adept than others at some constructive activity. Many women found him irresistible, including many wives of Duane's friends and relatives. Duane broke up the marriage of one of his brothers during a earlier brief period of parole and he later did the same for friends and his business partner. He got married himself along the way and fathered two legitimate children but treated them badly. One of Duane's friends ran a garage and one Saturday night, apparently just for the hell of it, Duane decided to break into the safe that his friend kept in the office. A passing police patrol noticed his flashlight beam and there followed a gun battle in which Duane was badly wounded. A couple of years later, fully recovered and again on parole, he returned to the building trades.

Bright and aggressive, Duane soon started a contracting business of his own which flourished, partly because of his "superficial charm." He became a successful businessman but not a successful human being. He had little capacity for love or empathy and little interest in the dull truth. As his financial position improved, Duane became an avid hunter, taking business associates big-game hunting in Canada and the West. Back from one such trip to Wyoming he showed off his trophy antlers and told me an elaborate story of how he had downed that running buck with one shot at nearly half a mile's range. It was a good example of a psychopathic lie: He'd had a successful hunting trip and I knew he was a good shot (but not that good) so the lie was pointless. Moreover, because he would not have believed such a story if I had told it, Duane should have been able to predict that I would not believe it either; this may have been an example of what Cleckley called a "specific lack of insight" or perhaps he just didn't care much whether I believed him or not. Duane enjoyed being admired and respected but what respect he achieved was elicited by skillful role-playing; those who knew him well understood that he was a manipulator, that his good fellowship was false.

On the other hand, I knew Duane as well as anyone and yet I let him swindle me out of $1,000 which, at the time, seemed like a lot of money. He had been on another hunting trip, to the Yukon, and told this plausible story of having stumbled upon a large deposit of long-fiber asbestos. He had brought samples back in his float plane and had them assayed to confirm the value of his find. Duane said needed $10,000 in expense money to stake and register a claim and he was letting a few friends buy one-tenth shares for $1,000 each. I think now that he may have actually found some ore and pursued the project far enough to decide there was no money in it, except what he could extract from a few gullible friends. You would not think me quite such a fool if you had been there yourself and heard Duane's casual, low-keyed pitch, full of circumstantial detail.

I might have used a more classic example of primary psychopathy, say, someone whose parents had been professional people and had nurtured him carefully and sent him to Groton, because then we could be surer that his antisocial predilections sprang mainly from within himself. But Duane is probably a more typical example of the species. He has a lot in common with Crystal Taylor whom I called a sociopath because I thought it likely that any pretty, extroverted, lively child, reared in Crystal's environment, might well turn out as she did. Duane's two brothers turned out well with the same parents he had (although it is true that they had a father longer than he did). If Duane's parents had been upper middle class and had sent him to Groton, I doubt that he would have done that first stretch in reform school for hot-wiring cars. If Duane's imaginary parents had been skilled enough and patient enough to control him without alienating him (e.g., if they had been the kind of parents who could get a bull terrier through obedience training), then Duane might have turned out very well indeed. We shall never know for sure.

Duane took up flying as an avocation and, with his quick mind and good memory, he soon became qualified well beyond the basic private-pilot level. He bought a plane with company funds and invited me to go up with him one weekend. I rashly accepted but, as we drove to the airport, I remembered too late that I was putting my fate in the hands of an callous dare devil who had skated his whole life on thin ice. But when we got in his new plane, equipped with the latest electronics, I discovered (with some relief) that Duane now saw himself as a skilled pilot and took great pride in his professionalism. He went conscientiously through his checklist before taking off and flew "by the book," not because he feared to take chances but as a matter of pride. I know from other evidence that he enjoyed encountering dangerous situations in the air, that he relished storms and fog, but he felt a superior contempt for unprofessional carelessness. He told me once that he could never remember experiencing "what other people talk about 'being afraid'" and I was inclined, in that instance, to believe him. By middle age, Duane seemed to have developed a kind of respectable, mature self-concept that was incompatible with the kind of aimless risk-taking that had characterized his early years.

The Neurobehavioral Theories of Fowles and Gray

Gray (1975, 1987a) identified in the brain what he calls the behavioral inhibition system (BIS), which is activated by cues associated with fear or with "frustrative nonreward" (i.e., not getting the expected reward) and that produces the experience of anxiety and the inhibition of ongoing behavior. The BIS organizes passive avoidance, that is, the inhibition of previously punished responses.

Another mechanism, the behavioral activation system (BAS), a term introduced by Fowles (1980), is activated by stimuli associated with reward or with escape from fear or pain. The BAS organizes approach behavior and also active avoidance, that is, behavior to escape from threat. Both Gray and Fowles noted that there are individual differences in the strength or reactivity of the BIS and that persons with

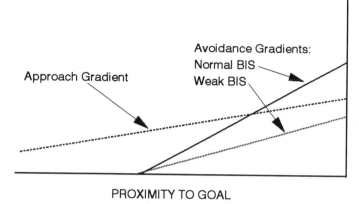

FIG. 7.1. Effect of a weak BIS, leading to failure of passive avoidance.

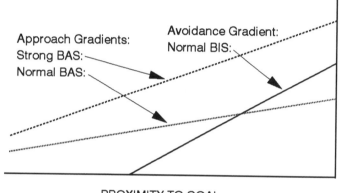

FIG. 7.2. Effect of an overactive BAS, also leading to a failure of passive avoidance.

a relatively weak BIS might show poor passive avoidance, low general anxiety, and the other characteristics of the primary psychopath. This formulation will be seen to be quite similar to my low-fear hypothesis.

Fowles and Gray also noted that persons with an unusually strong or reactive BAS might also manifest poor passive avoidance. The typical approach–avoidance conflict situation is illustrated in Fig. 7.1 in which the dashed line represents the individual's ("Adam") increasing incentive motivation as he approaches the goal (let us say, "Eve's" apple). The solid lines represent Adam's increasing anxiety and reluctance to go further as he nears that forbidden treat. If Adam's BIS is normally active, the steep avoidance gradient crosses the approach gradient—the strength of his fear equals the strength of his appetite—before he reaches the goal and he stops or passively avoids the temptation. If Adam has a weak BIS, then the two gradients do not cross and the apple is eaten. In Fig. 7.2, we see the similar effects of an overactive BAS. With a normal BIS and BAS, passive avoidance results, but if Adam has an unusually strong BAS—if the apple attracts him even more than it would you or me—then the gradients again fail to cross, the apple is eaten, and Exodus results.

This secondary psychopath, characterized by a strong BAS but a normal BIS, would appear to behave impulsively due to this failure of passive avoidance and would be likely to get into trouble as a result. Unlike the primary psychopath, however, he would be anxious during the commission of his crimes (assuming that he had a normal BIS) and would be likely to make a poor adjustment to the stresses of prison life.

Also unlike the primary type, the secondary psychopath should show high scores on negative emotionality or neuroticism, because the lure of temptation would be likely to cause him to select a stressful and disquieting lifestyle. Whether he would tend to be as free of guilt and empathic feeling as the primary type is an interesting question that I defer until chapter 10 where the Fowles–Gray theory is discussed in more detail.

Hare's Lateralization Theory: "Semantic Aphasia" Revisited

Hare, who must be regarded as the leading researcher in this area, published evidence that the psychopathic brain may be less strongly lateralized, that linguistic functions are less concentrated in the left brain hemisphere and emotional functions less focused in the right hemisphere, than is true for most of us. Supporting evidence from at least two laboratories suggests that the effect may be real and not merely an experimental artifact. In addition, recent studies by developmental psychophysiologists seem to indicate that there may be lateralization differences between young children with easy, tractable temperaments and those who might be characterized as difficult. On the other hand, the effects so far have been fairly weak, with many psychopathic subjects better lateralized than many nonpsychopaths. Moreover, it is not yet clear how reduced lateralization, even if it were characteristic of most psychopaths, could explain the phenomena of psychopathy. I consider Hare's contributions in detail in chapters 8, 9, and 11.

Inhibitory Defect or Underendowment

Some sociopathic individuals appear to act impulsively, "without thinking," without giving themselves time to assess the situation, to appreciate the dangers, to foresee the consequences, or even to anticipate how they will feel about their action themselves when they have time to consider it. These cases seem to involve a biological *inadequacy* of certain inhibitory control mechanisms and should be distinguished from Gottfredson's and Hirschi's "poor self-control," which those authors hold to be a consequence of inadequate socialization. That is, although many young children tend to act impulsively, watchful parents will reward more deliberate behavior and, if necessary, interrupt and punish heedless, thoughtless actions, teaching self-control as a part of the socialization process. Once again, however, self-control training is much harder with some children than with others.

Lesions in certain brain areas can cause a decrease in inhibitory control in animals and also in humans; the well-known case of Phineas Gage whose frontal lobes were damaged in a construction accident is one example. Gage had been a conscientious foreman of a railway track-crew prior to the accident but subsequently became "fitful, irreverent, indulging at times in the grossest profanity (which had not previously been his custom), manifesting but little deference for his fellows, impatient of restraint or advice when it conflicts with his desires, ... capricious" (Harlow, 1868, p. 327).

Gorenstein and Newman proposed in 1980 a disinhibitory theory of psychopathy based on similarities in the approach–avoidance behavior of experimental animals with lesions in certain brain regions (the septum, hippocampus, or frontal cortex) and the behavior in similar situations of some psychopaths or of strongly extroverted subjects. This model has been the basis for a program of research by Newman (1987) and his colleagues at the University of Wisconsin. Like Hare's lateralization model, mentioned earlier, Newman's theory postulates an essential defect in the structure or function of the psychopathic brain while the related theories of Lykken, Fowles, and Gray assume instead a mere difference in degree of some trait or some underlying brain process. The contributions of the Newman group are considered in chapter 12.

Inhibitory Overendowment

In chapter 3, it was suggested that individuals with a special talent for Freudian repression might be able to avoid fearful apprehension or escape the pangs of guilt simply by repressing awareness of stimuli, memories, or ideas that elicit these unpleasant feelings. Repression involves a different kind of inhibition than that invoked by Newman, an inhibition not of overt responding but of the processes of perception, recall, and cognitive processing. In chapter 13 I develop a theory of hysterical psychopathy based upon some psychophysical research that, for some reason, has not been followed up in the 65 years since it was published.

First, however, we should consider the important problem of diagnosis. Only a minority of antisocial individuals are primary psychopaths and we cannot efficiently test etiological hypotheses unless we can first devise clinical or behavioral criteria for identifying the people we are trying to understand.

8

The Classification of the Psychopathies

The first problem in doing useful research on psychopathy, research that is replicable and can be aggregated with the research of others, is the problem of diagnosis, of identifying a group of probands who can be said to belong to the same relatively homogeneous species or psychopathological type. Hare and his colleagues in British Columbia, Megargee and Moffitt in the United States, and Blackburn in England have been important contributors to this effort and their accomplishments comprise the topic of this chapter.

THE IMPORTANCE OF DIAGNOSIS

Whether we think of psychopaths as constituting a taxon, a category of individuals somehow qualitatively different from other people (as members of a species differ from nonmembers), or merely as persons at one extreme of some underlying continuous distribution of human variation, we cannot study these individuals in a useful, cumulative way unless we have an objective and reasonably valid diagnostic algorithm.

One approach has been to identify criterion groups clinically (e.g., persons diagnosed by psychiatrists as psychopathic deviates, or adolescents who are adjudicated delinquents) and then to construct self-report scales consisting of items which these groups tend to answer differently than do people in general. The Pd scale of the MMPI and the So scale of the CPI are examples of this approach. Both of these scales are elevated for most prison inmates however, and hence they are unable to discriminate between psychopaths and sociopaths generally. However, in the vast lore surrounding the MMPI, it came to be believed that "real" psychopaths have elevations both on Pd, the fourth scale of the standard set, and also on the Ma scale (Scale 9), thus producing a profile of scale scores in which Scales 4 and 9 are both much higher than the rest. Spielberger's Sociopathy (SPY) scale

(Spielberger, Kling, & O'Hagen, 1978) was constructed to distinguish prison inmates who have this "49" MMPI profile from inmates who do not. The sparse data so far available on the construct validity of the SPY scale are insufficient to justify its use as a sole basis for identifying primary psychopathy. Much the same verdict applies to the Antisocial Practices (ASP) scale (Butcher, Graham, Williams, & Ben-Porath, 1990) of the revised version of the MMPI (MMPI–2). Diagnosis based on MMPI profiles, as in the 49 profile just mentioned, seems more promising as will be seen in considering Megargee's work later in this chapter.

The CPI–So scale (Gough, 1994; Gough & Peterson, 1952) was constructed empirically by selecting from a larger item pool those items that discriminated delinquent from nondelinquent boys. The items are diverse, including some that relate to interpersonal difficulties, resentment toward family and authority, feelings of victimization and alienation, poor scholastic adjustment and rebelliousness. The So scale has been remarkably successful, not only in identifying delinquent youth and predicting future antisocial conduct but also in identifying the more highly socialized of normal subjects; "For 25 samples, involving over 10,000 subjects, the biserial correlation for the dichotomy of more-vs-less socialized was 0.73" (Schalling, 1978, p. 98). As shown in chapter 6, the heritability—in the general population—of the trait cluster measured by the So scale is on the order of 50%. Once again, however, there is no reason to suppose that the So scale, by itself, can discriminate psychopaths from sociopaths.

Hare's Psychopathy Checklist (PCL)

The most widely used approach to date has been to construct a rating scale to be completed by a clinician who knows the subject and his history, a scale that embodies many of the essential features of the criteria originally listed by Cleckley. Having clinicians make a global rating as to whether the inmate or patient is adequately described by Cleckley's 16 criteria, the method used by Lykken (1957) and subsequently by Hare and others, is imprecise; different clinicians may disagree and, as a result, groups classified in this way may not be homogeneous enough to yield the cleanest experimental results. Hare (1985, 1991) and his colleagues therefore developed the PCL. The current, revised, version of the PCL consists of 20 items to be rated by a clinician, based on interview and file data, with each item being rated *No* (0), *Maybe* (1), or *Yes* (2). The 20 items of the PCL are listed in Table 8.1.

Analysis of PCL ratings obtained on six samples of prison inmates have shown that the top two groups of eight and nine items, respectively, intercorrelate in such a way as to suggest that each group taps a separate underlying factor. The first group of items are more similar to the Cleckley criteria and one could get a high score on this Factor 1 without having accumulated a criminal record either as a juvenile or as an adult. In fact, Factor 1 correlates more strongly with the symptoms of Narcissistic Personality Disorder than with those of APD (Harpur, Hart, & Hare, 1993, Table 2) and they would plainly correlate better with the original Cleckley variables than do the remaining PCL items.

TABLE 8.1
Hare's PCL

---

1. Glibness/superficial charm.
2. Grandiose sense of self-worth.
3. Pathological lying.
4. Conning/manipulative.
5. Lack of remorse or guilt.
6. Shallow affect.
7. Callous, lack of empathy
8. Failure to accept responsibility for actions.

1. Need for stimulation/proneness to boredom.
2. Parasitic lifestyle.
3. Poor behavioral controls.
4. Early behavior problems.
5. Lack of realistic, long-term goals.
6. Impulsivity.
7. Irresponsibility.
8. Juvenile delinquency.
9. Revocation of conditional release.

1. Promiscuous sexual behavior.
2. Many short-term marital relationships.
3. Criminal versatility.

Note. The first group of items define Factor 1, the second group constitute
Factor 2, the last three items load about equally on both factors.

The second group of items are more like the APD criteria so that persons
diagnosed as APD are likely to get high scores on this Factor 2. Scored as a scale,
the APD criteria correlate about .6 with the PCL Factor 2 and about half that high
with Factor 1 (Harpur et al., 1993). Factor 1 can be said to describe a syndrome of
personality characteristics or traits, whereas Factor 2 describes a syndrome of
behavioral traits. The three remaining items of the PCL, which do not load strongly
on either factor, also are behavioral characterizations.

The two PCL factors correlate with one another only about .5 so that it is indeed
quite possible for someone to get a high score on one factor and a low score on the
other. This accords with the fact that not all Cleckley psychopaths qualify as ASP
nor are all ASPs primary psychopaths. Another important difference is that Factor
2 varies inversely with crystallized (e.g., verbal) intelligence, whereas Factor 1 is
unrelated to intelligence as Cleckley would have expected.[1]

---

[1]Harpur et al. (1989) reported correlations of −.04 and −.49, for Factors 1 and 2 respectively, with
crystallized intelligence. I am grateful to Dr. Scott Lilienfeld for pointing out to me the significance of
these correlations.

Improving the Diagnosis of Psychopathy

In the augmented-startle study by Patrick, Bradley, and Lang (1993), discussed in chapter 10, it was the personality component associated with Factor 1 of the PCL (PCL–1), rather than the antisocial behavior component measured by Factor 2 (PCL–2), that predicted the unusual response (or lack of response) of the psychopaths to the aversive slides. It seems to me that this result makes good sense. All of the sex offenders studied could be described as antisocial in some degree but we must assume that the etiology of this antisocial behavior varies from one subject to another. Some may have an insatiable sex drive, some are otherwise normal men whose sexual interest is for some reason restricted to children, while still others are simply sociopaths who take what they want, including sex, where they find it. We assume that one etiological subgroup have in common a psychopathic personality structure that did not result merely from inadequate parental socialization but, rather, from some constitutional peculiarity of their own and it is this peculiarity that we hope to tap into with our laboratory measures. We might expect the "normal" pedophiles to get relatively low scores on both factors of the PCL, whereas unsocialized sociopaths might get high scores on both, especially on PCL–2. Primary psychopaths also might get high scores on both factors but they are the only subgroup that we expect to get high scores only on PCL–1.

In Patrick's later study with federal prison inmates, PCL–2 was correlated with emotionality and impulsivity scores on the Emotionality–Activity–Sociability (EAS) Temperament Survey (A. Buss & Plomin, 1984) and with Tellegen's factor of negative affect (NA; Patrick, 1994). The PCL–1 factor, in contrast, was negatively correlated with EAS emotionality and with NA but positively with positive affect (PA). Once again, in this study, it was the inmates with high scores on PCL–1, rather than on PCL–2, who differed from nonpsychopaths on the augmented-startle measure of fearful apprehension.

These findings suggest that, in spite of its antecedents, the PCL may not be the optimum instrument for distinguishing the primary psychopath from other varieties of unsocialized offenders. The full PCL, with the overtly criminal behavior items included, is clearly not an appropriate tool for identifying the "successful psychopath," the individual with the psychopathic personality who does not appear in prison populations because he manages to stay within the law or, at least, to avoid criminal conviction. One might use just the Factor 1 items of the PCL for this purpose although with some loss of reliability.

One way to segregate the primary psychopaths more clearly would be to try to identify patterns of two or more indicators that are characteristic of this group. The APQ, discussed in chapter 9, or the Harmavoidance scale of the MPQ, should in theory work to improve classification based on the Cleckley criteria or the PCL alone. That is, if the low-fear hypothesis is valid, then the Cleckley or PCL–1-denominated psychopaths who are low in harmavoidance should constitute the purest group of primary psychopaths, whereas the prison inmates who are not psychopathic according to the PCL–1 and who are also high on harmavoidance should provide the best contrast.

It should be made clear that several "anxiety" scales exist which do not measure the fearfulness or harmavoidant trait but, instead, are loaded strongly on the superfactor of neuroticism.[2] Newman and colleagues at Wisconsin have sometimes employed one of these neuroticism measures (the Welsh Anxiety Scale) together with Hare's PCL, treating the subgroup of "low anxiety psychopaths" (prisoners high on the PCL but low on neuroticism) as if they were a purified group of "real" psychopaths. As discussed in chapter 12 where the Wisconsin work is critically reviewed, there is no clear theoretical justification for this practice. On the other hand, Patrick (1994) did find that Tellegen's NA, which is similar to neuroticism, correlated positively (.31) with PCL–2 but negatively (–.23) with PCL–1. Unfortunately, Patrick and his colleagues used a direct measure of NA and PA rather than the full MPQ and so were unable to determine whether, as I would have expected, the Harmavoidance scale and the constraint superfactor distinguished PCL–1 from PCL–2 more clearly than NA and PA.

TAXONOMIES OF CRIMINAL OFFENDERS

It will be remembered that the Cleckley criteria were originally intended to identify a group of *patients* (not necessarily adjudicated criminals) who constituted, Cleckley believed, a distinct taxon, a group who share certain qualitatively distinctive characteristics based on a common etiology. Because many, but not all, Cleckley psychopaths will become criminal, an adequate taxonomy of criminals will include a primary psychopathic taxon, if Cleckley's conjecture is correct. Over the past 100 years there have been numerous attempts, more systematic than mine in chapter 3, to classify criminal offenders into useful, relatively homogeneous groups or types. This literature is extensively reviewed by Megargee and Bohn (1979). Typologies have been based on the instant offense or on criminal career patterns, on social class or subculture or on roles played within the prison subculture itself, and on the basis of psychoanalytic or developmental theories.

More empirical typologies, using factor and cluster analytic methods applied to collections of demographic, rating, and self-report data, have also been developed, for example by Quay and his associates (1965, 1977). Quay identified four dimensions that, in turn, are thought to suggest four main types of delinquent, the "unsocialized-psychopathic," the "neurotic-disturbed," the "subcultural-socialized," and the "incompetent-immature." Other writers (Megargee & Bohn, 1979), attempting to integrate subgroups of the more than 30 extant criminal typologies, have arrived at sets of from three to six categories, each of which, like Quay's system, includes the three "genera" of my armchair taxonomy, the sociopaths (i.e., subcultural offenders), the psychopaths, and the neurotic characters.

We have already seen that MMPI mavens identify "true psychopaths" not just in terms of their elevation on the Pd scale, but by evaluating this scale relative to

---

[2]The Taylor Anxiety Scale, the Welsh Anxiety Scale, and the Spielberger Trait Anxiety Scale are all measures relatively unrelated to harmavoidance but which load strongly on neuroticism.

the rest of the profile (of nine scales), with particular attention to the Ma scale. It was natural, therefore, for Megargee to wonder whether certain MMPI profile types might not be characteristic of the criminal community and provide a basis for classifying offenders into groups that were relatively homogeneous in respect to their behavior in custody and after release.

Megargee's MMPI Profile Taxonomy

Based on a cluster analysis (Veldman, 1967) of MMPI profiles obtained from more than 1,200 inmates of a federal prison, Megargee and Bohn (1979) identified 10 profile types into which 96% of the offenders could be classified. A large and varied quantity of demographic, psychological, prison adjustment, and recidivism data was then collected in order to characterize each of these types, which Megargee labeled "Able, Baker, Charlie ... Jupiter" in order not to prejudge their essential characteristics. Group Able, comprising some 17% of the population, were the classic psychopaths, bright, engaging, active, self-assured, "not excessively aggressive, but does little to avoid hostile interactions," often from good homes, and among the most likely to be arrested again after discharge. Group Delta, containing another 10%, were similar in psychopathy to Group Able but came from the most socially deviant families, were aggressive and belligerent and, like the Ables, were recidivistic. Groups Charlie, How, and Jupiter (at least) seem to belong in the sociopathic genus; they are troublesome and poor bets for parole, tend to have dysfunctional families, and seem more stress reactive than the psychopaths. The men in Group Baker appear to be neurotic delinquents, and those in Groups Item and Easy seem to be psychologically normal, similar to the group in chapter 3 called "professional criminals" plus perhaps a few situational offenders. So, once again, the three "genera" of my taxonomy can be coordinated with one or more of Megargee's 10 MMPI patterns most commonly found among young male offenders.

It seems to me unfortunate that none of the researchers in this area have made use of Megargee's MMPI profile classification scheme. There has developed a tendency to treat the criminal population as if it consisted of just psychopaths and nonpsychopaths (or primary vs. secondary psychopaths). It would be of considerable interest to know how each of Megargee's types score on the two factors of Hare's PCL and it would not be surprising to find that, for instance, Megargee's Group Able proved to be more "psychopathic" in the laboratory than groups that are classified by, say, the PCL alone.

Moffitt's Dichotomy of Youthful Offenders

In an important essay, Moffitt (1993) pointed out that the sharp increase in the crime risk that begins about age 12 has largely tapered off some 20 years later so that a large fraction of criminal activity is "adolescence-limited." The 5% to 10% of males whose antisocial activities are "life-course persistent" typically show conduct disorder prior to puberty. Their criminal behavior is not necessarily more serious than that shown by some adolescence-limited delinquents but it is less sporadic, less likely to be limited to group action, and it begins earlier. Indeed, the best predictor of adult criminality is early onset of antisocial behavior problems in childhood (Farrington, Loeber, & Van Kammen, 1990).

Moffitt explained that the life-course persistent delinquents fail to learn the social skills and educational fundamentals that are expected to be acquired in a normal childhood so that, as their turbulent adolescence runs its course, healthy interpersonal relationships and legal avenues of economic independence are increasingly closed off to them. She does not consider adolescence-limited offending to be psychopathological; because most adolescent males break the rules now and then, such behavior indeed must be considered normative. Some adolescence-limited offenders contribute importantly to the aggregate problem of crime, but it is the early onset, persistent offender who constitutes the greater menace. This is both because he is persistent, contributing many more crimes per capita than his counterparts, most of whom become law-abiding young adults, but also because the early onset offender serves as the role-model, the peer group provocateur who, in Moffitt's plausible scenario, leads his better socialized but susceptible contemporaries astray. In terms of my armchair taxonomy in chapter 3, Moffitt's adolescence-limited offenders would be classified as dyssocial sociopaths. Most of this book and most of the other taxonomies discussed here are concerned with her much smaller group of life-course persistent offenders and with the subtypes within that family.

Ronald Blackburn and the European Perspective

In the United Kingdom, the English Mental Health Act of 1959 defined *psychopathic disorder* as "a persistent disorder or disability of mind (whether or not including significant impairment of intelligence), which results in abnormally aggressive behavior or seriously irresponsible conduct." Here is an omnibus definition that seems to include all recidivistic offenders plus any other irresponsible or aggressive individuals whose conduct is not actually illegal. Trying to impose some sort of taxonomic order on the zoo of murderers and other malefactors committed under this statute, the British psychologist, Ronald Blackburn (1975), also used the MMPI to identify four clusters or types into which he could classify most of the offenders in two samples. One type, whose mean profile is similar to Megargee's Group Able, he called *primary psychopaths*; they were undersocialized, impulsive, aggressive, extropunitive, and relatively free of anxiety or guilt. The *secondary psychopaths*, whose profiles resembled Megargee's Group How, were anxious, depressed, and emotional but also hostile, aggressive, impulsive, and undersocialized. A third group, like Group Item, were psychometrically normal, nonneurotic, and generally well controlled. The fourth group, similar to Group George, were "characterized mainly by social shyness, introversion, and depression, and although moderately hostile are not notably aggressive or impulsive" (Blackburn, 1975, p. 451).

Blackburn's primary psychopaths seem to correspond to the Cleckley syndrome with the addition of aggression and coerciveness. We might say that Blackburn's primary psychopaths represent what we might expect from those Cleckley psychopaths who are also aggressive enough to have indulged in violent crime. His secondary psychopaths are harder to classify on the evidence presented. They may be what I have called ordinary sociopaths, people with average temperaments who lack the restraints of conscience and empathic feeling due mainly to inadequate parenting, and whose antisocial behavior keeps them under more or less constant stress. Alternatively, they (or some of them) may be examples of the type of secondary psychopath suggested by the theories propounded by Gray and Fowles. Blackburn's third group, whose personalities appeared to be substantially normal, might represent some mixture of situational offenders plus people of the professional criminal type described in chapter 3. These ambiguities of interpretation would be lessened if one had information on the general socialization and family backgrounds of these inmates such as Megargee provides (Megargee & Bohn, 1979).

Blackburn's own interpretation, based on these and subsequent studies (ably summarized by Thomas-Peter, 1992) was that the inmates who produced his four MMPI types might best be understood as four clusters of points on a plane defined by the dimensions of antisocial aggression and social withdrawal. Thus, the psychopathic groups are both aggressive but differ in withdrawal, whereas the nonpsychopathic groups are relatively nonaggressive but also differ in social withdrawal. Blackburn (1987) subsequently developed a 40-item scale that measures these two factors, now called belligerence and withdrawal.

Blackburn's measures and classification scheme has not as yet been used in conjunction with the laboratory procedures that have distinguished the North American work in this area. Because he has worked primarily with violent offenders consigned to maximum security hospitals, while the North American workers have focused instead on a broader range of criminals and even noncriminals, the differences in the taxonomies generated may reflect not only differences in measures but in the populations studied. One thing that seems very clear is that the nonaggressive Cleckley psychopath does not appear to have occurred in Blackburn's samples in sufficient numbers to make his presence felt. To conclude, as do Blackburn and Maybury (1985), that a measure of hostile belligerence will segregate the Cleckley psychopaths from the rest of the inmates is simply unacceptable to anyone familiar with this syndrome or, indeed, to anyone conversant with Cleckley's case studies. Descriptors such as belligerent, hostile, and aggressive do not appear among Cleckley's 16 defining characteristics of the primary psychopath.

A Final Word on Taxometrics

The reader is reminded that my armchair taxonomy is not to be taken literally as a claim that criminals come in a variety of discrete types like the fruits and vegetables on a produce counter. On the other hand, it is hard to deny the impression that there are latent taxa within this domain, that—if we only knew the rules—many criminals could be usefully classified into one or more of some basic set of criminal types. Neither armchair nor cluster analytic methods are adequate to this task but the sophisticated taxometric methods recently developed by Meehl (1992) and his colleagues have great promise. A promising start in this direction was a study by Harris, Rice, and Quinset (1994) of 653 inmates of a maximum security prison in Canada.

These authors used Meehl's methods to show that the scores of these inmates on Hare's PCL suggest the existence of a taxon comprising about half the group, those who score the highest on Factor 2 of that scale. A similar taxon emerged from an analysis of data relating to childhood conduct disorder but not from data on adult criminal history. A possible interpretation of these findings might be that the data separate these serious offenders into two approximately equal groups, psychopaths on the one hand, whose difficult temperaments led to early-onset conduct disorder and delinquency, and sociopaths on the other. Factor 1 of the PCL, however, did not yield a taxonic split and this is puzzling since other findings discussed here suggest that it is Factor 1 that most clearly identifies the pure-case Cleckley psychopath. One possible explanation, mentioned by Harris et al., is that the PCL was scored entirely from file data and the Factor 1 items (e.g., shallow affect, lack of remorse) are especially difficult to rate accurately from the information contained in prison files.

I believe that future research employing these techniques may one day provide taxonomies of criminality and of psychopathology generally, systems of classification having a firmer empirical and logical foundation than any that currently exist.

Conclusions

An excellent review of the various measures that have been devised for identifying the primary psychopath is available in an unpublished doctoral dissertation by Lilienfeld (1990). Lilienfeld also developed a very promising self-report measure of his own that I hope soon will be published. In the meanwhile, use of Hare's PCL to identify study groups representative of psychopaths and nonpsychopaths, respectively, has become the standard practice among researchers in this field. The use of the CPI–So scale and, perhaps, the Harmavoidance scale of the MPQ as accessory criteria that may further refine the study groups would seem to be worth serious consideration. Finally, separate analyses based on the two factors of the PCL as in the work of Patrick (1994) is recommended. At the present stage of our knowledge, persons scoring high on the PCL–1, and perhaps also low on the CPI–So and on the MPQ–HA scales (and on MPQ–Constraint), should represent primary psychopathy in its purest form. Persons scoring high on the PCL–2, who have moderate to low scores on PCL–1, low scores on the CPI–So, and average to high scores on MPQ–NA may comprise the best available approximation to secondary psychopathy. As suggested earlier, it is at least possible that the Megargee MMPI profile types might also contribute usefully to the identification of more homogeneous experimental and comparison groups.

Finally, as suggested in chapter 9, the consistency of findings showing primary psychopaths to display less fearful apprehension in the Hare countdown situation, whether measured using electrodermal arousal or the startle-augmentation technique, suggests that the time may be approaching when a standardized psychophysiological test for diagnosing primary psychopathy might be devised.

9

A Theory of Primary Psychopathy

To begin with, both my father and my mother were "fearless ones." My father was decorated for bravery in WWI but, more importantly, he carried an aura of fearlessness about him. My mother lived in a tent just behind the front lines when my father was a front-line officer. My father assigned two troopers to look after her and each day the three of them would ride across the recent battlefield where they would locate the dead for the burial details. ... My mother died when I was 4 and my father later married an ex-Army nurse. She was tough as nails and very quick tempered, frequently hitting me ... I got pretty fed up with this sort of treatment and, one day when I was about 9, she hit me a vicious backhander across the face; I stood perfectly still with, I hope, no expression on my face but rather defying her to hit me again, looking her straight in the eye. She raised her hand again and I stood perfectly still, then her eyes widened and she snapped "Oh you are a little devil, get out of my sight!" and she never hit me again. It was a very good lesson for me as I later won several fights with bigger boys because I wouldn't show any fear or give up or show any pain when I was hit. When I boxed in the navy I sometimes lowered my guard and let my opponent hit me in the face because I found it discouraged them when they found they apparently couldn't hurt me.

Your points on antisocial behavior interested me because I had no fear of authority and none of punishment, as a result I became a "holy terror." I believe the three main reasons I didn't become a public enemy were, firstly, I admired soldierly conduct and disciplined people; second, I lived in the country where I could let off my boundless energy by chasing after rabbits, swimming, fishing, hunting, or (one of my favorites) leaping onto the backs of cattle when they were lying down, chewing their cud, and being taken for short wild rides before being bucked off, being flung off was always the most exciting part. Thirdly, and most importantly, the thing that slowed me down the most was, after a bad episode at school for which I received a public thrashing (which worried me not), a master whom I respected greatly said, "John, you let me down" in such a sad voice that if he had kicked me in the gut he couldn't have hit me harder.

—Letter from an adventurer who, among other exploits, had circumnavigated the globe single-handed in a small sailboat (8–17–1982)

When we say that criminality is a failure to inhibit or avoid antisocial behavior, we imply an impulse or temptation toward the forbidden act that is opposed by a restraining force that consists largely of fear of the consequences: fear of punishment, of feeling guilty, or the loss of self-esteem. Fortunately, most of us usually are spared the stress of this approach–avoidance conflict out of habit. We are so well socialized that we usually do the "right thing" automatically; feeling no temptation, we do not have to fight it. Frequently when we were growing up, however, and now and then even as adults, we have felt tempted to break the rules and have had to make a choice. The outcome of those choices depends on the relative strengths of the temptation and the countervailing socialized inhibition. As demonstrated in chapter 14, the most common reason for antisocial choices is weak inhibition due to inadequate socialization resulting from incompetent parenting. As discussed in chapter 3, there are some individuals who have been tolerably well socialized but who make certain kinds of antisocial choices because they are especially strongly tempted due to deviant desires or a susceptibility to passionate excess.

The primary psychopath makes antisocial choices when it pleases him or her for the first reason, because the fear of punishment and the coercive voice of conscience both are, for some reason, weak or ineffectual. But what makes the primary psychopath especially interesting is that his or her lack of antisocial inhibition is not merely the predictable consequence of incompetent parenting. We have pointed out repeatedly that some children are harder to socialize than others and the primary psychopath, like the bull terrier, is at the high end of this scale of difficulty. Most of the psychopaths that Cleckley described so vividly came from well-socialized traditional families and should, by rights, have turned out all right themselves. The reason why this group has been of special interest to psychopathologists is that they seem to lack conscience, moral values, and habits of good conduct because of some peculiarity in themselves rather than in their upbringing. For this same reason, it is sometimes forgotten that hard-to-socialize children also occur among the offspring of incompetent parents and are thus especially unlikely to achieve adequate socialization.

Cleckley's own theory was that these individuals lacked the normal emotional accompaniments of experience. A person who is color-blind may not understand that, when someone else says: "The traffic light is red," they are describing an experience that is qualitatively different than the one he has when looking at that same semaphore; for him, "red" means just that the larger, upper light is on. Similarly, Cleckley thought, when others say such things as "I was really embarrassed!" or "I'm sorry!" the psychopath does not realize that they are describing feeling states that he or she does not experience. Cleckley believed that the psychopath's "semantic aphasia" was pervasive and deep and that it constituted a grave personality disorder that distances the psychopath from the reality of human experience to a degree comparable to the effects of psychosis. It seemed to me, however, that a simpler hypothesis was both adequate and testable. (I should acknowledge here that I got this idea originally from my teacher, Paul Meehl, who got it from his teacher, Starke Hathaway.)

Like all mammals, we come equipped with a capacity to experience fear, an aversive state that elicits arousal and escape behavior. We have a repertoire of innate fears (sudden loss of support, the dark, the edges of cliffs, loud and unexpected noises, spiders and snakes, etc.) and we can also learn to fear stimuli or situations that have been associated in our past with strong feelings of fear or distress. We seem to acquire new fears by this simple process of Pavlovian conditioning but we learn to escape from fear, and to avoid fear-inducing stimuli, by what is called "operant" conditioning in which the escape or avoidance response is rewarded or reinforced by fear reduction.

Like all biological endowments, these fear-related tendencies or reactions obviously vary in degree from one person to another. Some children are so innately fearful, so unable to tolerate the whips and scorns of daily living that it compromises their adjustment. My idea was that children at the other end of this continuum, those whose innate fearfulness was weak or whose fear conditioning machinery was relatively sluggish, might tend to become primary psychopaths as they grow up.

As we have already seen, one can acquire two of the three components of socialization entirely through positive reinforcement. Loving mentors and prosocial role models can instill prosocial attitudes and altruistic habits without punishment or fear. My wife, who was always the most popular child in her room at school, went out of her way to be friendly and kind to the shy and unpopular among her classmates because her clever mother taught her the gratification associated with noblesse oblige. Any child with talent and a good teacher can discover the satisfactions of developing a skill and of doing a good job of work. An outgoing or attractive child can cultivate social skills and the ability to influence others entirely through the positive feedback that such skills entail. But we usually learn the third component of socialization, learn to avoid antisocial behaviors and to inhibit forbidden impulses, through punishment and the conditioned fear it leaves behind. My theory of primary psychopathy was that all the components of the syndrome outlined in Cleckley's 16 criteria might be expected to be found in a normal but relatively fearless child who had been subjected to the typical parenting methods that rely primarily on punishment for the development of conscience and the inhibition of antisocial behavior.

CAN THE THEORY ACCOUNT FOR
THE CLECKLEY CRITERIA?

Let us consider the Cleckley criteria, one by one, asking ourselves whether—given the typical rearing environment and typical parents—a relatively fearless little boy might grow up to have each characteristic. Keep in mind that the most useful test of any hypothesis is how well it fits the facts in comparison with competing hypotheses. Therefore, we should also ask ourselves, as we go along, whether some of the other theories that have been proposed for this condition—low-arousal and stimulus hunger, poor impulse control, delayed ego development, deficient serotonin activity, or reduced cerebral lateralization (reduced separation of the functions of the right and left halves of the brain)—can account for each of these same attributes; that is, does another etiological theory fit these descriptive criteria better—or as well?

Superficial Charm and Good Intelligence

This one is easy. I submit that insouciance—"want of concern, indifference"—is the essence of charm. Granted that a shy, sloe-eyed maiden may sometimes be described as "charming" in romantic novels but normally the people that we say are charming people are not shy but, rather, they are self-assured and socially adept, spontaneous and lively. A charming person is the candle flame that attracts us ordinary moths. Although the charmers may flatter us in passing with the heat of their apparent interest in us personally, still we know that a flame doesn't tend to bother with any one moth for very long.

Think of the reasons you might give in order to explain why you yourself were less charming at the party last night than you'd have liked to be: You were a little shy, a bit self-conscious, afraid to say the wrong thing, afraid to alienate, a little tongue-tied, inclined to get a bit rattled when it was your turn to say something, a bit inhibited: most of the reasons would turn out to be different manifestations of social fear. Why does the cocktail hour tend to make everybody slightly more charming, more interesting? because the alcohol releases inhibitions, assuages social fear.

The "good intelligence" criterion doesn't mean that psychopaths have higher than average IQs. Cleckley included this one for two reasons: (a) to point out that the psychopath's sometimes outrageous behaviors are not caused by simple stupidity; and (b) because the unafraid, unabashed, uninhibited psychopath always has his wits about him, does not get rattled, does not draw a blank when trying to think of something to say; that is, he tends to be able to make the most of what intelligence he has in those situations where you and I might be inclined to seem more foolish than we really are.

Absence of Delusions and Other Signs of Irrational Thinking

No problem here either. Like good intelligence, this specification is just to make clear that the psychopathic behaviors are not due to some defect in mentation. On the other hand, there is no clinical nor theoretical reason for supposing that psychopathy carries an immunity to psychosis and its symptoms. Psychopaths can be also stupid or crazy but psychopathy itself is not a consequence of psychosis or low intelligence.

Absence of "Nervousness" or Other Neurotic Manifestations

This one, of course, flows directly from the "relatively fearless" hypothesis. Notice that Cleckley does not mean by "nervousness" the opposite of "calm"; he means the neurotic's vulnerable state of jumpy oversensitivity or overstimulation. The only problem here is in making the correct clinical inference. We ordinary people are likely to interpret some of the psychopath's behaviors as indicating nervousness—and so is he, incidentally. If he is restless, bored, irritable, if he makes the *observer* feel nervous—we are likely to describe him as nervous. Meanwhile, the psychopath, not having experienced vulnerable oversensitivity but observing that other people who seem restless and edgy tend to describe themselves as nervous, might apply that same label to himself.

This is not to say that the psychopath is wholly incapable of real fear and nervousness, but merely that his or her reaction to a given stressor will be less than yours or mine would be. And, for this very reason, the psychopath is inclined to take more chances, to live closer to the edge, to experience more stress on a regular basis than you or I might tolerate. Cleckley's "absence of nervousness" has to be interpreted in relation to the circumstances; although Gary Gilmore was edgy and nervous on the evening before his execution, we need not on that basis revise our diagnosis that he was a Cleckley psychopath.

Unreliability

This is one of the important but derivative traits; if you meet the criteria following this one, you are likely to be considered unreliable. Would not you and I be less reliable than we now are if we stopped being capable of fear, shame, or guilt? I also think, however, that some psychopaths can be quite reliable about certain commitments, at least for a time, if doing so fits with some role that they enjoy or take pride in adopting.

Untruthfulness and Insincerity

You and I tend to tell the truth partly out of fear—fear of being caught, fear of being shamed, fear of feeling guilty. We even tend to lie, when we do lie, out of fear; we tell "white lies" when we fear hurting someone's feelings or alienating them, and we tell little "black lies" when we have been naughty and fear the consequences of our sins. Most people would lie more often (and more skillfully) if they were relatively free of fear. Sincerity is part of the social contract most of us live by because it makes us feel safer; it is a way of making allies, of creating a reassuring sense of solidarity with others. When we're in a high-stakes poker game where skillful bluffing and deception pays off, we try to stop being sincere because it's every man for himself there, but we don't dare to live our lives that way. If we were less fearful, perhaps we would treat larger blocks of our lives as if we were in a poker game.

Lack of Remorse or Shame

As Cleckley uséd the term, *shame* is a fear of what other people will think about us or our behavior; it begins as the feeling a child has when he or she has been caught doing something bad or forbidden. A child who is relatively fearless, who is relatively indifferent to punishment, may also be relatively indifferent to what other people think and relatively free of guilt.

It is important, however, to remember that our hypothesis does not say that the psychopath is indifferent to admiration, to the loving or admiring things that "people might say" about him or her. I think this is the one way to socialize or influence this type of individual, by creating relationships that are so satisfying, and a role in life or social image that is so gratifying that the child will make an effort to avoid losing either the relationships or his or her social position.

Empathy probably has roots that are similar to the origins of remorse and shame. The young child is a vulnerable sojourner in a dangerous world where big people with loud voices and hard hands can arbitrarily deprive and punish. The way to be safe in such a world is to learn the rules by which it operates, to find out what those big people want and like and what they don't want and dislike, and especially what makes them mad. This is one reason why young children are so fond of rules in games; "knowing the ropes" means knowing the rules that you that can hang onto (like ropes) to keep from sinking in dangerous waters. So the average child observes the grownups, imitates them, can be heard scolding her dolly or herself in words that mother sometimes uses scolding her. How assiduously the child works at this will depend in part on how fearful he or she is and in part on how well it pays off—if this child's world is unpredictable, if the adults are too inconsistent in their own behavior, then introjection of their attitudes may not work very well.

In general, however, it seems reasonable to say that we learn to see ourselves as others see us, to predict other people's behavior, and to "feel with" other people primarily as a way of achieving predictability and security. A child who feels less need for security, being less generally fearful and apprehensive, may not learn these skills as soon or as well as the average child does. Such a relatively fearless child therefore may be less inclined to feel shame or to introject such feelings so as to experience them as guilt.

Once again, however, it should be noted that predicting the behavior of others can be rewarded positively—by making it possible to achieve treats and caresses—as well as negatively by avoiding punishment. Some relatively fearless children, in the right environment, become quite skilled at predicting and, hence, manipulating the behavior of the big people.

Inadequately Motivated Antisocial Behavior

Fifteen-year-old Nicki, brought before the juvenile court judge after decamping from the Juvenile Center to spend a couple of days with a boy she met somewhere, referred to His Honor as "you asshole!" in response to a critical comment. Nicki, and her twin sister, Allie, were raised by middle-class, Lutheran adoptive parents who do not talk like that. Nicki was not greatly stressed nor righteously indignant at the time; the judge's comment irritated her so she called him an asshole; what's the big deal?

Antisocial behavior generally means yielding to some temptation that most people don't yield to out of fear of the consequences. But most of us would yield to some temptations if we were "adequately motivated"—if the pull of the temptation is stronger than the push of the restraining fear. If the restraining fear is weaker, as it was for Nicki, then the pull will overmaster it even when the pull is also relatively weak.

Notice that Cleckley said "inadequately motivated" rather than "impulsive" because the latter term is ambiguous. The same impulsive-appearing behavior could result from weak motivation overcoming still weaker restraint, as in Nicki's case, or when, as in the truly impulsive individual, the behavior is initiated before the actor has time to reflect upon the consequences—or by unusually strong motivation overcoming normal restraint. We shall see later that the antisocial behavior of another kind of psychopathy, the secondary rather than the primary or Cleckley type, may result from this sort of passionate excess of impulse strength.

Poor Judgment and Failure to Learn by Experience

When someone shows "inadequately motivated antisocial behavior," we commonly say he or she is displaying "poor judgment." Nicki showed poor judgment in her remark to the judge. QED.

"Failure to learn by experience" is too broad to be what Cleckley really meant. Taken literally, this would imply that the psychopath does not learn anything (how else does one learn except by experience?). What he plainly intended to say is that the psychopath does not tend to stop doing what he or she has been punished for doing. You and I learn to avoid punishment, it is thought, by a two-stage process. In Stage 1, the stimuli surrounding the forbidden behavior (including the impulse itself) are associated with the experience of punishment and become conditioned stimuli for fear. In Stage 2, the reoccurrence of these stimuli elicits fear, the fear elicits[1] avoidant behavior, the escape from the conditioned stimuli results in the relief of fear which, in turn, reinforces the avoidant behavior. A child or adult who is relatively fearless will experience a weaker fear response in Stage 2 and be less likely, therefore, to avoid the forbidden act.

It is important to realize that one can learn to avoid certain acts without the intermediation of fear or punishment. Suppose we want to teach a white rat not to press the food lever when a light is on, even though pressing the lever will yield a small amount of wet mash. We might rig up a second feeder on a side wall that provides even tastier morsels and arrange it so that avoiding the first lever, which turns the light off, and pressing the second one will produce this better treat whenever the light is on. Eventually the rat will learn the rules of this game and behave accordingly. An adult human can learn to avoid through positive reinforcement rather easier than the rat could because the human does not have to learn the contingencies by trial and error but can learn them by imitation or be told about them or reason them out.

Little Johnny, like most kids, tends to toss his candy wrappers out the car window and be generally a litterbug. Mom and Dad, whom Johnny admires, put their trash in a litter bag or in their pockets; they speak disdainfully of people they see littering,

---

[1]Skinnerians would say that fear, which is an involuntary reaction, is "elicited" but that avoidant behavior, which is an "operant" response, is "occasioned," not elicted.

implying that those who behave as they themselves do are superior to those who don't, and they also complement Johnny when he does put his gum wrapper in the litter bag. In time, behaving properly in this sense can be rewarding in the same way as dressing up to look good or making a skillful play at second base is rewarding, even to a psychopath. Nicki might not call the judge an asshole if Nicki could develop a role or image or style of behavior that was admired by people Nicki admired and that made her feel good about herself—and which was incompatible with saying such things to a judge. But it is not easy to get Nicki far enough into such a role to make it valuable to her and, moreover, these spur-of-the-moment peccadilloes are harder to inhibit except by the minatory impact of punishment.

Pathological Egocentricity and Incapacity for Love

Most egocentric people are not psychopaths. For example, many chronically sick people and many old people become almost totally preoccupied with themselves. Someone who does not care much about what other people think, who is disinclined to empathize with others, who has never learned to take satisfaction in nurturing others, who lives life like it was a big poker game, winner take all—in short, an unsocialized person—is likely to be described as egocentric. I think egocentricity is another derivative symptom.

What do you mean by "love"? One meaning is to value or to cherish; you can love your new car, your new dress, your new boyfriend, your new baby—so can the psychopath. Another meaning is to need, to depend on, to be unable to live without. Suppose you were charming, carefree, attractive to others, easily adaptable, unworried about what tomorrow may bring—would your relations with your loved ones then have the same quality of *needing*? Loving couples become intertwined at all levels, literally part of each other's lives so that the loss of the loved one leaves the life space empty. But we do this intertwining in part for security, we "cling to" each other. The psychopath has less need for such security.

But of course we also intertwine in affectionate embrace for positive reasons, not just for security. A relatively fearless person can form close, affectionate relationships perhaps more easily than someone inhibited by the usual amount of social fear. If the relatively fearless child's relationships with parents and friends work out positively, produce the pleasures that we social animals are able to experience through mutual closeness, then that child could be said to be loving and affectionate, just as my psychopathic cat and my bull terrier are both loving and affectionate. Too often, however, the relatively fearless child will have stormy and unrewarding relationships with those closest to him; new friends and new conquests will be more rewarding at least until they too turn sour due to the new friends' reactions to the child's psychopathic behavior.

Although the psychopath might cherish and be proud of his or her new baby, he or she is unlikely to be as nurturant and as patient with that child as a normal parent would be because these qualities of parenting require empathy and at least some degree of fearful apprehension (and, yes, some capacity for guilt), tendencies which, as we have seen, the psychopath lacks. Just as he or she might disdainfully discard a hitherto cherished possession once it is damaged, the psychopathic parent is more likely to turn his or her face away from a child who has become a burden rather than a joy—as all children do from time to time. Although psychopaths can succeed in many of life's challenges, I suspect that the unrelenting demands of parenthood may be the one challenge that no true psychopath is ever likely to answer.

I believe that relatively fearless people can learn to love, to be tender and affectionate, but, when they do, will not be inclined to suffer the "tyranny of love" that we more vulnerable people are subject to. However, I believe that relatively fearless people seldom have the kinds of rewarding experience in intimate relationships that are required to induce tenderness and affectionate intimacy because other people, especially family and childhood acquaintances, react against their uninhibited, unsocialized behavior. A child who develops in an environment in which more and better gratification can be achieved through affiliation and prosocial behavior than through defiance and rule-breaking will tend to become a better socialized adult, whatever his or her innate temperament may be.

General Poverty in Major Affective Reactions

I think this one is derivative too and also a bit of an overstatement. I believe that a psychopath can get really angry, for example, although some things that might make me angry—because they hurt or threaten me in some way—might not bother the psychopath who doesn't feel the same hurt. Cleckley's cases fly off the handle easily when frustrated but as quickly get over their pique and seldom bear a grudge. But Cleckley's case histories are mostly of young, middle-class psychiatric patients, not prison inmates who often have more to be angry about.

I see no evidence that the psychopath cannot feel ecstatic or joyful or delighted and there is no reason to suppose that he or she cannot be truly depressed, either, which means "alone and parted far from joy and gladness" and is due to a disorder of brain chemistry. On the other hand, the psychopath may be invulnerable to neurotic or reactive depression, stemming from feelings of guilt, failure, and personal inadequacy. Some clinicians may find it difficult to think of the psychopath as being joyful but that is because they have not seen him just after he has effected a successful escape or bank robbery or high-stakes swindle. Joy requires a degree of excitement, which you and I can feel in making love or in greeting old friends, experiences that may not excite the psychopath as much as they do us. But winning the lottery would probably delight him even more than it would me because I would start worrying about my grandchildren being kidnaped and the psychopath would not.

My clinical impression is that psychopaths are also less vulnerable to the torments of jealousy than you and I may be. Evolutionary psychologists expect jealousy to be controlled by a separate "mental organ" because of the way in which this human disposition is thought to have evolved, differently in men than in women. Yet I think there is a link between jealousy and fear in the sense that fearful, insecure people seem to be more vulnerable to jealous concerns, perhaps because they would be less confident of securing a replacement for a lover who strays. My guess is that the psychopath is never what one would call a jealous person but, confronted by what appears to be clear evidence of flagrant infidelity or of rejection by a partner, I suspect that even a psychopath would get angry and perhaps, like Othello, dangerously violent. The recent case of Sol Wachtler, the 62 year-old chief judge of the State of New York, appears to be an interesting example (Franks, 1992). When Wachtler's ex-mistress traded him in on a younger man, the judge embarked on a Byzantine plot of harassment that required a major FBI task force to unravel. Wachtler's attorneys will no doubt contrive a defense based on some other psychiatric condition but I suspect that a careful study of the judge's biography would reveal instances of artfully concealed rule-bending and manipulation beginning in his youth.

Specific Loss of Insight

Here, Cleckley referred to the psychopath's inability to see himself as others see him, to predict or to appreciate how other people will react emotionally to his (or her) behavior. If it is true that the psychopath has attenuated feelings of fear, remorse, concern for others, and if he or she has not worked as hard to learn to predict how others will feel or react, has not tried to internalize other people's attitudes, then it is not surprising that he or she will find it difficult to see himself or herself as others do.

Unresponsiveness in Interpersonal Relations

This criterion also seems to me to be derivative from the low fear hypothesis. If the man I am talking to cares less about what I think, how I feel, than is customary in human interactions, and if he does not even make the usual polite effort to simulate interest in me or my views, I am likely to consider him to be "unresponsive." I think many psychopaths, at least when engaged in manipulation or otherwise having fun, can be quite responsive in their own way, which may not be your way.

Fantastic and Uninviting Behavior, With Drink and Sometimes Without

Here we can think of John Belushi in the movie *Animal House*. Why do you not belch and break wind and throw food around and do all those things he got paid lots of money for doing? Because you'd feel embarrassed, that's why. Not all psychopaths behave this way but most of them could, if they wanted to, more easily than you could. It is interesting to note that many adult psychopaths make less use of drink and downer-type drugs than other people do because they have less need for the disinhibiting or tranquilizing effects of these compounds. However, in keeping with their propensity for risk-taking, psychopaths are more likely to abuse alcohol and especially stimulant drugs such as cocaine than is the average citizen.

Suicide Rarely Carried Out

David Bjorkman, grandson of a prominent Minneapolis merchant, was a likable, generous, primary psychopath who, throughout most of his adult life, made his living selling drugs.

> Everybody who knew him was charmed by David. "He had a salesman's personality," his mother said. "He could have been successful as a legitimate salesman. But the other life was more exciting and the remuneration was so much greater." And he was a great salesman. He was busted once in Missouri for transporting marijuana under an assumed name. "He literally talked his way out of jail," his mother said. "I couldn't believe it. I thought he was in jail and in big trouble and then I get a call, 'Mom, the phoenix has risen.'" (Grow, 1994)

David also sold his mother on setting up a large, sophisticated, indoor marijuana farm in the basement of her home. Before long Mom found herself serving a 1-year term in a federal prison. David, convicted as a "drug kingpin," was given 25 to 40 years. Depressed and in poor health, David killed himself in prison. "'That's like David,' said his mother. 'The big, flamboyant gesture.'"

Psychopaths can get depressed and sometimes kill themselves in earnest. But, more often than most people, some psychopaths, especially women, will make histrionic suicide "attempts" as a means of manipulating others or just on impulse. You and I are less likely to do this because we are less impulsive and because we fear the consequences.

Sex Life Impersonal, Trivial, and Poorly Integrated

Van Hoffman's biography of Roy Cohn provides a good illustration of the sort of thing that Cleckley had in mind. However, as he admitted, the psychopath with his charm and lack of ordinary inhibitions often makes a strong impression on his or her sex partners. If I were revising Cleckley's criteria, I would rewrite this one simply as "lack of sexual inhibition." Like anyone else, the psychopath's sex drive may be strong or weak but he or she is especially unlikely to restrain it.

Failure to Follow any Life Plan

A person who does not worry about the future is, of course, less likely to plan for it. A fearless, difficult-to-socialize child may be sufficiently gratified by the opportunities of the moment so as never to discover the greater satisfactions of developing his or her skills and achieving higher worldly success. But Cleckley himself described psychopaths who had earned medical degrees, graduated at the top of the class in law school, and achieved eminent status in various fields. I would classify Roy Cohn and Lyndon Johnson as primary psychopaths and yet they both followed life plans with great success. The key is the early success they had and the rewards that drew them on.

Summary

Like the ability to experience pain, the fear mechanism is especially useful early in life before the individual's judgment and reason are sufficiently dependable guides to behavior. A child born with a congenital insensitivity to pain is unlikely to survive to maturity intact unless carefully and skillfully monitored and guided. I once examined such a child who had been reared by indifferent and incompetent foster parents. He was bound to a wheelchair, having broken many bones during his first few years, and the distal phalanges of all his fingers were missing, as were the front third of his tongue and both lips—he had been allowed to simply chew them off! Once maturity has been safely attained, we might all be better off if we could turn down both our pain reactors and our fear reactors (turn them down but not off). It is important to see that being relatively fearless does not imply an indifference to the consequences of one's actions. I do not need the goad of dread in order to work to attain something I want or to prevent the loss of something I value. But a child whose goals are unformed and whose understanding of how the world works is still vague will be less likely to select constructive behaviors (and avoid reckless ones) on purely rational grounds without the push of conscience and the restraint of fear to help provide direction.

TESTING THE LOW-FEAR HYPOTHESIS

Psychologists and psychiatrists are notoriously glib about stretching or squeezing their theories to fit the facts. Although the low fear-quotient theory passes the glib test reasonably well, can it make predictions that pass experimental test? In 1954, I did an experiment to test some predictions from this theory and I describe that study in some detail, in spite of its antiquity, for three reasons: First, that study initiated a long series of studies by others, notably by Hare at the University of British Columbia, that now constitute an impressive literature of experimental psychopathology. Second, these subsequent studies have repeatedly replicated and extended my original results. It may seem odd to take pride in the fact that these findings have stood up to replication by others but the truth is that this is a relatively rare event in psychopathological research. Third, progress in psychological science is slow and this study, although venerable, is still informative and, I think, it remains a good example of how one fairly solid brick was added to the foundations of what may one day be an edifice of understanding.

I tested the following three predictions: First, compared to ordinary criminals and also to normal subjects, Cleckley psychopaths should score lower on a test of general fearfulness. Second, in a conditioning situation, where the sound of a buzzer is frequently followed by a painful electric shock, the psychopaths should show weaker physiological signs of a fear reaction upon hearing the buzzer. Third, in a task where certain responses are punished by a painful shock, and where it is possible to learn to avoid making these punished responses, psychopaths should show relatively poorer avoidance learning because they should be less fearful of the shock.

The Subjects

The first step was to select the experimental group, the primary psychopaths (Group 1). At one mental hospital and two prisons, I asked the institution psychologists to nominate inmates who, in their opinion, met all of Cleckley's 16 criteria. They also nominated a second group of persons with extensive records of antisocial behavior, people who already had been classified as psychopaths, but whom they felt did not meet the Cleckley criteria. I referred to this group then as "neurotic" sociopaths (Group 2) on the then-popular assumption that the basis for their persistent antisocial behavior was some sort of acting-out of neurotic conflicts. It turned out, in fact, that this group had by far the highest scores on a measure of neuroticism and, because of this combination of antisocial and neurotic traits, these people resembled those who have been subsequently referred to as *secondary* psychopaths by Blackburn (1988) and others. There were 19 primary psychopaths in Group 1 and 20 secondary psychopaths in Group 2. I also recruited 15 normal subjects (Group 3) matched for age, education and sex with the other two groups.

The ideal Cleckley psychopath comes from a traditional two-parent middle-class home. Individuals reared in dysfunctional or single-parent homes or in high-crime neighborhoods might meet most of the Cleckley criteria because of inadequate parenting even without the aid of deviant temperamental endowment. The best way to identify a homogeneous group of 200-proof primary psychopaths for experimental purposes would have been to add to the Cleckley criteria the requirements that they were raised in reasonably stable two-parent homes because this would increase the odds of psychopathy versus sociopathy. The family backgrounds of my psychopathic subjects, however, were evaluated from the institution records and "with certain notable exceptions, these records painted a uniformly morbid picture" so I was unable to exclude individuals whose lack of socialization might be attributed to inadequate parenting.[2] Nevertheless, Group 1 seemed to have contained a high enough proportion of primary psychopaths for the experiment to work. (If I were to repeat this experiment now, I would recruit middle-class malefactors from among juvenile offenders, adult probationers, and from psychiatric hospitals rather than using primarily prison inmates. As an additional refinement, I would use the first factor of Hare's PCL, discussed in chapter 8, to assess the Cleckley criteria and perhaps also require low scores on my APQ, the MPQ Harmavoidance scale, or the MPQ constraint superfactor.)

Prediction 1: Low Fearfulness

To test the first prediction, I wanted a questionnaire or self-report measure of general fearfulness. Although there were several tests available that claimed to measure "anxiety," it was apparent that these were all measures of what is now

---

[2]See Lykken (1955, p. 23). Siddle and Trasler (1981, pp. 284–285) reported, incorrectly, that I excluded subjects whose family background was markedly sociopathic or deviant and also subjects with strongly adverse or neuropathic heredity. My original intent was to use these exclusion criteria but it turned out that only a handful of candidates then would have remained.

called *neuroticism*. People who are nervous, dissatisfied, and self-critical get high scores on these anxiety tests. Therefore, I constructed my own instrument, the APQ. Each item of the APQ invited the subject to suppose that one of two events had to happen but that he could choose which he would prefer as the lesser of evils. All of the alternatives were events or experiences that most people would consider unpleasant. For most of the items, the paired alternatives consisted of one event that was unpleasant because it was frightening or embarrassing whereas the other was onerous—perhaps boring or arduous, frustrating or uncomfortable—but not frightening. Here are a couple of examples:

1. (a) Being in a bank when suddenly three masked men with guns come in and make everyone raise their hands. (b) Sitting through a 2-hour concert of bad music.
2. (a) Being sick to your stomach for 24 hours. (b) Being chosen as the "target" for a knife-throwing act.

These various events had been previously rated for general unpleasantness by a group of young adults so that I was able to pair alternatives for which the average unpleasantness ratings were about equal. The theory of the test was simple; someone whose general fearfulness was lower than average should more frequently choose the frightening experiences as preferable to the onerous but nonfrightening alternatives. Therefore, the low-fear quotient theory predicted that, compared to Groups 2 and 3, the primary psychopaths in Group 1 should get lower scores (should more often choose the frightening alternative) on this self-report measure of fearfulness. This first prediction was supported by the findings.

It is worth noting that some of the APQ items consisted of paired onerous or paired frightening items that did differ in rated unpleasantness. This provided a validity key; people responding honestly and thoughtfully should always choose the less unpleasant alternative in these items as the lesser of evils. The inclusion of these validity items helped to conceal the purpose of the test so that graduate students in clinical psychology, shown the test items, were unable to guess what the test was intended to measure. This was useful because I did not want inmates who were trying to project a tough and fearless image to be motivated to make dishonest choices.

Prediction 2: Poor Fear Conditioning

After the subject had filled out the APQ, I attached a pair of electrodes to his nondominant hand. Through these electrodes I could safely administer a harmless but painful electric shock. I told the subject I wanted to measure his pain threshold and that I would turn up the shock, one step at a time, until he was unwilling to let me go any higher. This "tolerance threshold" was the level of shock used in the subsequent procedures. Because the shock was on continuously during the threshold measurement, its subjective intensity at the threshold was considerably weaker than that same intensity seemed to be later when the shocks came on suddenly at full strength and lasted just half a second. This insured that the later shocks would continue to command the subject's attention and respect.

The next step was to apply a pair of recording electrodes to two fingers of the subject's other hand. Through these electrodes, I would measure the electrical conductance of the skin. The skin on the palms and soles is penetrated by thousands of tiny sweat glands and the activity of these glands largely determines the skin's electrical properties. If we record the conductance on a moving paper chart, we will see wavelike increases in conductance every time the subject is stimulated, as when we speak to him or sound a buzzer or administer a shock. These waves are called electrodermal responses (EDRs) and they are produced by sweat gland activity in response to the stimulus. For a given subject, the size of each EDR will be proportional to the subjective intensity of the stimulus. Thus, a strong stimulus (or a weak stimulus that has special significance) will produce a larger EDR than a weaker or less significant stimulus.

I explained to the subject that, in this second part of the experiment, he would from time to time hear the sound of a buzzer or feel a brief electric shock. The subject was then blindfolded and told to sit still and try to relax. During the ensuing 30 minutes or so, the buzzer was sounded repeatedly for 5 seconds at 20- to 60-second intervals. On the first 6 trials, the buzzer was presented alone. On the next 11 trials, a shock was delivered when the 5-second buzzer terminated; these were the conditioning trials. Finally, another 16 buzzer-alone trials were given in order to track the extinction of the subject's conditioned response to the buzzer. The low fear-quotient theory predicted that the primary psychopaths in Group 1 should show a smaller conditioned EDR to the buzzer—less physiological disturbance in anticipation of the imminent shock—than the subjects in the other two groups. This prediction too was born out.

Prediction 3: Poor Avoidance Learning

Measuring avoidance learning in order to test the third prediction from the theory provided an interesting challenge. The task I proposed to use was a kind of mental maze involving a series of 20 choice-points with four alternatives at each choice-point. The subject was seated before a cabinet from which projected four levers. On the front panel was the label: "Minnesota Leadership Assessment Test" and below this an electrically operated counter and two signal lights, one red and one green. The subject was told that one of the four levers would be correct at each choice-point and that pressing that lever would flash the green light and move him forward to the next choice-point. Pressing any of the three incorrect levers would flash the red light and cause an error to be recorded on the counter. The subject understood that the first time through the maze would be a matter of trial and error; at the end, the green light would stay on, I would record how many errors he had made, and then reset the machine for another trial. His task was to try to remember the sequence of correct levers so that, eventually, he would be able to traverse the maze without error.

So far, this task has no obvious relationship to avoidance learning. The subjects who were willing to perform it (none declined) were presumably motivated by curiosity, perhaps by a desire to be compliant or to prove to me or to themselves how clever they were. We know, of course, that psychopaths can learn most things as well as anyone else can. I had every reason to suppose that the psychopaths would learn this maze task at least as readily as the other subjects did. Suppose I were to modify the task so that the subject received an electric shock every time he made an error. Then we could say that we had added shock-avoidance as a motive for quick learning. How might we expect this to affect the mean performance of the three groups? I would have expected the psychopaths to do as well or better than the other subjects because they are still motivated to learn the maze, just as they were without shock, and their lesser fear of the shock might make them less prone to shock-induced disruptions of their concentration.

To measure pure avoidance learning, however, what I needed was to somehow disassociate the motivations and reinforcement involved in learning the correct responses—let's call that the *manifest* task—from the motivations and reinforcement involved in avoiding the shocks—the *latent* task. This was accomplished by arranging things so that just one of the three incorrect levers at each choice-point produced a shock. The average person now wants to accomplish the manifest task, to learn the maze, but in the meanwhile he also wants to avoid those painful shocks if he can. That is, there is an implicit incentive for him to learn the latent task of avoiding the shock-producing errors. On the back of the machine, out of the subject's view, was a second counter that recorded the number of shocked errors committed on each traverse of the maze. The subjects in Groups 2 and 3 were expected to start out making about one-third of their errors on the shocked levers but to decrease this proportion toward zero as they learned which levers were dangerous on which trials. (I made this a little easier by arranging things so that the levers toward the left were more likely to be shocked than the two on the right.) The primary psychopaths, however, were expected to be less concerned about the shocks, to focus their attention on learning the correct levers, and therefore to show less avoidance of the errors that were punished by shock. Once again, this prediction from the low fear-quotient hypothesis was supported by the findings.

Disconfirming Low-Powered Theories

Theories in psychology, like my theory of primary psychopathy, tend to be low-powered theories that cannot make precise quantitative predictions. The best one can do typically is to say that Group A should be higher (or lower) than Group B on some measure or, perhaps, that Variable X should be positively correlated with Variable Y; how much higher or how strongly correlated can seldom be specified. But Group A is almost certain to be either higher or lower than Group B on any variable I specify; it would be reckless to suppose that psychopaths, for example, have precisely the same average height or IQ or musical ability as nonpsychopaths. The differences may be trivial and meaningless but, if we measure accurately and select large enough groups, we will almost certainly obtain a difference. This means that, if my theory predicts Group 1 to be lower than Group 2 on some variable, then I have about a 50:50 chance of being proved right—even if my theory is foolish and wrong! Therefore, unlike the physicist whose theory allows him to predict the mass of the Q-meson within very narrow limits and whose theory is strongly affirmed by a good experiment that gets a result within those limits, the psychologist's theories are seldom strongly supported by just one confirmed prediction (cf. Lykken, 1968b; Meehl, 1967). The confirmation of three separate predictions, on the other hand, provides more substantial reassurance that the theory may have something to it.

Replicating the Study

After publication of this study in 1957, its various components have been constructively replicated by others. Schachter and Latané (1964) replicated the APQ and avoidance-learning findings in a different Minnesota prison in 1964 and Schoenherr (1964) also replicated the avoidance results that same year. Hare (1965a) replicated the EDR conditioning finding in Canada and again later (Hare & Quinn, 1971); Ziskind, Syndulko, and Maltzman replicated it in 1978.[3] Schmauk (1970) replicated the avoidance finding, using both electric shock and "social disapproval" as a punishment, and then he proceeded to show that, when loss of money was substituted for electric shock as a punishment, the psychopaths avoided punished errors as well as the control subjects. This result emphasizes that the psychopath is perfectly capable of learning to avoid what he really wants to avoid (e.g., loss of money, in a prison setting) but he is likely not to bother to avoid eventualities to which he is indifferent.

The APQ measure of general fearfulness has had a less consistent replication history. In three out of five studies, the APQ failed to separate prison inmates classified as psychopathic from those that were not (the three failures were Borkovec, 1970; Hare, 1972; Schmauk, 1970). On the other hand, college students with low APQ scores report more minor legal offenses, more drinking, and more speeding tickets than more fearful students (Hauser, 1959; London, 1965). Delinquents in two institutions scored lower than normal adolescents and those scoring below the median had double the recidivism rate of those scoring high (Chabot, 1968; Higgins, 1973). At a juvenile corrections facility in California, adolescents with the lowest APQ scores were 66% White and from middle-class backgrounds; two thirds of them were heavily involved with drugs or alcohol by age 12 and, for 88%, there was total loss of parental control by age 14. The wards with average or fearful scores were only 12% White, from high-crime neighborhoods, not yet substance abusers, and only 20% were out of control by age 14. Based on these findings, the institution's psychologist concluded that there may be two routes to chronic delinquency, one via school failure, subcultural environment, and unstable

---

[3]Raine (1988) asserted that "some studies (see Passingham, 1972, for a review) failed to replicate Lykken's findings" (p. 236). Passingham, however, cited no failures to replicate Lykken's findings nor have I (or, apparently, Raine) been able to find any.

family, and the other resulting from a relatively fearless temperament (Timothy Miller, personal communication, September 1, 1983).

In another study with college student subjects, who also completed a neuroticism (N) scale and an adjective checklist ("Indicate which of the following adjectives do or do not describe yourself"), Katzenmeyer (1967) located 25 subjects with high scores on both the APQ (fearful) and on N (self-critical), another 25 with low scores on both, 25 with high APQ and low N, and 25 with low APQ and high N. The adjectives that reliably discriminated each quadrant from the other three are listed in Table 9.1 and the picture they paint is revealing. People who are both fearful and neurotic describe themselves as anxious, irritable, tense and touchy, whereas the fearful but low-N subjects say they are cautious, conservative, conventional, responsible, and unselfish—that is to say, well socialized. The subjects with low APQ scores attribute to themselves many of the qualities of the Cleckley psychopath but those with low N report the more attractive of those qualities whereas those with high N scores admit the less desirable aspects of the Cleckley syndrome.

Thus, the fearless low-N subjects say they are charming, confident, daring, humorous, but *not* awkward, nervous, or shy. The relatively fearless high-N people, in contrast, are bossy, deceitful, immature, quarrelsome, rebellious, selfish, but *not* cooperative, helpful, honest, persistent, or self-denying. This cross-classification nicely illustrates both the good and bad features of being either high or low on the fearfulness dimension, making the most of the tendency for high-N people to look at themselves critically whereas low-N people are more inclined to emphasize the positive.

Because the APQ really does measure fearfulness, unlike most "anxiety" scales, which measure neuroticism, Tellegen made use of some of the APQ items to construct the Harmavoidance scale of his MPQ, where it loads, not on the negative emotionality (or neuroticism) superfactor, but rather on (absence of) constraint. In a large study of the MPQ profiles of psychiatric patients, the group diagnosed as antisocial personality had the highest scores of any group on aggression, and the lowest on harmavoidance and constraint (DiLalla & Gottesman, 1993). People who are high on constraint find that much of the world is out-of-bounds for them, either because they disapprove of it or because they are afraid of it. They are conventional and aversively oversocialized. People low on constraint are relatively fearless, impulsive, nontraditional free spirits and quite a few of them are in jail.

Other Tests of the Low-Fear Hypothesis

Tolerance for Electric Shock

Numerous other studies have tested new and different predictions that also flow from the low fear hypothesis, many of them the work of Hare and his collaborators. Hare and Thorvaldson (1970) compared psychopathic and nonpsychopathic prisoners on their tolerance for electric shock. People who have worked with electric shock know that much of the aversiveness of moderate levels of shock is due to the unfamiliar quality of the sensation which, because it is so strange, elicits fear. Once

TABLE 9.1
How People in Each Quadrant, in the Cross-Classification of APQ and
Neuroticism Scores, Describe Themselves

High APQ ("Fearful")		Low APQ ("Fearless")	
	High Neurotic		
More:	Anxious	More:	Bossy
	Disorderly		Distractible
	High-strung		Deceiptful
	Irritable		Dissatisfied
	Tense		Immature
	Touchy		Impatient
			Opinionated
			Quarrelsome
			Rebellious
			Selfish
			Temperamental
Less:	Adaptable	Less:	Cooperative
	Calm		Friendly
	Cheerful		Helpful
	Contented		Honest
	Cool		Patient
	Healthy		Persistent
	Relaxed		Self-denying
			Thoughtful
	Low Neurotic		
More:	Catious	More:	Charming
	Conservative		Confident
	Conventional		Daring
	Foresighted		Deliberate
	Formal		Good-natured
	Handsome		Humorous
	Unselfish		Natural
	Wholesome		
Less:	Cynical	Less:	Awkward
	Demanding		Dependent
	Dominant		Nervous
	Frivolous		Preoccupied
	Indifferent		Shy
	Lazy		Talkative
	Rebellious		
	Restless		
	Sarcastic		
	Self-centered		

Note. Each adjective listed occurred significantly more (or less) often in that quadrant than in each of the other three.

one is accustomed to the sensation and fear is overcome, one can tolerate stronger shocks than before. The truth of this proposition is illustrated in the following anecdote.

In 1969, I was preparing to conduct a study of what I call the *preception* phenomenon, the ability to modulate the subjective strength or impact of a stimulus when that stimulus is made predictable in time (Lykken, 1962; Lykken & Tellegen, 1974; Lykken, Tellegen, & Macindoe, 1972). In the case of negative preception, the effect is to reduce the impact of an aversive stimulus such as a painful shock. I proposed to administer a series of trials in which the subject would hear a 1-second warning tone beginning just 5 seconds prior to a brief painful shock (the predictable trials) intermixed with unpredictable trials in which the shock might occur at any time from 0.5 to 15 seconds after the tone onset; the subjects knew in advance which type of trial was to come next. The impact of the shock was measured by means of the cortical response (brain wave response) evoked by the shock. I expected that, for most subjects, the slow components of the cortical response would be larger for strong than for moderate shocks, and also stronger for less than for more predictable shocks. In setting up this experiment, like all sensible psychological researchers, I called upon my wife to serve as a pilot subject. After wiring her up with the needed electrodes, I proceeded to ascertain her tolerance threshold for shock, increasing the intensity until she told me that it hurt; this was at a setting of 70 on the arbitrary 100-point scale of the stimulator. We then proceeded with the experimental run and, to my annoyance, there was no difference in the size of her cortical responses to the predictable and less predictable shocks. When I reported this to her, indignantly, she told me that if the shocks really had to hurt for the experiment to work, I had better increase the intensity because she was just ignoring them. Therefore, little by little, I turned the knob until it reached maximum intensity, 100. "That should work," she reported. We then ran the experiment again and got the expected result (see Fig. 9.1).

During the next week, I ran 12 male university students in this study. All of them refused shock levels higher than 75 and 9 of the 12 showed a clear preception effect.

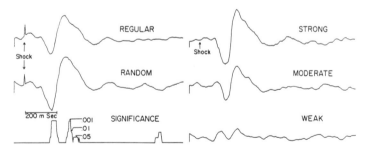

FIG. 9.1. These are Harriet Lykken's ERPs or brainwave responses to a series of electric shocks. Each segment is the average of eight trials. On the right are her responses to shocks of three different intensities that were presented at random intervals. This set of responses demonstrates that her ERPs do in fact get larger as the shock becomes more intense. On the left, above, are her responses to strong shocks delivered at regular intervals, so as to be predictable in time. On the left, below, are her responses to strong shocks delivered at random intervals, so as to be less predictable. The bottom line on the left plots the statistical significance of the difference between the two upper curves at each time point.

The following weekend, my three young sons visited the lab and wanted to try out the shock that they had heard about and which they knew their mother had taken at the maximum intensity of 100. The 14-year-old went first and made it all the way to 100. So did the 12-year-old. The 10-year-old boy kept going all the way to 85, higher than any of the university men.

Now my wife is tough—she delivered all three of her sons by natural childbirth without anesthesia—and it may be she was somewhat less frightened with me at the controls than some stranger. My sons were all protected (as well as competitively motivated) by their knowledge that their mother had "gone to 100," so I think it reasonable to conclude that they were simply less fearful than the men and the same objective shock therefore produced less of an impact. (I return to this notion of "preception" later on.)

Hare and Thorvaldson expected that psychopaths, being less fearful, could tolerate stronger shock than the control subjects but they also suspected that the psychopaths might not be willing to demonstrate their greater tolerance without incentive. Therefore, after each subject had indicated that the shock had reached as high a level as he was prepared to take, he was offered an inducement of cigarettes for each additional increment that he permitted. As expected, there were no group differences in the unmotivated thresholds but, once it had been made worth their while, the psychopaths tolerated significantly stronger shocks than the controls did. In later studies, Hare and his colleagues found that, compared to nonpsychopaths, psychopaths give smaller electrodermal responses to painful shock and to the insertion of a hypodermic needle.

EDR Activity While Anticipating Shock

Waid (1983) studied young adults scoring high or low on the So scale of the CPI; the low-scorers were denominated "delinquency-prone." Using a 5-second 92 db noise burst as his aversive stimulus, Waid found that low-So subjects gave smaller EDRs in anticipation of the blast and also to the blast itself. Using my "preception" paradigm, Waid found that another sample of low-So subjects also showed decreased EDR responses to the noise but the effect was as great when the blast was coincident with the warning signals as when it came later, indicating that the "delinquency-prone" subjects were not achieving their decreased responsiveness by more efficient preception. Lippert and Senter (1966) compared the spontaneous EDRs emitted by two groups of adolescent delinquents, one diagnosed as psychopathic and the other as adjustment reaction. Spontaneous EDRs are thought to be reactions to internal stimuli and they increase in frequency when subjects are tense, excited, or apprehensive. The group differences were small under resting conditions but, while the subjects were waiting in anticipation of an electric shock, the nonpsychopaths showed a sharp increase in spontaneous EDRs whereas the psychopathic group did not. Sutker (1970) found that the amplitude of these spontaneous anticipatory EDRs was smaller in psychopaths than in nonpsychopathic subjects.

Hare's Countdown Paradigm

Using a rather similar anticipation paradigm that he first developed in 1965, Hare measured palmar skin conductance while the subject watches a counter or other indicator moving slowly and inexorably toward a point at which the subject knows he will receive an aversive stimulus. This "countdown" paradigm has replaced my conditioning paradigm because it is simpler and better. Pavlovian conditioning in humans is hard to disentangle from the effects upon responding of the subject's expectations about stimulus contingencies. With Hare's method, all the subjects have the same accurate appraisal of the situation so that their physiological arousal tends to follow a more consistent and unambiguous course. In numerous studies, using both shock and an aversively loud noise as the anticipated stimulus, Hare has found that psychopaths show substantially less palmar sweating in anticipation of the noxious stimulus and that the increase in electrical conductance starts later and does not rise so high as in control subjects (Hare, 1965b, 1966; Hare & Craigen, 1974; Hare, Frazelle, & Cox, 1978). In a recent and detailed review of the relationship between electrodermal activity and antisocial behavior, Fowles (1993) concludes that: "there are many findings that support an inference of electrodermal hyporeactivity among psychopaths. At present, the strongest findings seem interpretable as reflecting a weak response to the anticipation of punishment ... " (p. 237; see also Fowles & Missel, 1994).

THE STATUS OF THE LOW-FEAR HYPOTHESIS

The idea that the syndrome of primary psychopathy could result from the rearing by typical parents of a child who is normal in all respects save for a below-average endowment of innate fearfulness still seems to me, after 40 years, to have much to recommend it. It has been tested in a variety of studies in numerous laboratories and it has survived these tests. It gives a plausible account of the various components of the syndrome, more plausible I think than any of the competing theories. Moreover, unlike any of the competing hypotheses, most of which assume some qualitative innate defect of the central nervous system rather than a simple parametric difference, the low fear hypothesis is compatible with the fact that about half of the MZ cotwins of psychopathic probands do not meet criteria for psychopathy themselves.[4] The low-fear hypothesis does not claim that persons with the genetic talent for psychopathy must fail to become adequately socialized but merely that they are more likely to fail, given typical parenting. It is not difficult to imagine circumstances in which even MZ twins might gradually diverge in the warmth of their relationships with their parents—the "good twin, bad twin" situation—with the good twin being positively reinforced for his comparatively tractable behavior and developing a socialized self-image that he values and wishes

---

[4]No twin study of psychopathy based on the Cleckley criteria has yet been done, however. It is possible, although I think it unlikely, that MZ concordance for psychopathy defined by Hare's PCL might be higher than 50%.

to maintain. Theories that posit a deep-seated defect of inhibitory control or of language processing or the like would seem to require that the cotwins of primary psychopaths must be psychologically abnormal themselves. Because the low-fear hypothesis is a developmental theory based on principles of gene–environment correlation and interaction, it is compatible with the clinical observation that there seem to be many individuals with the genetic talent for psychopathy and who manifest some of the facets of the syndrome who, because of special talent or opportunity, manage to become tolerably socialized and even to achieve great worldly success—as explorers (Sir Richard Burton), military heroes (John Paul Vann, Chuck Yeager), celebrity lawyers (Roy Cohn), financiers (Charles Keating, II), chief judges (Sol Wachtler), or even as prime ministers (Winston Churchill) or presidents (Lyndon Johnson).

Nevertheless, since it was first proposed in 1957, the low-fear hypothesis has not been taken very seriously, even by researchers whose own findings have contributed to its empirical support. Because the theory has never been refuted, I attribute this neglect to two factors: First, I have to confess to having been a neglectful parent of my (adopted) brainchild, having sent it forth on its own without further support after that initial study. Even better mousetraps need to be actively merchandised before a doubtful public will accept them. Second, there seems to be an irresistible tendency for psychopathologists to assume that underlying every syndrome there must be a lesion, that there must be something qualitatively wrong with the psychopath's brain. Now that the field is coming to realize that people create their own environments and that merely quantitative differences in genetic temperament can culminate, over years of development, in qualitative differences in psychological adjustment or achievement, perhaps the time is ripe for the low-fear hypothesis of primary psychopathy to be reconsidered. There may well be other etiologies leading to the psychopathy syndrome; it would be rash to suppose that a low fear endowment accounts for every case. Yet, it seems to me at least equally rash to deny that this simple factor could account for some cases and I find it hard to believe that it does not in fact account for many.

10

Primary and Secondary Psychopathy

THE CONTRIBUTIONS OF FOWLES AND GRAY

I have always been leery of psychologists who invoke complex neurophysiological models to account for the facts of psychopathology. We know of course that brain mechanisms must underlie the phenomena that we study as psychologists but the human brain is still largely uncharted territory, our certain knowledge about on a par with those 16th-century maps of the New World, "Here be monsters!" Yet psychologists are inclined to feel that physiological concepts are somehow more scientific than psychological ones. One of the few examples of such physiologizing that has seemed to me to be productive is Fowles' elaboration of the neurobehavioral motivation theory propounded by the British psychologist, Jeffrey Gray (Fowles, 1980, 1987, 1988). Perhaps this is because Gray's theory (1975, 1987a) is firmly rooted in psychological research (mostly animal research) and consists of a functional mechanism, situated in the "conceptual nervous system" rather than in the central nervous system of the neurophysiologist, a mechanism that can account for many research findings and which has successfully predicted many others. Gray has then proceeded to try to coordinate the components of his mechanism to known brain structures and processes, to marry the conceptual with the central nervous systems in the hope that each may somewhat illuminate the other.

Gray's (1987b) model distinguishes three separate systems for the control of emotional behavior:

> a fight/flight system, responsible for organizing behavior in response to uncondi-
> tioned punishment or unconditioned nonreward; a behavioral inhibition system (BIS),
> responsible for organizing behavior in response to stimuli that signal these uncondi-
> tioned aversive events; and an approach system (now often call the behavioral
> activation system, or BAS, in Fowles' terminology), responsible for organizing
> behavior in response to stimuli that signal unconditioned rewards or nonpunishment.
> (p. 495)

Gray further postulated that there are innate individual differences in the activity or sensitivity of each of these three systems. Thus people with hyperactive fight–flight systems respond more intensely to unconditioned aversive stimuli such as pain. People with an active BIS respond especially strongly to conditioned stimuli that have been associated with aversive stimuli in the past. An interesting illustration of the independence of these first two systems is the fact that analgesics such as morphine reduce the response to actual pain but do not diminish the fear reaction, mediated by the BIS, in response to conditioned cues or signals for pain. Conversely, anti-anxiety drugs or tranquilizers have the obverse effect of reducing fear but not the unconditioned distress produced by pain. People with a strong BAS respond with greater-than-average intensity or enthusiasm to conditioned stimuli associated with reward or pleasure and also to the experience associated with the escape from a threat situation.

The BAS responds to signals of reward that elicit either *hope* (incentive cues for positive reinforcers such as food or sex) or *relief* (e.g., cues for cessation of pain or the achievement of safety). The effect of the BAS response to such signals of hope or relief is to activate behavior toward these goals. The BIS responds to signals of *punishment* and also to signals of *frustrative nonreward*; the effects of the BIS are to inhibit activity, including the activity of the BAS. The fight–flight system is associated with the reticular activating system of the brain stem and is activated by both the BAS and the BIS, but the latter two systems can also be regarded as specialized arousal systems in their own right. BIS activation is experienced as anxiety or frustration but Gray argues that these states are essentially identical and are affected in the same way by psychotropic drugs. Thus, stimuli associated with punishment or with frustration activate the BIS and produce slowing or inhibition of the responses leading to that punishment or nonreward. The BIS is specifically inhibited by alcohol, barbiturates, and the anti-anxiety drugs such as benzodiazepine, so these agents reduce the BIS' inhibition of punished behavior; these drugs therefore tend to inhibit passive avoidance and also the extinction of previously rewarded responses.

The subjective effects of BAS arousal—hope or relief—also are equivalent; whether I am hurrying home to get my dinner or to escape a swarm of bees, the anticipation feels much the same and the achievement of my goal is similarly rewarding in both cases. Stimuli associated with pleasure activate the BAS which tends to instigate approach or consummatory behavior. Some stimulant drugs, such as cocaine, may activate the BAS directly.

Conflict

Approach–avoidance conflict involves an opposition of the BAS and the BIS and, as Miller (1944) pointed out, as an individual moves toward some goal, the avoidance impulse starts later but increases faster than does the impulse to approach. The sight of a forbidden cookie (or sex object) activates both systems, the BAS tending toward approach and the BIS toward avoidance. The approach gradient (illustrated in Fig. 7.1) is less steep than the avoidance gradient; this means that, from the vantage point of the kitchen door, the cookie attracts more than it repels and the child approaches but, when he gets too close, the BIS prevails and he backs off. The height of the gradients at this (or any) point is a measure of the arousal level of the respective systems. If the child is very hungry and also very fearful of the consequences of cookie-stealing, then his interaction with the cookie will involve the clash of two strong forces and, whichever one prevails, the experience will be more upsetting for him than if either his fear or his appetite had been weaker.

Increasing BAS activity, either by increased incentive (a better cookie) or drive (greater hunger) or by appropriate drugs, makes the approach gradient steeper so that it crosses the avoidance gradient at a higher point (see Fig. 7.2). That means, paradoxically, that the child with the stronger positive motivation gets more anxious in a conflict situation because he gets closer to the cookie before the gradients cross and he stops or turns back. Attenuating BIS activity with, say, alcohol may permit the goal to be achieved because this flattens the avoidance gradient, thus reducing the inhibition of the approach response.

Active Versus Passive Avoidance

Passive avoidance means inhibiting previously punished behavior; it is associated with anxiety and is managed by the BIS. In Gray's theory, punishment and "frustrative nonreward" (the omission of an expected reward) are functionally equivalent. Suppose I am accustomed to reaching into the cookie jar when I get home from school. If, today, when I reach in for a cookie and encounter instead a mouse trap that snaps painfully on my finger, I am less likely tomorrow to emit that usual response. By the mechanism of Pavlovian conditioning, the punishment today has attached a fear response to the impulse to reach into the jar. The next time I feel that impulse, the BIS is activated; this produces a feeling of anxiety, it inhibits the BAS and the approach responses that the BAS controls, and I am likely to give the cookie jar a miss.

Gray argued that finding the cookie jar empty, with no mousetrap but also with none of the cookies I have come to expect, has essentially the same effect. It is well known that the withholding of the expected reward tends to produce extinction of the approach response. In Gray's theory, this frustrative nonreward has the same effect as punishment; the BIS is activated, the BAS is inhibited, and a feeling of distress (anxiety) is produced. One piece of evidence for the equivalence of punishment and nonreward is that anti-anxiety drugs moderate the effects of both. Tomorrow, if I have had a couple of drinks before I visit the kitchen, I am more likely to try the cookie jar again, whether today I was punished by the mousetrap or frustrated by finding an empty jar.

Active Avoidance

Active avoidance is actively escaping from danger. The standard theory for explaining active avoidance held that punishment produces Pavlovian conditioning of a fear response to stimuli present at the time of punishment and that any action that takes the animal away from those conditioned fear stimuli is rewarded by cessation of the fear. Gray cited numerous studies that show this theory to be incomplete. Specifically, he argued that, just as fear can become conditioned to danger signals—which are stimuli associated with punishment—so also can "relief" become conditioned to "safety" signals—stimuli associated with the escape from fear. The mouse encounters a cat (danger signal) and flees into a nearby hole (active avoidance response); the mouse's fear is reduced by this escape from the danger signals and this "relief" response of fear reduction becomes conditioned to the stimuli of being safe inside the hole.

The addition of this relief response idea to the traditional theory allows Gray to explain phenomena that make trouble for the standard model. For one thing, conditioned safety signals can reduce fear in new situations. Thus, for example, a young child who is frightened in a new environment can be comforted by holding the teddy bear or the quilt from his bed, safety signals associated with a place where he has felt secure. Second, safety signals can be reinforcing even when fear is negligible; that is, stimuli associated with escape from fear or the avoidance of expected punishment act like stimuli that have been associated with positive rewards, they serve as rewards in their own right. This is important because it helps explain why active avoidance behaviors are so resistant to extinction.

Consider the shuttle box, an apparatus with two chambers connected by a doorway; the laboratory rat must learn to move from the black chamber to the white chamber (or vice-versa) whenever the flashing light indicates that shock is imminent. Moving from one chamber to the other is active avoidance and is under BAS control; each successful avoidance of the shock is rewarded by the conditioned relief response. Before this active avoidance response is learned, however, the animal will have been shocked a few times in each compartment. This means that the active avoidance response will be opposed by BIS inhibition because the response of entering the other chamber now involves approaching a place where the animal has previously been shocked. Thus, active avoidance is opposed by passive avoidance in this situation. Therefore, and this is the kind of finding that helps confirm Gray's formulation, one can speed up shuttle box performance—enhance active avoidance of the shock—by reducing BIS activity, using anti-anxiety drugs.

As indicated earlier, an active avoidance response, once established, is exceedingly hard to extinguish. In the shuttle-box experiment, for example, dogs or rats will continue to perform flawlessly for hundreds of trials without experiencing additional shocks and also without exhibiting signs of fear. Gray explained this resistance to extinction by pointing out that the avoidance response is reinforced each time by the safety signals that accompany avoidance. Studies have shown that the rewarding effect of safety signals is relatively independent of the amount of fear elicited by the warning signals and is itself unusually resistant to extinction (Gray, 1987a). This may help explain why most of us "do the right thing" habitually without feeling any fear of the punishment that might ensue if we failed to do so, why I habitually go in and pay after filling up my tank with gas instead of just driving off, for example. I do not have to experience the temptation to drive off, followed by a fear of feeling guilty or of being arrested, in order to maintain this behavior because "doing the right thing" is a safety signal that is inherently reinforcing. (If one also takes pride in being a good citizen, and feels superior to those who are less good, then doing the right thing is doubly reinforcing.)

Many nonpsychopathic children will now and then react aggressively to parental interference: being told to do something or to stop doing something or being disciplined may provoke an emotional display ranging from whining and crying to a violent temper tantrum. If the parent then backs off and lets the child win, that aggressive behavior becomes a successful method of active avoidance. Gray's theory and data tell us that, once entrenched, this tendency to avoid by aggression will be hard to extinguish. As Patterson's research has demonstrated (see chap. 14), such "coercive cycles" are an important method by which little sociopaths can be manufactured in the home.

Impulsivity

If we define *impulsivity* as behavioral excess or as engaging actively in goal-seeking or approach behavior even though the path may be a risky one, then we might get impulsive behavior either from BAS activity that is too strong or from BIS activity that is too weak.

Fowles (and Gray himself) suggested that psychopathy might be understood as a consequence of a weak or deficient BIS. Because BIS activation is associated with anxiety, a weak BIS means a relative absence of anxiety or fear. A weak BIS means weak inhibition of behavior either in response to punishment or in response to nonreward. Moreover, remembering the shuttle box example, risky *active* avoidance responses, such as lying or assaulting the source of the threat, are more likely if the BIS is weakened. Finally, the experimental findings discussed in chapter 9—weak EDR anticipation of punishment, and poor passive avoidance— are also compatible with the weak BIS hypothesis.

Notice, however, that impulsive psychopathic *behavior* results, according to Gray's model, whenever either BIS inhibition is too weak or when BAS activation is too strong. That means we could get two types of psychopathic behavior, one resulting from a weak BIS and the other from a BAS that is unusually active. The weak BIS would produce a Cleckley or primary psychopath for the same reasons discussed in chapter 9; the weak-BIS model is equivalent to what I have more mundanely referred to as the low fear hypothesis. Because of his weak BIS, the transgressions of the primary psychopath will be accompanied by relatively little emotional arousal. In a relatively tranquil environment, he will tend to be underaroused and bored and, for that reason, he is likely to seek out a more stimulating environment, one that may involve greater temptation and also greater risk.

The Secondary Psychopath

The individual with a normal BIS but an unusually active BAS might resemble what Blackburn and others called a secondary psychopath. He will not show weak electrodermal arousal in anticipation of shock nor poor passive avoidance in a laboratory task that does not strongly engage his interest; in the Lykken maze task, for example, he may be just as concerned about those shocks as any normal person would. On the other hand, he is likely to show poor passive avoidance in the real world when he is confronted with incentives that attract him strongly enough to overcome his fear. This secondary psychopath may therefore show considerable anxiety in relation to his psychopathic behavior because his BIS is normal and it is his overactive BAS that pushes him into stressful situations.

Fowles pointed out that, because people tend to create their own environments, people with active BIS systems may actually lead low stress lives because they will tend to avoid stressful situations; that is, in responding to self-report measures of "trait-anxiety" or neuroticism, they may describe themselves as generally calm and at peace with their world. This is how the high-fearful, low-neurotic subjects described themselves in the APQ study summarized in Table 8.1. Conversely, people with active BAS systems may tend to lead stressful lives because the pleasures they so avidly seek may tend to be surrounded by higher levels of risk. The reactions expected of persons on a variety of measures whose BIS or BAS systems are unusually strong or unusually weak are summarized in Table 10.1.

Fowles Redux

In his most recent formulation, Fowles (Fowles & Missel, 1994) analyzed the proposal by Crider (1994) that electrodermal *lability-stability* measures a personality dimension that is associated with psychopathy. An early longitudinal study by Jones (1950, 1960) involved 11 laboratory assessments of 100 adolescents who

TABLE 10.1
The Expected Effects of Having a Strong or Weak BIS or BAS

Variable	BIS		BAS	
	Strong	Weak	Strong	Weak
Fearfulness	High	Low	Avg.	Avg.
MPQ constraint	High	Low	Avg.	High
Passive avoidance (lab situation)	High	Low	Avg.	High
Passive avoidance (real life)	High	Low	Low	Avg.
Active avoidance	Avg.?	High	High	Low
Impulsiveness	Low	High	High	Low
Negative emotionality	Avg.	Avg.	High[a]	Avg.
Positive emotionality	Avg.	Avg.	High	Low
Drugs of abuse	Downers	Uppers	Downers	Uppers
Sensation seeking	Low	High	High	Avg.
Extinction after nonreward	Fast	Slow	Slow?	Fast?

Note. If one system is strong or weak, it is assumed in the table that the other system is average.

[a]If the strong BAS leads to risk-taking and antisocial behavior, the associated stress is likely to elevate negative emotionality.

were followed from age 12 to age 18. In each assessment, EDRs were recorded during a free association task in which the stimuli were words of varying emotional significance. By averaging over the 11 assessments, highly reliable estimates were obtained of each youngster's EDR reactivity or lability. Then the 20 most and 20 least reactive subjects were compared in terms of staff and peer ratings of their personality characteristics. The low-reactive subjects were found to be more talkative, animated, assertive, aggressive, and attention-seeking than the high-reactive group.

In a related study, Block (1957) measured EDR reactivity of 70 medical students in a lie-detector situation. Once again the 20 most and 20 least reactive subjects were selected for comparison on an 18-hour personality assessment involving Q-sort ratings and Adjective Checklist ratings by several independent staff psychologists. The low EDR-reactors were found to be hostile, independent, critical, and rebellious while the high-reactors were more submissive, inclined to withdraw in the face of adversity, vulnerable, fearful, ethically consistent, and more easily exploited. On the Adjective Checklist, the reactors were cautious, dependent, mannerly, idealistic, and suggestible, whereas the nonreactors were clever, cool, evasive, ingenious, leisurely, opportunistic, and realistic.

Fowles and Missel (1994) agreed with Crider (1993) that such findings strongly suggest the existence of a normal personality dimension, associated with EDR reactivity to stimuli of intermediate arousal value (the verbal stimuli in both the Jones and the Block studies were less intense than painful shocks but substantially more evocative than, e.g., meaningless tones). Because normals who are EDR low-reactors in these situations are described as assertive, aggressive, rebellious, cool, and opportunistic, whereas high-reactors are fearful, vulnerable, passive, and ethically consistent, it seems reasonable to suppose that it is the low-reactive individuals who would be at risk for psychopathy. Crider, following Raine and Venables (1984), suggested that the low-reactors (EDR stabiles) might be "schizoid psychopaths" but Fowles and Missel (quite rightly, in my view) found little support for this idea in the research literature generally or even in the evidence advanced by its proponents.

Fowles and Missel were uncertain, however, as to whether low EDR reactivity to emotional words on a word-association test, or to questions on a lie detector test (really a guilty knowledge test, see chap. 11), can be interpreted the same way as low EDR reactivity to threat of physical punishment, as an indicant of weak BIS reactivity. It seems to me that the answer to this question clearly is "Yes." An average subject hooked up to a polygraph and required to quickly associate to emotional words, or to try to conceal which number or color he or she has chosen, feels a certain mild anxiety or risk of self-exposure with each stimulus. The apprehension is not as great as one feels when a painful shock impends but it is qualitatively similar. If one were alone in the laboratory responding to tape-recorded words or questions, knowing that no one was monitoring the polygraph record and drawing inferences about one's secret self, the result would almost certainly be a change in the low-reactive direction. Pending someone's doing such an experiment, I am satisfied that the data reviewed by Fowles and Missel are fully compatible with the Fowles–Gray–Lykken theory that (at least one form of) primary psychopathy is a consequence of a weak BIS which, in the absence of unusually skillful parenting, is likely to lead to a failure of normal socialization.

It seems to me, in fact, that the Fowles–Gray–Lykken theory provides the firmest available foundation on which to build the future experimental study of psychopathic personality. It assimilates the Lykken low-fear theory, now the "weak-BIS" theory; it suggests a second type of secondary psychopathy, the "strong-BAS" individual; and it may also suggest a third type in which it is the fight–flight mechanism that is congenitally underactive. It is possible that there may also be psychopaths whose machinery for the processing of language is somehow compromised as Hare believes (see chap. 11); "septal-defect" psychopaths, as Newman and Gorenstein suggested (see chap. 12); and "hysterical" psychopaths with hypertrophied mechanisms for repression or dissociation or "preception," mechanisms that are exhaustible through overuse (chap. 13). These other types, if they exist, will require different theoretical models, or elaborations of the Gray model. It would be prudent for investigators to keep in mind the probability that experimental subjects selected by means of the Hare PCL are likely to comprise a genus rather than a single species.

THE POTENTIATED STARTLE PARADIGM

An interesting new technique in psychopathy research is to be found in a recent study using Lang's startle reflex paradigm (Lang, Bradley, & Cuthbert, 1990). The subject views a series of slides depicting attractive or heartwarming scenes (e.g., sunsets, puppies), neutral or utilitarian scenes (e.g., a hair dryer, a workman), and disturbing or frightening scenes (e.g., an accident victim, a vicious dog). Unpredictably during this slide viewing, loud but very brief noise pips are presented that tend to elicit a reflex eyeblink response. Electrodes on the subject's forehead measure the activity of the corrugator muscle that causes frowning while another electrode beneath the left eye measures the eyeblink. What is interesting about this paradigm is that Lang and his colleagues have consistently found that the emotional valence of the slide being viewed modulates the strength of the startle reflex. Compared to the neutral slides, pleasant or positively valenced slides produce weaker startle while disturbing or negatively valenced slides produce stronger startle.

Patrick et al. (1993) used this paradigm with three groups of male felons who had been convicted of sex offenses. Group P included those who had the highest scores on Hare's PCL (discussed in chap. 8), Group NP comprised those with the lowest scores, while a mixed Group M had intermediate scores. Groups NP and M both showed the pattern of startle reflex modulation found in normal subjects, weakest startle during the positive slides and strongest during the negative ones. Both groups showed a marked increase in corrugator or frowning activity while watching the negative slides. Group P, in contrast, did not frown during the negative slides and their startle reflex diminished for both the positive and negative slides as compared with the neutrals. That is to say, the psychopathic subjects behaved as if the negative slides merely engaged their interest, like the positive scenes, without at the same time causing an emotional disturbance of the kind that, in the other subjects, potentiated their startle response.

The authors pointed out that their results are compatible with Lykken's low-fear hypothesis and to the related theory propounded by Gray. That is, pictures of accident victims, mad dogs, and other scary scenes are interesting and would not produce frowning or potentiate startle if they did not generate a fear response. Thus, an experienced surgeon might respond to the accident victim slide just as the psychopath does because his or her prior experience has extinguished the emotional response to this type of stimulus.

If this interpretation is correct, then normal subjects, who typically display augmented startle while viewing disturbing pictures, should not show this augmented reaction if premedicated with an anti-anxiety drug. Patrick (1994) tested this prediction and found that diazepam (Valium) blocked startle potentiation in a dose-dependent way. Interestingly, however, it was found that both skin conductance and heart rate responses were reliably greater to the aversive and to the neutral slides whether the subjects had received diazepam or a placebo, suggesting that the startle potentiation effect may be a more sensitive or more specific indicant of fear differences than the autonomic variables.

Most importantly, the psychopathy finding has been replicated "constructively" (Lykken, 1968b) and therefore can probably be trusted. Patrick (1994) and his colleagues assessed a large sample of inmates at a federal prison in Florida using Hare's PCL plus other self-report temperament scales to identify four groups of inmates: 18 nonpsychopaths; 14 *detached* offenders, who were high on PCL–1 but not on PCL–2 and most resembled the Cleckley prototype; 8 antisocial inmates, who had a background of persistent antisocial behavior (were high on PCL–2) but without the emotionally detached personality of the psychopath (not high on PCL–1; these would be called sociopaths in the usage employed in this book); and 18 PCL-denominated psychopaths, who showed both the antisocial behavior history of the sociopath (high on PCL–2) and the emotional detachment of the psychopath (high PCL–1).

In this study, the aversive slide viewing was replaced by something similar to Hare's countdown paradigm. During an initial baseline phase, subjects viewed a simple visual stimulus for 6-second periods during some of which an acoustic startle probe (a 50-msec, 50 db noise burst) was presented. In the test period, the subjects knew that these 6-second intervals would each terminate in an aversive noise blast (a 500-msec, 110 db noise blast). Startle probes were presented during 9 of the 14 blast-anticipation periods and also during 6 of the intertrial intervals. A pilot study with normal subjects had shown that this blast-anticipation situation reliably produced augmented startle.

As expected, the psychopathic and detached groups showed reliably less startle-potentiation than the nonpsychopathic and the antisocial subjects. These findings confirm once again that the psychopath's anticipation of a disturbing or aversive event seems to generate less fearful apprehension than the same situation produces in nonpsychopaths and also that this difference is associated with the psychopathic personality (high PCL–1) rather than with a history of antisocial behavior (PCL–2). The consistency of such findings has been great enough as to suggest the possibility of creating a psychophysiological diagnostic test that might prove to have greater validity than existing procedures based on clinical ratings or on self-report.

11

Further Contributions of R. D. Hare

Since 1965, the most productive and significant player among psychopathy researchers has been Robert Hare, at the University of British Columbia. Hare's early work replicated and extended my 1957 study, providing additional support for the conclusion that the Cleckley psychopath experiences less fearful apprehension of impending aversive stimulation than does the typical nonpsychopathic prison inmate. Realizing that studies of "the psychopath" could not hope to produce cumulative, useful results unless different investigators were studying roughly the same species, Hare proceeded to develop the PCL (see chap. 8) with which it is possible to identify among prison inmates a reasonably homogeneous core group of primary psychopaths.

Heart Rate Changes During the Hare Countdown

We have also seen that one of Hare's important innovations was the simple but revealing "countdown" paradigm. The subject hears a recorded voice counting backwards "9" through "0" at intervals of about 3 seconds, having been told in advance that an aversive stimulus (a painful shock in the good old days or a loud noise blast in these weak, piping times of human subjects committees) will be delivered coincident with "0" (Hare, 1966).

One of the most replicable findings in all of experimental psychopathology is that primary psychopaths will show relatively little electrodermal arousal during the Hare countdown, whereas control subjects, including prison inmates denominated nonpsychopaths by the Hare PCL, will show higher arousal from the start of the countdown with a larger and earlier increase in skin conductance as the count approaches 0.

When he began monitoring heart rate (HR) as well as skin conductance during this paradigm, Hare made the intriguing discovery that the same psychopaths who were evincing minimal EDR activity, and therefore probably little premonitory

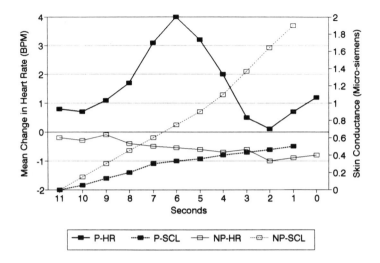

FIG. 11.1. Autonomic changes during countdown (psychopaths vs. nonpsychopaths). The solid lines show how the skin conductance level (SCL) increases during the Hare countdown, much more for nonpsychopaths than for psychopaths (all subjects are prison inmates). The dashed lines show a remarkable increase in heart rate (HR) for the psychopaths during the same countdown (redrawn from Hare, 1987b).

apprehension of the aversive stimulus, were simultaneously producing greater cardiac acceleration than the control subjects; see Fig. 11.1. This phenomenon has been repeatedly replicated.[1]

Schachter and Latané (1964) previously reported paradoxical increases in HR in psychopaths or relatively fearless normal subjects, and Valins (1966) had found that normals with low scores on a measure of fearfulness anticipated weak tones or shocks with decreased HR but loud tones or strong shocks were awaited with increased HR; Valins's more fearful subjects showed deceleration even prior to the strong stimuli. I had suggested that these findings might be understood in terms of the earlier report by J. Lacey and B. Lacey that normal subjects show cardiac deceleration when attempting to detect or respond to external stimulation but acceleration when the external stimulation was aversive or distracting (B. Lacey & J. Lacey, 1974; Lykken, 1967). Perhaps cardiac acceleration is a "defensive reflex," as Sokolov (1960) contended, and reflects the operation of an inhibitory control mechanism that diminishes the impact of an aversive stimulus.

It had been demonstrated by Lykken et al. (1972) that relatively fearless subjects show more HR acceleration than average subjects do prior to a painful electric shock but then respond less to the shock itself (see Fig. 11.2). Hare (1978b) suggested that, if increased HR is indicative of some sort of inhibitory or coping

---

[1]Hare and Quinn (1971); Hare (1978a, 1978b, 1982); Hare and Craigen (1974); Hare, Frazelle, and Cox (1978); and Tharp, Maltzman, Syndulko, and Ziskind (1980) found that psychopaths (compulsive gamblers) showed higher HR during the countdown but the differences were not statistically significant.

response, then a reduction in the concurrent EDA activity may reflect the success of that coping response.

Ogloff and Wong (1990) recently modified the Hare countdown by providing a response button that, if pressed just after the "1" count, would prevent the aversive stimulus (a loud tone) from occurring. Ogloff and Wong found that criminal

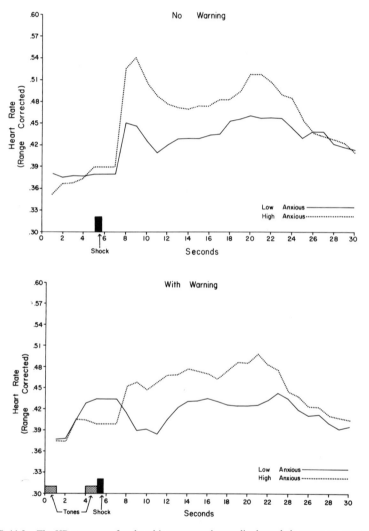

FIG. 11.2. The HR response of male subjects grouped accordingly to their scores on a test of fearfulness or "anxiety." At the top, both groups have similar HRs before the shock but the more fearful men show a much stronger HR response after the shock is delivered. In the lower panel, the strong electric shock is made predictable by preceding it with two warning tones. Now the least fearful subjects show higher HRs while waiting for the shock but no reaction at all to the shock itself (both groups accelerate some 10 seconds after the shock, associated with making verbal ratings of shock intensity). Modified from Lykken et al. (1972).

psychopaths showed the usual low levels of EDR activity during both the normal and modified countdown but showed cardiac acceleration only in the former situation where the aversive stimulus could not be prevented. These results seem to confirm that cardiac acceleration shown by psychopaths and other low-fear subjects in anticipation of an aversive stimulus does in fact reflect some sort of reflexive coping response that adaptively inhibits anticipatory arousal perhaps because, based on our 1972 "preception" findings, this coping response reduces the impact of the aversive stimulus. When an operant response is available that prevents the aversive stimulus entirely, the coping response signaled by the HR increase is unnecessary and does not occur.

It is apparent that cardiac acceleration is an ambiguous indicant that does not always betoken the operation of an effective inhibitory response. Ogloff and Wong's nonpsychopathic prisoners showed elevated skin conductance and cardiac acceleration during not only the standard countdown when the stimulus was unavoidable but also somewhat smaller increases in both variables even during the modified paradigm when the aversive stimulus could be avoided by a button press. During the normal countdown, the HR increase was in fact larger for the non-psychopaths than for the psychopaths (unlike earlier findings by the Hare group). The NP subjects showed greater HR lability than the psychopaths so that range correction (Lykken, 1972) indicated that the psychopaths accelerated 36% of their range compared to only 21% for the nonpsychopaths; thus, the Ogloff and Wong results do agree with those of the Hare group when range-corrected. There is no denying, however, that fearful subjects sometimes show strong HR increases together with marked EDA activity before, and strong reactions after, the anticipated aversive stimulus so it is clear that the occurance of an effective coping response cannot be reliably inferred from anticipatory cardiac acceleration. What the Ogloff and Wong study appears to indicate is that, in subjects who anticipate an aversive stimulus with little EDR activity and, therefore, with little fearful arousal, anticipatory cardiac acceleration is probably associated with some sort of inhibitory coping response because the acceleration disappears when such coping is rendered unnecessary by the availability of an effective operant avoidance response.

Can Psychopaths Beat the Lie Detector?

Because most psychopaths are experienced and accomplished liars and, because they tend to be less apprehensive in response to threat, one might suppose that their physiological responses while lying would be weaker than those shown by non-psychopaths. Waid and Orne (1982) subjected "delinquency-prone" young adults (selected for low scores on the CPI–So scale) to a mock lie detector test and found that their electrodermal responses while lying were significantly weaker than those of control subjects, both during the test proper and while the polygraph was turned off and the subjects thought that their responses were not being monitored.

Raskin and Hare (1978), however, found that psychopathic prison inmates were as likely to fail a standard control-question polygraph test (CQT) as were non-psychopathic inmates in a mock-crime situation in which inmates successful in beating the lie detector could win $20. Patrick and Iacono (1989) got similar results in a different prison and using better controls.

One fails such a polygraph test if the relevant or "Did-you- do-it?" questions produce stronger physiological reactions (EDRs, blood pressure changes, irregular breathing) than the "control" questions (e.g., "Prior to last year, did you ever lie to get out of trouble?") In real-life criminal investigations, suspects are inclined to regard the relevant questions as strong, aversive stimuli whether they are guilty or not; that is why an innocent suspect has nearly a 50–50 chance of failing a conventional polygraph test when administered by the police.[2] Both because of his weaker fear response, and because of the desensitizing effect of his extensive experience in lying, the psychopath should respond less strongly to both the relevant and the control questions of the CQT. In the studies by Raskin and Hare and by Patrick and Iacono, however, the PCL-designated psychopaths who were "guilty" of the mock crimes tended to respond more strongly to the relevant than to the control questions and were correctly classified as deceptive.

I am not persuaded, however, that these findings can be safely extrapolated to real-life criminal interrogation. We should recall that: "When a felon's not engaged in his employment … his capacity for innocent enjoyment is just as great as any honest man's." In real life, the relevant or "Did- you-do-it?" question elicits a strong reaction from the nonpsychopathic crook because he is afraid of discovery and punishment. In the mock crime situation, only the control questions (e.g., "Have you ever betrayed someone who trusted you?") are veridical because the relevant questions refer to mock crimes the subject committed under orders and cannot be punished for. (That is why most laboratory studies of the lie detector produce many fewer false–positive errors than in real life.) Psychopaths, however, should not be greatly disturbed by such references to their past misdeeds and should not respond strongly to the "control" questions. We must remember, however, that the psychopath likes games, takes pride in being a good liar, and would like to show off by beating the polygraph. That appetitive motivation may cause the psychopath to respond more strongly to the relevant questions in these gamelike conditions and thus fail the lie detector.

Patrick and Iacono attempted to induce a sense of threat in their subjects by telling them that the names of those who failed the test would be posted and that too many failures would cause all participants to lose the promised rewards. Because some of these men were aggressive and dangerous, this manipulation should have added a sense of menace to the proceedings and there is evidence that it did just that. Probably because of the success of this maneuver, 44% of Patrick and Iacono's "innocent" subjects failed their tests; although they were truthfully denying the mock crimes, they were apparently apprehensive about failing the test just as are innocent suspects in real-life situations and this made them react strongly

---

[2]See Lykken (1981, 1988). Another method of polygraphic interrogation, designed to determine, not whether the suspect is lying, but whether he has guilty knowledge of the crime in question, promises to have considerably greater accuracy than lie detection in forensic applications. The Guilty Knowledge Test is described in the cited references.

to the relevant questions. But this threat should not have been as effective with the psychopathic inmates as with the others and therefore they should not have responded as strongly to the relevant questions—unless, as suggested, the psychopaths were responding to the challenge rather than to the threat.

There is no doubt that the typical psychopath is not emotionally distressed when lying in real life. As Hare himself has emphasized, psychopaths lie "much more persistently and blatantly, and with considerably more panache, than do most people" (Hare, Forth, & Hart, 1989, p. 25). If we compare the demeanor and the physiological responses of 10 psychopaths and 10 nonpsychopaths, all of them guilty of some crime, while they each try to convince a detective of their innocence, most experts would expect the psychopaths to appear more at ease, both behaviorally and physiologically. However, if they are even more "at ease" while answering CQT control questions, then the psychopaths, like their more nervous companions-in-crime, would be likely to fail the CQT. The fact that the CQT compares responses within subjects, rather than between subjects, means that being generally less (or more) responsive should not greatly influence the outcome.

Alternatively, in these two mock-crime studies, it may be that the psychopaths regarded denying the relevant questions as a challenging game that they wanted to win, thus defeating themselves. It seems to me that we cannot decide this question with confidence until we have data on a number of primary psychopaths who have attempted to beat the CQT in real-life situations with their freedom hanging in the balance.

Meanwhile, however, when he is selling you the Brooklyn Bridge or promising that he will never cheat on you again, you can be sure that the psychopath will appear relaxed and confident and that he will look earnestly straight into your eyes.

Hare's Search for the Origins of Cleckley's "Semantic Aphasia"

Cleckley has long argued that the speech of psychopaths is a mechanically correct artifact that masks a profound, deep-seated semantic disorder, and that only appears to represent the inner human intention, thought, or feeling. The precise nature of this putative disorder is unclear, although it may involve some sort of dissociation between the formal, semantic, and affective components of language, perhaps because of conflict or poor integration between the cerebral hemispheres or between semantic and emotional processes. These are highly speculative possibilities, but they may provide a clue to the often baffling inconsistency between what psychopaths say and what they actually do, a discrepancy that seems to involve much more than simply lying, dissimulation, and hypocrisy. (Hare & McPherson, 1984, p. 148)

As this quotation attests, Hare has long been partial to the view that something must be wrong with the psychopath's brain. The contrasting view, and the one to which I subscribe, is that the psychopath begins life as a normal child with less than the average endowment in harmavoidance or BIS reactivity, a difference that is not pathological in itself but which does make him more difficult to socialize. This diathesis–developmental model, it seems to me, makes it easier to understand how MZ twins can be discordant for psychopathy, why children who grow up without normal parenting or socializing influences can be behaviorally so similar to psychopaths and yet differ from them in their physiological responses in Hare's countdown situation, and why some noncriminals behave like psychopaths in that same countdown but make their living as police officers (who tend to have elevated MMPI–Pd scores), test pilots or business entrepreneurs rather than as bank robbers or confidence men. (This last claim is pure speculation but one on which I would give very good odds.)

Cleckley, however, was convinced that psychopathy is a neuropsychiatric disorder, as qualitatively different from normality as the most profound psychosis, although masked by an appearance of normal mentation. Hare, too, although his own research has provided substantial support for the low fear hypothesis, seems to regard psychopathy as a discrete diagnostic entity, a taxon all members of which share the same underlying central nervous system (CNS) defect. For the past 15 years or so, the research of Hare and his students has been aimed at characterizing this putative defect: specifically, at identifying a basic difference in the way the psychopathic brain processes language or especially emotive language.

Most humans process verbal information faster and more accurately when it is presented to the right visual field or to the right ear because these sensory portals connect most directly to the left hemisphere of the brain which, for most people, is primarily responsible for processing language. In the first study in this series, Hare (1979) found that both psychopaths and nonpsychopaths performed better in identifying words presented to the right than to the left visual field (LVF), that is, both groups showed a left-hemisphere superiority on this task. Hare and Jutai (1986), however, found that when words had to be classified as to semantic category (e.g., "living things") the two groups differed, with psychopaths making fewer errors on words presented to the LVF, whereas nonpsychopaths showed the usual right visual field (RVF) or left-hemisphere superiority. Hare and McPherson (1984) used a dichotic listening task in which different one-syllable words are presented simultaneously to the left and right ears and the subject's task is to report the words heard. Most people tend to report more of the words presented to the right ear, the usual left-hemisphere superiority, but the psychopaths in this experiment showed a significantly smaller right-ear advantage, even when told in advance to attend just to the right ear.

Two other studies from Hare's lab (Williamson, Harpur, & Hare, 1990, 1991) seem to be regarded as the most direct tests of the idea that the psychopath processes language differently than nonpsychopaths do. The first of these indicated that psychopaths react less strongly than nonpsychopaths do to the emotional connotations of descriptive statements or pictures. These are interesting findings but they cannot be said to indicate a defect in the psychopath's linguistic processing per se; the low-fear hypothesis also predicts a weaker reaction to disturbing emotional stimuli, including the implications or connotations of emotional words or pictures.

The other study, based on 8 psychopaths and 8 nonpsychopaths, compared reaction times and event-related potentials (ERPs or brain-wave responses) in a task in which the subject was required to identify words versus nonwords that were presented to the left or right visual fields. The words were either neutral, negative, or positive in emotional tone. It was expected that there would be group differences resulting from differences in the lateralization of the processing of emotional words; these differences were not found. However, combining over positive and negative valence and over visual fields, it was found that the nonpsychopaths responded faster to emotional than to neutral words whereas psychopaths did not. Moreover, the groups differed in a number of aspects of the shapes or components of their ERPs and the psychopaths showed less difference in their ERPs to the neutral and emotional words than the nonpsychopaths did. This also is a provocative study but the samples are very small and a great deal of *ex post facto* analysis was involved. It would not seem unreasonable to regard this as a pilot study requiring replication before we invest heavily in interpreting the results.

In another ERP study (Jutai, Hare, & Connolly, 1987), subjects were required to press a response button each time the less frequent of two phonemes was presented binaurally. This is the familiar "odd-ball" task in which one expects to see, after the targets but not after the more frequent nontarget stimuli, a long-latency ERP component called the P–300 (because it is a positive-going wave that peaks about 300 msec after the stimulus). Both groups showed the expected ERP results and, moreover, they did not differ in an ERP-based measure of CNS arousal. When the task was made more difficult, by having the subjects simultaneously play an interesting video game in which they could win money, striking differences were observed in the target-related ERPs of the two groups; the nonpsychopaths showed essentially the same target ERP as in the single-task test, although the P–300 was smaller and had a longer latency, suggesting that the two tasks competed for similar processing resources. But the psychopathic prisoners also showed a pronounced and protracted slow-wave response (i.e., their P–300 waves returned much more slowly to baseline) and this effect was much stronger in the left or language hemisphere than on the right.

This was an unexpected finding and our understanding of the function of these ERP components does not permit us to be sure what these results mean. They might mean (and this is the interpretation that the authors favor) that psychopaths have "limited left-hemisphere resources for processing linguistic stimuli" (Jutai et al., 1987, p. 175). Hare and his colleagues prefer this interpretation because it supports in a general way their hypothesis that the "mental organ" or brain structure for processing language is somehow defective in psychopathic individuals.

Critique

It is too early to be sure what we can make of Hare's studies of "semantic aphasia." I am sure the authors would acknowledge that an important first step is independent replication of the general proposition that at least certain language functions are less lateralized in psychopaths than in nonpsychopaths. The next step will be harder, namely, explaining how such a difference in lateralization might be expected to lead to inadequate socialization and the various dispositional peculiarities of the Cleckley psychopath.

Another problem arises from the fact that many left-handed people also are less lateralized for language functions and yet most left-handers are not psychopaths. Hare and his colleagues may be on the track of a neuropsychological marker that characterizes (one subtype of) the primary psychopath and this will be valuable even if the causal connections between this marker and the psychopath's personality and social behavior remain somewhat obscure.

A problem of another kind has been pointed out to me by Scott Lilienfeld. Because Factor 2 of Hare's PCL varies inversely with verbal intelligence (see chap. 8), PCL-denominated psychopaths will have less verbal facility than comparison groups with lower PCL scores. This is yet another reason for using, either the PCL-1 alone, or some other similar diagnostic instrument that, like Factor 1, is truer to the Cleckley syndrome. Moreover, it reminds us that direct assessment of intelligence would be an obvious precaution in studies of alleged peculiarities of language processing. Intelligence modulates so many psychological processes that one should also want the reassurance provided by knowing how X and Y are related after the influence of intelligence has been accounted for.

It must be remembered that, as is true of all the research discussed in this book, every study that reports a significant difference between psychopaths and non-psychopaths also has found substantial overlap between the two groups. That is, for example, we can be confident that each of Hare's studies found some psychopaths who were *more* lateralized than the average nonpsychopath and some nonpsychopaths less lateralized than the average psychopath. Therefore, as is true for every theory we consider here, the reduced lateralization theory will have to be able to explain why some well-lateralized people become psychopathic and why some poorly lateralized people do not. The low-fear hypothesis must meet the same challenge and does so by arguing that low-fear boys with the right parents can grow up to be heroes instead of psychopaths, and that average-fear boys with truly inadequate parents can grow up to be feral sociopaths and phenocopies of true psychopaths.

As is true for each alternative theory also, we should keep in mind that there is no law of nature requiring that all psychopaths must have the same etiology or belong to the same breed of cat. Perhaps some PCL-denominated psychopaths are low-fear types while others are poorly lateralized types. It may require another 30 years of research before we can decide these issues with any confidence.

Asymmetry of Cortical Activation

Possibly related to Hare's lateralization theory is some well-replicated research by Davidson and colleagues showing in both adults and children that persons characterized by negative emotionality tend to show greater EEG activation in right-frontal brain areas whereas less-inhibited subjects with a more positive outlook show relatively greater frontal activation on the left side (Davidson, in press; Davidson & Fox, 1989; Finman, Davidson, Coltin, Straus, & Kagan, 1959; Tomarken, Davidson & Henriques, 1990). Calkins, Fox, and Marshall (in press) showed that infants selected for irritability and negative affect at 4 months, showed greater right-frontal EEG activation at 9 months and more inhibited behavior at 14 months, than infants who seemed happy and responsive at 4 months. Fox et al. (1994) found that left-frontal activation is associated with greater social competence and less withdrawal tendency in 4-year-olds.

Even more intriguing is Kagan's (1994) finding that lateral asymmetries in hand and finger temperature are a robust predictor of this same temperamental difference in children. "Many more inhibited than uninhibited children have a cooler right middle or index finger and always have a cooler ring finger. This asymmetry is, of course, related to the findings by Davidson and Fox" (Kagan, personal communication, June 13, 1994). The infants whom Kagan classifies as uninhibited do not all grow up to be psychopaths, of course, but one suspects that the infant psychopath would be more likely to belong to this than to the inhibited group. Taken altogether, it seems clear that the last word has not yet been said about brain lateralization and psychopathy.

12

Theories of Frontal Lobe Dysfunction

In 1980, Gorenstein and Newman, then both graduate students at the University of Indiana, published a theoretical article in which they suggested parallels between psychopathy and behaviors seen in laboratory rats with lesions of the septum and frontal cortex of the brain, areas thought to be involved in the inhibitory regulation of behavior. Such animals are less deterred than normal rats by punishment of previously rewarded responses and seem less able to inhibit responses when periods of nonresponding are required to achieve a food reward. Because these behaviors are reminiscent of the actions of some psychopaths, it was suggested that psychopathy in humans might be a consequence of inherited or acquired defects in the septal or frontal brain areas.

A well-known example of what they had in mind is Phineas Gage, a 19th-century railway foreman who was injured in an explosion that drove a steel bar through his frontal skull. Miraculously recovered, Gage displayed a marked personality change, becoming impulsive, irresponsible and indifferent to social proprieties. The four main features of frontal lobe damage in humans are slowing, perseveration, deficient self-awareness, and a concrete attitude and inability to plan or sustain goal directedness. The latter three of these defects might seem similar to aspects of psychopathy. It is thought that the frontal lobe of the brain is involved in programming complex acts and sustaining goal-directed behavior and that frontal lobe injury produces a deficit in behavioral flexibility and perseverance (i.e., in perseveration combined with lack of perseverance; Luria, 1972).

After their 1980 article, Gorenstein and Newman pursued in their doctoral dissertations different lines of investigation suggested by their theory linking psychopathy to septal or frontal brain defect. In the years since then, Newman, now at the University of Wisconsin, has become a psychopathy researcher second in productivity only to Hare and his colleagues at British Columbia. I review in some detail, especially Newman's attempts to confirm his brain defect theory of psychopathy, because I think it is a saga that illustrates many of the reasons why experimental psychopathology takes such a circuitous path in its slow progress toward useful understanding.

PERFORMANCE OF PSYCHOPATHS ON STANDARD
TESTS OF BRAIN DAMAGE

A variety of standard neuropsychological tests have been devised for assessing possible frontal lobe damage. These include the Wisconsin Card-Sorting Task (WCST), in which the patient is required to sort a deck of cards into piles according to criteria that change from time to time. Frontal patients tend to perseverate on previously learned criteria. The Sequential Matching Memory Test (SMMT) uses a series of cards bearing plus or minus signs; the cards are displayed one at a time and the patient must report the sign that occurred two cards earlier. Frontal patients are said to show deficits on the SMMT. Although it is not clear why this should be, patients with bilateral frontal lesions also produce more reversals in perception of the Necker Cubes, a drawing of two linked cubes in which first one, then the other cube appears to be nearer the viewer. Previous investigators (Waid & Orne, 1982) reported that "undersocialized" subjects had more trouble than control subjects on the Stroop test, which involves the fast-paced naming of the color of color names (e.g., "GREEN") printed in a different colored ink.

As his doctoral dissertation research, Gorenstein (1982) tested the frontal lobe theory by administering these neuropsychological tests to groups of psychopaths and controls. His psychopathic group consisted of male psychiatric patients, most of whom were in treatment for substance abuse, who met APD criteria and also had low CPI–So scores. On the WCST, the psychopaths made more perseverative errors (but not more nonperseverative errors) and they made more errors also on the SMMT. There were no significant differences on the Stroop or on an anagrams test but the psychopaths did report more Necker Cube reversals.

Hare (1984) attempted to replicate Gorenstein's findings using prison inmates sorted into groups that scored high, medium, or low on his PCL. Hare found no group differences on the WCST, the SMMT, or the Necker Cube, nor were there differences when he reclassified the groups like Gorenstein's, using combined APD criteria and the So scale. In a later study (Hart, Forth, & Hare, 1990), a variety of neuropsychological tests were administered to inmates classified low, mixed, or high on Hare's checklist, again finding no group differences.

For one investigator, testing his own theory, to get positive results that other investigators, dubious about the theory, cannot replicate is an all too common occurrence in the biological sciences. In selecting subjects, in the administration of the tests or measures, and in the analysis of the resulting data, there are many small subjective decisions that an investigator has to make and each one provides an opportunity for the expectations of the researcher to cumulatively bias the outcome. Psychologists as old as I am have learned never to trust an experimental finding, especially if it is surprising or interesting, until it has been replicated, preferably by someone who was disposed not to believe it originally.

In 1992, however, Newman and his students tried yet again, administering a battery of neuropsychological tests to prisoners classified as psychopathic or not, using Hare's PCL. On the theory that psychopaths have a defect in "verbal-left hemisphere functioning and frontal lobe (executive) functioning" (Smith, Arnett, & Newman, 1992, p. 1234), psychopaths were expected to score more poorly than the controls on six of the tests but no group differences were found. However, when the authors restricted their analysis to just those subjects scoring below the median on a neuroticism ("anxiety") measure, then two of the six tests predicted to show a difference did in fact do so. The low-neurotic psychopaths scored lower than the low-neurotic controls on the Block Design subtest of the WAIS–R (an IQ test) and on one part of the Trail Making Test (which requires drawing a pencil line connecting circles marked 1, A, 2, B, 3 ... in that order). The difference on this second test, however, turns out to have been associated with neuroticism, not with psychopathy.[1] In summary, these investigators managed to confirm one out of the six theoretical predictions made, provided that we allow them to restrict their analysis to subgroups that are not recognized by the theory. Taken all together, it seems fair to say that the search for neuropsychological evidence of frontal lobe or "verbal-left hemisphere" defect in psychopaths has been unsuccessful.

Psychopathic Behavior in Patients With Frontal Lobe Damage

The studies reviewed here indicate that brain damage of the sort detectable by neuropsychological tests cannot plausibly account for most psychopathic behavior but, as the Phineas Gage example suggests, these is no doubt that patients with frontal lobe damage commonly exhibit abnormalities of conduct that are strongly reminiscent of psychopathy. Neurologist A. R. Damasio and colleagues recently described a 35-year-old professional man, "EVR," who was successful, happily married, and "who led an impeccable social life, and was a role model to younger siblings" (Damasio, Tranel, & Damasio, 1990, p. 81). EVR developed a brain tumor that required surgical excision of the frontal orbital (behind the eyes) brain cortex on both sides. After recovery, his IQ and memory test scores were uniformly in the superior range, and his performance on the WCST and on several other tests designed to detect frontal lobe damage was entirely normal. EVR's social conduct, however,

> was profoundly affected by his brain injury. Over a brief period of time, he entered disastrous business ventures (one of which led to predictable bankruptcy), and was divorced twice (the second marriage, which was to a prostitute, only lasted 6 months). He has been unable to hold any paying job since the time of surgery, and his plans for future activity are defective. (p. 82)

Previously a model citizen, EVR now meets adult criteria for APD.

---

[1] Both subgroups of psychopaths had intermediate scores while the high and low neurotic controls scored high and low, respectively, on the Trail Making Test.

In the psychophysiology laboratory, EVR gave normal electrodermal responses to simple stimuli such as a hand clap or taking a deep breath but his response to meaningful pictures was unusual. He was shown a series of 40 slides, 30 of them depicting neutral scenes but 10 of which, the "targets," were selected to be arousing or disturbing pictures of disasters, mutilated bodies, frontal nudity, and the like. EVR attended to the pictures with apparent interest but showed essentially no EDR responses to any of them (this was the "passive" condition). When the slides were presented again with instructions to describe what was going on (the "active" condition), EVR gave a substantial EDR to the targets but not to the neutral slides. On a different day, using a new set of slides, again with 10 disturbing target slides, EVR was tested three times, in the passive, active, and passive conditions, and he again showed negligible EDR activity when not required to make a verbal response but a consistent EDR to the target slides in the active condition. The patient reported that he was interested in the tests and that he had been surprised by his own lack of emotional response to the scenes that he thought should have disturbed him.

Damasio et al. proceeded to recruit four more patients who had bilateral frontal lesions similar to EVR's and who also displayed severe defects in social conduct, judgment, and planning, acquired after their brain damage. Five patients with nonfrontal brain damage and five normal controls were also recruited and all subjects were run through the same laboratory paradigms as EVR and with quite consistent results. Both the normals and the nonfrontal brain-lesioned patients showed substantially stronger EDRs to the target, than to the nontarget, slides, in both the active and passive conditions. Two of the new frontal patients showed negligible EDR to any of the slides, even in the active condition, whereas the other two, like EVR, showed a much weaker response to the targets in the passive than in the active condition. All subjects showed normal strong EDR activity in response to movement or sudden noises.

This interesting study suggests, at least to me, that EVR and the other frontal patients would very likely have responded like primary psychopaths in the Hare countdown experiment and also in the Lykken avoidance learning task. Stimuli that they were perfectly able to identify, and the significance of which they understood well at a cognitive level, did not produce the normal emotional reaction with its attendant EDR. At least in EVR's case, we know that conventional neuropsychological indicators of frontal lobe damage would not have been revelatory. In all five frontal cases the damage had occurred acutely and the behavioral changes could plainly be traced to that event but this study clearly suggests that more subtle damage or even congenital injury to the orbital frontal cortex might produce both the behavioral and laboratory signs of primary psychopathy without other more obvious evidence of brain defect. Modern brain-imaging techniques now make it possible to measure differences in focalized activity between, say, murderers and control subjects; see Raine (1993; chap.6) for an introduction to this new line of investigation. These findings do not, of course, demonstrate that all—or even many—primary psychopaths have lesions or qualitative defects in their frontal cortex areas, but merely that frontal lesions can produce a syndrome very similar to primary psychopathy.

NEWMAN'S PERSEVERATION THEORY
OF PSYCHOPATHY

Newman was especially intrigued by the fact that rats with septal brain lesions tend to perseverate in emitting responses that have previously been rewarded, even after the rewards have stopped and, indeed, even when these responses have begun to be followed by punishment. The card-sorting test, described earlier, is intended to detect this kind of aberration in human subjects but, as we have seen, the WCST does not in fact distinguish psychopaths from normals. Nevertheless, Newman persisted (I will not say "perseverated") in designing several ingenious new tests of perseveration and in testing them on prison inmates.

For his doctoral dissertation, Newman introduced a go/no-go discrimination task in which subjects are rewarded for responding to "correct" cues and punished for responding to "incorrect" cues (Newman, Widom, & Nathan, 1985). The idea is that, to avoid punishment (loss of a token), the subject must withhold a response that has frequently resulted in reward (gain of a token). Newman's subjects were boys' school inmates classified according to their scores on the MMPI–Pd Scale (used as an indicant of psychopathy) and on the Welsh Anxiety Scale (an MMPI scale that measures neuroticism). Subjects were rewarded by tokens redeemable for cigarettes or candy. Both tasks involved learning by trial and error that four of eight two-digit numbers were (arbitrarily) correct. In Task 1, each response (tapping the card on which the number was printed) was rewarded or punished; non-responses produced no reinforcement. On this task, it was expected that psychopaths, due to their brain defect, would become so involved in producing the rewarded responses that they would, in effect, fail to notice which numbers were incorrect and caused them to lose a token when tapped; the psychopaths would therefore produce more errors of commission and lose more of their tokens. Such errors, which involve actively tapping a card with an incorrect number on it, constituted a failure of passive avoidance of a punishable response.

In Task 2, no punishments were used; the subject was given tokens for tapping the correct numbers and also for not tapping the incorrect ones. In this case, Newman "predicted that equating the outcome of appropriate responding and appropriate response inhibition would prevent one response strategy from becoming dominant and interfering with the other" (Newman et al., 1985, pp. 1318–1319). That is, Newman expected that the low-neurotic psychopathic subjects would give more passive avoidance errors (tapping the incorrect numbers) than the low-neurotic nonpsychopaths on Task 1 and that there should be no differences on Task 2. It should be mentioned that the perseveration hypothesis also predicts that the psychopaths, but not the controls, should show more errors of commission in Task 1 than in Task 2.

In fact, the low-neurotic psychopaths did more frequently tap the incorrect numbers than did the low-neurotic nonpsychopathic subjects. Using a rather liberal method of analysis, this difference was found to be statistically significant. On Task 2, where no group differences were predicted, the groups did differ significantly on the errors of omission. Moreover, low-neurotic psychopaths failed to show significantly more errors of commission in the reward–punishment condition than they did in the reward-only condition. My reading of this study therefore is that it failed to unequivocally produce the predicted findings although managing to produce a significant but inexplicable group difference on another variable.

Newman and Kosson (1986) repeated this two-task experiment using prison inmates classified by Hare's checklist. This time the task was computerized and Task 2 was changed to involve only punishment; the subjects started with 40 tokens and lost one each time they responded to an "incorrect" number or failed to respond to a "correct" number. Psychopaths showed the same high error rate on both tasks, contrary to expectation. Nonpsychopaths showed fewer errors of commission on Task 1, the reward–punishment task, than when punishment was the only contingency. As I understand it, the two task conditions should have shown different results only for the psychopaths and only on errors of commission. One possible explanation is Newman's, namely, that the punishment-only task was "harder" than the reward–punishment task. But the actual tasks were identical, differing only in whether the correct numbers were identified by their choice being rewarded, or by their neglect being punished. In any case, the psychopaths did produce more errors of commission than the nonpsychopaths in the reward–punishment task so, as in 1983, this study could be said to have confirmed one of two predictions from the perseveration hypothesis and also to have produced one unanticipated finding, the significant difference in the nonpsychopathic group's response to the two tasks. It should be mentioned that the Welsh Anxiety Scale was administered also to these subjects, as in 1983, but was not used to classify the groups and, indeed, the mean neuroticism scores for the two groups were approximately equal.

In 1990, another part of the 1986 study was reported (Kosson, Smith, & Newman, 1990), a test of Black prison inmates on the same paradigm as used with the White inmates in that study. This time the difference between psychopaths and the nonpsychopaths was not significant in either condition.

In the same year, another set of three studies with white inmates was reported (Newman, Patterson, Howland, & Nichols, 1990). The first of these employed the reward plus punishment condition of Newman and Kosson but omitted both the reward-only and the punishment-only control tasks that had muddied the waters in 1983 and 1986, respectively. As in 1986, the PCL was used to classify inmates as psychopathic or nonpsychopathic but this time the only data reported are for those subjects in both groups who also scored below the median on the Welsh measure of neuroticism. The low-neurotic psychopaths produced more errors of commission than the low-neurotic nonpsychopaths. One can compute from the information provided that the high-neurotic nonpsychopaths produced even more errors of commission than the low-neurotic psychopaths but this was due to an unusually high error rate for 4 of the 13 subjects in this discarded group.

Perseveration as Playing Long Odds

Newman, Patterson, and Kosson (1987) changed the game. Their inmate subjects, who were classified according to the PCL, played a computer card game. If the next card shown was a face card, they won (5¢); if a numbered card, they lost.

Before each card was presented, the computer asked: "Do you want to play?" The game ended whenever the subject decided not to take the next card. Nine of the first 10 cards were winners but, after every 10 cards, the probability of losing was increased in 10% increments. Psychopaths "perseverated" in this game, continuing to play longer, 90 cards on average, than the nonpsychopaths, who averaged 62 cards. When subjects were required to wait for 5 seconds after each card before continuing the game, both groups stopped play after an average of 48 cards had been played.[2]

The authors interpreted the results of this study as providing "unambiguous evidence of response perseveration in psychopaths" (Newman et al., 1987, p. 147) and in one sense this is plainly true; the psychopaths kept on playing longer than the control subjects did. But Newman and his colleagues treat this as evidence for some kind of brain defect whereas I would be inclined to treat this finding as a predictable result of the psychopath's well-known penchant for risk-taking. Suppose we let people in general gamble small stakes on a game in which the odds are clearly known. Most people will agree to play at odds of 9–1; many will agree at odds of 50–50; fewer will agree as the odds get worse. If we suppose that all these inmates perceived, as they played, that the odds were gradually getting worse, are we obliged to say that those who continued longer have defective nervous systems? Many people try long shots just for the fun of it, especially, perhaps, if the game is an interruption of boring prison routine. Perhaps Newman's psychopaths cared less than the nonpsychopaths about losing and/or enjoyed playing the game more, at least until the 5-second wait for each card made the game too tedious. It has to be remembered that the kind of perseveration seen in patients with frontal lobe damage is something more than a mere proclivity to gamble at long odds. We have already seen that neuropsychological tests designed to detect true perseveration do not show this defect in the psychopath.

On the other hand, the Fowles–Gray weak-BIS theory directly predicts slower extinction of conditioned operant responses in the primary psychopath. Just as he is less fearful of cues for punishment, so is he less distressed by "frustrative nonreward" and therefore the psychopath is less inclined to stop playing what has been a rewarding game just because he has started to lose.

Inability to Delay Gratification

Newman, Kosson, and Patterson (1992) tested the notion that psychopaths are less able than normals to "delay gratification." Prison inmates were once again divided into two groups according to their scores on Hare's PCL and then subdivided at the median on the Welsh neuroticism measure (oddly, there were 84 subjects above the

---

[2]Shapiro, Quay, Hogan, and Schwartz (1988) used this same task with students at a Forida school for seriously emotionally disturbed children. Nine youngsters with the highest scores on the Conduct Disorder (CD) scale of Quay's Revised Behavior Problems Checklist (Quay & Peterson, 1987) played an average of 78 cards, whereas a comparison group with lower CD scores played on 48 cards. On the reasonable assumption that many psychopaths present with CD as children, this result is consistent with the data of Newman, Patterson, and Kosson.

median and only 74 below it). The four groups played a different computer game for money, in one of three conditions. On each trial of the reward condition (R), they could either press Button A immediately or wait 10 seconds and then press Button B. Button A provided a 40% probability of winning whereas Button B promised 80%. Because the number of trials was fixed at 50, one would make more money by waiting 10 seconds each time for Button B—but the subjects were not told about the 50 trial limit! Therefore, a not unreasonable assumption would be that the game would last for a set length of time. In that case, an option would be to press Button A as fast as possible, thus achieving a better payoff from many low-odds trials than could be achieved from fewer high-odds trials. As it turned out, the groups did not differ significantly in how often they chose the delay option.

In the equal delay (EQ) condition, both the high- and low-probability choices required a 10-second delay; not surprisingly, all groups more often chose the high probability option under this condition. Finally, in the reward-plus-punishment (R+P) condition, Button A earned 5¢ 70% of the time and lost 5¢ 30% of the time, while Button B, which required the 10-second delay, won 90% and lost just 10% of the time. In the other two conditions, the low-neurotic psychopaths had more frequently chosen Button B (contrary to expectation, in the case of Condition R) but in the R+P condition, this group chose Button B least often, although the difference was not significant. However, the authors take the surprising step of subtracting the scores on condition EQ from those on condition R+P which has the effect of giving the low-neurotic psychopaths a score that is significantly different from that of the low-neurotic nonpsychopaths and this outcome is said to "lend some support for the predictions made for psychopaths and control subjects" (Newman, Kosson, & Patterson, 1992, p. 634). Other studies using a different method of assessing willingness to delay gratification, in adolescent delinquents and in adult prison inmates, have also produced complex and conflicting results (Blanchard, Bassett, & Koshland, 1977; Unikel & Blanchard, 1983).

Critique

Most researchers would agree that analyzing raw experimental data is rather like interrogating a criminal suspect; one often has to squeeze a little to get at the truth. But there is the ever-present danger, if one squeezes too hard, that the result will be a false confession, that one will "find out" what one hoped or expected to find out, whether it is true or not.

The first problem I see with this corpus of studies is the inconsistent use of a neuroticism measure in the selection of the psychopathic subjects. It is true that some other investigators, beginning with Lykken (1957), distinguished "primary" psychopaths, who fit the Cleckley criteria, from "secondary" or "neurotic" psychopaths who do not, but that is precisely what Hare's PCL is intended to do. Newman and colleagues use the PCL alone in five studies when it seemed to give them the group differences they are looking for[3] but they resort to subclassification by Welsh

---

[3]See Newman and Kosson (1986); Kosson and Newman (1986); Newman, Patterson, and Kosson (1987); Kosson, Smith, and Newman (1990); and Howland, Kosson, Patterson, and Newman (1993).

neuroticism score in five other studies where the psychopath versus nonpsychopath differences were nonsignificant.[4] Such inconsistency does not inspire confidence.

Second, in the Newman, Kosson, and Patterson (1992) delay of gratification study, the authors plainly would have been pleased to find that the low-neurotic psychopaths made the delay choice significantly less often in both the R and the R+P conditions, because that surely is predicted from the hypothesis that psychopaths (or, at least, "low-neurotic psychopaths") have a CNS defect that makes them relatively incapable of delaying gratification. The hypothesis makes no prediction of group differences in the EQ condition in which both choices involved the same delay. Neither of the two predicted results eventuated. However, both low-neurotic groups differed in opposite directions from the condition averages in R+P and in EQ so that by scoring the former relative to the latter, the group differences were enhanced to statistical significance. This is squeezing too hard.

In the case of the go/no-go learning paradigm used in 1986, it was the nonpsychopaths, rather than the psychopaths, who were affected by the two conditions. When punished either for responding at the wrong time or for failing to respond at the right time, both groups made lots of wrong responses. When punished only for responding at the wrong time (and rewarded for responding at the right time), the nonpsychopaths (but not the psychopaths) made fewer errors. This difference did not hold up in the study with Black inmates. Even if had held up or if it could be replicated with other White subjects, it is not the effect predicted by the theory. The theory says that psychopaths should perseverate in making sometimes-rewarded responses and hence make more errors on the reward–punishment condition than on the punishment-only condition. The theory does not predict that the nonpsychopaths should differ in their response to the two conditions.

The clearest finding, that psychopaths tend to gamble longer and at poorer odds than nonpsychopaths, is what one would expect of these devil-may-care, sensation-seeking individuals—and what one would predict if psychopaths are less distressed both by threat of punishment and by losing a bet, as the Fowles–Gray theory postulates. To speak of these results as evidence of "response perseveration" similar to the behavior of laboratory rats with septal lesions, however, is to suggest a kind of mindless, uncontrollable characteristic of the behavior that goes well beyond what has been demonstrated. Are we to conclude that the millions of Americans who weekly buy tickets in the 50-million-to-one-shot lotteries all have septal lesions? Suppose we were to repeat this experiment with the following additional instruction: "The inmate who has the most tokens in hand when he quits playing will be given immediate parole." If then the psychopaths continued to play after the odds had turned against them, one might be willing to conclude that they had a defect in their brains but not, I think, on the evidence so far provided.

That being said, however, clinical evidence indicates that the psychopathic syndrome can result from frontal lobe injury in the absence of other symptoms of

---

[4]See Newman, Patterson, Howland, and Nichols (1990); Newman, Kosson, and Patterson (1992); Smith, Arnett, and Newman (1992); Arnett, Howland, Smith, and Newman (1993); a combination of the MMPI–Pd scale and the Welsh was employed in one instance (Newman, Widom, & Nathan, 1983).

brain damage. This, in turn, suggests that more subtle perinatal injury or developmental defects in frontal lobe structure could produce primary psychopathy. The low-fear or weak-BIS hypothesis implies that *something* is different in the emotional machinery of the psychopathic brain and that difference could result either from genetic or developmental factors.

For many years I have assumed that the relatively fearless child, who may mature as a psychopath unless the parents are skillful and diligent, is a product of the great genetic lottery that takes place at conception. Just as a child, at that lottery, might happen to receive less than his fair share of each parent's "smart genes" or "tall genes," and grow up relatively dim or short in consequence, so might he receive a short ration of "fear genes," either by the luck of the draw or because his parents themselves were relatively fearless people and had fewer "fear genes" to pass along. We do know that the adult trait of harmavoidance is fairly strongly influenced by genetic factors; yet the brain is such an unimagineably complex mechanism that it is also reasonable to suppose that little accidents of development, as the machinery is being fabricated from the genetic blueprint, might also produce from time to time behavioral inhibition systems that are less that normally effective. One thing that seems clear is that it would be of great interest to study the temperaments, autonomic responding, and avoidance behavior of the parents, siblings, and especially the discordant cotwins of primary psychopaths. The genetic hypothesis does not require that psychopathy itself run in families but it does require that the underlying diathesis—the lessened fearfulness—should show itself among the first-degree relatives.

13

Other Theories of Psychopathy

In this chapter, I discuss three additional approaches to an understanding of psychopathic behavior, the *psychoanalytic* approach, which I find intractably mysterious, the *neurochemical* approach, which appears able to account for an important subspecies of "dystempered" psychopathy involving impulsive aggression, and a largely speculative proposal of my own, the *hysterical psychopath*.

Psychoanalytic Theories

The etiological hypotheses that are discussed in this book are relatively common-sensical, inevitably speculative to a degree, but at least testable. It is only fair to alert the student to the fact that there is another, quite separate, theoretical tradition based on psychoanalytic principles. This psychodynamic approach seems to rely for its confirmation largely on clinical impressions and the Rorschach test. I do not attempt to characterize these theories further because I frankly do not understand them. Here is an example:

> The developmental origins of the psychopathic personality are characterized by a precocious separation from the primary parent during the symbiotic phase of maturation; failures of internalization that begin with an organismic distrust of the sensory-perceptual environment; a predominate, archetypal identification with the stranger selfobject (*sic*) that is central to the conceptual self and object fusions within the grandiose self-structure during the period of separation-individuation; a failure of object constancy and a primary narcissistic attachment to the grandiose self; and states of relatedness (separate from the *traits* of primary narcissistic attachment) that are aggressively and sadomasochistically pursued with actual objects. This coexistence of benign attachment and aggressively pursued, sadistically toned attempts to bond is pathognomic of the psychopathic process. (Meloy, 1988, p. 59)

The Low Serotonin Syndrome

Serotonin (5-hydroxytryptamine or 5HT) is one of the important cerebral neuro-transmitters. The 5HT system consists of numerous fiber bundles arising in the midbrain and projecting diffusely to the medial and lateral forebrain, the periventricular system, and the cerebral cortex (Spoont, 1992). The functions of this system seem to consist of modulating, coordinating and constraining signal transmission in these higher centers. In animals, experimentally reducing 5HT availability produces a reduction in passive avoidance and an increase in irritable aggression (Lewis, 1991).

The catabolism of 5HT takes place in the brain, producing a compound known as 5–HIAA which, in humans, can be measured in the cerebrospinal fluid as an indicant of 5HT activity. Aggressive tendencies have repeatedly been found to correlate negatively with 5–HIAA in young men, with low levels commonly observed in impulsive–aggressive offenders, in men who had attempted some violent form of suicide, and in nonviolent but impulsive arsonists (Lewis, 1991). Many of these findings suggest that Gray's BIS (chap. 10) may depend on serotonin activity. Soubrie (1986), however, pointed out that humans with reduced serotonin activity are both more impulsive and also more anxious, whereas weak-BIS activity, whether congenital or produced by antianxiety drugs, is expected to produce a kind of carefree impulsivity.

Linnoila and Virkkunen (1992) argued that reduced serotonin activity compromises blood glucose metabolism and that it is during periods of transient hypoglycemia that aggressive and impulsive outbursts occur. These authors postulate a "low serotonin syndrome" in which deficient 5HT output disturbs both glucose metabolism and diurnal rhythm regulation.

> Hypoglycemia directly lowers the threshold for impulsive behavior, while alterations in the normal day–night rhythm are conducive to chronic low-grade dysphoria or dysthymia. Alcohol, which elicits an acute increase in serotonin release, may provide temporary relief from the dysphoric mood. Chronic alcohol consumption, however, exacerbates the serotonergic deficit. Combined with the anxiolytic effects of alcohol, which loosen reinforced contingencies, this further increases the propensity for impulsive and violent behavior. (pp. 49–50)

Thus, among those individuals whom I labeled as *distempered*, nonprimary psychopaths, we may expect to find a subgroup displaying impulsive, sometimes violent behavior, dysphoric mood, and a history of early onset alcoholism (Cloninger, Bohman, & Sovardsons's, 1981, male-limited Type II alcoholism), who will be found to have abnormally low levels of 5–HIAA in their spinal fluid as well as low minimum blood glucose levels.

Although this low serotonin syndrome model is still speculative, the foregoing discussion illustrates an important fact. Persisting antisocial behavior is a final common pathway with a multiplicity of different starting points. Not all psychopaths are deficient in serotonin levels but those who are should be separated from the experimental study group first before testing different etiological hypotheses on the remainder. Experimental psychopathologists are too easily satisfied by finding statistically significant mean differences, in the predicted direction, between their experimental and control groups—even when there is substantial overlap so that many patients or inmates score in the normal direction, and many normals in the pathological direction, on the variable hypothesized to be causative. By excluding cases that are better explained in other ways, one might hope gradually to reduce this overlap and thus to refine our understanding.

The Hysterical Psychopath

Heymans' Law of Inhibition

In a series of studies published in 1928, Spencer and Cohen found very high correlations (.8 to .9 and higher) between the simple sensory threshold and the increase in that threshold when measured in the presence of an additional, "inhibitory" stimulus (Spencer, 1928; Spencer & Cohen, 1928a, 1928b). These findings, obtained both across a sample of 50 subjects measured once and also across 50 daily measurements on the same individual, were interpreted to support a theory advanced earlier by a Dutch psychologist named Heymans. Heymans held that the sensory threshold is normally elevated well above its physiological minimum by an active process of afferent inhibition and that this inhibition, in turn, is a function of the aggregate intensity of all ambient stimulation. The higher a subject's simple threshold, the higher his immediate capacity for inhibition and therefore the more will his threshold be further elevated by increasing ambient stimulus levels.

In their study of the single subject over 50 days, Spencer and Cohen also correlated his simple (brightness) threshold against the amount of sleep the subject had on the preceding night (all measurements were made first thing in the morning). This correlation was about +.60 over all 50 days and about +.80 over just the final 25 days when the threshold data were presumably the most reliable. Correlations between thresholds and the subject's self-ratings of his "freshness" were of about the same magnitude.

It is at first surprising that fatigue lowers sensory thresholds rather than raising them; on the other hand, most people would agree that they are more irritable, more distractible, more sensitive to pain, and the like, at the end of a tiring day than when they are well rested. One of my colleagues for many years conducted studies of the effect of noise on human hearing and hired healthy undergraduates to sit in a large room filled with loudspeakers that intermittently produced extended blasts of 120 db white noise. The subjects could read or try to relax during their 6-hour session except while undergoing periodic hearing tests.

Subjects willing to tolerate these conditions were presumably self-selected for having what the Russian physiologists called "strong nervous systems"; they were healthy and resilient young people who felt relatively invulnerable to strong stimulation. However, a common report of these subjects was that, after completing a day's stint in this simulated boiler factory, they felt irritable, nervous, unable to relax, and overresponsive to noises and they had difficulty sleeping that first night. These observations are compatible with Heymans' theory that the sensorium is tonically protected by an inhibitory process that reduces the impact of strong stimulation but which is exhaustible, working most efficiently when the individual is well rested but leaving him or her hypersensitive and vulnerable after protracted overuse.

If such an inhibitory mechanism exists, its efficiency must vary not only within individuals, as a function of "freshness" as Spencer and Cohen demonstrated, but also between individuals, as a function of genetic endowment. If such inhibition can substantially reduce the impact of strong external stimulation, then it is not implausible that it might also serve to modulate the impact of internal stimulation, including the impact of thoughts about the possible bad consequences of one's actions or the impact of conditioned stimuli for fear. Thus, although Adam's avoidance gradient is normally steep enough to prevent him from grasping the apple, if Eve tempts him after a good night's rest she might find that Heymans' inhibition softens the impact of Adam's thoughts of future punishment, flattening that gradient enough to satisfy the serpent.

It should be emphasized that this conjectured form of tonic inhibition is different from—and, indeed, works in opposition to—the inhibition involved in Gray's BIS (discussed in chap. 10). An individual with an unusually strong tonic inhibitory system of the type described by Heymans might very well exhibit periods or binges of psychopathic behavior alternating with interludes of tremulous vulnerability such as I believe I have seen in some patients. Several of the subjects in my 1957 study displayed a curious pattern of electrodermal activity that is suggestive in this regard (Lykken, 1968a). Like the primary psychopaths, they showed little palmar sweating after the buzzer signaled the imminence of painful shock. Unlike the primaries, and unlike any of the other subjects studied, these few individuals showed an unexpected *decrease* in skin conductance beginning after they were first told about the shocks or, in one case, after the first shock was actually delivered. These striking decreases in conductance imply a corresponding decrease in general arousal, a kind of "turning off the lights" response one might expect from a subject who is told that a 30-minute rest period is about to begin and that he or she should try to sleep. We do not expect such a response at the start of what the subject knows will be 30-minutes of intermittent buzzers and electric shocks and it seems reasonable to speculate that these subjects were preparing for the ensuing stress by invoking some sort of generalized inhibition.

All but one of these subjects were criminal psychopaths assigned to the non-primary group. The exception was a young woman from the normal group; she and her parents were Christian Scientists and she told me that her faith enabled her to control her emotions better than most of her friends; another possibility is that her inhibitory capacities enabled her to be a successful Christian Scientist. Because I have never gotten around to pursuing these speculations systematically since they were first outlined in 1968, I hope that some young investigator might find them worth looking into.

It is interesting that people with high scores on both positive and negative emotionality (extraversion and neuroticism), people whom both Blackburn and Gray would identify as similar to "secondary" psychopaths, tend to be un-deraroused in the morning and overaroused at night (Revelle, Humphreys, Simon,

& Gilliland, 1980). Perhaps this reflects the fact that such people are better shielded by protective inhibition in the mornings, when they are rested, but are more reactive to stimulation and thus more vulnerable in the evenings when the inhibitory mechanism is fatigued. In the Hare countdown situation, subjects like these should show low skin conductance and perhaps cardiac acceleration, the so-called "defensive reflex" that I think is associated with preception, at least if they are tested in the mornings. They should also show a higher than normal increase in sensory thresholds when measured in the presence of competing or masking stimulation. It seems reasonable to expect that their detection thresholds for electric shock should be higher than normal, the threat of the situation serving to elicit the protective inhibitory response. Moreover, if there is a relationship between Heymans' inhibition and the operation of the conjectured preception mechanism, secondary psychopaths, when they are well rested, should also show greatly attenuated response to aversive stimuli that are made predictable in time.

Donna

When I was a graduate student in the 1950s, the Psychiatry Department of the Minneapolis General Hospital boasted one full-time psychologist, a part-time psychiatrist (the chief, who came around three mornings a week to do rounds and to push the button on the electroconvulsive shock machine), and lots of very crazy patients. In the summer of 1953, the psychologist went off for a 3-month tour of Europe while I took her place, trying not to look too foolish to the veteran psychiatric nurses who really ran the place. It was there I met Donna, a tall, thin 19-year-old made by the same firm that created the then-young actress, Audrey Hepburn. It was hard to believe that Donna was in the psychiatric ward on referral from the county jail; she had been picked up with a man trying to burglarize a pharmacy for drugs. It was almost *impossible* to believe that Donna was a heroin addict and had spent the previous 3 months in Chicago, working as a prostitute to support her pimp and her habit.

You must picture a shy, tremulous, soft-spoken girl, demure and vulnerable, who could hardly bring herself to speak of these experiences, just as I could hardly imagine her enacting them. The court agreed to put Donna on probation contingent on my taking her as a patient and the head of psychiatry at the university hospital agreed to have her transferred there when the summer was over. I saw her daily for the 6 weeks that she remained an inpatient, then once a week for several months, then intermittently over the next 15 years.

During those years, Donna completed a kind of Rake's Progress in reverse, from prostitute and heroin addict, to becoming the star turn at a local lesbian bar, to a serious relationship with a Black Army lieutenant, and finally to a reasonably stable marriage with a young musician. There was much backsliding along the way, binges of wild self-indulgence, impromptu romances, unplanned trips with new acquaintances. I would not hear from her for months at a time and then I would hear a faint, frightened voice on the phone: "Dr. Lykken? Can I see you?" I would pry out of her a summary of what she had been up to this time and always the protagonist of those wild adventures seemed unconnected to the farouche and vulnerable girl who was reluctantly recounting them. It was hard to believe that the person I had come to know was capable of doing the things that other Donna did; my Donna could barely talk about them, much less do them. I saw the other Donna just once, when she dropped in for an unscheduled social visit; it was the only time I saw her laugh or heard her swear. Having burned thus fitfully but at both ends, Donna's candle guttered out; she died of uterine cancer when she was 36.

It is noteworthy that alleged examples of multiple personality, such as Cleckley and Thigpen's *The Three Faces of Eve*, often include at least one "personality," like Eve Black, one of Eve's three "faces," who appears to be a psychopath. It may also be relevant that hysterical personality disorder may have a familial linkage to psychopathy, occurring in higher than normal frequency among the relatives of psychopaths. It is also thought that hysterics often are the sex or marriage partners of psychopaths, due to the former's tendency to repress awareness of the dangers of such liaisons, but this assortative mating hypothesis has not been systematically investigated.

Postscript

The theory presented in this section is sheer speculation and one possibly compatible case history does not constitute evidence either. I hope some reader may be intrigued enough at least to replicate Spencer and Cohen's work with up-to-date techniques. Donna's history, although it does not prove the theory of hysterical psychopathy, does something more important. Neither Cleckley's theory, Hare's or Newman's, or the Fowles–Gray–Lykken theory of psychopathy will account satisfactorily for Donna's case. This chapter emphasizes once again that there is more than one kind of psychopath and more than one valid theory of psychopathy, including at least one that has not yet been seriously studied. I think we know how to rear fearless children so that they do not turn out as psychopaths. Until we understand the other psychopathies as well as this type, we shall not be able to identify the children at high risk or design preventive treatment for these other psychopathic diatheses.

PART IV

THE SOCIOPATHIC
PERSONALITIES

14

The Sociopath or Common Criminal

Illegitimacy is the single most important social problem of our time—more important than crime, drugs, poverty, illiteracy, welfare, or homelessness, because it drives everything else.

—Charles Murray (1993)

IS SOCIOPATHY INCREASING?

Because most crime is committed by unsocialized young men, and because most unsocialized young men qualify as *sociopaths* rather than as *psychopaths* as these terms are defined herein, we can safely deduce the increase in sociopathy from the increase in the crime rate. During the year in which this book was written, one frequently encountered statements in the press and elsewhere suggesting that the citizen's sense that crime is increasing is illusory, that crime in the United States peaked in 1980 and has decreased since then. That it is these dubious reassurances that are illusory is illustrated in Fig. 14.1. We see there that rate of index (all serious) crime has increased more than 300% since 1960. Meanwhile, the rate of violent crime (murder, aggravated assault, forcible rape, and robbery, per 100,000 population) increased about 300% from 1960 to 1980, decreased somewhat to 1984, then once again began to rise to over 500% by 1990. Part of that increase in the crime rate from 1960 through about 1975 resulted from the passage of post-war "baby-boomers" through the period of highest crime risk (the ages 15 to 25, as we have seen previously). Also plotted in Fig. 14.1 is the percentage of the total population in this high-risk age group each year. What accounts for the continuing increase in crime after the baby-boomers reached maturity is the principal subject of this chapter.

Figure 14.2 shows a still more alarming statistic. The rate of violent crime committed by juvenile offenders has greatly increased also, more than 220% since

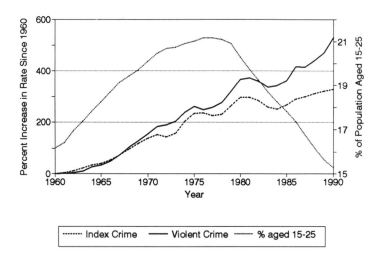

FIG. 14.1. Percent increase in the rate (per 100,000 population) of index (major) crimes and crimes of violence in the United States. The increase from 1963 to about 1978 was due partly to the proportion of the population who were age 15 to 25 (the "baby-boomers") and thus at highest risk for crime. The dotted line shows the rise and fall in the size of this high-risk group, estimated from the number of births 15 to 25 years earlier. The post-1980 increase in crime rate requires further explanation (sources: FBI, 1992; National Center for Health Statistics, 1993a).

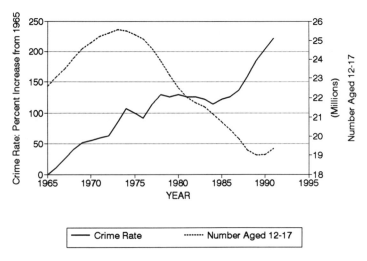

FIG. 14.2. The increase in the rate of violent crime (crimes per 100,000 population) committed by juveniles. The rate in 1991 was 222% higher than the rate in 1965. The dashed line plots the number of individuals in this 12- to 17-year age group. The size of this segment of the U.S. population might help explain the increase in juvenile violence from 1965 to 1974 (and, perhaps, the leveling of the curve until about 1984) but it clearly cannot explain why juvenile violence increased so sharply after 1984 (sources: FBI, 1992; National Center for Health Statistics 1993a).

1965. These are muggings, rapes, drive-by shootings, gang-style executions—crimes of violence committed by youngsters and, as the figure shows, this frightening increase in juvenile crime cannot be explained just by the numbers in this age group.

THE CAUSES OF SOCIOPATHY

The Effect of Father Absence

In the 1950s, most children learned to tell right from wrong at home, in the bosoms of their families. Today, one fourth of all U.S. children under the age of 18 do not have a family in the customary sense. According to U.S. Census figures, one third of these fatherless children were born out-of-wedlock (55% of the Black children) and many of their mothers were themselves poorly educated and poorly socialized. The proportion of all live births that were births to unwed mothers in the United States has increased from about 5% in 1960 to nearly 30% today (Eckholm, 1992; Fuchs & Reklis, 1992; Murray, 1993). Not coincidentally, the number of families receiving Aid to Families with Dependent Children (AFDC) grew from less than 1 million in 1960 to about 6 million in 1990 (DeParle, 1992). Nearly one fourth of never-married 18- to 44-year-old U.S. women have produced at least one child (U.S. Census Bureau figures, cited by Ingrassia, 1993). Each year in the United States about 1 million adolescent girls are impregnated and about 50% of these pregnancies come to term (Byrne, Kelley, & Fisher, 1993, p. 102). About 97% of unmarried mothers currently elect to keep their children and attempt to raise them, usually with welfare assistance (Lewin, 1992).

What about teenage pregnancy? In the United States since 1987, at least 11% of all females aged 15 to 19 became pregnant in any given year. The rate of teenage pregnancy in the United States is higher than that of any other industrialized nation, twice as high as the next highest competitor (England and Wales), three times the rates of Sweden and Denmark, seven times the rate of the Netherlands (Jones et al., 1987). I do not mean to suggest that all illegitimate offspring of unmarried teenage mothers grow up unsocialized but it is a fact that an unacceptably high proportion of them do so.

On the other hand, many do not grow up at all; of the 61 children murdered in Chicago during 1993, 51 of them were the offspring of unmarried teenage mothers; only 10 were living with both biological parents (Johnson & McMahon, 1994).

> In a fit of anger, Tina threw two-year-old Amber to the floor and hit her in the face with a full baby bottle. Charged with criminal battery, Tina got probation. Tina lived with Amber, baby Andrew, and her boyfriend, the burglar. When an investigator came by he found the children filthy, with full diapers and genital rashes. The home was filthy, crusted and rotted food. ... Tina smoked crack and boozed with friends at night, slept during the day. Child Protection offered Tina "drug rehab and counseling for 'self-esteem,' and they also wanted to send a homemaker along to teach her to keep

her house clean." It didn't work. Early one afternoon, Tina woke up and found the baby, Andrew, face down in the bathtub, drowned. The police could never establish what happened. Now Amber is in foster care, Tina is pregnant again, still living with her burglar boyfriend. (Royko, 1993, p. 3)

Nationwide, some 1,300 young children died from familial abuse in 1993 (Ingrassia & McCormick, 1994), only a few of them in homes where their biological father also lived. Most were the victims of their single-mothers' boy-friends or of those harried, heedless, hapless mothers themselves. Somewhat luckier, perhaps, are the 22,000 newborn infants each year whose mothers abandon them at birth, "boarder babies" left in the birth hospital for an average stay of 22 days (and an average cost of $13,000) before being transferred into foster care (Ritter, 1993).

In the public schools, truancy among pupils in the early grades ("baby truancy") has increased alarmingly; in Minneapolis in 1992, 70% of those truant youngsters, who averaged 22 unexcused absences, come from fatherless homes (Chandler, 1993). Because it is symptomatic of a failure of parental control, truancy presages more serious problems later. Of the swelling tide of adjudicated delinquents currently in custody, that same proportion —70%—come from homes with no resident father (Sullivan, 1992).

As psychologists Draper and Belsky (1990) report:

Adolescents and young adults who are the products of father absence show early sexuality; a rather antagonistic, deprecating attitude toward members of the opposite sex; and a lack of interest in developing a durable, bonded relationship with a mate. Father-absent boys also exhibit more hypermasculine behavior, aggressive acting out, excessive boasting and risk-taking behavior ... (p. 142)

The list of cultural, social, economic, familial, and biological factors that have been cited as causes of crime is a long one and familiar but, for each of these factors, there are many affected individuals—many youngsters exposed to TV violence, drugs, gangs and guns, or subjected to ethnic prejudice, to poverty, or to various forms of abuse or deprivation—who do not become delinquent or criminal. The only sine qua non on this list of causal variables is the combination of biological susceptibility with inadequate parenting. The self-controlled, socialized child manages to resist temptation, to tolerate and in some way surmount disadvantage, without resorting to crime and violence.

The Socialization of Children

The socialization of children, the instilling of self-control and prosocial values, is traditionally achieved by the consistent nurturing and good example of both a mother and a father who are themselves tolerably mature and socialized. Parenting is one of the most difficult and demanding of human responsibilities; if would-be parents in modern Western cultures had to pass a licensure examination, it is likely that many couples from all strata of society would remain childless. In his classic study of *The Young Delinquent*, Cyril Burt (1945) concluded that: "the commonest and the most disastrous conditions [conducing toward delinquency] are those that centre about the family" (p. 185). More than 40 years later, the Cambridge Study of Delinquent Youth found family criminality and "parental mishandling" to be primary risk factors for adolescent criminality (Farrington & West, 1981). The most recent survey of the relevant literature (Yoshikawa, 1994) reaches the same conclusion. Although not all delinquents become criminal adults, adult criminality is almost invariably preceded by juvenile conduct disorder (Robins, 1966). Moreover, while offenses can be classified as violent or nonviolent, offenders are typically versatile, impulsively reacting to the exigencies of the moment (Farrington, 1979; Gottfredson & Hirschi, 1990). Thus, the antecedents of violent and nonviolent criminality are substantially the same.

An Indochinese Experiment. The recent influx of displaced families from Southeast Asia has provided a natural experiment on the importance of parenting, an experiment with striking conclusions. Most of the more recent immigrants were peasant families, unable to speak English when they arrived from refugee camps where their children had fallen a year or more behind in formal education. Caplan, Choy, and Whitmore (1992) studied a representative sample of 200 such Indochinese families settled in five urban areas across the United States. Living in relatively poor neighborhoods and attending the much-maligned U.S. public schools where the instruction was in, to them, a foreign language, 79% of these children had a grade point average of 3.0 ("B") or better, in spite of their special handicaps in English, history, and social studies courses. It need hardly be added that these children are greatly underrepresented in delinquency statistics. Caplan et al.'s explanation for this success story emphasizes the traditional values and solidarity that these families brought with them, qualities that have produced similar successes among other ethnic groups in this country since its beginning.[1]

In traditional societies, where children are reared in and by an extended family, young people have an opportunity to learn how to be a parent and, moreover, the responsibility for socializing children is shared by numerous adults. In what we call the developed countries, children depend for their socialization instead on untutored, inexperienced, often part-time parents, and on day care, the schools, and the streets. Inadequate or incompetent parenting leads to insecure attachment bonding that forecasts "low levels of empathy, compliance, cooperation, and self-control" (Draper & Belsky, 1990, p. 151). The best measure of parental competence is the success of the product and, by this index, these immigrant Indochinese parents were more competent than many of their American-born counterparts.

---

[1]Not all Southeast Asian families are successful after transplantation to the United States (Ingrassia, 1994). When the parents themselves are slow to adapt to the new culture, their children may find the lure of the peer culture irresistible. One suspects that Asian families with several children are more cohesive and better able to maintain their traditional values.

Remember that the process of socialization involves: monitoring the child's behavior, recognizing deviant behavior when it occurs, punishing that deviant behavior, selectively reinforcing prosocial alternatives to antisocial behavior, and explaining why some things are wrong and others right. All five of these facets of parenting are much more difficult to do than to describe, even for mature, loving, middle-class couples who can share the load. All five are particularly difficult for an immature, uneducated, undersocialized single mother to accomplish. As Burt (1948) put it, "Should one of the livelier boys, possessor of far more energy, leisure, and shrewdness than his worn and distracted mother, take to unprincipled mischief, it will be much easier for him to play upon her feelings than for her to appeal successfully to his; he can laugh, argue, intimidate; and turn himself to any disobedience that he chooses" (p. 97).

The Single-Parent Family

It seems plausible to suppose that boys raised in a home with a resident father are, in consequence, more likely to assume the existence of a higher authority who is more powerful than they are and whose rules are dangerous to flout. According to Smith and Jarjoura (cited in Moynihan, 1993), "Neighborhoods with larger percentages of youth (those aged 12 to 20) and areas with higher-percentages of single-parent households also have higher rates of violent crime. The relationship is so strong that controlling for family configuration erases the relationship between race and crime and between low income and crime" (p. 24). J. Q. Wilson (1991) went so far as to suggest the provision of boarding schools in which to socialize "boys growing up in a fatherless family." Not all fatherless children turn to crime, of course, but even a few percent of 15 million guarantees that the criminal justice system will continue to be a growth industry.

The Search Institute Study

The Search Institute of Minneapolis recently conducted a survey of more than 46,000 Grade 6–12 students in 111 communities across the United States (Benson & Roehlepartain, 1993). The sample did not include most large city school systems and, of course, youngsters who had already dropped out of school or were incarcerated were also excluded. About 8,200 of those surveyed came from single-parent families, nearly all of them marriages broken by death or divorce rather than families headed by a never-married mother. The data are reported for the sexes combined. For all of these reasons, this large sample underestimates the frequency of delinquent behaviors and also the expected differences between two- and single-parent homes.

The Search Institute found that sixth- to eighth-grade youngsters living in one-parent families were twice as likely as those from two-parent families to use illegal drugs, to be sexually active, to engage in vandalism, to skip school frequently, and to steal things from stores. The single-parent children were also twice as likely to have used a weapon at least twice "to get something from another person," to have been in trouble with the police, to have been physically or sexually abused by an adult, and to plan on quitting school before graduation. Students classified as high risk for delinquency and crime because they had engaged in five or more of the list of at-risk behaviors constituted 21% of the sixth to eighth graders from single-parent families and 43% of those in Grades 9–12 who were living with a single parent. Had the Search Institute used never-married mothers, rather than divorced or widowed mothers, to comprise their single-parent group, we can be confident that the differences in delinquency rates between the single and two-parent samples would have been larger still.

Many of the biological parents of the children of never-married single mothers contributed genetic tendencies that exacerbate the difficulties of socialization as do, of course, the "mean streets" of the communities in which many of these children live. The relationship of criminality to biological and genetic factors has been controversial since Lombroso but, as we have seen, studies relating criminality in adoptees to criminality in their biological and adoptive parents indicate that this complex phenotype, like most other psychological characteristics, is influenced by genetic differences between people. No one, of course, argues that there are specific genes for criminality. But, as suggested in Burt's example, there are aspects of innate temperament and aptitude that make some children more difficult to socialize than others and some of these attributes—relative fearlessness, aggressiveness, stimulus-seeking, risk-taking proclivities, impulsiveness, low IQ—can be expected to be more common both in the unmarried mothers of these 5 million youngsters and in the biological fathers who have planted their seed and gone their ways.[2] The other commonly cited villains—poverty, drug abuse, street gangs, ethnic xenophobia, a handgun for everyone, and so on—should perhaps be regarded as potentiating variables, fuel for the fires started by the massive failure of primary socialization in biologically susceptible young males.

There is no doubt that these two key factors, biological susceptibility and parental inadequacy, vary in their relative importance from case to case. In his *The Mask of Sanity*, Cleckley contended that the primary psychopath was a sort of biological accident that could befall the best of parents. It is also possible that a few criminals are actually created by Faginlike parents from boys with unexceptional temperaments. But most delinquents of the group destined to become adult criminals, possibly violent criminals, begin as relatively fearless, impulsive, stimulus-seeking, often ungifted children who would be difficult—but not impossible—for any parent to socialize, children who are often too difficult a problem for their feckless biological parent(s) to be able or willing to contend with.

Peter Cantu

This 19-year-old Houston school drop-out directed the gang rape and murder of two teenage girls in 1994. A month earlier, he remarked to his former shop teacher

---

[2]See Horn et al. (1976). The biological parents of adopted-away children, also, show higher than average rates of criminality and, thus, higher levels of hard-to-socialize temperaments on average, and the adoptees whose biological parents were criminal are themselves more likely to develop criminal ways; see Baker et al. (1989).

that "I'd like to kill somebody just to see what it feels like." A few months before that, at the Astrodome, he prowled the hallways bumping into people; when one protested, Cantu pulled a knife and tried to stab him, slashing his shirt before being overpowered by a security guard. There had been numerous prior arrests dating back to the sixth grade for car thefts, disruption at school, attacking teachers and other students. School officials "held many conferences with his mother, but made no headway because Cantu refused to listen and his mother defended him." One of his violent outbursts was sparked when a school security guard took away his beeper, a little luxury provided by his mother because he was a "good boy" (Harper, 1994.) Peter Cantu may have had a difficult temperament but he surely had incompetent parents. His father was said to have epilepsy and did not attend his son's murder trial. Peter's mother continued to insist that he was a good boy even after a jury sentenced him to be executed.

But most of our current harvest of antisocial youth were reared in homes without any resident biological father, most often by a poorly educated, poorly socialized mother subsisting on welfare. We have been producing bumper crops of these nascent felons as a direct consequence of two recent social trends. The first is the sharp increase in the divorce rate, which has more than doubled since the 1950s (Whitehead, 1993). The second and more serious development has been the sharp and continuing increase in the rate of illegitimate births, from about 4% in the 1950s to nearly 30% in the mid-1990s (Eckhom, 1992; Murray, 1993).

More than 80% of babies born just after World War II were reared by both biological parents who were married to each other. Not all those fathers were Ward Cleavers, of course (he was the wise, caring father on "Leave It To Beaver," a TV program that my sons grew up with), but at least they were there, bringing home the hamburger and helping mom to set some limits. In 1990, 19% of White, 62% of Black, and 30% of Hispanic children under age 18 lived with only one parent, usually the mother (Reiss & Roth, 1993). More than 50% of U.S. children born in 1988 will spend all or part of their childhood in a mother-only family (about 45% of White children and about 85% of Black children) where they will be five times as likely to spend years in poverty, much more likely to drop out of school, to show emotional and behavioral problems, seven times more likely to get into trouble with the law, more likely to suffer physical or sexual abuse—than children reared in intact families (McLanahan & Garfinkel, 1988; Whitehead, 1993).

In a small Minnesota town, an 18-year-old unmarried mother of two became so upset by her baby's continued crying that she stuffed toilet paper down the infant's throat and held it there until the infant quieted—and died ("Woman Admits Killing Baby Daughter," 1993). The young mother now faces years in prison for murder in the second degree. Just another one of millions of mothers, children themselves, who wanted babies, had them, and then found they could not cope. They all are our responsibility to care for, the mothers, the surviving babies, those babies grown up and then *their* babies. Some might even argue that our responsibility should have started earlier, that children, as well as irresponsible adults, should somehow be dissuaded from having babies in the first instance.

I have not been able to find good estimates of the proportion of these children, reared by single mothers, who become felons or welfare dependents. If we turn the question around, however, asking what proportion of school truants, school drop-outs, teenage pregnancies, illegitimate birth parents, adjudicated delinquents, or prison inmates were reared in fatherless homes, the evidence is clear—from two thirds to three fourths of the people in each of the these categories come from families in which the biological father was absent for long periods or never present from the start.[3] Fatherless children are more likely to drop out of school, to get involved with drugs, or to suffer child abuse and, when the "father is present in the household, teen-age girls get pregnant 50% less frequently than their fatherless counterparts" (Kristol, 1994).

Mealey's "Integrated Evolutionary Model"

In an important paper, Mealey (1995) offered a taxonomy of antisocial personality, based on sociobiological principles, that is very similar to the one outlined here (see also Harpending & Sobus, 1987). Mealey's "primary sociopaths," like my psychopaths, are individuals who possess a genotype that "results in a certain inborn temperament or personality, coupled with a particular pattern of autonomic hypoarousal that, together, design the child to be selectively unresponsive to cues necessary for normal socialization and moral development" (Mealey, 1994, p. 29). Her "secondary sociopaths" (my sociopaths) are "individuals who are not extreme on the genetic sociopathy spectrum, but who, because of exposure to environmental risk factors, pursue a life history strategy that involves *frequent* but not necessarily emotionless cheating" (p. 30).

Because it is the temperamental risk factors that are heritable, Mealey pointed out that the heritability of psychopathy will be higher than for sociopathy and the sex difference in heritability of antisocialiality should decrease as one moves from middle-class environments with better parenting to underclass environments with poorer parenting. A similar conclusion emerges from the arguments advanced herein.

The Effect of Home Environment

We have seen that most psychological traits show very little lasting influence of the rearing environment. Unrelated foster-siblings brought up together by the same adoptive parents are no more alike as adults than random pairs of people, in IQ, in personality, and in most other respects (Plomin & Daniels, 1986). But, if the trait

---

[3]According to Louis Sullivan (1992), formerly secretary of Health, Education and Welfare, "Approximately 70% of juveniles in long-term correctional facilities did not live with their father while growing up." Only 20% to 30% of the antisocial boys studied at the Oregon Social Learning Center come from intact families (Forgatch, Patterson, & Ray, 1994). Raspberry (1993), like Moynihan (1993), said that controlling for father absence erases the relationship between low income and crime; it doesn't quite, but it comes close. See also Loeber and Dishion (1983), Patterson and Capaldi (1991), and Whitehead (1993).

we are measuring is socialization or criminality, and if many of these pairs of unrelated siblings are placed to be reared by immature, uneducated, unsocialized single mothers, then we will get a different result. The experiment has not been done, of course, although it has been approximated in the fact that a significant number of the siblings now being reared by single mothers have different fathers. But this is an experiment that does not have to be conducted in order for us to make a confident guess about its outcome. Although half of tomorrow's adolescents will have been reared with little or no help from the biological father, "only" about 25% of today's adolescents come from fatherless homes. Yet about 70% of adjudicated delinquents were reared in such homes (Sullivan, 1992), indicating a risk of delinquency about *seven times* higher for children from father-absent than from father-present homes.[4]

Twin studies have demonstrated a significant genetic influence on the symptoms of APD and also on the full-blown manifestation of that personality disorder (DiLalla & Gottesman, 1993; Grove, Eckart, Heston, & Bouchard, 1990). Moreover, it is probable that the biological parents of today's fatherless children possessed, on average, genetic characteristics that made them relatively harder to socialize; even by today's frayed standards, both the siring and what I will call the "daming" of an illegitimate child are behaviors that most of the truly socialized tend to avoid.[5] It is likely that the offspring of these parents, in consequence, tend to be somewhat more difficult to socialize than children growing up in two-parent families. That is, part of the increased risk of criminality in this group may be due to genetic factors. The evidence discussed in chapter 6 indicated that adopted-away sons are at about 50% greater risk if their biological fathers were criminal than if they were not. However, it is apparent that this modest increase in genetic risk cannot account for the sevenfold increase in the observed risk for delinquency among father-absent children.

Patterson's "Three-Step Dance"

Not only the absent fathers, but a large proportion of the single mothers who retain custody of the child may be antisocial. Gerald Patterson and his colleagues (Forgatch, Patterson, & Ray, 1994; Patterson & Capaldi, 1991) demonstrated that antisocial mothers are more likely to separate from their child's father and more likely to be deficient in child monitoring and discipline. Their research strongly supports the conclusion that contextual variables such as social disadvantage and stress, "will have an impact on child adjustment only if parenting practices are disrupted" (Forgatch et al., 1994). It has also demonstrated the vicious cycle in

---

[4]If R_F = the delinquency rate for the 75% of children raised with fathers present and R_{NF} = the rate for the 25% of children raised with no father, then $(.25\ R_{NF}):(.75\ R_F) = 7:3$, the ratio of fatherless delinquents to delinquents reared with fathers. This means that the ratio of the two delinquency rates, $R_{NF}:R_F$, equals $(7 \times .75):(3 \times .25) = 7$.

[5]In their sample of more than 13,000 Danish adoptees, Baker, Mack, Moffit, and Mednick (1989) found that 28% of the biological parents had a criminal conviction, compared with only 6% of the adoptive parents.

which stress → poor parental practices → antisocial child behavior → increased parental stress.

In his classic developmental studies of antisocial youth, Patterson demonstrated the continuing series of "three-step dances" in which the harried mother asserts a command ("do this" or "stop doing that") to which the child responds with tears or an argument or a temper-tantrum, which in turn causes the mother to back off (Patterson, Reid, & Dishion, 1992, p. 11). Patterson (1993) called these mother–child pas de deux *coercive cycles*, each one of which reinforces the child's defiant response, leading to a widening repertoire of coercive, antisocial behaviors. Moreover, as Gray demonstrated (see chap. 10), active avoidance responses are long-lasting and hard to extinguish. When a child reacts aggressively to parental admonitions or interference and the parent backs off, then aggression becomes the way that child will actively avoid constraint or punishment and, once learned, such lessons last.

Longitudinal studies have shown that mothers of boys who are willful and hot-tempered as children tend to become more permissive of such behavior and that these children become increasingly aggressive during childhood (Olweus, 1979). This may be why boys who display temper tantrums as children are more than twice as likely to be arrested before reaching adulthood (Sampson & Laub, 1993).

Most parents have participated in such three-step dances and know how easy it is to take that misguided third step of backing off and how tempting it is, next time, to avoid taking the first step of giving the command that is likely to elicit the coercive response. Most parents can sympathize with the single mother's tendency to relax her monitoring of the defiant child's behavior, to avoid intervening or to fail to follow-through when her intervention is defiantly resisted. But it is exactly these repeated interactions that constitute the process of socialization. With a temperamentally defiant child, socialization will fail unless, most of the time, the parent takes the first step whenever intervention is required, and then refuses the third step of backing off, refusing to let the child's coercive response be successful.

> In the week before her 3-year-old son died, Tonia Nelson spent much of her time writing a love letter to his killer. "Everytime I start writing you Jerry gets all upset," said the letter to her boyfriend, Douglas Oaks. "He is throwing my shoes against the wall, slamming dressers around. He always tells me stop writing. ... Doug, could you please take Jerry for a weekend ... or for a full week? ... I'm going crazy. ... It's 12:25, he's not sleeping yet. Doug what is your secret the kid won't listen." Douglas Oak's secret was one that children learn every day, even in seemingly untroubled places like Henry County [Illinois]: He beat the hell out of the boy. (S. Johnson, 1993, p. 1)

Doug, the mother's current boyfriend, gave little Jerry a fatal beating the next week and now both he and the mother are in prison. Most child abuse is committed, not by strangers or biological kin, but by affines, usually the mother's boyfriend or new husband (Daly & Wilson, 1988). Tonia Nelson was a single mother at 16; little Jerry was illegitimate. The sad question we must ask here is: What if Doug had been hit by a truck and little Jerry had survived to adolescence? Even in their small town of Cambridge, Illinois, far from the special problems of the metropolitan inner city, can one imagine little Jerry doing well in school, delivering newspapers, joining the Boy Scouts, going to church, falling in love with a nice local girl, and progressing toward a place in the society of law-abiding men? I suggest that no such happy outcome would have been likely, hardly even imaginable: Not with such a start in life or with such a mother.

In 1993 two English boys, 11 years old, were sentenced in Liverpool to indeterminate incarceration, "at the Queen's pleasure," for abducting a 2-year-old child, beating him to death, and then leaving his body on the railroad tracks to be cut in half by a passing train. Known by the authorities to be out-of-control, persistent truants, these boys were being reared by single mothers. About the same time, in the small town of Mankato, Minnesota, a 56-year-old man was severely beaten in his apartment, left hopelessly brain-damaged. He was a known homosexual and his assailants were several teenage boys who had gotten drunk, armed themselves with lengths of 2×4 boards, and gone to the man's home "to teach him a lesson." The mother of the 16-year-old ringleader was interviewed on television; she was, predictably, a single mom.

Crime Runs in Families

If there are two children in a family, each of whom has a temperament that inclines him or her toward defiance, the parent who does Patterson's three-step dance with one is likely to do it with both. Moreover, as Patterson (1986) also demonstrated, aggressive (and, likely, other antisocial) behavior in one sibling potentiates similar behavior in the other. My conjecture, therefore, is that the trait of socialization, and its component trait of criminality, are probably the striking exceptions to the rule that the rearing family environment has little lasting effect. We know that 53% of juveniles in long-term correctional institutions come from homes in which another family member has been incarcerated (Bureau of Justice Statistics, 1988). In 1991, 31% of adult inmates in U.S. state prisons had a brother who had also been in prison (Bureau of Justice Statistics, 1993). There is no doubt at all that criminality runs in families; what I am suggesting is that only part of this familial effect is due to genetic transmission and that much of it results from incompetent parenting. To test this hypothesis properly with conventional twin or family designs requires adequate sampling of the low end of the socialization continuum and this is seldom achieved by behavior geneticists. The sampling problem is further complicated by the tendency, especially for juvenile corrections institutions, to maintain astonishingly limited records which, nonetheless, are made surprisingly inaccessible to researchers.[6]

---

[6]In my county, the juvenile corrections facility does not know the make-up of a resident's family, whether there is a father in the home, whether the parents or siblings have arrest records; they do not even know officially whether the resident himself has been previously arrested. In view of the importance of better understanding these youngsters, and the ease with which such data could be collected on admission, it seems a shame that better records are not kept.

In their intensive reanalysis of the data from Sheldon and Eleanor Glueck's (1950) classic longitudinal study of 1,000 delinquent and nondelinquent youth, Sampson and Laub (1993) demonstrated that, compared to the nondelinquents (some of whom could be better described as noncaught delinquents), the delinquent boys were several times more likely to be arrested as adults and seven times more likely to be dishonorably discharged from the military. They then painstakingly separate effects of poverty, crowding, parental deviance, child's temperament, family disruption, and the like, and they concluded that "mother's supervision has by far the largest effect on delinquency" (p. 93). The Gluecks did not measure father's supervision and there were apparently few or no cases of illegitimacy among their sample of White males born from 1924 to 1935 in lower class neighborhoods of central Boston. There was, however, a strong relationship ($\phi = .62$) between delinquency and parental separation or divorce (Sampson & Laub, 1993).

These data strongly support Gottfredson and Hirschi's (1990) and Patterson et al.'s (1989) contention that it is inadequate parental supervision that leads to delinquency and crime and that genetic factors that make the child "difficult" have their effect by further straining already limited parental supervisory resources. The other data cited in this chapter, together with ordinary common sense, impel the additional conclusion that both paternal and maternal supervision are likely to be poorest when the fathers are not even present.

Fatherless Rearing is the Major Cause of Crime

In their important and controversial book, Herrnstein and Murray (1994) argued that most of the baleful characteristics of the underclass—poverty and unemployment, crime, welfare dependency, illegitimacy, bad parenting—can be attributed in part to the lower mean IQ of the members of that blighted segment of society. They provide abundant evidence showing that, indeed, each of these tendencies increase as IQ decreases. The mean IQ for White males sentenced to a correctional facility is 10 points lower than for those never booked by the police. White women with IQs from 75 to 90 are twice as likely to produce an illegitimate child as are women with IQs in the average range from 90 to 110; the odds double again for women below IQ 75.

However, as Herrnstein and Murray acknowledged, low IQ cannot explain the marked and steady *increases* in illegitimacy and crime that have occurred in the United States since about 1960. Beginning in the 1970s, the rate of violent crime continued to increase, substantially higher than the rate to be predicted from the proportion of the population that were then in the high-risk age group. The argument of this chapter suggests that we should look to incompetent parenting for an explanation of this continuing increase. We have seen that males reared without a father are some seven times more likely to contribute to the crime statistics than are men raised by both biological parents. Figure 14.3 shows the proportion of men aged 15 to 25 who were born out-of-wedlock and the proportion whose parents had divorced (the elevation of the later curve, peaking around 1955–1960, resulted from the sharp increase in the divorce rate during and just after World War II). I shall

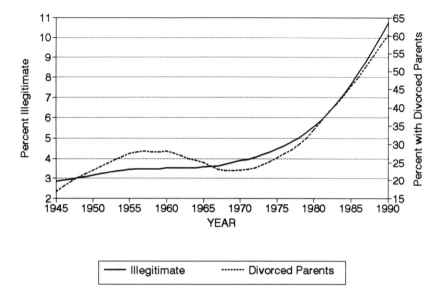

FIG. 14.3. The percentages of the high-risk group of 15- to 25-year-old males who either were born out-of-wedlock or whose parents had divorced. The elevation in the children-of-divorce curve around 1955–1960 resulted from the sharp increase in divorces during and just after World War II. Both curves bend sharply upwards in the mid-1970s, suggesting that fatherless rearing, which would be at high levels for both these subgroups, might account for the continuing rise in the rates of crime and violence (sources: National Center for Health Statistics, 1993a, 1993b).

arbitrarily assume that about one-fourth of divorced fathers essentially abandon their parental responsibilities. By adding one fourth of those with divorced parents to those with never-married mothers, I create a crude estimate of the total proportion of this high-risk group who were reared without fathers. The sharp bend upwards during the 1970s in this proportion suggests that fatherless rearing may be the explanation for the rising crime rate that we seek. The confirmation is displayed in Fig. 14.4 which shows that a combination of the two predictors, the percentage of the population who were high-risk males and the proportion of these who were reared without fathers, very closely tracks the growth in the violent crime rate since 1960.

However, this sort of regression analysis can be deceiving, especially if the variable to be predicted displays such a steady secular trend. The U.S. Justice Department cannot provide comparable crime rate data prior to 1960 when the increase shown in Fig.14.4 began. We can test the hypothesis a different way by attempting to predict, from the same two variables, the rise and fall in the proportion of all those arrested each year who were in the 15- to 25-year age group; good estimates of this proportion are available back to 1940. Figure 14.5 shows that the arrest rate of the high-risk group is not well predicted just from the group's relative size. In Fig. 14.6 we see, however, that the fall and rise of criminal activity is nicely estimated when we include as a predictor even a crude estimate of the proportion of the high-risk group who were reared without fathers.

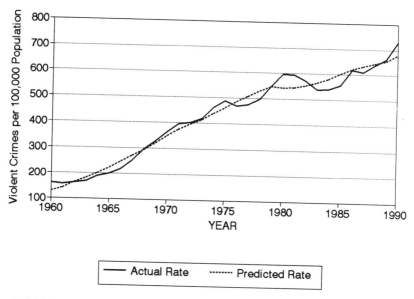

FIG. 14.4. The violent crime rate predicted from the variables plotted in Fig. 14.1 and 14.3. The relative size of the high-risk group, plus the proportion of males in this group who were reared without fathers jointly estimate the rising rate of violent crime with considerable fidelity.

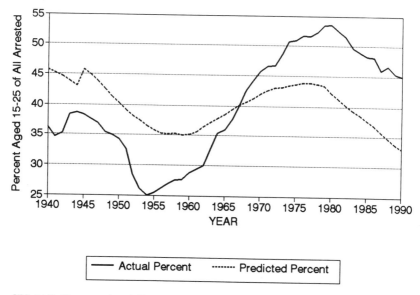

FIG. 14.5. The proportion of all those arrested in the United States from 1940 to 1990 who were in the 15- to 25-year age group. Also plotted is the arrest rate as predicted from the proportion of the total U.S. population who were in this high-risk age group (sources: FBI, 1993; National Center for Health Statistics, 1993a).

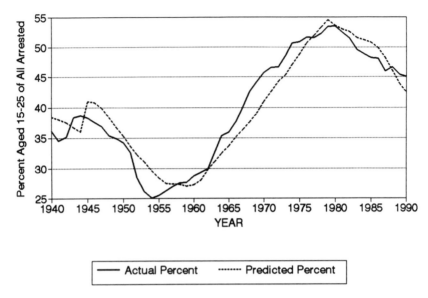

FIG. 14.6. Percent arrested who were age 15 to 25, plus the values predicted from both the relative size of this age group and the proportion of its members who were reared without fathers. The fatherless percentage was estimated from the sum of divorces 20 to 30 years earlier (sources: FBI, 1993; National Center for Health Statistics, 1993a, 1993b).

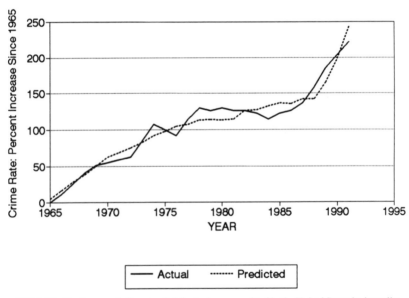

FIG. 14.7. The increase in the rate of violent crime committed in the United States by juveniles, together with the values predicted from the relative size of the 12- to 17-year age group and the proportion of that group reared without fathers (source: FBI, 1993; National Center for Health Statistics, 1993a, 1993b).

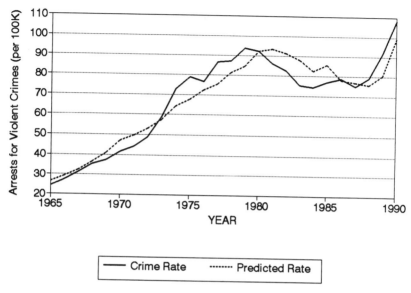

FIG. 14.8. Rate of arrest for violent crimes of U.S. White juveniles age 12 to 17, per 100,000 total White juveniles. Also plotted are the values predicted from the relative size of this group and the proportion that were born out-of-wedlock (source: FBI, 1993).

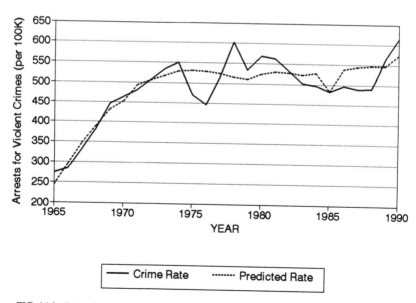

FIG. 14.9. Rate of arrest for violent crimes of U.S. Black juveniles age 12 to 17, per 100,000 total Black juveniles. Also plotted are the values predicted from the relative size of this group and the proportion that were born out-of-wedlock (source: FBI, 1993).

As another demonstration of the central role played by the absence of fathers in the criminal propensities of their offspring, I have applied the same analysis to the data on violent crimes among juveniles shown in Fig. 14.2. In Fig. 14.7 we see that the increase in juvenile crime also is reasonably well predicted from the proportion of the population who are in this age group together with the proportion of juveniles who have been reared without fathers.

Both the incidence of violent crime and the proportion of juveniles who were born out-of-wedlock differ greatly for White and Black youngsters and this fact provides the opportunity for a final test of the hypothesis that fatherless rearing is the major proximate cause of delinquency and crime. In the absence of race-specific divorce data, I have used as estimates of father-absence just the proportion of each group of juveniles who were born out-of-wedlock. The results, shown in Fig. 14.8 and 14.9, again seem to confirm the hypothesis.

The conclusion indicated by these data is this: Although criminals average lower in intelligence than noncriminals, most men with low IQs do not commit violent crimes. It is not low IQ that leads a man to murder, assault, rape, and rob people; it is, rather, incompetent and fatherless rearing that produces sociopaths who murder, assault, rape, and rob people.

15

The Question of Race

Thus, when it comes to the homicidal violence of the contemporary inner city, we are dealing with very bad boys from very bad homes, kids who in most cases have suffered or witnessed violent crimes in the past. These juveniles are not criminally depraved because they are economically deprived; they are totally depraved because they are completely unsocialized.

—J. J. DiIulio, Jr. (1995)

"No matter how one adjusts for other demographic factors, Blacks tend to be overrepresented by a factor of four to one among persons arrested for violent crimes, and by a factor of nearly three to one among those arrested for property crimes" (J. Wilson & Herrnstein, 1985, pp. 461–462). To put it differently, if the Black crime rate were no higher than the rate for Whites, violent crimes in the United States would decrease by half. As can be seen in Fig. 15.1, the arrest rate of juveniles for violent crimes was about six times higher for Blacks than for Whites by 1992. Black male juveniles were seven times more likely to murder someone (or to be murdered themselves) in 1980 than were Whites of the same age; by 1990, the ratio had increased to 8:1 (FBI, 1992). In 1987, arrest rates for robbery were 15 times higher, and for assault 7 times higher, for Blacks than for Whites (Blumstein & Cohen, 1987). Although one might suspect that the criminal justice system is quicker to arrest and to convict Black than White suspects, reports by victims of the race of the person who robbed or assaulted them correspond closely to the proportions of Blacks and Whites arrested for such crimes (J. Wilson & Herrnstein, 1985).

"In 1988, in the nation's 75 most populous urban counties, Blacks were 20% of the general population but 54% of all murder victims and 62% of all defendants" (DiIulio, 1994). In Little Rock, Arkansas, victims of more than 80% of the violent crimes (97% of Black victims) reported during 1991 identified the assailant as Black (Uyttebrouck, 1993). Although African Americans make up only one-eighth of the population of the United States (one third of the population of Little Rock), one gets the impression that many more than one eighth of the perpetrators of the

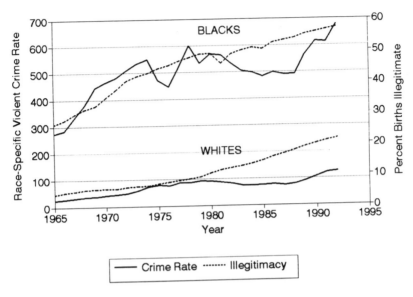

FIG. 15.1. Rates of arrest (per 100,000 of the reference group) of persons age 12 to 17 for violent offenses, plotted separately for Black and White juveniles. Also plotted are the rates of illegitimacy for the two races. In 1992, White illegitimacy had reached nearly the 1965 Black rate, which presaged the breakdown of the Black family and, as shown in chapter 14, which accounts for most of the sharp rise in Black juvenile crime (sources: FBI, 1993; National Center for Health Statistics, 1993a, 1993b).

violent crimes that we read about daily or see reported on the television are Black and this impression is correct; in 1991, Blacks accounted for 32% of U.S. property crime and 45% of violent crime (FBI, 1992).

In 1965, when the Black illegitimacy rate had climbed to about 25%, Daniel Patrick Moynihan wrote his famous memorandum on the breakup of the Black family, predicting much of the social dislocation that has since come to pass (see Rainwater & Yancey, 1967). Figure 15.1 shows that White illegitimacy, which was only about 5% in 1965, is now fast approaching the level that, in the Black community, presaged all those dire consequences. In his analysis of 1980 data from 150 U.S. cities, Sampson (1987) found that the strongest predictor of both homicide and robbery by Black juveniles was the local percentage of Black households headed by females. Sampson also found a similar relationship within the White community, where the percentage of families headed by females was a strong predictor of both juvenile and adult offending.

BLACK CRIME AND BLACK ILLEGITIMACY

Can we now account for the higher crime rate among Black than White youth in terms of the much higher rate of illegitimacy in the Black community? Specifically, young Black men are about six times more likely commit a violent crime than are young White men. We know that boys raised in fatherless families are about seven times more likely to become delinquent or criminal than are boys raised by both biological parents. And we know further that about half of the rising tide of never-married mothers in the United States are Black women.[1] Because Black mothers constitute only about one seventh of all mothers in the United States, this suggests that the rate of unwed motherhood among Blacks is about six times the rate for Whites.[2] In 1986, however, the Children's Defense Fund reported that, in American cities, compared to White children, Black children "were 12 times as likely to live with a parent who never married" (cited in Garmezy, 1991, p. 416). "During the 1970s, Black teenagers who had never been married were *ten times* as likely to have been pregnant as were White teenagers who had never been married. In addition, unmarried young Black women who get pregnant are more than twice as likely as unmarried pregnant White women to have their babies" (Nettler, 1989, p. 246). Our question is this: How much of the 6:1 excess in crime rate of Blacks over Whites can be accounted for directly by the fact that the proportion of children being reared by unmarried single mothers is from 6 to 12 times higher among Blacks than Whites?

It turns out that the ratio of the Black-to-White crime rates that is predicted directly from the ratio of Black-to-White illegitimacy is somewhere between 3.4:1 and 4.4:1.[3] Thus, illegitimacy predicts most of the excess Black crime rate, leaving a ratio of Black-to-White crime on the order of 1.5:1 yet to be accounted for.

It is important to remember that more than two thirds of all Index or violent crimes are committed by a relative handful of chronic offenders, whether White or Black (Gottesman & Goldsmith, 1994). Within these recidivist groups, the average frequency of offending while free and on the streets is high but about equal across

---

[1]U.S. Census Bureau figures released in July 1993, cited by Ingrassia (1993).

[2]If R_B is the illegitimacy rate for Blacks and R_W the rate for Whites, and N_B = the total number of Black mothers, then $R_B N_B$ = the number of unwed Black mothers and we know that the numbers of unwed Black and White mothers are about equal: $R_B N_B \approx R_W N_W$. Therefore, the ratio of the illegitimacy *rates* for Blacks versus Whites or $R_B{:}R_W$ must equal the ratio of total White to total Black mothers: $N_W{:}N_B \approx 6{:}1 = 6$.

[3]Let: $P(C|1)$ & $P(C|2)$ be, respectively, the probability that a man will be a criminal, given that he is reared in a one or a two-parent home; then, if S = the ratio of crime risk for fatherless boys to the risk for boys reared with two parents, we can write:

$S = P(C|1) : P(C|2) = 7$.

Let $P(1|B)$ = the probability that a man will have been reared in a one-parent home, given that he is Black; then, if R = the ratio of Black to White illegitimacy (or fatherlessness), we can write:

$R = P(1|B) : P(1|W)$ and R is in the range from 6 to 12.

Let $P(C|B)$ = risk for delinquency and crime if one is Black; and

RC = the expected ratio of the Black-to-White crime rates, then

$RC = P(C|B){:}P(C|W) = R * [(S-1)*P(1|B)+1] : (S-1)* P(1|B)+R]$.

If $P(1|B)$, the Black illegitimacy rate, equals .70, then RC will range from 3.06 to 3.85 as R ranges from 6 to 12. If the Black illegitimacy rate equals .90, the corresponding predictions for the ratio of Black to White crime are 3.1:1.4. I conclude that illegitimacy differences alone predict a difference in Black–White crime of about 4:1. If the true RC is equal to 6, then the residual crime rate ratio yet to be explained is about 6:4 = 1.5:1.

I am indebted to J. D. Lykken for correcting my algebra.

races (Blumstein & Cohen, 1987). What we are trying to explain, then, is not an average difference in propensity toward crime between the vast majority of Blacks and the similar majority of Whites. What we are trying to explain is why the small fraction of Blacks who are chronic offenders is some six times larger than the even smaller fraction of Whites who are responsible for most White crime. If sociopathy results from the inadequate parenting of biologically susceptible youngsters, and if rearing by unmarried single mothers (who more often provide inadequate parenting) is 6 to 12 times higher among Blacks than Whites in present-day America, then most of the Black–White difference in the rate of production of sociopaths can be accounted for.

Genetic Racial Differences

Are there racial differences in the genetic factors that make a child difficult to socialize? There is still a strong tendency among intellectuals to reject any idea of racial differences out of hand but this tendency can only be described as mindless. Five hundred years ago, my Norwegian ancestors differed both physically and psychologically from the natives of the Italian peninsula and from the people on the islands of Japan. Where there are physical differences, indicating a relatively isolated gene pool, there will also be psychological differences. I don't know if the average IQ of the Vikings was higher or lower than the Italian or the Japanese averages but it would be silly to imagine that the three values were somehow magically identical.

Although there has been considerable interbreeding, Black with White, in the United States (as in my own immediate family), it remains true that Blacks breed primarily with Blacks and Whites with Whites. Therefore, there remain physical differences, on the average, between American Blacks and Whites (differences that are responsible for the much higher incidence of outstanding athletes among Blacks than Whites) and there surely are psychological differences as well. One firmly established difference is in mean IQ, which is some 15 points higher in Whites than in Blacks (Herrnstein & Murray, 1994). There is no argument about this fact but there is a lot of argument about how much of this difference is due to genetic differences and how much can be explained by differences in prenatal and postnatal care and nurturing.

Some people argue that the difference represents test bias and that a test designed to measure the intellective talents that are more emphasized within the Black culture would show smaller or opposite differences. No such test has been successfully devised, however, probably because "street smarts" and what the IQ tests measure are basically the same thing. It is a good guess, in fact, that the leaders of urban street gangs would prove to have higher IQs as conventionally measured than their subordinate members.[4] Herrnstein and Murray (1994) pointed out that if IQ

---

[4]Kody Scott, the Los Angeles gang leader known as Monster, was interviewed in prison for the TV program "60 Minutes." He is more articulate and has a better working vocabulary than the average college graduate and I would estimate his verbal IQ to be at least 125.

tests were biased against Blacks, they would *underpredict* Black performance in the real world—in school, business, industry, and the military—yet dozens of studies agree in showing that these tests predict just as well for Blacks as for Whites. Moreover, other studies show that the Black–White difference in IQ is at least as great on tests or test items "that appear to be culturally neutral [as] on items that appear to be culturally loaded" (p. 282).

As to the question of how much of the Black–White difference in average IQ is due to *genetic* differences between the two racial demes, I doubt that a dispositive answer will be given until a neurophysiological measure, if one exists, of Spearman's general intelligence or *g* factor has been discovered. Meanwhile, however, I think it is instructive to ask just how large the observed Black–White difference really is. We know that the correlation in IQ of adult MZ twins, who are genetically identical, is about .80 (Pedersen et al., 1992). This means that the typical pair of adult MZ twins will differ in measured IQ by about 8 points.[5] For fraternal twins and ordinary siblings, the same computation indicates a mean absolute difference of about 14 IQ points. Therefore, we can say that the average difference in IQ between the average White and the average Black American is about equal to the average difference between siblings of either race.

We know that brighter youngsters are less likely to become delinquent (White, Moffitt, & Silva, 1989) and that criminal offenders have a lower average intelligence than nonoffenders; the Black–White difference in IQ may thus contribute to the difference in antisocial tendency. For example, the preponderance of criminals have IQs in the range from 75 to 105 (J. Wilson & Herrnstein, 1985) and about 66% of Blacks score in this range compared to 58% of Whites, suggesting that IQ alone could account for a Black–White crime ratio of about 1.14:1, leaving a ratio of about 1.3:1 yet to be explained after controlling for the higher incidence of inadequate socialization that results from the high Black rate of illegitimate births.

Irrespective of race, the IQs of the parents of illegitimate children are on average substantially lower than the IQs of those parents who wait until they are mature, married, and self-supporting before having children. Among White women, as we saw in chapter 14, those with IQs of 75 or below are twice as likely to produce an illegitimate child as are women with IQs from 75 to 90, and four times as likely as women in the broad average range from 90 to 110 (Herrnstein & Murray, 1994). In the large National Longitudinal Survey of Youth[6] (NLSY) sample, one third of illegitimate children were born to mothers in the bottom 10% of the IQ distribution and 85% to mothers with IQs less than 100. That is to say that we can safely expect that the IQs of the legitimate children of competent, mutually committed parents will average significantly higher than the IQs of children born out of wedlock. If we could somehow reduce the incidence of the latter, therefore, the IQs of the next generation should rise and, since illegitimacy is currently so much higher among

---

[5]If R is the twin correlation, the mean absolute difference between cotwins will be $|D| = 1.13(SD_{IQ})(1 - R)^{1/2} = 1.13(16)\sqrt{.2} = 8$ points (Plomin & Defries, 1980).

[6]The NLSY, a survey of labor market experience of youth, was begun in 1979 with 12,686 participants who were chosen to be representative of the general U.S. population.

American Blacks than Whites, this same social change—which should largely eliminate the current disparity in Black versus White crime rates—should also tend to reduce the current disparity in Black versus White IQs.

Other Factors

It seems to me that the residual excess of Black–White crime rate is plainly attributable to poverty and cultural aggregation. That is, a higher proportion of Black than White youth who would otherwise be tolerably socialized now must nonetheless grow up on the mean streets of urban ghettos inhabited by feral youth and adolescent street gangs, an environment that must increase the crime risk for any youngster immersed in it.[7] In some of these neighborhoods, the most competent of parents would be lucky to raise law-abiding, economically independent off-spring. (On the other hand, one could argue that truly competent parents would not try to rear children in such circumstances.) And, because of the low sex ratio that currently exists among urban Blacks and the resulting failure of male–female pair-bonding (see later), Black youth remain longer in this subculture, through the age when young White men are withdrawing from the risky adolescent culture into marriage and family responsibilities.

Why is the Black Rate of Illegitimacy so High?

We might also ask whether there is a genetic basis for this high current difference in illegitimacy rates in American Blacks versus Whites. It has been argued that this is instead a cultural phenomenon imposed during slave times when Black families were cruelly separated. Wilson and Herrnstein cited evidence, however, that there was not an excess of female-headed Black families in the South after slavery or even in New York early in this century. "In 1925, for example, 84 percent of all native Black families and 86 percent of West Indian Black families living in central Harlem were headed by males, and in most of the female-headed households, the woman was not a teenager but over the age of 30" (J. Wilson & Herrnstein, 1985, p. 480). "In every census from 1890 to 1960 the percentage of African American households with two parents remained essentially unchanged at about 80%" (Westman, 1994, p. 187). According to Lemann (1993), "a generation of historical scholarship ... stands in refutation of the idea that slavery destroyed the Black family" (p. 30). Therefore, both the legacy-of-slavery hypothesis and also the suggestion of a gene-based racial difference in pair bonding or in family structure have to be rejected.

The Vicious Circle of Illegitimacy

It is important to understand that there is a positive feedback to illegitimacy, that people reared without fathers, both males and females and teenagers as well as

---

[7]Kotlowitz's (1992) *There Are No Children Here* provides a vivid and dismaying firsthand picture of one such environment, the Henry Horner housing project on Chicago's near west side.

adults, tend to beget illegitimate children themselves in ever-widening circles. Here is a vignette that poignantly displays the mother's point of view:

> Fourteen-year-old Taisha Brown is thinking of having a baby.... Around her way—a housing project in the South Bronx—lots of girls have babies. Her 16-year-old cousin just gave birth a few months ago, and she enjoys helping with the infant. "I love babies," the braided, long-legged youngster says sweetly. "They're so cute. My mother already told me, 'If you get pregnant, you won't have an abortion. You'll have the baby, and your grandmother and I will help out.' ... Why do I need to worry about a father? My mother raised me and my sister just fine without one." (Hymowitz, 1994, p. 19)

Meanwhile, what are the potential "fathers" thinking about?

> While the girls play mother, some of the lost boys of never-never land seek sexual adventure to test their early manhood. They often brag about their conquests, which they achieve with promises—sneakers, clothes, a ride in a nice car—and with flattery. "You know I love you, baby," they'll tell a girl. "You're so pretty." Fathering children is a sign of manhood. (Hymowitz, 1994, p. 22)

Illegitimacy feeds on itself and the rising curve of illegitimate births is the same kind of growth function that describes the increase of a cancer or the spread of a contagion. The antidote for this contagion is nicely suggested by the following anecdote:

> I recently watched a girl of about 12 walking down the street with her parents [this is a Black girl in the South Bronx]. As she skipped along next to them, busily chattering, she held her father's hand and occasionally rested her head against his arm. The introduction of a serious boyfriend into this family romance is unlikely to come soon. Marion Wright Edelman's aphorism has received a wide currency: "The best contraceptive is a real future." It would be more accurate to say, "The best contraceptive is a real father and mother." (Hymowitz, 1994, p. 29)

The question we must ask, therefore, is not why Black illegitimacy is so high but, rather, what precipitated the sharp upward spiral as recently as the 1950s.

The Sex-Ratio Hypothesis

The most plausible explanation for the breakdown of the urban Black family structure is that it is a consequence of the substantial excess of young Black women to young Black men that presently exists in these communities.[8] At any given time, currently, approximately one fourth of young Black men from central city areas are in jail or prison. Together with the extremely high rate of death by homicide in this same group, this yields a male:female sex ratio for Black young people not much greater than .50 in the areas where illegitimacy rates are highest. Basic principles of evolutionary psychology suggest that, with an excess of females, young males can be expected to adopt the strategy of mating with multiple partners in preference to an exclusive bonding with one woman.

---

[8]This was suggested to me by David Buss in the spring of 1994.

Guttentag and Secord (1983) investigated the demographic correlates of the sex ratio over diverse cultures and convincingly document this conjecture, concluding that high adult male:female ratios "create male fidelity and family commitment" whereas low sex ratios have the opposite effect, independently of race. The ratio of marriage-aged Black men to women in Chicago and other Northern cities was about 1:1 as recently as 1950 but had dropped below .70 by 1975, due in part to the greater proportion of women than men in the Black migration from the rural South. During this same time period, the proportion of illegitimate births among Blacks rose from 17% to about 50%. This sex-ratio disparity not only accounts for the current high Black rate of illegitimacy but must independently contribute to the increased crime rate. Unattached young men without wives or family responsibilities are for that reason alone at greater risk for crime. Even among the Gluecks' 500 delinquents, those who formed strong marital attachments were at less than half the risk for adult crime as those who did not (Sampson & Laub, 1993).

In China, pressures to limit offspring have led to the aborting or infanticide of females so that the next generation will show a relative excess of breeding-age males. Then each young Chinese man who can find a mate will be especially likely to cleave to her exclusively with traditional family bonds and to invest his energies in nurturing her offspring. If that proves to be the case, then we should expect the next Chinese generation to produce children who are unusually well-socialized to their own culture and that the Chinese will enjoy a correspondingly low rate of crime and violence.

Other Alleged Causes of Black Crime

Unemployment

It is natural to suppose that crime is a reaction to joblessness and, because unemployment is so high among Black Americans generally and among Black youth in particular, there are many who think that providing more jobs, through "enterprise zones" and other initiatives, will solve the problem. In the United States, however, the crime rate has been highest when business is booming and unemployment is low. Sociologist David Rubinstein (1992) pointed out that the homicide rate in the United States peaked just before the Great Depression: "Between 1933 and 1940, the murder rate dropped nearly 40%. Property crimes reveal a similar pattern." From 1940 to 1960 the homicide rate was fairly stable and then increased sharply as the economy picked up, peaking in 1974. "Between 1963 and 1973, homicides in New York City tripled." During this same period, unemployment *decreased* by about 50%.

On the other hand, Sampson (1987) showed that, "while male joblessness has little or no direct effect on crime, it has the strongest overall effect on family disruption, which in turn is the strongest predictor of Black violence" (p. 377). The advent of reliable mechanical cotton pickers soon after World War II, followed in the 1960s by chemical methods of weed control that were cheaper than human "cotton choppers," produced between 1940 and 1970 a great northward migration of some 5 million Black people, mostly former sharecroppers or their families from the Mississippi Delta and the Cotton Belt, headed for Chicago, Detroit, and other Northern cities where job prospects were better. As chronicled by Lemann (1993), it was the serflike conditions under which sharecroppers existed that initiated the disruption of the Black family and a high proportion of these northward migrants were poorly educated Black women, often with their children, fleeing these intolerable conditions toward the illusory promise of a better life in the big cities.

In our worst urban ghettos, there are assuredly people who would be glad to work if jobs were available, and still more people who would work if they had skills to qualify. But if factories and other job opportunities were established throughout South Central Los Angeles, it would be naive to imagine that the local crime rate would plummet in consequence. Many of those unsocialized young people have never even known anyone who held a full-time job and jobs are not on their personal agendas. Having fun and hanging out and crime is on their agendas. Working for a living is for socialized people.

Black Rage

"Black rage" is frequently invoked, by certain Black leaders and also by the media, as an explanation for the antisocial conduct of Black youth. When a gang of toughs murdered an Hasidic Jewish passerby in the Crown Heights section of Brooklyn in 1991 and then went on a rampage of burning and looting, their behavior was explained as a rage reaction to the accidental death of a Black child when a Jewish leader's car ran out of control up on the sidewalk. The Los Angeles riots of 1992, which destroyed $1 billion worth of property and took some 50 lives, were attributed to rage over a jury's failure to convict policemen who had beaten a Black man named Rodney King. Black leaders who preach messages of anger and hatred enjoy an enthusiastic following, perhaps because, paradoxically, it feels good to be able to say: "I'm mad as hell and I'm not going to take it any more!"—it engenders a transient feeling of strength and pride. Football players, like soldiers charging into battle, cultivate a similar synthetic rage because it gives them confidence and energy.

Many Black people (and many Whites as well) did experience genuine outrage as they viewed the video pictures of the Rodney King beating. But the citizens whose sense of social justice was outraged were not out burning buildings and looting stores. The people who empathized with Rodney King were not stabbing harmless Hasidim or pulling innocent truck drivers from their cabs and beating them nearly to death. The young Black men who broke all the bones in Reginald Denney's face in that South Central Los Angeles intersection were dancing with glee, not with rage, their faces wreathed in proud smiles.[9] The looters and rioters in these affairs were having the time of their lives, as high and excited as kids at an amusement park. It may be that interracial xenophobia and resentment lowers

---

[9]One of the men later convicted for beating Reginald Denney confessed that he had not heard about the Rodney King verdict and did not know, when he happily joined in the mayhem, what the riot was about.

the barriers that conscience and empathic feeling raise toward most crime, in the special case of interracial crime. But the fact is that most crime by far is either White-on-White or Black-on-Black. Truly socialized people seldom riot, destroying the infrastructure of their own neighborhoods. When socialized people are angry they bring a lawsuit or, like Martin Luther King, they hold a peaceful demonstration. When unsocialized people get angry (or when they are bored and want a good time) they beat and burn, rape and pillage, and their victims are whomever is handy.

The Impact of Black Crime on the Black Community

Because the victims of Black criminals are overwhelmingly likely to be Black citizens, the African American community has an obvious and pressing interest in reversing the upward spiral of Black crime. But there is another and equally exigent concern as well. It seems to me that by far the greatest obstacle to continuing, or even maintaining, the extraordinary improvements that have occurred during my lifetime in race relations and in the opportunities available for Black people in this country is the fact that the one eighth of the population who are of African descent are responsible for nearly one half of the crime. I hate the idea that my two grandsons who have African heritage and who look now as if destined to become large, physically intimidating men, are likely to engender fear and distrust in all strangers they encounter as they move from adolescence to maturity.

But I believe that most of this imbalance in the crime statistics is directly attributable to the near disappearance of the traditional two-parent family within the Black community. That fact does not really need the statistical corroboration I have assembled here; it must be apparent to any citizen who keeps up with the horror stories that have become regular fare in our news reports. One especially notorious example surfaced one midnight, February 1, 1994, when four Chicago police officers entered a house in which they thought a drug pusher might be hiding. Instead of a pusher they found 19 children aged 1 to 14, sleeping six to a bed or on piles of dirty clothes on the dirty floor or tussling with a dog over a half-chewed bone (Ingrassia & McCormick, 1994). The interior was a scene of total squalor, filthy, crumbling, the kitchen stove inoperable, the dishes crusted with last week's food. The 6 single mothers of this brood were out partying at the time. Five of them were sisters, aged 21 to 31, themselves illegitimate offspring of a prior generation. Their AFDC payments plus food stamps came to $4,500 a month but it had not been spent on the children.

What kind of future can we imagine for these children "reared" in such circumstances, those who survive to adolescence? Will they be average citizens, law-abiding, self-supporting, generally a credit to their race? Or are they overwhelmingly likely to be criminals, prostitutes, drug addicts, welfare recipients, doomed to replicate the sequence once again with children of their own? And how many such children will there be the next time around?—the 6 mothers had produced 19 children by an average age of 25, leaving plenty of time for another dozen before their biological clocks run down.

Even allowing for the inevitable early mortality expected in this group, these 6 mothers might reasonably anticipate as many as 100 grandchildren, most of them as unsocialized as themselves. This case is exceptional only because so many mothers and children happened to be living under one roof. There are hundreds of thousands of such mothers and of such children in the United States today. Nearly half of them are White but the proportion who are Black is vastly greater than the proportion of Blacks in the population. What can the future hold for our society, for the problems of crime and violence, for racial amity in this country, for my "Black" grandchildren—if this exponential increase in the numbers of fatherless, feral, sociopathic children, half of them Black children, is allowed to continue?

My grandsons' African-American grandparents raised seven children in the old-fashioned way with both biological parents each doing their jobs (both at home and at work) and those seven offspring are all good, law-abiding citizens. Maybe the mother could have done it alone but, when I look at her four tall, venturesome sons, I am inclined to doubt it. The mother of my three sons is a remarkable woman and had an instinctive gift for parenting that I, as a psychologist, could appreciate but never equal. Yet even she, I think, might have been severely tested had she been forced to raise them on her own.

Conclusions

Most people who are victims of poverty, minority status, or who are exposed to the prevalence of drugs, guns, violent programs on television, and the many other alleged causes of crime commonly alluded to, do not in fact resort to antisocial, criminal behavior. I have argued that the one fundamental source of common criminality—or, in psychiatry's lexicon, of APD—is the failure of too many parents to perform their primary function of socializing their offspring. The probability of such failure is increased by a higher incidence among the offspring of these incompetent parents of traits of temperament that make those children harder than average to socialize.

From an evolutionary point of view, it seems probable that most children of our species would become adequately socialized if they could grow up within a stable extended family structure similar to that of our ancestors during the Pleistocene or to, say, the Amish culture of today. Reared in the modern way by two parents working alone, parents who have had little opportunity to learn parenting skills during their own growing-up period, a higher proportion of youngsters will be inadequately socialized and the crime rate will increase. Reared by a single mother, with no equally committed biological father present to share the load, to provide a male role model and paternal authority, the incidence of failed socialization must substantially increase.

At least 10 million such children under the age of 18 are being raised in the United States by divorced women many of whose ex-husbands have essentially abandoned their parental responsibilities. Rearing by a single mother who is immature, poorly educated and poorly socialized herself, yields a child who, if he or she avoids a career of social dependency and crime, deserves our wonderment and special approbation. More than 5 million such children, born out of wedlock, are growing up in the United States today where it can be said that we are operating a veritable factory of crime (National Center for Health Statistics, 1993b).

In a recent widely cited article entitled "The Coming White Underclass," Murray (1993) pointed out that, in 1991, more than 700,000 babies were born in this country to single White mothers, representing 22% of all White births or very nearly the 25% rate that, in 1965, led Moynihan to make his dire but accurate prediction of the growth of the Black underclass. One way to equalize the crime rates, White with Black, would be to just dream on. The incidence of Black single-parenthood cannot go much higher while, if present trends continue, the White rate will catch up. Then the young man you see approaching on the deserted city street at night will be equally dangerous whether he is White or Black. A better way, it seems to me, would be to start doing something now to reverse the rates of illegitimacy and incompetent parenting in both communities.

16

Preventing Antisocial Personality

From the wild Irish slums of the 19th Century Eastern seaboard to the riot-torn suburbs of Los Angeles, there is one unmistakable lesson in American history: a community that allows a large number of young men to grow up in broken families, dominated by women, never acquiring any stable relationship to male authority, never acquiring any set of rational expectations about the future—that community asks for and gets chaos. Crime, violence, unrest, unrestrained lashing out at the whole social structure—that is not only to be expected; it is very near to inevitable.

—Daniel Patrick Moynihan (1969)

In this last chapter, I recapitulate the main themes of this book and then consider briefly the important but difficult question of what might be done to minimize crime and violence by reducing the proportion of antisocial personalities in our midst.

A SUMMING UP

Psychopathy

Like the other social animals, *homo sapiens* became adapted through natural selection to live together in reasonable harmony in extended family groups, our *environment of evolutionary adaptation*. We can assume that, in ancestral times, truly antisocial personalities were rare and, in most cases, were the consequence of temperamental and other innate characteristics that made those individuals unusually resistant to socialization. We have called such persons *psychopaths*. Although it seems likely that there are numerous genetic dispositions that, alone or in combination, might contribute to such refractoriness, we have suggested that a common risk factor for primary psychopathy is simply a low endowment in ordinary fearfulness or, in terms of the Fowles–Gray model, a weak BIS.

225

Overactivity in another brain mechanism, which Fowles and Gray refer to as the BAS, might be responsible for what has been called secondary psychopathy. In these individuals, yielding to temptation may result not from a weakened inhibition but, rather, from overeager impulse strength. Unlike the primary type, the secondary psychopath may be vulnerable to the stresses of his risky lifestyle, capable of normal fear and, if he has been tolerably socialized, of normal guilt.

Other deviations, innate or acquired through developmental injury or accident, can make a child difficult to socialize or may overmaster normal socialization from time to time. We have referred to these as the *distempered psychopathies*. A choleric tendency or hypersexuality are two examples. There seems to be good evidence that abnormalities in the prefrontal area of the brain can produce psychopathic behavior. The *low serotonin syndrome* appears to be associated sometimes with violent aggression and dysphoric mood. A more speculative possibility is that hypertrophied repressive or dissociative tendencies may yield bouts of apparently carefree self-indulgence alternating with periods of guilty or anxious regret. What seems clear is that there are several "psychopathies" and that future research must find a way of distinguishing among them.

Although the various tendencies that make a youngster difficult to socialize are mostly innate and usually genetic, it seems clear that there are not genes for criminality as such, that most difficult-to-socialize children could in principle be socialized given the right rearing environment, and that, in such cases, at least some of the problematic traits (e.g., relative fearlessness or an ardent lust for life) might then become social and communal assets rather than just liabilities.

Sociopathy

Most modern humans do not live in the environment of evolutionary adaptation and, because their rearing environments are not optimal for our species, larger proportions of modern children remain unsocialized than is true in most traditional societies or than probably was true in ancestral times. Antisocial personalities whose innate endowments are in the broad normal range we refer to as *sociopaths*. However, because socialization is the product of genetic characteristics and the quality of socializing experiences (i.e., of parenting), the psychopath and the sociopath are endpoints of a continuum. Many psychopaths were less than optimally reared and many sociopaths began life with difficult temperaments. Because most antisocial personalities tend to breed carelessly and then function poorly as parents, antisocial personality is a familial trait.

Most psychological traits, including the ones most relevant to socialization, owe the larger portion of their variance to genetic differences and very little of their variance to lasting effects of home environment. Probably for the very evolutionary reasons just reviewed, socialization is an important exception to these rules. Genetic effects on socialization are significant but somewhat weaker than on aptitudes and on most traits of personality while the effects of the rearing environment are substantial and enduring.

Unlike the great apes, we are a pair-bonding species. This is a go|
suppose that even in ancestral times fathers played an important |
socializing role. Being reared by both committed biological parents may not be
quite as efficient and effective as when the extended family also participates on a
daily basis; nevertheless, evolutionary considerations suggest what modern empirical research has demonstrated, that both parents working together are far more
effective as socializing agents on the average than is one parent working largely
alone. The current trend toward single parent households, due either to early
divorce or to the rapid increase in illegitimacy, is beyond doubt the primary source
of the concurrent increase in the proportion of sociopaths in our society and in the
rates of juvenile crime and violence.

TREATMENT

Some of the antisocial subspecies or types listed in chapter 3 are potentially
reformable. Most adolescents whose delinquency does not begin until their teen
years will reform more or less spontaneously as they mature. As Moffitt (1993)
pointed out, these youngsters acquire the rudiments of socialization during childhood and, importantly, they learn at least the basic skills in school so that, when
they do decide to leave the primrose path of dalliance, they are prepared for
employment or for further training. If their adolescent outlawry does not go too far
(e.g., if it does not get them convicted for some serious offense) then, as they
become more aware of the high cost–benefit ratio of their dyssocial lifestyle and
tired of keeping their consciences shut up in some mental closet, many late-onset
delinquents rejoin the main stream.

Many of the people classified under character neurosis can be helped and thus
reformed by counseling or psychotherapy. Like late-onset delinquents, they also
tend to be basically socialized and, because they are unhappy people, they are
inclined to want to change, to try something or to be something different. One of
the reasons why the primary psychopath is a poor therapeutic bet is that he lacks
this motivation; it is the psychopath's family and associates who suffer the pain of
his condition, not the psychopath himself. The paranoid personality is also a poor
risk for treatment because he projects blame for his misfortunes onto others and
because his suspicious nature makes a useful therapeutic relationship hard to
establish.

Some distempered psychopaths also can be helped to reform their ways. The
premenstrual syndrome generally responds to hormone therapy and the hypersexed
male can moderate his lust by means of chemical treatment that reduces his
production of testosterone. Although it is believed in some quarters that rape is
motivated by aggression rather than by sexuality, it is a fact that castration, whether
surgical or chemical, reduces the incidence of repeat offenses among rapists to a
low level (and is the only treatment that does seem to be reliable; see Bremer, 1959).
Traditional insight therapy ought to be effective with the hysterical psychopath; at
least it appeared to work, eventually, with Donna (see chap. 13).

Most confirmed psychopaths and early onset sociopaths, however, do not seem to be reformable. The only real solution to the serious problem posed by these outlaws is prevention. As we have seen, the number of recidivistic sociopaths among us is increasing faster than the general population and the conclusion seems inescapable that this increase is due largely to the parallel increase in the proportion of incompetent or overburdened single-parent households.

PREVENTION

Preventing Primary Psychopathy

By definition, the child whose innate temperament makes him or her a potential psychopath must remain at high risk unless the parents are unusually skillful or unless they have skillful help. On the other hand, I believe that the principles involved in the successful socialization of "difficult" children are the ones that also work the best with children of average temperament. The rules for training a bull terrier are the same as those that work with beagles; the task of rearing a bull terrier is merely harder and more demanding and the price of failure greater. In the early years, the main objective in rearing any child is the creation of a strong and loving parental bond. Unless the parents can genuinely enjoy holding the toddler, feeding her, playing with him, reading her stories, then professional help should be sought because that early emotional relationship is the basis on which later successful parenting depends.

As the child's behavioral repertoire expands, the potential primary psychopath will not be shy or timorous but, on the contrary, venturesome and sometimes aggressive. Careful monitoring then is required as well as patient and consistent intervention whenever necessary. A good parent will not rely heavily on punishment (and not at all on heavy punishment) because it does not work with the potential psychopath and can have bad side effects with most children. Sometimes a hard swat on the behind may be necessary to get the youngster's attention but that is about all that corporal punishment is good for. Whether the child seems to have the "talent" for primary psychopathy or not, he or she must learn that tantrums do not work and that disobedience costs more than it pays. In addition, the good parent tries to develop in the child the self-concept that he or she is the sort of a person who does the right thing and is therefore deserving of love, praise, and respect. While they are still bigger and smarter than their youngster, parents should be able to accomplish this or, if their efforts seem not to be working, to seek help before it is too late.

I think that parents, whether their child is "difficult" or not, should make a conscious effort to treat their youngster with respect, to really listen to what he or she has to say and to be responsive, to treat him or her like a person and not like a "dumb kid." Many adults shift into a patronizing or condescending mode when they interact with children and this does not help to sustain a strong parent–child bond. To the infant the parent is the source of all good things; to the older child, the parent should continue to be the principal source of interest, support, encouragement, affection, information, admiration—that is, still the source of most of the good things that youngster wants and needs. To the extent that such a relationship exists, then the parent's values will tend to become the child's values.

A venturesome and relatively fearless child can and will do things—things he finds gratifying and fun—which the average child is too timid to attempt or carry off successfully. Many of these attractive temptations will be illicit or dangerous. The challenge to any parent of such a child is to direct his interest toward exciting activities that are also constructive. Suppose that Kody Scott's ("Monster's") biological father, said to have been a professional football player, had started teaching his daredevil son the rudiments of that game when Kody was very small. Suppose dad had enrolled him in a Little League team and shared his triumphs and disappointments with him. What committed Kody to a life of crime early on was his discovery that he was *good* at it, he could dominate other boys, beat people up, become feared and respected by his peers. What if he had learned instead that he could dominate and be respected on the football field? What if he had learned in that context that it is more gratifying to win within the rules than by flouting them?

Pride

I believe that pride can be an effective antidote to psychopathy. Winston Churchill was a fearless boy and a bad student who seldom did anything right until he finally (on his third attempt) got admitted to the military college at Sandhurst and began playing polo for which he had a gift. His heroics on horseback, in polo and later in battle, gave the young Winston status among his fellows and a sense of pride and accomplishment that undergirded his later political career. As was true for many upper class Englishmen of his generation, Churchill's nanny, Mrs. Everest, and his strict schoolmasters were effective substitute parents while the remote Lord and Lady Randolph Churchill were more like dreams of glory, incentives to great accomplishment which, happily, Winston had the gifts to achieve (Carter, 1965).

Preventing Sociopathy

Reversing the current trend, in which increasing proportions of young Americans are growing up unsocialized, is a major—I would say *the* major—social problem of our time. Solving this problem will be difficult and expensive, yet not nearly so expensive as not solving it. If my analysis is correct, the essence of the solution is to reduce the numbers of youngsters being reared by incompetent or indifferent or unsocialized parents.

Parental Guidance

The solution, I believe, has three parts. The first component would involve providing guidance and help to those struggling parents who are motivated to rear their children successfully but who lack the skills and resources. We know already that half-way measures do not work, nor programs that involve only the children, programs like Head Start or even the expensive Milwaukee project (Jensen, 1989) from which the children daily return to still pathogenic home environments. Approaches such as the promising FAST Track program (Conduct Problems Prevention Research Group, 1992) that involves the child's parents and school teachers as well as the child and his peers, are very expensive. We must remember, however, that each sociopath costs society at least $1.5 million over his first 50 years.[1] Therefore, an investment of as much as $150,000 in each of 10 high-risk youngsters, if it succeeds in turning just one potential criminal into a socialized wage-earner will leave us financially ahead at the end of the day.

Alternative Rearing Environments

The second component of a workable solution to sociopathy is to provide alternative rearing environments for the many youngsters whose parents cannot or will not make effective use of help and guidance. Competent parenting is one of the most difficult, and plainly one of the most important, jobs that any of us ever undertake and yet it is one of the most unappreciated and underpaid. One reason children are left too long with abusive or incompetent parents is that social workers have been taught to believe that the biological relationship compensates somehow for almost all deficiencies of parental commitment or skill. The much-touted "family preservation" movement, that has dominated thinking in this area since the 1970s, has been based on wishful thinking and a cruel refusal to face the facts of life on the urban streets (MacDonald, 1994). Another reason why our children are left too long at risk, however, is that foster homes are in such short supply. In my own county, children taken from abusive parents (more than 90% of whom are single mothers) sometimes have to be placed with known criminals.[2] Moreover, both the licensure requirements and the supervision of the existing placements are generally negligible.

Because a good foster home can often prevent the production of a sociopath, can avoid a $1.5 million debit in society's balance sheet, surely it would be a sound investment to pay a trained foster mother as much as she would make in a full-time office job. And surely in these times when most couples feel they need two incomes to make ends meet, there must be many women who would prefer to work as a professional foster parent at home rather than in most conventional jobs outside. Surely there must be men who would be happy to quit their outside jobs and stay home to collaborate with their wives full time in providing foster care for several children—if the compensation were adequate. We know enough about parenting, about what works and what does not, to devise courses of instruction, say at the community college level, that could be used as prerequisites to licensure for foster

---

[1]Westman (1994) estimated a cost of $51,362 per year or $3 million over 60 years and this is without including the cost of other people's property destroyed or stolen or the high cost of Medicaid treatment of abused children or of premature "crack babies" or those with infantile alcohol syndrome.

[2]Information provided by a social worker in Hennepin County (MN) who prefers to remain anonymous (January 1995).

parents. Social workers would be needed to regularly inspect and monitor these homes, to organize periodic group meetings of foster parents where they can discuss problems and compare notes. But an adequate foster home structure would also free up a lot of social worker time now expended in dreary and largely ineffectual contacts with incompetent biological parents. The professionalization of foster care would be a cost-effective and salutary step in the right direction.

Another option, suitable especially for the older boys, would be the establishment of boarding schools as suggested by J. Wilson (1991). A large number of well-socialized former noncommissioned officers are currently being released by the armed forces, men who with proper training and close supervision could staff such schools as strong role models capable of maintaining order with a look or a word as a good father does.

On the assumption that welfare is at last to be reformed in the United States so that all adult recipients who can work must work, at either a job or at supervised and meaningful job training, then a large system of day-care facilities for infants and young children will have to be established. The 70-year experience of the Israeli kibbutzim (Aviezer et al., 1994) can provide a guide for how to do this. At these day-care centers, small enough to permit the one-on-one attention that encourages healthy bonding, each child's physical, intellectual, and emotional development could be monitored so that intervention, if needed, can be timely. Moreover, these same centers could provide a jobs program for the former welfare mothers, providing on-the-job training that could make them into better mothers.

Parental Licensure

All of these programs, if properly implemented, could reduce the production of new sociopaths and thus improve the safety and the quality of life for all of us. But, by themselves, such programs would constitute only a temporary expedient. Suppose we come to a river and find it full of children being swept down by the current, thrashing and struggling to keeps their heads above water. We can leap in and save a few but they keep coming and many drown in spite of our best efforts. This is Harris' (cited in Shanker, 1993) analogy for attempts to socialize children in the public schools. It is time to go upstream, Harris insists, to see what is pushing all those children into that river of no return. What we shall find upstream is increasing numbers of immature or indifferent or unsocialized or incompetent people, most of them unmarried and many economically dependent, who are having children whom they cannot or will not competently rear. The *licensure of parenthood* is the only real solution to the problem of sociopathy and crime.[3]

ROBERT: EXECUTED AT 11

Although Robert Sandifer was just a diminutive 11-year-old, he had been wanted for three days in the slaying of a 14-year-old girl. He was found Thursday lying in a pool of blood, believed to have been the victim of the gang he embraced. (McMahon, 1994, p. 1)

---

[3]Westman (1994) made an eloquent and convincing case for licensing parents.

This recent news report poignantly illustrates the kind of thing that we shall find upstream of Harris' river. Robert was always a difficult child, aggressive and hard to discipline, resembling in this his father who is currently in prison; most 11-year-old boys would not be as reckless and venturesome, even if allowed to run loose as Robert was. His mother, Lorina, was 18 when Robert was born and only 15 when she had her first illegitimate child (the first of seven; Robert was her third). Lorina or her boyfriend responded to Robert's difficult temperament by abusing the toddler. His grandmother, Jannie Fields, had herself been just 16 when she gave birth to Robert's mother and, with AFDC assistance, she has had 13 more children. In addition to child abuse, Lorina has some 30 criminal convictions, mostly for drug and shoplifting offenses; thus we know that Jannie's own track record as a parent was a poor one. Nevertheless, for reasons reviewed earier, county social workers placed the 3-year-old Robert and several of his siblings in her feckless care when Robert was found covered with bruises, scratches, and cigarette burns.

The grandmother provided "no discipline" at all and, between the ages of 9 and 11, Robert was prosecuted eight times for felonies including burglary, arson, car theft, and armed robbery. By age 10, he had a tattoo on his arm signifying membership in the Black Disciples street gang. Then, one Sunday in August 1994, apparently on orders from older gang members, Robert fired a gun several times at some boys in the street, permanently crippling one of them. Three hours later and two blocks away, Robert started shooting again, this time accidentally killing a 14-year-old girl. Robert eluded a police search for 3 days until two gang comrades, aged 14 and 16, put two bullets in Robert's brain and left him under a bridge.

According to the *New York Times* story (Terry, 1994), the neighbors blame the gangs and the guns in Robert's neighborhood and one cannot deny that an 11-year-old is a lot more dangerous with a gun in his hand and older gang members telling him where to point it. But it is obvious that the real problem was two (or more) generations of incompetent parenting. Cook County's Public Guardian, Patrick Murphy, got it right: "'This kid was a time bomb waiting to explode.' Mr. Murphy said. 'He was turned into a sociopath by his family'" (p. A10).

Although there are thousands of juvenile murderers in the United States, Robert was unusual and newsworthy whereas Robert's parents and grandparents are commonplace; there are millions of indifferent or incompetent mothers who hold parental rights over millions of fatherless children. Not all of these, perhaps, but millions still, are growing up like wild things, in environments of filth, chaos, violence, substance abuse, child abuse, and crime. Juvenile corrections agencies, child protection agencies, probation and parole officers, the adult prison system— all are overwhelmed. The cases that get into the newspapers are the tiny tip of the iceberg.

Mike Royko (1994), the Chicago columnist, asks despairingly what can we do to prevent the manufacture of juvenile sociopaths: "Robert's dad is a criminal and ... his mother is a drug user and a fool.... Obviously, these two boobs should not have had children. But how do we stop them? Tie her tubes? Snip his organs? No, because that's unconstitutional and will remain so unless we become a totalitarian state" (p. 3). I think Royko is unduly pessimistic about the possibilities of a long-term solution.

What is constitutional and what is not is decided in the end by the Supreme Court and usually on the basis of contemporary social realities. The licensure of parenthood would not in my view constitute a totalitarian step. No average mom and dad would be discommoded by a statute that required biological parents to meet the criteria demanded of couples who wish to adopt a child. Fifteen-year-old Lorina and her then-boyfriend, however, would have found themselves up on charges. She would have been required to name the father (or the possible fathers if, indeed, she had ever known their names) and modern DNA analyses would make it possible to prove out parenthood. If she wished to carry her baby to term, Lorina might have been required to spend those months in a maternity home, working at useful lessons by day and supervised by night, to ensure that the infant got a healthy start in life. The baby would be taken into foster care at birth and the mother sent back to school or work. The father's wages (if he could be identified) would be taxed until he had paid off the costs of the confinement. If either Lorina or the boyfriend were to be involved in a second unlicensed pregnancy, they would have to submit to the implantation of a long-acting antifertility drug.

A society that enforces parental licensure, but one in which mature married couples who are self-supporting, noncriminal, and not mentally ill can expect to receive a licence if they want one, does not seem to me to deserve the epithet "totalitarian." Such a society, however, would surely be a safer, happier one for children to grow up in and one in which the incidence of 11-year-old murderers would be negligible.

References

Alexander, F. (1930). The neurotic character. *International Journal of Psychoanalysis, 2*, 292–311.

Alport, G. W. (1937). *Personality: A psychological interpretation*. New York: Henry Holt.

American Psychiatric Association. (1994). *Diagnostic and statistical manual of mental disorders, (DSM–IV)*. Washington, DC: Author.

Apter, M. J. (1992). *The dangerous edge*. New York: The Free Press.

Arnett, P. A., Howland, E. W., Smith, S. S., & Newman, J. P. (1993). Autonomic responsivity during passive avoidance in incarcerated psychopaths. *Personality and Individual Differences, 14*, 173–184.

Aviezer, O., Van IJzendoorn, M., Sagi, A., & Schuengel, C. (1994). "Children of the dream" revisited: 70 years of collective early child care in Israeli kibbutzim. *Psychological Bulletin, 116*, 99–116.

Baker, L. A., Mack, W., Moffitt, T., & Mednick, S. A. (1989). Sex differences in property crime in a Danish adoption cohort. *Behavior Genetics, 19*, 355–370.

Baumrind, D. (1971). Current patterns of parental authority. *Developmental Psychology Monograph, Vol 4. Part 1, Part 2.*

Baumrind, D. (1980). New directions in socialization research. *American Psychologist, 35*, 639–652.

Baumrind, D. (1993). The average expectable environment is not good enough: A response to Scarr. *Child Development, 64,* 1299–1317.

Belsky, J., Steinberg, L., & Draper, P. (1991). Childhood experience, interpersonal development and reproductive strategy: An evolutionary theory of socialization. *Child Development, 62*, 647–670.

Benson, P. L., & Roehlepartain, E. C. (1993). *Youth in single-parent families*. Minneapolis, MN: The Search Institute.

Biederman, J., Faraone, S., Keenan, K., Benjamin, J., Krifcher, B., Moore, C., Sprich-Buckminster, S., Ugaglia, K., Jellinek, M., Steingard, R., Spencer, T., Norman, D., Kolodny, R., Kraus, I., Perrin, J., Keller, M., & Tsuang, M. (1992). Further evidence for family-genetic risk factors in Attention Deficit Hyperactivity Disorder. *Archives of General Psychiatry, 49*, 728–738.

Blackburn, R. (1975). An empirical classification of psychopathic personality. *British Journal of Psychiatry, 127*, 456–460.

Blackburn, R. (1987). Two scales for the assessment of personality disorder in antisocial populations. *Personality and Individual Differences, 8*, 81–93.

Blackburn, R. (1988). On moral judgments and personality disorders: The myth of psychopathic personality revisited. *British Journal of Psychiatry, 153*, 505–512.

Blackburn, R., & Maybury, C. (1985). Identifying the psychopath: The relation of Cleckley's criteria to the interpersonal domain. *Personality and Individual Differences, 6*, 375–386.

Blanchard, E. B., Bassett, J. E., & Koshland, E. (1977). Psychopathy and delay of gratification. *Criminal Justice and Behavior, 4*, 265–271.

Block, J. (1957). A study of affective responsiveness in a lie-detection situation. *Journal of Abnormal and Social Psychology, 55,* 11–15.

Blumstein, A., & Cohen, J. (1987). Characterizing criminal careers. *Science, 237,* 985–991.

Borkovec, T. D. (1970). Autonomic reactivity to sensory stimulation in psychopathic, neurotic, and normal juvenile delinquents. *Journal of Consulting and Clinical Psychology, 35,* 217–222.

Bouchard, T. J., Jr., Lykken, D. T., McGue, M., Segal, N. L., & Tellegen, A. (1990). Sources of human psychological differences: The Minnesota Study of Twins Reared Apart. *Science, 250,* 223–228.

Bouchard, T. J., Jr., & McGue, M. (1981) Familial studies of intelligence: A review. *Science, 212,* 1055–1059.

Bouchard, T. J., Jr., & McGue, M. (1990). Genetic and rearing environmental influences on adult personality: An analysis of adopted twins reared apart. *Journal of Personality, 58,* 263–292.

Bowlby, J. (1969). *Attachment and loss* (Vol. 1). London: Hogarth.

Bremer, J. (1959). *Asexualization: A follow up study of 244 cases.* New York: Macmillan.

Bureau of Justice Statistics. (1988). *Survey of youth in custody, 1987.* Rockville, MD: U.S. Department of Justice.

Bureau of Justice Statistics. (1993). *Survey of state prison inmates, 1991.* Rockville, MD: U.S. Department of Justice.

Burks, B. S., & Tolman, R. (1932). Is mental resemblance related to physical resemblance in sibling pairs? *Journal of Genetic Psychology, 40,* 3–15.

Burt, C. L. (1945). *The young delinquent.* (4th ed.). London: University of London Press.

Buss, A. H., & Plomin, R. A. (1984). *Temperament: Early developing personality traits.* Hillsdale, NJ: Lawrence Erlbaum Associates.

Buss, D. M., Larsen, R., Westen, D., & Semmelroth, J. (1992). Sex differences in jealousy: Evolution, physiology, and psychology. *Psychological Science, 3,* 251–255.

Buss, D. M., & Schmitt, D. P. (1993). Sexual strategies theory: An evolutionary perspective on human mating. *Psychological Review, 100,* 204–232.

Butcher, J. N., Graham, J. R., Williams, C. L., & Ben-Porath, Y. (1990). *Development and use of the MMPI-2 content scales.* Minneapolis: University of Minnesota Press.

Byrne, D., Kelley, K., & Fisher, W. A. (1993). Unwanted teenage pregnancies: Incidence, interpretation, and intervention. *Applied, & Preventive Psychology, 2,* 101–113.

Cadoret, R. J., Cain, C., & Crowe, R. R. (1983). Evidence for a gene–environment interaction in the development of adolescent antisocial behavior. *Behavior Genetics, 13,* 301–310.

Calkins, S. D., Fox, N. A., & Marshall, T. (1995). Behavioral and physiological antecedents of inhibition in infancy. *Child Development,*

Caplan, N., Choy, M. H., & Whitmore, J. K. (1992). Indochinese refugee families and academic achievement. *Scientific American, 266,* 36–42.

Capron, C., & Duyme, M. (1989). Assessment of effects of socioeconomic status on IQ in a full cross-fostering study. *Nature, 340,* 552–553.

Carey, G. (1992). Twin imitation for antisocial behavior: Implications for genetic and family environment research. *Journal of Abnormal Psychology, 101,* 18–25.

Caro, R. A. (1982). *The years of Lyndon Johnson: The path to power.* New York: Knopf.

Caro, R. A. (1988). *The years of Lyndon Johnson: Politics of power.* New York: Knopf.

Carter, V. B. (1965). *Winston Churchill: An intimate portrait.* New York: Konecky & Konecky.

Casseno, D. (1993, June 13). He's in prison for good, but not before a murder. *Minneapolis Star Tribune,* p. 1.

Cattell, R. B. (1982). *The inheritance of personality and ability: Research methods and findings.* New York: Academic Press.

Chabot, D. R. (1968). *An investigation of the effects of an increased emotional state on the reliability of the MMPI in an adolescent population.* Unpublished doctoral dissertation, University of Minnesota, Minneapolis.

Chandler, K. (1993, March 21). Hennepin County tries to stem "baby truancy." *Minneapolis Star-Tribune,* p. 15A.

Chomsky, N. (1986). *Knowledge of language: Its nature, origin, and use.* New York: Praeger.

Christiansen, K. O. (1968). Threshold of tolerance in various population groups illustrated by results from Danish criminological twin study. In A. V. S. de Reuck & R. Porter (Eds.), *Ciba Foundation Symposium on the mentally abnormal offender* (pp. 107–116). London: Churchill.

Christiansen, K. O. (1977). A review of studies of criminality among twins. In S. A. Mednick & K. O. Christiansen (Eds.), *Biosocial bases of criminal behavior* (pp. 45–85). New York: Gardner.

Cimerman, A. (1981). "They'll let me go tomorrow": The Fay case. *Criminal Defense, 8,* 7–10

Cleckley, H. (1941). *The mask of sanity.* St. Louis: C.V. Mosby.

Cleckley, H. (1955). *The mask of sanity* (3rd ed.). St. Louis: C.V. Mosby.

Cleckley, H. (1982). *The mask of sanity* (rev. ed.). St. Louis: C.V. Mosby.

Cloninger, C. R., Bohman, M., & Sigvardsson, S. (1981). Inheritance of alcohol abuse. *Archives of General Psychiatry, 38,* 861–868.

Cloninger, C. R., & Gottesman, I. I. (1987). Genetic and environmental factors in antisocial behavior. In S. A. Mednick, T. E. Mofitt, & S. A. Stack (Eds.), *The causes of crime: New biological approaches* (pp. 92–109). Cambridge: Cambridge University Press.

Cloninger, C. R., Sigvardsson, S., Bohman, M., & von Korring, A. (1982). Predisposition to petty criminality in Swedish adoptees. II. Cross-fostering analysis of gene–environment interaction. *Archives of General Psychiatry, 39,* 1242–1247.

Conduct Problems Prevention Research Group. (1992). A developmental and clinical model for the prevention of conduct disorder: The FAST Track Program. *Development and Psychopathology, 4,* 509–527.

Cortés, J. B., & Gatti, F. M. (1972). *Delinquency and crime: A biopsychological approach.* New York: Academic Press.

Crider, A. (1993). Electrodermal response lability-stability: Individual difference correlates. In J. C. Roy, W. Boucsein, D. Fowles, & J. Gruzelier (Eds.), *Progress in electrodermal research.* London: Plenum.

Cromwell, P. F., Olson, J. N., & Avary, D. W. (1991). *Breaking and entering: An ethnographic analysis of burglary.* Newbury Park, CA: Sage.

Crowe, R. R. (1975). Adoptive study of psychopathy: Preliminary results from arrest records and psychiatric hospital records. In R. Fieve, D. Rosenthal, & H. Brill (Eds.), *Genetic research in psychiatry* (pp. 111–132). Baltimore, MD: Johns Hopkins University Press.

Daly, M., & Wilson, M. (1988). *Homicide.* New York: Aldine de Gruyter.

Daly, M., Wilson, M., & Weghorst, S. (1982). Male sexual jealousy. *Ethology and Sociobiology, 3,* 11–27.

Damasio, A. R., Tranel, D., & Damasio, H. (1990). Individuals with sociopathic behavior caused by frontal damage fail to respond autonomically to social stimuli. *Behavioral Brain Research, 41,* 81–94.

Davidson, R. J. (1992). Anterior cerebral asymmetry and the nature of emotion. *Brain and Cognition, 6,* 245–286.

Davidson, R. J., & Fox, N. A. (1989). Frontal brain asymmetry predicts infants' response to maternal separation. *Journal of Abnormal Psychology, 98,* 127–131.

Dawkins, R. (1976). *The selfish gene.* Oxford: Oxford University Press.

Dawkins, R. (1982). *The extended phenotype.* Oxford: Oxford University Press.

Degler, C. N. (1991). *In search of human nature.* New York: Oxford University Press.

DeParle, J. (1992, January 12). Recession is not the only suspect in the nation's surging welfare rolls. *New York Times,* p. 4A.

Dienstbier, R. A. (1984). The role of emotion in moral socialization. In C. E. Izard, J. Kagan, & R.B. Zajonc (Eds.), *Emotions, cognition and behavior* (pp. 484–514). New York: Cambridge University Press.

DiIulio, J. D., Jr. (1994, Fall). The question of Black crime. *The Public Interest,* 3–32.

DiIulio, J. D., Jr. (1995, Winter). White lies about black crime. *The Public Interest,* 30–44.

DiLalla, L. F., Gottesman, I. I., & Carey, G. (1993). Assessment of normal personality traits in a psychiatric sample: Dimensions and categories. In L. J. Chapman, J. P. Chapman, & D. Fowles (Eds.),

Progress in experimental personality and psychopathology research (pp. 145–162). New York: Springer.

Dobzhansky, T. (1956). What are adaptive traits? *Natural History, 90*, 337–347.

Dodge, K. A., Bates, J. E., & Pettit, G. S. (1991). Mechanism in the cycle of violence. *Science, 250*, 1678–1683.

Dollard, J., & Miller, N. E. (1950). *Personality and psychotherapy*. New York: McGraw-Hill.

Draper, P., & Belsky, J. (1990). Personality development in evolutionary perspective. *Journal of Personality, 58*, 141–162.

Dunn, J. (1992). Siblings and development. *Current Directions in Psychological Science, 1*, 6–9.

Dunn, J., Brown, J., Slomkowski, C., Tesla, C., & Youngblade, L. (1991). Young children's understanding of other people's feelings and beliefs: Individual differences and their antecedents. *Child Development, 62*, 1352–1366.

Dunn, J., & Plomin, R. (1990). *Separate lives: Why siblings are so different*. New York: Basic Books.

Eckholm, E. (1992, July 26). Solutions on welfare: They all cost money. *New York Times*, p. 1.

Eckman, P. (1985). *Telling lies: Clues to deceit in the marketplace, politics, and marriage*. New York: Norton.

Ekman, P., & Friesen, W. V. (1974). Detecting deception from the body or face. *Journal of Personality and Social Psychology, 29*, 288–298.

Epps, P., & Parnell, R. W. (1952). Physique and temperament of women delinquents compared with women undergraduates. *British Journal of Medical Psychology, 25*, 249–255.

Eron, L. D., & Huesman, L. R. (1984). The relation of prosocial behavior to the development of aggression and psychopathology. *Aggressive Behavior, 10*, 201–212.

Eron, L. D., & Huesman, L. R. (1990). The stability of aggressive behavior—Even unto the third generation. In M. Lewis & S. M. Miller (Eds.), *Handbook of developmental psychopathology* (pp. 147–156). New York: Plenum Press.

Eysenck, H. J., & Eysenck, S. B. G. (1978). Psychopathy, personality and genetics. In R. D. Hare & D. Schalling (Eds.), *Psychopathic behavior: Approaches to research* (pp. 197–224). Chichester, England: Wiley.

Falconer, D. S. (1989). *Introduction to quantitative genetics*. New York: Wiley.

Farrington, D. P. (1979). Longitudinal research on crime and delinquency. In N. Morris & M. Tonry (Eds.), *Crime and justice: An annual review of research* (Vol. 1, pp. 209–348). Chicago: University of Chicago Press.

Farrington, D. P. (1986). Stepping stones to adult criminal careers. In D. Olweus, J. Block, & M. Radke-Yarrow (Eds.), *Development of antisocial and prosocial behavior: Research, theories and issues* (pp. 359–384). New York: Academic Press.

Farrington, D. P. (1991). Childhood aggression and adult violence: Early precursors and later-life outcomes. In D. J. Pepler & F. H. Rubin (Eds.), *The development and treatment of childhood aggression* (pp. 5–29). Hillsdale, NJ: Lawrence Erlbaum Associates.

Farrington, D., Loeber, R., & Van Kammen, W. (1990). Long-term criminal outcomes of hyperactivity-impulsivity-attention deficit and conduct problems in childhood. In L. N. Robins & M. Rutter (Eds.), *Straight and devious pathways from childhood to adulthood* (pp. 62–81). New York: Cambridge University Press.

Farrington, D. P., & West, D. J. (1981). The Cambridge Study in delinquent development. In S. A. Mednick & A. E. Baert (Eds.), *Prospective longitudinal research* (pp. 207–227) New York: Oxford University Press.

Farwell, B. (1963). *Burton: A biography of Sir Richard Francis Burton*. New York: Holt, Rinehart & Winston.

FBI. (1992). *Uniform crime reports for the United States, 1991*. Washington, DC: U.S. Department of Justice.

FBI. (1993). *Age-specific arrest rates and race-specific arrest rates for selected offenses, 1965–1992*. Washington, DC: U.S. Department of Justice.

Finman, R., Davidson, R. J., Colton, M., Straus, A., & Kagan, J. (1989). Psychophysiological correlates of inhibition to the unfamiliar in children. *Psychophysiology, 26*(4A), S24.

Fletcher, R. (1991). *Science, ideology, and the media: The Cyril Burt scandal.* London: Transaction Publishers.

Flynn, J. R. (1987). Massive IQ gains in 14 nations: What IQ tests really measure. *Psychological Bulletin, 101,* 171–191.

Forgatch, M. S., Patterson, G. R., & Ray, J. A. (1994). Divorce and boys' adjustment problems: Two paths with a single model. In E. M. Hetherington, D. Reiss, & R. Plomin (Eds.), *Stress, coping, and resiliency in children and the family* (pp. 96–110). Hillsdale, NJ: Lawrence Erlbaum Associates.

Fowles, D. C. (1980), The three arousal model: Implications of Gray's two-factor learning theory for heart rate, electrodermal activity, and psychopathy. *Psychophysiology, 17,* 87–104.

Fowles, D. C. (1987). Application of a behavioral theory of motivation to the concepts of anxiety and impulsivity. *Journal of Research in Personality, 21,* 417-435.

Fowles, D. C. (1988). Psychophysiology and psychopathology: A motivational approach. *Psychophysiology, 25,* 373–391.

Fowles, D. C. (1993). Electrodermal activity and antisocial behavior: Empirical findings and theoretical issues. In J. C. Roy, W. Boucsein, D. Fowles, & J. Gruzelier (Eds.), *Progress in electrodermal research* (pp. 223-237). London: Plenum.

Fowles, D. C., & Missel, K. (1994). Electrodermal hyposreactivity, motivation, and psychopathy: Theoretical issues. In D. C. Fowles, P. Sutker, & S. H. Goodman (Eds.), *Experimental personality and psychopathology Research* (pp. 263–284). New York: Springer.

Fox, N. A., Rubin, K., Calkins, S., Marshall, T., Coplan, R., Porges, S., Long, J., & Stewart, S. (1995). Frontal activation asymmetry and social competence at four years of age. *Child Development,*

Frank, G. (1966). *The Boston strangler.* New York: New American Library.

Franks, L. (1992, December 21). To catch a judge: How the F.B.I. tracked Sol Wachtler. *The New Yorker,* pp. 58–66.

Freeman, D. (1992). Paradigms in collision. *Academic Questions, 5,* 23–33.

Fuchs, V. R., & Reklis, D. M. (1992). America's children; Economic perspectives and poly options. *Science, 255,* 41–46.

Fulker, D. W., Eysenck, H. J., & Zuckerman, M. (1980). The genetics of sensation seeking. *Journal of Personality Research, 14,* 261–281.

Garmezy, N. (1991). Resiliency and vulnerability to adverse developmental outcomes associated with poverty. *American Behavioral Scientist, 34,* 416–430.

Glueck, S., & Glueck, E. (1950). *Unraveling juvenile delinquency.* Cambridge, MA: Harvard University Press.

Glueck, S., & Glueck, E. (1956). *Physique and delinquency.* New York: Harper.

Gorenstein, E. E. (1982). Frontal lobe functions in psychopaths. *Journal of Abnormal Psychology, 91,* 368–379.

Gorenstein, E. E., & Newman, J. P. (1980). Disinhibitory psychopathology: A new perspective and a model for research. *Psychological Review, 87,* 301–315.

Gorsuch, R. L. (1988). Psychology and religion. In M. R. Rosenzweig & L. Porter (Eds.), *Annual review of psychology* (Vol. 39, pp. 201–221). Stanford, CA: Annual Reviews.

Gottesman, I. I. (1991). *Schizophrenia genesis: The origins of madness.* New York: W. H. Freeman.

Gottesman, I. I., Carey, G., & Hanson, D. R. (1983). Pearls and perils in epigenetic psychopathology. In S. B. Buze, E. J. Earls, & J. E. Barrett (Eds.), *Childhood psychopathology and development* (pp. 287–300). New York: Raven Press.

Gottesman, I. I., & Goldsmith, H. H. (1994). Developmental psychopathology of antisocial behavior: Inserting genes into its ontogenesis and epigenesis. In C. Nelson (Ed.), *Threats to optimum development: Biological, psychological and social risk factors* (pp. 69–104). Hillsdale, NJ: Lawrence Erlbaum Associates.

Gottfredson, M. R., & Hirschi, T. (1990). *A general theory of crime.* Stanford, CA: Stanford University Press.

Gough, H. G. (1987). *CPI administrator's guide.* Palo Alto, CA: Consulting Psychologists Press.

Gough, H. G. (1994). Theory, development, and interpretation of the CPI Socialization Scale. *Psychological Reports,* Monograph Supplement 1–V75.

Gough, H. G., & Peterson, D. R. (1952). The identification and measurement of predispositional factors in crime and delinquency. *Journal of Consulting Psychology, 16,* 207–212.

Gove, W. R., & Wilmoth, C. (1990). Risk, crime, and neurophysiological highs: A consideration of brain processes that may reinforce delinquent and criminal behavior. In L. Ellis, & H. Hoffman (Eds.), *Crime in biological, social and moral contexts* (pp. 261–293). New York: Praeger.

Gray, J. A. (1975). *Elements of a two-process theory of learning.* New York: Academic Press.

Gray, J. A. (1987a). Perspectives on anxiety and impulsivity: A commentary. *Journal of Research in Personality, 21,* 493–509.

Gray, J. A. (1987b). *The psychology of fear and stress. 2nd Ed.* Cambridge: Cambridge University Press.

Grove, W. M., Eckert, E. D., Heston, L., & Bouchard, T. J., Jr. (1990). Heritability of substance abuse and antisocial behavior: A study of monozygotic twins reared apart. *Biological Psychiatry, 27,* 1293–1304.

Grow, D. (1994, April 2). *Minneapolis Star Tribune,* pp. 1A,8A.

Guttentag, M., & Secord, P. F. (1983). *Too many women? The sex ratio question.* Beverly Hills, CA: Sage.

Hamparian, D. M., Davis, J. M., Jacobson, J. M., & McGraw, R. R. (1985). *The young criminal years of the violent few.* Washington, DC: National Institute for Juvenile Justice and Delinquency Prevention.

Hare, R. D. (1965a). A conflict and learning theory analysis of psychopathic behavior. *Journal of Research in Crime and Delinquency,* 12–19.

Hare, R. D. (1965b). Psychopathy, fear arousal and anticipated pain. *Psychological Reports, 16,* 499–502.

Hare, R. D. (1966). Temporal gradient of fear arousal in psychopaths. *Journal of Abnormal and Social Psychology, 70,* 442–445.

Hare, R. D. (1972). Psychopathy and physiological responses to adrenalin. *Journal of Abnormal Psychology, 79,* 138–147.

Hare, R. D. (1978a). Psychopathy and electrodermal responses to nonsignal stimulation. *Biological Psychology, 6,* 237–246.

Hare, R. D. (1978b). Psychopathy and physiological responses to threat of an aversive stimulus. *Psychophysiology, 15,* 165–172.

Hare, R. D. (1979). Psychopathy and laterality of cerebral function. *Journal of Abnormal Psychology 88,* 605–610.

Hare, R. D. (1982). Psychopathy and physiological activity during anticipation of an aversive stimulus in a distraction paradigm. *Psychophysiology, 19,* 266–271.

Hare, R. D. (1984). Performance of psychopaths on cognitive tasks related to frontal lobe function. *Journal of Abnormal Psychology, 93,* 133–140.

Hare, R. D. (1985). Comparison of procedures for the assessment of psychopathy. *Journal of Consulting and Clinical Psychology, 53,* 7–16.

Hare, R. D. (1991). *The Hare Psychopathy Checklist–Revised.* Toronto: Multi-Health Systems.

Hare, R. D. (1993). *Without conscience: The disturbing world of the psychopaths among us.* New York: Pocket Books.

Hare, R. D., & Craigen, D. (1974). Psychopathy and physiological activity in a mixed-motive game situation. *Psychophysiology, 11,* 197–206.

Hare, R. D., Forth, A. E., & Hart, S. D. (1989). The psychopath as prototype for pathological lying and deception. In J. C. Yuille (Ed.), *Credibility assessment* (pp. 25–49). New York: Kluwer Academic Publishers.

Hare, R. D., Frazelle, J., & Cox, D. N. (1978). Psychopathy and physiological responses to threat of an aversive stimulus. *Psychophysiology, 15,* 165–172.

Hare, R. D., & Jutai, J. W. (1986). Psychopathy, stimulation seeking, and stress. In J. Strelau, F. Farley, & A. Gale (Eds.), *The biological bases of personality and behavior* (Vol. 2, pp. 175–184). Washington, DC: Hemisphere.

Hare, R. D., & McPherson, L. M. (1984). Psychopathy and perceptual asymmetry during verbal dichotic listening. *Journal of Abnormal Psychology, 93,* 141–149.

Hare, R. D., & Quinn, M. J. (1971). Psychopathy and autonomic conditioning. *Journal of Abnormal Psychology, 71,* 223–235.

Hare, R., & Thorvaldson, S. (1970). Psychopathy and response to electrical stimulation. *Journal of Abnormal Psychology, 76,* 370–374.

Harlow, J. M. (1868). Recovery from the passage of an iron bar through the head. *Publications of the Massachusetts Medical Society, II,* 327.

Harpending, H. C., & Sobus, J. (1987). Sociopathy as adaptation. *Ethology and Sociobiology, 8,* 63S–72S.

Harper, J. (1994, February 10). Death penalty for Cantu. *Houston Post,* p. A1.

Harpur, T. J., Hare, R. D., & Hakstian, A. R. (1989). Two-factor conceptualization of psychopathy: Construct validity and assessment implications. *Psychological Assessment, 1,* 6–17.

Harpur, T. J., Hart, S. D., & Hare, R. D. (1994). The personality of the psychopath. In P. T. Costa & T. A. Widiger (Eds.), *Personality disorders and the Five-Factor Model of personality* (pp. 198–216). Washington, DC: American Psychological Association.

Harris, G. T., Rice, M. E., & Quinset, V. L. (1994). Psychopathy as a taxon: Evidence that psychopaths are a discrete class. *Journal of Consulting and Clinical Psychology, 62,* 387–397.

Hart, S. D., Forth, A. E., & Hare, R. D. (1990). Performance of criminal psychopaths on selected neuropsychological tests. *Journal of Abnormal Psychology, 99,* 374–379.

Hartl, E. M., Monnelly, E. P., & Elderkin, R. D. (1982). *Physique and delinquent behavior: A thirty-year follow-up of William H. Sheldon's "Varieties of delinquent youth."* New York: Academic Press.

Hartshorne, H., & May, M. (1928). *Studies in the nature of character.* New York: Macmillan.

Hauser, K. (1959). *The relationship between normal anxiety and minor crimes.* Unpublished doctoral dissertation, University of Minnesota, Minneapolis.

Hearnshaw, L. S. (1979). *Cyril Burt: Psychologist.* London: Hodder, & Stoughten.

Herrnstein, R. J. (1973). *IQ in the meritocracy.* Boston: Atlantic–Little, Brown.

Herrnstein, R. J., & Murray, C. (1994). *The bell curve..* New York: The Free Press.

Higgins, P. (1973). *Evaluation of the Minnesota Youth Advocacy Program.* Unpublished doctoral dissertation, University of Minnesota, Minneapolis.

Hillerman, T. (1989). *Talking God.* New York: Harper & Row.

Hinde, R. A. (1986). Some implications of evolutionary theory and comparative data for the study of human prosocial and aggressive behavior. In D. Olweus, J. Block, & M. Radke-Yarrow (Eds.), *Development of antisocial and prosocial behavior* (pp. 340–356). New York: Academic Press.

Hoffman, M. L. (1988). Moral development. In M. H. Bornstein & M. Lamb (Eds.), *Developmental psychology: An advanced textbook* (pp. 497–548). Hillsdale, NJ: Lawrence Erlbaum Associates.

Horn, J. M., Plomin, R., & Rosenman, R. (1976). Heritability of personality traits in adult male twins. *Behavior Genetics, 6,* 17–30.

Horowitz, M. (1993, December). In search of Monster. *The Atlantic Monthly,* pp. 28–37.

Howland, E. W., Kosson, D. S., Patterson, C. M., & Newman, J. P. (1993). Altering a dominant response: Performance of psychopaths and low socialization college students on a cued reaction time task. *Journal of Abnormal Psychology, 102,* 379–387.

Huesman, L. R., Eron, L. D., Lefkowitz, M. M., & Walder, L. O. (1984). Stability of aggression over time and generations. *Developmental Psychology, 20,* 1120–1134.

Hutchings, B., & Mednick, S.A. (1977). Criminality in adoptees and their adoptive and biological parents: A pilot study. In S. A. Mednick & K. O. Christiansen (Eds.), *Biosocial bases of criminal behavior* (pp. 127–141). New York: Gardner.

Hymowitz, K. S. (1994, Autumn). The teen mommy track. *The City Journal,* 19–29.

Ingrassia, M. (1993, August 2). Daughters of Murphy Brown. *Newsweek,* p. 58.

Ingrassia, M. (1994, April 4). America's new wave of runaways. *Newsweek*, p. 64.

Ingrassia, M., & McCormick, J. (1994, April 25). Why leave children with bad parents? *Newsweek*, pp. 52–53.

Jankowiak, W. R., & Fischer, E. F. (1992). A cross-cultural perspective on romantic love. *Ethnology, 31*, 149–155.

Jary, M. I., & Stewart, M. A. (1985). Psychiatric disorder in the parents of adopted children with aggressive conduct disorder. *Neuropsychobiology, 13*, 7–11.

Jensen, A. R. (1989). Raising IQ without increasing g? A review of the Milwaukee Project: Preventing mental retardation in children at risk. *Developmental Review, 9*, 234–258.

Jensen, A. R. (1991). IQ and science: The Burt affair. *The Public Interest, 105*, 93–106.

Johnson, A. M. (1949). Sanctions for superego lacunae of adolescents. In K. Eissler (Ed.), *Searchlights on delinquency* (pp. 224–245). New York: International Universities Press.

Johnson, S. (1993, May 16). Killing our children. *Chicago Tribune*, p. 1.

Johnson, S., & McMahon, C. (1994, January 2). Killing our children. *Chicago Tribune*, pp. 1, 6, 7.

Jones, H. E. (1950). The study of patterns of emotional experession. In M. L. Reymert (Ed.), *Feelings and emotions: The Mooseheart Symposium* (pp. 161–168). New York: McGraw-Hill.

Jones, H. E. (1960). The longitudinal method in the study of personality. In I. Iscoe & H. W. Stevenson (Eds.), *Personality development in children* (pp. 3–27). Chicago: University of Chicago Press.

Jones, E. F., Forrest, J. D., Goldman, N., Henshaw, S., Lincoln, R., Rosoff, J. I., Wetsoff, C., & Wulf, D. (1987). *Teenage pregnancy in industrialized countries*. New Haven, CT: Yale University Press.

Joynson, R. B. (1989). *The Burt affair*. London: Routledge.

Juel-Nielsen, N. (1965). Individual and environment: A psychiatric–psychological investigation of MZ twins reared apart. *Acta Psychiatric Scandinavia Suppl. 183*. Copenhagen: Munksgaard.

Jutai, J. W., Hare, R. D., & Connolly, J. F. (1987). Psychopathy and event-related brain potentials (ERPs) associated with attention to speech stimuli. *Personality and Individual Differences, 6*, 175–184.

Kagan, J. (1987). Introduction. In J. Kagan, & S. Lamb (Eds.), *The emergence of morality in young children* (pp. ix–xx). Chicago: University of Chicago Press.

Kagan, J. (1994). *Galen's prophecy*. New York: Basic Books.

Karpman, B. (1941). On the need for separating psychopathy into two distinct clinical types: symptomatic and idiopathic. *Journal of Criminology and Psychopathology, 3*, 112–137.

Katz, J. (1988). *Seductions of crime: Moral and sensual attractions in doing evil*. New York: Basic Books.

Katzenmeyer, C. G. (1967). *Revision, standardization and validation of the Lykken Activity Preference Questionnaire*. Unpublished doctoral dissertation, University of Minnesota, Minneapolis.

Kochanska, G. (1991). Socialization and temperament in the development of guilt and conscience. *Child Development, 62*, 1379–1392.

Kochanska, G. (1993). Toward a synthesis of parental socialization and child temperament in early development of conscience. *Child Development, 64*, 325–347.

Kornhauser, R. (1978). *Social sources of delinquency*. Chicago: University of Chicago Press.

Kosson, D. S., & Newman, J. P. (1986). Psychopathy and the allocation of attentional capacity in a divided-attention situation. *Journal of Abnormal Psychology, 95*, 257–263.

Kosson, D. S., Smith, S. S., & Newman, J. P. (1990). Evaluation of the construct validity of psychopathy in black and white male inmates: Three preliminary studies. *Journal of Abnormal Psychology, 99*, 250–259.

Kotlowitz, A. (1992). *There are no children here*. New York: Doubleday.

Kristol, I. (1994, November 3). Children need their fathers. *New York Times*, p. A15.

Lacey, B. C., & Lacey, J. I. (1974). Studies of heart rate and other bodily processes in sensorimotor behavior. In P. A. Obrist, A. H. Black, J. Brener, & L. V. Dicara (Eds.), *Cardiovascular psychophysiology: Current issues in response mechanisms, biofeedback, and methodology* (pp. 275–295) Chicago: Aldine–Atherton.

Lang, P. J., Bradley, M. M., & Cuthbert, B. N. (1990). Emotion, attention, and the startle reflex. *Psychological Review, 97*, 377–398.

Lemann, N. (1993). *The promised land: The great Black migration and how it changed America.* New York: Alfred A. Knopf.

Levin, M. (1992). Responses to race differences in crime. *Journal of Social Philosophy, 23,* 5–29.

Lewin, T. (1992, February 27). Fewer children up for adoption, study finds. *New York Times,* p. A15

Lewis, C. E. (1991). Neurochemical mechanisms of chronic antisocial behavior (psychopathy). *Journal of Nervous and Mental Disease, 179,* 720–727.

Lewontin, R. C. (1982). *Human diversity.* New York: Scientific American Books.

Lewontin, R., & Gould, S. (1978). The spandrels of San Marco and the Panglossian paradigm: A critique of the adaptationist paradigm. *Proceedings of the Royal Society of London, 205,* 581–598.

Lilienfeld, S. O. (1990). *Development and preliminary validation of a self-report measure of psychopathic personality.* Unpublished doctoral dissertation, University of Minnesota, Minneapolis.

Lindner, R. M. (1944). *Rebel without a cause.* New York: Grune & Stratton.

Linnoila, V. M. I., & Virkkunen, M. (1992). Aggression, suicidality, and serotonin. *Journal of Clinical Psychiatry, 53[10, suppl],* 46–51.

Lippert, W. W., & Senter, R. (1966). Electrodermal responses in the sociopath. *Psychonomic Science, 4,* 25–26.

Loeber, R., & Dishion, T. J. (1983). Early predictors of male delinquency: A review. *Psychological Bulletin, 94,* 69–99.

Loehlin, J. C., & Nichols, R. C. (1976). *Heredity, environment and personality: A study of 850 sets of twins.* Austin: University of Texas Press.

London, H. (1965). *An inquiry into boredom and thrill-seeking.* Unpublished doctoral dissertation, Columbia University, New York.

Lore, R. K., & Schultz, L. A. (1993). Control of human aggression: A comparative perspective. *American Psychologist, 48,* 16–25.

Luria, A. R. (1973). *The working brain.* New York: Basic Books.

Lykken, D. T. (1955). *A study of anxiety in the sociopathic personality.* Unpublished doctoral dissertation, University of Minnesota, Minneapolis.

Lykken, D. T. (1957). A study of anxiety in the sociopathic personality. *Journal of Abnormal and Social Psychology, 55,* 6–10.

Lykken, D. T. (1962). Preception in the rat: Autonomic response to shock as a function of length of the warning interval. *Science, 137,* 665–666.

Lykken, D. T. (1967). Valins' "Emotionality and autonomic reactivity": An appraisal. *Journal of Research in Personality, 2,* 49–55.

Lykken, D. T. (1968a). Neuropsychology and psychophysiology in personality research. In E. Borgotta & W. Lambert (Eds.), *Handbook of Personality Theory and Research* (pp. 413–509). New York: Rand McNally

Lykken, D. T. (1968b). Statistical significance in psychological research. *Psychological Bulletin, 70,* 151–159.

Lykken, D. T. (1972). Range correction applied to heart rate and to GSR data. *Psychophysiology, 9,* 373–379.

Lykken, D. T. (1981). *A tremor in the blood: Uses and abuses of the lie detector.* New York: McGraw-Hill.

Lykken, D. T. (1982a, September). Fearlessness. *Psychology Today,* pp. 6–10.

Lykken, D. T. (1982b). Research with twins: The concept of emergenesis. *Psychophysiology, 19,* 361–373.

Lykken, D. T. (1988). The case against polygraph testing. In A. Gale (Ed.), *The polygraph test: Lies, truth and science* (pp. 111–125.) London: Sage.

Lykken, D. T., Bouchard, T. J., McGue, M., & Tellegen, A. (1992). Emergenesis: Genetic traits that do not run in families. *American Psychologist, 47,* 1565–1577.

Lykken, D. T., Bouchard, T. J., McGue, M., & Tellegen, A. (1993). Heritability of interests: A twin study. *Journal of Applied Psychology, 78,* 649–661..

Lykken, D. T., & Katzenmeyer, C. (1973). Manual for the Activity Preference Questionnaire (APQ). In *Psychiatric Research Reports,* Minneapolis: University of Minnesota.

Lykken, D. T., & Tellegen, A. (1974) On the validity of the preception hypothesis. *Psychophysiology, 11,* 125–132.

Lykken, D. T., & Tellegen, A. (1993). Is human mating adventitious or the result of lawful choice? A twin study of mate selection. *Journal of Personality and Social Psychology, 65,* 56–68.

Lykken, D. T., Tellegen, A., & Macindoe, I. (1972). Preception: Autonomic response to shock as a function of predictability in time and locus. *Psychophysiology, 9,* 318–333.

Lytton, H. (1990). Child and parent effects in boys' conduct disorder: A reinterpretation. *Developmental Psychology, 26,* 683–697.

Maccoby, E. E. (1992). The role of parents in the socialization of children: An historical overview. *Developmental Psychology, 28,* 1006–1017.

MacDonald, H. (1994, Spring). The ideology of "family preservation." *The Public Interest,* 45–60.

Manchester, W. (1986). *The last lion: Winston Spencer Churchill; Visions of glory, 1874–1932.* New York: Little, Brown.

Manchester, W. (1988). *The last lion: Winston Spencer Churchill; Alone, 1932–1940.* New York: Little, Brown.

Martin, N. G., Eaves, L. J., Heath, A. C., Jardine, R., Feingold, L. M., & Eysenck, H. J. (1986). Transmission of social attitudes. *Proceedings National Academy of Sciences, 83,* 4364–4368.

Matheny, A. P., Wilson, R. S., & Dolan, A. B. (1976). Relations between twins' similarity of appearance and behavioral similarity: Testing an assumption. *Behavior Genetics, 6,* 343–352.

Mayr, E. (1963). *Animal species and evolution.* Cambridge, MA: Harvard University Press.

McCartney, K., Harris, M. J., & Bernieri, F. (1990). Growing up and growing apart: A developmental meta-analysis of twin studies. *Psychological Bulletin, 197,* 226–233.

McGue, M. (1989). Nature–nurture and intelligence. *Nature, 340,* 507–508.

McGue, M., Bacon, S., & Lykken, D. T. (1992). Personality stability and change in early adulthood: A behavioral genetic analysis. *Developmental Psychology, 29,* 96–109.

McLanahan, S., & Garfinkel, I. (1988). *Single mothers, the underclass, and social policy* (Institute for Research on Poverty Discussion Paper No. 868–88). Madison: University of Wisconsin.

McMahon, C. (1994, September 4). Robert, executed at 11. *Chicago Tribune,* p. 1.

Mead, M. (1928). *Coming of age in Samoa.* New York: William Morrow.

Mead, M. (1949). *Male and female: A study of the sexes in a changing world.* New York: William Morrow.

Mealey, L. (1995). The sociobiology of sociopathy: An integrated evolutionary model. *Behavioral and Brain Sciences, 18.*

Mech, L. D. (1970). *The wolf.* Minneapolis: University of Minnesota Press.

Meehl, P. E. (1967). Theory-testing in psychology and physics: A methodological paradox. *Philosophy of Science, 34,* 103–115.

Meehl, P. E. (1977). Specific etiology and other forms of strong influence: Some quantitative meanings. *Journal of Medicine and Philosophy, 2,* 33–53.

Meehl, P. E. (1992). Factors and taxa, traits and types, differences of degree and differences in kind. *Journal of Personality, 60,* 117–174.

Mednick, S., Gabrielli, W., & Hutchings, B. (1984). Genetic influences in criminal convictions: Evidence from an adoption cohort. *Science, 224,* 891–893.

Mednick, S., Gabrielli, W., & Hutchings, B. (1987). Genetic factors in the etiology of criminal behavior. In S. A. Mednick, T. E. Moffitt, & S. A. Stack (Eds.), *The causes of crime: New biological approaches* (pp. 74–91). Cambridge: Cambridge University Press.

Megargee, E. I., & Bohn, M. J., Jr. (1979). *Classifying criminal offenders: A new system based on the MMPI.* Beverly Hills, CA: Sage.

Mellen, S. L. (1981). *The evolution of love.* San Francisco: W. H. Freeman.

Meloy, J. R. (1988). *The psychopathic mind: Origins, dynamics, and treatment.* Northvale, NJ: Jason Aronson.

Menninger, K. (1938). *Man against himself.* New York: Harcourt-Brace.

Miller, N. E. (1944). Experimental studies of conflict. In J. McV. Hunt (Ed.), *Personality and the behavior disorders* (Vol. 1, pp. 431–465). New York: Ronald Press.

Moffitt, T. E. (1993). Adolescence-limited and life-course-persistent antisocial behavior: A developmental taxonomy. *Psychological Review, 100,* 674–701.

Monahan, J. (1993). Mental disorder and violent behavior: Perceptions and evidence. *American Psychologist, 47*(4), 511–521.

Moynihan, D. P. (1969). America. In D. P. Moynihan (Ed.), *On understanding poverty* (pp. 42–65). New York: Basic Books.

Moynihan, D. P. (1993). Defining deviancy down. *The American Scholar, 62,* 17–30.

Munsinger, H. (1977). The identical-twin transfusion syndrome: A source of error in estimating IQ resemblance and heritability. *Annals of Human Genetics, London, 40,* 307–321.

Murphy, J. M. (1976). Psychiatric labeling in cross-cultural perspective. *Science, 191,* 1019–1028.

Murray, C. (1993, October 29). The coming white underclass. *The Wall Street Journal,* pp. 1, 2.

National Center for Health Statistics. (1993a). *Vital statistics of the United States, 1989, Vol.I, Natality* (DHHS Pub. No. [PHS] 93–1100). Washington, DC: U.S. Government Printing Office.

National Center for Health Statistics. (1993b). *Vital statistics of the United States, 1989, Vol.III, Marriage and divorce* (DHHS Pub. No. [PHS] 93–1103). Washington, DC: U.S. Government Printing Office.

Nettler, G. (1989). *Criminology lessons.* Cincinnati, OH: Anderson.

Newman, J., Freeman, F., & Holzinger, K. (1937). *Twins: A study of heredity and environment.* Chicago: University of Chicago Press.

Newman, J. P. (1987). Reaction to punishment in extroverts and psychopaths: Implications for the impulsive behavior of disinhibited individuals. *Journal of Research in Personality, 21,* 464–480.

Newman, J. P, & Kosson, D. S. (1986). Passive avoidance learning in psychopathic and nonpsychopathic offenders. *Journal of Abnormal Psychology, 95,* 252–256.

Newman, J. P., Kosson, D. S., & Patterson, C. M. (1992). Delay of gratification in psychopathic and nonpsychopathic offenders. *Journal of Abnormal Psychology, 101,* 630–636.

Newman, J. P., Patterson, C., & Kosson, D. (1987). Response perseveration in psychopaths. *Journal of Abnormal Psychology, 96,* 145–148.

Newman, J. P., Patterson, C. M., Howland, E. W., & Nichols, S. L. (1990). Passive avoidance in psychopaths: The effects of reward. *Personality and Individual Differences, 11,* 1101–1114.

Newman, J. P., Widom, C. S., & Nathan, S. (1985). *Journal of Personality and Social Psychology, 48,* 1316–1327.

Ogloff, J. R., & Wong, S. (1990). Electrodermal and cardiovascular evidence of a coping response in psychopaths. *Criminal Justice and Behavior, 17,* 231–245.

Olweus, D. (1979). Stability of aggressive reaction patterns in males: A review. *Psychological Bulletin, 86,* 852–875.

Partridge, G. E. (1930). Current conceptions of psychopathic personality. *American Journal of Psychiatry, 10,* 53–99.

Passingham, R. E. (1972). Crime and personality: A review of Eysenck's theory. In V. D. Nebylitsyn & J. A. Gray (Eds.), *Biological bases of individual behavior* (pp. 127–139). New York: Academic Press.

Patrick, C. J. (1994). Emotion and psychopathy: Startling new insights. *Psychophysiology, 31,* 415–428.

Patrick, C. J., Bradley, M. M., & Lang, P. J. (1993). Emotion in the criminal psychopath: Startle reflex modulation. *Journal of Abnormal Psychology, 102,* 82–92.

Patrick, C. J., & Iacono, W. G. (1989). Psychopathy, threat, and polygraph test accuracy. *Journal of Applied Psychology, 74,* 347–355.

Patterson, G. R. (1982). *Coercive family process.* Eugene, OR: Castalia.

Patterson, G. R. (1986). The contribution of siblings to training for fighting: A microsocial analysis. In D. Olweus, J. Block, & M. Radke-Yarrow (Eds.), *Development of antisocial and prosocial behavior: Research, theories and issues* (pp. 235–262). New York: Academic Press.

Patterson, G. R. (1992). Coercion and the early age of onset for arrest. In J. McCord & R. E. Tremblay (Eds.), *Coercion and punishment in long-term perspective* (pp. 217–234). Cambridge: Cambridge University Press.

Patterson, G. R., & Capaldi, D. M. (1991). Antisocial parents: Unskilled and vulnerable. In. P. A. Cowan & M. Hetherington (Eds.), *Family transitions* (pp. 195–217). Hillsdale, NJ., Lawrence Erlbaum Associates.

Patterson, G. R., DeBaryshe, B., & Ramsey, E. (1989). A developmental perspective on antisocial behavior. *American Psychologist, 44*, 329–335.

Patterson, G. R., Reid, J. B., & Dishion, T. J. (1992). *Antisocial boys.* Eugene, OR: Castalia.

Pedersen, N. L., Plomin, R., Nesselroade, J., & McClearn, G. (1992). A quantitative genetic analysis of cognitive abilities during the second half of the life span. *Psychological Science, 3*, 346–353

Pepler, D. J., & Rubin, F. H. (1991). *The development and treatment of childhood aggression.* Hillsdale, NJ: Lawrence Erlbaum Associates.

Plomin, R., & Daniels, D. (1986). Why are children in the same family so different from one another? *Behavioral and Brain Sciences, 10*, 1–16.

Plomin, R., DeFries, J. C., & Loehlin, J. C. (1977). Genotype–environment interaction and correlation in the analysis of human behavior. *Psychological Bulletin, 84*, 309–322.

Plomin, R., Foch, T. T., & Rowe, D. C. (1981). Bobo clown aggression in childhood: Environment, not genes. *Journal of Research in Personality, 21*, 391–402.

Plomin, R., Nitz, K., & Rowe, D. C. (1990). Behavioral genetics and aggressive behavior in childhood. In M. Lewis & S. M. Miller (Eds.), *Handbook of developmental psychopathology* (pp. 119–133). New York: Plenum.

Price, B. (1950). Primary biases in twin studies: A review of prenatal and natal difference-producing factors in monozygotic twins. *The American Journal of Human Genetics, 2*, 293–352.

Quay, H. C. (1965). Personality and delinquency. In H. C. Quay (Ed.), *Juvenile delinquency* (pp. 1–17). New York: Litton.

Quay, H. C. (1977). Measuring dimensions of deviant behavior: The Behavior Problem Checklist. *Journal of Abnormal Child Psychology, 5*, 277–287.

Quay, H. C., & Peterson, D. R. (1975). *Manual for the Behavior Problem Checklist.* Unpublished manuscript.

Raine, A. (1988). Antisocial behavior and social psychophysiology. In H. L. Wagner (Ed.), *Social psychophysiology and emotion: Theory and application* (pp. 193–213). New York: Wiley.

Raine, A. (1993). *The psychopathology of crime.* San Diego: Academic Press.

Raine, A., & Venables, P. H. (1984). Elecrodermal nonresponding, antisocial behavior, and schizoid tendencies in adolescents. *Psychophysiology, 21*, 421–433.

Rainwater, L., & Yancey, W. (1967). *The Moynihan Report and the politics of controversy.* Cambridge, MA: MIT Press.

Raskin, D. C., & Hare, R. D. (1978). Psychopathy and detection of deception in a prison population. *Psychophysiology, 27*, 567–575.

Raspberry, W. (1993, May 20). No doubt about it: Kids need their dads. *Washington Post*, p. A6.

Reed, T. E. (1984). Mechanisms for the heritability of intelligence. *Nature, 311*, 417.

Reiss, A. J., Jr., & Roth, J. A. (Eds.). (1993). *Understanding and preventing violence.* Washington, DC: National Academy Press.

Revelle, W., Humphreys, M. S., Simon, L., & Gilliland, K. (1980). The interactive effect of personality, time of day, and caffeine: A test of the arousal model. *Journal of Experimental Psychology: General, 109*, 1–31.

Rice, E. (1990). *Captain Sir Richard Francis Burton.* New York: Scribners.

Richmond, R. (1994, March 28). A look at the real Schindler tells the searing story. *Los Angeles Daily News*, p. 17.

Ritter, J. (1993, December 3). Abandoned at birth. *USA Today*, pp. 1, 2.

Robins, L. N. (1966). *Deviant children grown up.* Baltimore: William & Wilkins.

Robins, L. N. (1978a). Etiological implications in childhood histories relating to antisocial personality. In R. D. Hare & D. Schalling (Eds.), *Psychopathic behavior: Approaches to research* (pp. 255–272). Chichester, U.K.: Wiley.

Robins, L. N. (1978b). Sturdy childhood predictors of adult antisocial behavior: Replications from longitudinal studies. *Psychological Medicine, 8,* 611–622.

Robins, L. N., & Regier, D. A. (1991). *Psychiatric disorders in America.* New York: The Free Press.

Robins, L. N., Tipp, J., & Przybeck, T. (1991). Antisocial personality. In L. N. Robins & D. A. Regier (Eds.), *Psychiatric disorders in America* (pp. 258–290). New York: The Free Press.

Rowe, D. C. (1983). Biometrical genetic models of self-reported delinquent behavior: A twin study. *Behavioral Genetics, 13,* 473–489.

Royko, M. (1993, May 30). Family a priority: What about kids? *Chicago Tribune,* p. 3.

Royko, M. (1994, September 2). Who's to blame? The obvious targets. *Chicago Tribune,* p. 3.

Rubinstein, (1992, November 9). Joblessness and crime. *Wall Street Journal,* p. 1.

Ruffié, J. (1986). *The population alternative.* New York: Random House.

Rush, B. (1812). *Medical inquiries and observations upon the diseases of the mind.* Philadelphia: Kimber & Richardson.

Sacks, O. (1995, January 9). A neurologist's notebook: Prodigies. *The New Yorker,* pp. 44–65.

Sampson, R. J. (1987). Urban black violence: The effect of male joblessness and family disruption. *American Journal of Sociology, 93*(2), 348–382.

Sampson, R. J., & Laub, J. H. (1993). *Crime in the making.* Cambridge, MA: Harvard University Press.

Satterfield, J. H. (1987). Childhood diagnostic and neurophysiological predictors of teenage arrest rates: An eight-year prospective study. In S. A. Mednick, T. E. Moffitt, & S. A. Stack (Eds.), *The causes of crime: New biological approaches* (pp. 146–167). Cambridge: Cambridge University Press.

Scarr, S., & McCartney, K. (1983). How people make their own environments: A theory of genotype–environment effects. *Child Development, 54,* 424–435.

Scarr, S., & Weinberg, R. A. (1978). The influence of "family background" on intellectual attainment. *American Sociological Review, 43,* 674–692.

Schachter, S., & Latené, B. (1964). Crime, cognition and the autonomic nervous system. *Nebraska Symposium on motivation, 12,* 221–273.

Schalling, D. (1978). Psychopathy-related personality variables and the psychophysiology of socialization. In R. D. Hare & D. Schalling (Eds.), *Psychopathic behavior: Approaches to research* (pp. 85–106). Chichester, U.K.: Wiley.

Schiff, M., Duyme, M., Dumaret, A., & Tomkeiewicz, S. (1982). How much could we boost scholastic achievement and IQ scores? A direct answer from a French adoption study. *Cognition, 12,* 165–196.

Schmauk, F. (1970). Punishment, arousal, and avoidance learning in sociopaths. *Journal of Abnormal Psychology, 76,* 325–335.

Schoenherr, J. C. (1964). *Avoidance of noxious stimulation in psychopathic personality.* Unpublished doctoral dissertation, University of California at Los Angeles. (University Microfilms No. 8334)

Schulsinger, F. (1972). Psychopathy: Heredity and environment. In S. A. Mednick & K. O. Christiansen (Eds.), *Biosocial bases of criminal behavior* (pp. 109–126). New York: Gardner.

Shakur, S. (A.K.A. Monster Kody Scott). (1993). *Monster: The autobiography of an L.A. gang member.* New York: Atlantic Monthly Press.

Shanker, A. (1993, July 5). A million drowning children. *New Republic,* p. 21.

Shapiro, S. K., Quay, H. C., Hogan, A. E., & Schwartz, K. P. (1988). Response perseveration and delayed responding in undersocialized aggressive conduct disorder. *Journal of Abnormal Psychology, 97,* 371–373.

Sheehan, S. (1993a, January 11). A lost childhood. *The New Yorker,* pp. 54–66.

Sheehan, S. (1993b, January 18). A lost motherhood. *The New Yorker,* pp. 52–79.

Sheldon, W. H. (with the collaboration of C. Dupertius & E.McDermott). (1949). *Varieties of delinquent youth.* New York: Harper.

Sherman, P. W., Jarvis, J., & Braude, S. (1992). Naked mole rats. *Scientific American, 267*(2), 72–78.

Shields, J. (1962). *Monozygotic twins brought up apart and brought up together.* London: Oxford University Press.

Siddle, D. A. T., & Trasler, G. B. (1981). The psychophysiology of psychopathic behavior. In M. J. Christie & P. G. Mellett (Eds.), *Foundations of psychosomatics* (pp. 283–303). London: Wiley.

Siegman, A. W. (1966). Father absence during early childhood and antisocial behavior. *Journal of Abnormal Psychology, 71,* 71–74.

Skeels, H. M. (1966). Adult status of children with contrasting early life experiences. *Monographs of the Society for Research in Child Development, 31*(3, Whole No. 105).

Smith, S., Arnett, P., & Newman, J. P. (1992). Neuropsychological differentiation of psychopathic and non-psychopathic criminal offenders. *Personality and Individual Differences, 13,* 1233–1243.

Sokolov, E. N. (1960). Neuronal models and the orienting reflex. In M. A. B. Brazier (Ed.), *CNS and behavior* (Vol. 3, pp. 70–93). New York: Josiah Macey, Jr. Foundation.

Soubrie, P. (1986). Reconciling the role of central serotonin neurons in human and animal behavior. *Behavioral and Brain Science, 9,* 319–364.

Spencer, L. T. (1928). The concept of the threshold and Heyman's law of inhibition. *Journal of Experimental Psychology, 11,* 88–97.

Spencer, L. T., & Cohen, L. H. (1928a). Correlation of the visual threshold and Heyman's coefficient of inhibition in a single individual with uniocular vision. *Journal of Experimental Psychology, 11,* 194–201.

Spencer, L. T., & Cohen, L. H. (1928b). The relation of the threshold to estimates of daily variation in freshness. *Journal of Experimental Psychology, 11,* 281–292.

Spielberger, C. D., Kling, J. K., & O'Hagen, S. E. (1978). Dimensions of psychopathic personality: Antisocial behavior and anxiety. In R. D. Hare & D. Schalling (Eds.), *Psychopathic behavior: Approaches to research* (pp. 23–46). Chichester: Wiley.

Spitz, H. H. (1986). *The raising of intelligence: A selected history of attempts to raise retarded intelligence.* Hillsdale, NJ: Lawrence Erlbaum Associates.

Spoont, M. R. (1992). Modulatory role of serotonin in neural information processing: Implications for human psychopathology. *Psychological Bulletin, 112,* 330–350.

Sullivan, L. (1992, January 6). *Families in crisis.* Prepared address by the then Secretary of Health and Human Services, delivered before the Council on Families in America of the Institute for American Values.

Sutherland, E., & Cressey, D. (1978). *Principles of criminology* (10th ed.). Philadelphia: Lippincott.

Sutker, P. B. (1970). Vicarious conditioning and sociopathy. *Journal of Abnormal Psychology, 76,* 380–386.

Tellegen, A., & Waller, N. (1994). Exploring personality through test construction: Development of the Multidimensional Personality Questionnaire. In S. R. Briggs & J. M. Cheek (Eds.), *Personality measures: Development and evaluation* (Vol. 1, pp. 133–161). Greenwich, CT: JAI Press.

Tellegen, A., Lykken, D. T., Bouchard, T. J., Wilcox, K., Segal, N., & Rich, S. (1988). Personality similarity in twins reared apart and together. *Journal of Personality and Social Psychology, 54,* 1031–1039.

Terry, D. (1994, September 9). When children kill children: Boy, 11, is wanted in Chicago. *New York Times,* pp. A1, A12.

Tharp, V., Maltzman, I., Syndulko, K., & Ziskind, E. (1980). Autonomic activity during anticipation of an aversive tone in noninstitutionalized sociopaths. *Psychophysiology, 17,* 123–128.

Thomas-Peter, B. A. (1992). The classification of psychopathy: A review of the Hare vs. Blackburn debate. *Personality and Individual Differences, 13,* 337–342.

Tomarken, A. J., Davidson, R. J., & Henriques, J. B. (1990). Resting frontal brain asymmetry predicts affective responses to films. *Journal of Personality and Social Psychology, 59,* 791–801.

Toobin, J. (1994, March 7). The man who kept going free. *The New Yorker,* pp. 38–53.

Tooby, J., & Cosmides, L. (1992). The psychological foundations of culture. In J. H. Barkow, L. Cosmides, & J. Tooby (Eds.), *The adapted mind: Evolutionary psychology and the generation of culture* (pp. 19–136). Oxford: Oxford University Press.

Tracy, P. E., Wolfgang, M. H., & Figlio, R. M. (1990). *Delinquency in two birth cohorts.* New York: Plenum Press.

Unikel, I. P., & Blanchard, E. B. (1983). Psychopathy, race, and delay of gratification by adolescent offenders. *Journal of Nervous and Mental Disease, 156,* 57–60.

Unlucky 13th. (1991, July 21). *Minneapolis Star-Tribune,* p. A1.

Uyttebrouck, O. (1993, April 14). Police study links blacks to 80% of violent crimes. *Arkansas Democrat Gazette,* p. 1.

Valins, S. (1966). Emotionality and autonomic reactivity. *Journal of Experimental Research in Personality, 2,* 41–48.

Vanderbilt, A. T., II. (1989). *Fortune's children: The fall of the House of Vanderbilt.* New York: Morrow.

Veldman, D. J. (1967). *Fortran programming for the behavioral sciences.* New York: Holt, Rinehart & Winston.

Virkkunen, M. (1987). Metabolic dysfunctions among habitually violent offenders: Reactive hypoglycemia and cholesterol levels. In S. A. Mednick, T. E. Moffitt, & S. A. Stack (Eds.), *The causes of crime: New biological approaches* (pp. 292–311). Cambridge: Cambridge University Press.

Waddington, C. H. (1957). *The strategy of the genes.* London: Allen & Unwin.

Wagenbichler, H. (1993). The Yugoslav tragedy. *The Social Contract, 3,* 235–239.

Waid, W. M. (1983). Psychophysiological processes in delinquency-prone young adults. In B. A. Maher & W. B. Maher (Eds.), *Progress in experimental personality research* (pp. 181–213). New York: Academic Press.

Waid, W. M., & Orne, M. T. (1982). Reduced electrodermal response to to conflict, failure to inhibit dominant behaviors, and delinquency proneness. *Journal of Personality and Social Psychology, 43,* 769–774.

Waller, N. G., Kojetin, B. A., Bouchard, T. J., Jr., Lykken, D. T., & Tellegen, A. (1990). Genetic and environmental influences on religious interests, attitudes, and values: A study of twins reared apart and together. *Psychological Science, 1,* 1–5.

Watson, J. B. (1924). *Behaviorism.* Chicago: University of Chicago Press.

Westman, J. C. (1994). *Licensing parents: Can we prevent child abuse and neglect?* New York: Plenum Press.

White, J. L., Moffitt, T. E., & Silva, P. A. (1989). A prospective replication of the protective effects of IQ in subjects at high risk for juvenile delinquency. *Journal of Consulting and Clinical Psychology, 57,* 719–724.

Whitehead, B. D. (1993, April). Dan Quayle was right. *The Atlantic,* pp. 47–84.

Widom, C.P. (1989). The cycle of violence. *Science, 244,* 160–166.

Williamson, S., Harpur, T. J., & Hare, R. D. (1991). Abnormal processing of affective words by psychopaths. *Psychophysiology, 28,* 260–273.

Williamson, S., Harpur, T. J., & Hare, R. D. (1992). *Psychopathy and sensitivity to emotional valence.* Unpublished manuscript.

Willerman, L., Loehlin, J. C., & Horn, J. M. (1992). An adoption and a cross-fostering study of the Minnesota Multiphasic Personality Inventory (MMPI) Psychopathic Deviate Scale. *Behavior Genetics, 22,* 515–529.

Wilson, E. O. (1975). *Sociobiology.* Cambridge, MA: Harvard University Press.

Wilson, E. O. (1978). *On human nature.* Cambridge, MA: Harvard University Press.

Wilson, R. S. (1983). The Louisville Twin Study: Developmental synchronies in behavior. *Child Development, 54,* 298–316.

Wilson, J. Q. (1991). Boarding schools might help today's "warrior class." *American Enterprise Institute Newsletter, 3.*

Wilson, J. Q., & Herrnstein, R. J. (1985). *Crime and human nature.* New York: Simon & Schuster.

Woman admits killing her daughter. (1993, January 6). *Minneapolis Star-Tribune,* p. 53.

Yoshikawa, H. (1994). Prevention as cumulative protection: Effects of early family support and education on chronic delinquency and its risks. *Psychological Bulletin, 115,* 28–54.

Zahn-Waxler, C., & Kochanska, G. (1988). The origins of guilt. In R. A. Thompson (Ed.), *Nebraska symposium on motivation* (Vol. 36, pp. 76–131). Lincoln: University of Nebraska Press.

Ziskind, E., Syndulko, K., & Maltzman, I. (1978). Aversive conditioning in the sociopath. *Pavlovian Journal, 13*, 199–205.

Zuckerman, M. (1989). Personality in the third dimension: A psychobiological approach. *Personality and Individual Differences, 10*, 391–418.

Author Index

Subject Index